I0114738

Homelessness in America

Homelessness in America

The History and Tragedy of
an Intractable Social Problem

Stephen Eide

ROWMAN & LITTLEFIELD
Lanham • Boulder • New York • London

Published by Rowman & Littlefield
An imprint of The Rowman & Littlefield Publishing Group, Inc.
4501 Forbes Boulevard, Suite 200, Lanham, Maryland 20706
www.rowman.com

86-90 Paul Street, London EC2A 4NE

Copyright © 2022 by The Rowman & Littlefield Publishing Group, Inc.

All rights reserved. No part of this book may be reproduced in any form or by any electronic or mechanical means, including information storage and retrieval systems, without written permission from the publisher, except by a reviewer who may quote passages in a review.

British Library Cataloguing in Publication Information Available

Library of Congress Cataloging-in-Publication Data

Names: Eide, Stephen, 1979– author.
Title: Homelessness in America : history and tragedy of an intractable social problem / Stephen Eide.
Description: Lanham : Rowman & Littlefield, [2022] | Includes bibliographical references and index. | Summary: "This book examines the history, governmental and private responses, and future prospects of this intractable challenge. Stephen Eides explains why homelessness persists in America and offers concrete recommendations for how we can do better for the homeless population"— Provided by publisher.
Identifiers: LCCN 2021059344 (print) | LCCN 2021059345 (ebook) | ISBN 9781538159576 (cloth) | ISBN 9781538159583 (ebook)
Subjects: LCSH: Homelessness—United States—History.
Classification: LCC HV4505 .E43 2022 (print) | LCC HV4505 (ebook) | DDC 362.5/920973—dc23/eng/20211213
LC record available at https://lccn.loc.gov/2021059344
LC ebook record available at https://lccn.loc.gov/2021059345

Contents

List of Figures and Tables

Preface

Homelessness has, for years, ranked as one of urban America's most pressing social challenges. As we push into a post-pandemic future and new decade, cities' prospects are uncertain. But homelessness is destined to be one concern the future will share with the recent past.

The overarching frame within which this book examines homelessness is a rethinking of the concept itself. "Homelessness" is an elusive concept. The term was not much in use prior to 1980. The continued reliance on it, by policymakers, scholars, and the public, causes us to group many disparate kinds of social problems together. Opioid addiction. Single-parent families. Public health emergencies stemming from encampments. Able-bodied men without work. People with untreated schizophrenia. Viewing all such challenges as so many parts of a larger challenge with "homelessness" clouds our thinking and frustrates debate over solutions. It guarantees we'll be talking past one another.

The history of homelessness is bound up with industrialization and urbanization, the opening and closing of the West, the Great Depression, and the post-World War II decline and revival of great American cities. Though we've used different terms ("tramp," "hobo," "bum," etc.) at other times, something like homelessness has always been with us and the debate over causes and solutions has always involved conflicts over cherished values. We're committed to civil liberties, but we also feel obliged to help those who can't—and sometimes won't—help themselves. Individualism can, when misguided, lead to homelessness, but individualism also stands as a goal of policy, insofar as people who aren't economically independent tend not be very well integrated into ordinary society. Capitalism has produced historically unprecedented levels of prosperity but has also caused great social disruption. In designing our safety net, we want both the nimble touch only charitable organizations can provide but also the awesome power of government to coerce, regulate, tax, and spend. We've rid cities of most of their worst "slums" and lowest-quality housing but at the cost of eliminating many low rent options on which the poor used to rely.

The modern homelessness era got going around 1980. Homelessness often stands as a proxy for the debate over neoliberalism and the ambivalence of urban renaissance. The cities with the worst homelessness crises rank among America's most successful. How much progress can we credit the last four decades with if they also witnessed the emergence and persistence of modern homelessness? At the same time, homelessness can't be attributed to some cold-hearted plot to deny resources to the poor. Homelessness's root causes are connected with a range of improvements: better housing standards for the poor, increased respect for civil liberties, and higher expectations for the treatment of mental illness. In this respect, there's a certain tragedy to the homelessness challenge. Modern homelessness emerged as a side effect of reform, and thus some tough choices will be involved in addressing its causes.

To reckon with the tragic aspect of homelessness is not to say that we can't do things better. In addition to explaining why homelessness persists in America and correcting popular misconceptions about it, this book will offer a number of recommendations for how to improve our response to homelessness. It's easy to become demoralized about social policy challenges such as homelessness that we debate constantly and yet never manage to make any progress with. But there's a lot that can be done, actually.

Acknowledgments

I want to thank my family for all their guidance and support, especially my parents, Gordon and Annie Eide, and my wife, Irene Flowers Eide.

I want to thank my employer, the Manhattan Institute. The support of Reihan Salam and Bernadette Serton was especially pivotal. Other colleagues, past and present, that made this book possible are Brian Anderson, Seth Barron, Paul Beston, Brandon Fuller, Nicole Gelinas, Carolyn Gorman, Vanessa Mendoza, Larry Mone, and Troy Senik.

Thanks to Kevin Corinth, Howard Husock, and Elizabeth Sinclair-Hancq for reviewing portions of the manuscript.

I would like to thank the New York Public Library and the member libraries of Connecticut's Bibliomation system.

I want to thank Jon Sisk and the team at Rowman & Littlefield.

There were a lot of strong contenders for the book's dedication. But, given the topic, DJ Jaffe's qualifications stood out. DJ, a heroic advocate for the mentally ill, passed away while this book was being written. He was a valued mentor both intellectually and morally. Hopefully, DJ would have liked *Homelessness in America*.

1

"Homelessness"

An Elusive Concept

Americans react to homelessness with a mix of anger, compassion, perplexity, and frustration. Little progress ever seems to be made. Homelessness persists, despite years of being a top priority of politicians in major cities and despite the billions in public resources devoted to it. Ideally, when spending on a social problem goes up, public concern over that problem goes down. Homelessness in America has not followed that trajectory. Whether the economy's expanding or in recession seems to make no difference with respect to encampments and other forms of homelessness-related public disorder. In recent decades, major cities have managed to drive down murder rates, improve schools, restore built environments, and revitalize economies. Middle-class families have put down roots in neighborhoods once given up for dead. But solutions to homelessness have eluded even the most successful cities. In fact, the healthiest cities seem to face the worst homelessness crises. Youngstown, Ohio, a long-struggling Rust Belt city, faces a long list of challenges: little economic development for generations, a loss of more than half the population since the post–World War II golden age, and an astronomical poverty rate. But there's less public concern about homelessness in Youngstown than there is in San Francisco, though no one would consider Youngstown more successful than San Francisco.

To understand America's homelessness challenge, one must begin by grasping the somewhat artificial nature of the term itself. In the 1970s, progressive advocates began promoting "homeless" to replace less sympathetic terms like "vagrant" and "bum." Debate was then raging about the legacy of the Great Society. A historic expansion of public programs had left in its wake an array of serious social challenges including crime and entrenched poverty. Many, including Ronald Reagan, were challenging the then-conventional wisdom on domestic policymaking in America. But progressives opposed retrenchment due to the harm they said it would pose to many disadvantaged populations including those they described as "homeless." They knew that those on whose behalf they were advocating had many problems other than a lack of stable housing. But investing in housing gained a logic and sense of urgency by emphasizing the shared struggle of "homelessness" among welfare mothers, drug addicts, the long-term unemployed, and the mentally ill. In short, asserting the existence of a homelessness crisis highlighted the need for expanding subsidized housing at a time when government's commitment to that and related priorities appeared to be wavering. In a 1992 interview, here's how Nancy Wackstein, a former New York City bureaucrat and former homeless advocate, put it to the *New York Times*: "Like every advocate in town, I had hewed to the party line that the solution to homelessness is housing. The belief was that if you focused on drug problems or family breakdown, you played into that blaming-the-victim mentality. You didn't want to say that people's problems were a result of their own actions because then you would get no public support for helping them."[1]

Advocates' strategy succeeded in the near term and in the long term.[2] By the mid-1980s, everyone—journalists, politicians, ordinary Americans concerned with urban decay—was speaking of "the homeless." The number of listings for "homelessness" in the *Reader's Guide to Periodical Literature* grew from zero in 1980 to thirty-two in 1984.[3] The *New York Times* ran four articles on the subject in 1978; by 1987, that figure had climbed to 370.[4] Governments set up agencies dedicated to helping "the homeless," distinct from their existing network of safety net services and benefits. A homeless services system took shape toward the end of the Reagan administration. It was briefly imbued with the "workfare" philosophy influential during the Clinton years. That changed, though, during the George W. Bush era of "compassionate conservativism," as policymakers began to prioritize connecting people with permanent housing over other more rehabilitative goals. Homeless advocates' influence grew steadily throughout the Bush and Obama years. Governments at all levels committed themselves to the nationwide campaign to "end homelessness." Thus emerged the reigning standard of success in homelessness policymaking, namely, how many housing units a government has recently made available to its homeless population.

Fifteen plus years into the campaign to end homelessness, we haven't ended homelessness. Major cities have not even seen much of a reduction. During the 2010s, homelessness rose 30 percent, 47 percent, 92 percent, and 40 percent in Seattle, New York, Los Angeles, and San Francisco, respectively.[5] These cities have all participated enthusiastically in the campaign to end homelessness. And we continue to struggle with the semantics of the thing, a struggle that ultimately reflects our confusion about what kind of problem "homelessness" is.

Some prefer "house-less," "the unhoused," or "undomiciled." *The Associated Press Stylebook* recently directed journalists to drop "the homeless" on the grounds of its being a "dehumanizing collective noun."[6] Per the *AP*, homelessness status must only be a qualifier (e.g., "person experiencing homelessness," "people without houses," "residents without addresses," etc.). The advocacy community has long portrayed homeless Americans as being like anyone else, save for the fact that they lack permanent housing.[7] But that "just folks" ethos tends to obscure non-economic factors such as serious mental illness and drug addiction that often cause someone to lose their housing. For someone living out of a tent on the streets of San Francisco, their lack of housing is not simply one attribute among many. It's the whole reason why concerns over them run so high in the Bay Area, far higher than levels of public concern for basic poverty. It's why, nationwide, we've created scores of new government agencies and nonprofits, staffed with hundreds, even thousands, of employees, and raised billions in dedicated funding. Thus, deemphasizing the importance of individuals' homelessness status, for fear of stigmatizing them, may well reduce the overall urgency over solutions.[8]

Speaking of homelessness as an experience is no more illuminating than speaking of it as an attribute. People respond, psychologically, to losing their housing in many different ways. Everyone is shaped by encounters with adversity, but homeless individuals experience many forms of adversity and it's not clear why one form of adversity should define someone's identity more than any other. From the perspective of a director of a homeless shelter, the largest difference among his clients may be between those determined to change their lives and those with less motivation. Those can be very different cohorts, which makes their experiences of homelessness very different, too. Individuals with "lived experience" regularly participate in panel discussions and serve on task forces, but they tend to be drawn from the ranks of the more functional homeless adults. They represent a certain kind of the "experience" of homelessness, but not every kind, and arguably not the most important kind. The homeless individuals we'd most like to help are those least likely to be interested in serving on a task force.

People who live in encampments are often described as uniquely "vulnerable," but that distracts from their toughness. The street population endures, for years, conditions that most of us couldn't tolerate for hours. Their toughness may explain their "service resistance"—the propensity of many on the street to decline help when offered. A further complication with the "vulnerable" description is that some homeless people are predatory. They rob and assault, and even sometimes kill, other homeless people. Some people lose their housing less because of their vulnerability than an assertiveness or other trait that makes them difficult to live with. Not all the homeless are equally vulnerable.

A doubled-up family living with friends or relatives sleeps in a home to which they have no legal claim of ownership or tenancy. They are unquestionably "housing insecure," but is that the same thing as homelessness? Dating back to the nineteenth century, "homelessness" has always connoted "place-lessness," the lack of a defined position in a social order. Note this definition of "homeless" from 1933 by Nels Anderson, an eminent sociologist: "a destitute man, woman, or youth, either a resident in the community or a transient, who is without domicile at the time of enumeration. Such a person may have a home in another community, or relatives in the local community, but is for the time detached and will not or cannot return."[9] A mentally ill single adult sleeping under an overpass has likely exhausted resources available to him from the informal safety net of friends and family, whereas that's not so for a single mother and her two kids rooming with her sister in an apartment in a neighborhood in which all parties have lived their entire lives. That single mother is not place-less. Government has an obligation to both the unsheltered and housing-insecure populations, but clearly different forms of assistance will be required to fulfill that obligation.

POLICY AND SEMANTICS

To speak of "root causes," is to speak of causes not correlations. "Homelessness" overlaps with numerous other social problems: incarceration, doing poorly in school, chronic unemployment, family separation and foster care, substance abuse, mental illness, domestic violence, public disorder, and so on. Clear-minded policymakers avoid presuming that "nothing causes anything" and try to parse the ultimate origins of social problems from the effects. Judgments about causes determine how to prioritize solutions to social challenges. Public officials only have so much time and political capital and, moreover, sometimes solutions run counter to one another. The "root causes" of crime are debated endlessly in the criminal justice reform debate. Those calling for defunding the police and transferring resources to social services argue that the best way to drive down crime is to address socioeconomic disadvantage. When someone gets sent to jail or prison, it would be unenlightened simply to process them through without giving any consideration to their behavioral health problems, lack of education, and employment prospects.[10]

By contrast, the homelessness debate minimizes "root cause"-type complexities and trains its focus on housing. Someone evicted due to a short-term bout with unemployment. A thirty-year-old man with schizophrenia who has lived on the streets almost his whole adult life. A young man who, on a lark, moved to the streets of San Francisco and has a family back in the Midwest who would willingly take him back. A single mother living in a welfare hotel with two small children. For all these diverse cases, in the world of homeless services, the attitude tends to be to just get people housed as soon as possible and for as long as possible. We'll work on the mental illness, sobriety, and unemployment issues later, which, after all, can't be resolved properly until secure housing is in place. In fact, this is less an attitude than a philosophy, known as "Housing First." Housing First dominates homeless services nationwide. Its influence has come at a cost, though, because when governments focus so intensely on housing, other concerns tend to become afterthoughts.

The number of homeless people, the rate of homelessness, can rank as one measure of how successful a community is in its fight against poverty. But that measure is only fair to use when taken as one among many measures of success on poverty-related issues, including education, crime, unemployment, and income. Detroit has a poverty rate about three times that of San Francisco (30 percent versus 10 percent). But San Francisco has a homelessness rate more than five times that of Detroit (920 per 100,000 versus 180 per 100,000, approximately). Which city is better at fighting poverty? A thirteen-year-old who's been struggling in school for years, emotionally and academically, could benefit from having stable housing. At the same time, Detroit has only a modest number of homeless children and yet its schools don't perform very well. Studies of the effect of subsidized housing programs on their formerly homeless recipients tend to show far more robust success rates in terms of keeping people "stably housed" than improving their lives in a more substantive sense. Defining a homeless, mentally ill person as a "seriously mentally ill person" instead of a "person experiencing homelessness" points to a different standard of policy success.

Going back to the nineteenth century, social reformers have held that decent, affordable housing contributes to human flourishing. Jacob Riis was just as firm in that belief as modern-day proponents of universal housing choice vouchers and Housing First.[11] Over the generations, government has made housing more decent by prohibiting extremely low-quality forms of housing and made it more affordable through various subsidy programs. But the contribution of housing policy to human flourishing is harder to assess. Decades of experience with public housing and voucher programs demonstrate that it is possible for people to be stably housed and continue to struggle with unemployment, crime, and education. Subsidized housing, like any other form of government assistance, undoubtedly provides a sense of relief. But can it do more than that? Housing is not the same thing as treatment.

Of late, homeless policymaking's housing-oriented focus has not proven successful in the jurisdictions facing the most serious homelessness crises. Throughout the 2010s, levels of spending on homelessness were rising in a number of jurisdictions, thanks to a combination of voter approvals for new taxes for homeless services (Measure H [2017 Los Angeles County], Proposition HHH [Los Angeles City 2016], and Proposition C [San Francisco 2018]) and healthy local economies. US Department of Housing and Urban Development (HUD) data show that, during the 2010s, the number of permanent supportive housing units in New York City and California rose by about one-third and two-thirds, respectively.[12] But in both cases, homeless rose over that span, too.

The Housing First goal aims too high and too low. It aims too high because it has not succeeded in ending homelessness. It aims too low because it expects too much from stable housing alone. High-quality research commissioned by HUD found that providing housing vouchers to a large cohort of homeless families had a dampening effect on the adult heads' level of employment, which was already low. Other studies of subsidized housing have come to similar conclusions about programs having a negative or, at best, neutral effect on employment and behavioral health measures. In the later decades of the twentieth century, cities across the nation dismantled thousands of units of public housing. They would not have done so if subsidized housing led to as much human flourishing as many had hoped. The 2018 ProPublica

"Right to Fail" report and accompanying *Frontline* documentary profiled a group of mentally ill individuals who had been put into an independent living setting by a lawsuit against New York State.[13] Despite being housed, these individuals were living in waste-strewn apartments swarming with bugs and had gruesome infections and other health problems. Independent, subsidized housing for them meant mental and physical decompensation, death, and extreme social isolation. Half of all fatal police shootings of mentally ill people occur at the victim's house.[14]

Now, to say that the "housing, housing, housing" approach has not thus far been very successful is not to say that it can't be successful. In the Biden era, truly historic investments in subsidized housing are under discussion. The more than $20 trillion spent since the war on poverty's began hasn't ended poverty, but it has brought relief to the lives of many people, as some conservatives have conceded.[15] Government can be effective without being efficient. But in what way would a massive investment in subsidized housing benefit the most disadvantaged Americans? Relief is not the same thing as flourishing, though flourishing is sometimes what's promised. These, among many other considerations, point to the need for a close examination of the homeless population and their specific needs.

CONCLUSION

"Homelessness" is a sociological term. "Home" has more social valence than "house." Going back centuries, the term "homelessness," though used more rarely and in a different way than now, has always had a sense of "place-lessness" or "family-lessness."[16] Someone without a home is even more desperate than someone without housing. By providing people with housing, government can help people find a home. But subsidized housing cannot guarantee someone a family, job, sobriety, or social integration. Reckoning with "family-lessness" and "place-lessness" prompts an appreciation of the social, more than economic, nature of the homelessness challenge and points to the need for coupling the redistribution of housing resources with efforts at rehabilitation, education, and training. To help people with their needs, social policymakers should define groups by their needs. The needs of the homeless population are very diverse. We are no more certain about how to separate the social and economic elements of the challenge when it emerged four decades ago than we are closer to "ending" homelessness.

"Homeless" is not likely to go the way of obsolete terms such as "idiot," "lunatic," "bum," and "derelict" anytime soon, because it points to a solution that is still broadly influential. Any attempt to replace "homeless" would raise awkward questions about why chronically unemployed non-disabled adults, single-parent families, and untreated schizophrenics were all grouped together in the first place. "Homeless" in some modified term is likely to be with us, though we could stand to be much clearer in how we talk about the problem. That should begin with thinking more clearly about it.

In pursuit of more clarity, the following chapters will turn to the history of homelessness in America. We are now in the third iteration of the campaign to end homelessness in America. The first focused on the "tramps" prevalent in the early twentieth century; the second focused on Skid Row neighborhoods, circa 1950. These efforts have differed significantly in their rhetoric, structure, and target population, because the character of the homeless population has changed. Always, though, the efforts have been buoyed by hopes of social reform. In the lead-up to the Great Depression, reformers' concerns centered mainly around the labor market. Housing itself was less of a concern, as cheap housing existed in wide abundance then, whereas steady work was harder to find. Many of the reforms they recommended were enacted, eventually, during the New Deal, most notably unemployment insurance. However, their effect is hard to evaluate since private developments in the area of transportation and the broader economy also had a big effect on homelessness. In the postwar era, the homeless population was smaller but also less employable. That campaign to end homelessness focused on urban renewal and rehabilitation. Skid Row was one of the main neighborhoods targeted by cities in their effort to revitalize themselves by getting rid of so-called slum housing. To varying degrees of vagueness, planners believed that somehow Skid Row denizens would be provided for and their lives improved for the better. Urban renewal did not much improve the lives of the homeless, but it did destroy their housing and neighborhoods. In response, the homeless population, in the later decades of the twentieth century, began devising new accommodations out of tents, train stations, and other public spaces. The current, third campaign to end homelessness in America focuses on housing, like the second. However, instead of aiming to end homelessness by eliminating substandard housing, its strategy centers around expanding permanently subsidized housing. When someone, for whatever reason, loses permanent housing, the government should promptly transfer housing to them, and for as long as they need it. This effort has not yet succeeded in ending homelessness any more than previous efforts did.

Homelessness has always been with us but the character of the challenge has changed dramatically. History is essential in understanding the root causes of the current challenge and the service systems we've built to respond to it. The next three chapters, this book's first section, will lay out the history.

The second section of this book turns from history to ideas. Evidence ("the facts") is important in policy debates, but so are values and the ideas that frame which solutions we consider as acceptable. In its policy response to homelessness, government seeks to be compassionate, to re-integrate homeless adults and families back into society, and to minimize harm. Harm reduction, compassion, and integration: these ideas all hold a certain appeal, but they are not without complications. Chapters 5, 6, and 7 will sort through these complications and contradictions.

There is no one type of "homelessness." But nor are there infinite types. Understanding homelessness in its modern variety requires understanding four main problems: the problems of poor families, especially those headed by a single mother; untreated mental illness; public disorder; and inadequate low-rent housing in major cities. Each of those four problems can be traced to a major development or policy change from the late twentieth century. Chapters 8 to 11 will take up the family, mental illness, public disorder, and housing. The conclusion (chapter 12) will recommend some reforms that reflect the underlying complexity of homelessness.

Homelessness is a bad thing. But, as we'll see, most of its underlying causes, certainly in its current form, developed because of good things that happened or at least attempts to make things better. Frequently, in policymaking, attempts to solve one problem create new ones. That is substantially the story with modern homelessness. Modern homelessness came about from the unintended consequences of good government reform, which should create a measure of humility amidst current debates over reform and America's homelessness crisis.

2

The Romantic Era

Post-Civil War to the 1920s

Throughout human history, there have always been those who were poor and stood, somehow, at a remove from ordinary society—those who lacked a place in an existing social order, such as exiles and mendicants.[1] The outcast has been a staple character in world literature since Greek tragedy. Before the term gained its current significance, "homelessness" implied a combination of place-lessness and poverty. Cain may have been the first homeless man.[2] Someone is most likely to have no social place if they have no money, no job, and no contact with their family. It is possible for a poor person to be well-integrated into a community, such as if they're a member of a generally poor community, or if their family takes care of them. It is also conceivable to lack a distinct place in a social order and have means (Captain Nemo). But modern homelessness, the social policy challenge of interest to this book, lies at the intersection of place-lessness and poverty.

The epic of American homelessness begins in the post-Civil War era. At that time, the American social scene witnessed the development of large masses of adult men who were poor, mobile, and apparently unattached to any family or community. These "wandering poor" were the premodern homeless. They emerged as a consequence of industrialization, urbanization, and the development of the Great American Common Market. Railroads—the transcontinental spike was driven in May 1869—facilitated the cheap and rapid movement of goods and people. Everyone has seen old photographs of men "riding the rails,"[3] a dangerous business that, every year in the late nineteenth century, claimed the lives of thousands and injured thousands more.[4] Railroads opened up new markets for agricultural products. Farmers realized that railroads gave them a way to sell their sugar beets, wheat, fruit, hops, and so forth, not just to neighboring communities but all over America. They were therefore motivated to farm harder, thus creating a near insatiable demand for labor.[5] The wandering poor met this demand.

Cities functioned as vast labor exchanges. Cities provided information about current and upcoming opportunities for picking fruit, digging ditches, harvesting ice, digging tunnels, husking corn, logging, plowing, pitching hay, sinking telegraph poles, building dams for rivers, oil-well drilling, working in canneries, and digging mine-shafts.[6] You went to the city to learn about jobs outside the city, to access railroad interchanges, and, when the seasonal farm work wound down, to go on a spree and hibernate throughout the winter.[7] In twenty-first-century America, New York and Los Angeles lay claim to the title of homeless capitals of the United States. New York is home to the largest homeless population, while Los Angeles is home to the largest unsheltered population. But in the late nineteenth and early twentieth centuries, Chicago held the title.[8] As the nation's largest rail hub, Chicago functioned as the labor market exchange for much of the rapidly developing Heartland and West.

The premodern homeless didn't call themselves "the wandering poor." "Homeless" and "homelessness" were used by some sociologists and reformers[9] but they did not have the popular currency they have now. The premodern homeless referred to themselves using a colorful variety of terms that journalists and scholars have long taken keen interest in documenting.[10] All have since fallen into obscurity with the exception of "bum," "hobo," and "tramp." Generally, the hobo worked and moved, the tramped moved and didn't work, and the bum didn't move and didn't work.[11] Bum," "tramp," and "hobo," to the modern ear, sound politically incorrect. But they were not tools of oppression. They demarcated social distinctions in an order designed by the premodern homeless themselves.[12] As explained by Charles Hoch and Robert Slayton, "Like African tribes that maintained minute status differentiations based on ancestry and familial relationships, the homeless and nearly homeless of the United States' industrial age created fine distinctions that defined status."[13] In modern times, we use "homeless" to group disparate types of hard-up individuals into one category so as to imply that what's most defining about all of them is their lack of permanent housing. "Hobo," "tramp," and "bum" left more ambiguity as to how much these men had in common with one another. Both tramps and hoboes took pride in not being bums, even though many bums were old, disabled former hoboes and tramps. Physical disability was a significant driver of premodern homelessness, due to the aforementioned hazards of freighthopping and rigors of a life of manual labor. A spirited debate over who reigned supreme, the hoboes or the tramps, turned mainly on the value of work. The tramps' ability to live by their wits and avoid work gave them a claim to elite status among some members of the late nineteenth-century underclass and many writers.[14] Others ranked hoboes as higher due to their work ethic and saw the tramps as parasites. A genuinely free man worked: that was, after all, one of the principles for which the Civil War was fought.[15] Someone who appears idle and can give no account of his idleness immediately drew scrutiny in nineteenth-century America. When those men started showing up in small communities in very large numbers, they touched off a broad public policy debate.

Though hard employment data are elusive, probably, larger numbers of the premodern homeless worked than do the homeless in twenty-first-century America.[16]

One telling detail is the extraordinary seasonality and cyclicality of premodern homelessness. In the late nineteenth- and early twentieth-century period, the numbers of destitute single men fluctuated greatly in response to both the cycles of the economy and the manual labor market's seasonal rhythms.[17] Nowadays, homelessness rates depend on cities' climates but have little to do with the seasons.[18] Modern homelessness has a more structural character: it does not necessarily rise during recessions and has not been known, in cities like New York and San Francisco, to decrease much during times of economic expansion.

They were not considered working class, however. The work they did, generally, was temporary and unskilled. The seasonal fluctuations of the size of the premodern homeless, and their gradual decline throughout the first half of the twentieth century, indicate that they mainly did casual, manual labor. They also were known for odd jobs like repeat-voting for corrupt political machines.[19] Social observers at the time saw these men as troubled and downwardly mobile. Their health was appalling.[20] All hoboes risked winding up as bums without a course correction—meaning, opting for "steady work" over casual labor.[21] Social reformers did not see casual labor as a step on the way to working class status, but an alternative to it. Someone who never moved on and up from a life of temporary jobs would never join ordinary American society.

THE ROMANCE OF THE ROAD

The premodern homeless shared with their twenty-first-century counterparts a lack of upward mobility. But they were very mobile in a horizontal sense. They traveled far and wide on the railroads. Many rode a defined "circuit" across a handful of cities and gigs over the course of a year.[22] (The only "circuit" the modern homeless ride is the "institutional circuit," from jails to mental hospitals to homeless shelters.) These "knights of the tie and rail" eschewed steady work for independence and adventure. In our day, homeless advocates strenuously deny that anyone chooses to be homeless. The hobos and tramps of the late nineteenth century took pride in having chosen to be homeless.[23] Their memoirs amply document that, for many of them, taking to the road was a voluntary act.[24] Thanks to admirers such as Jack London, Carl Sandburg, O. Henry, and Walt Whitman, the ideal of hoboes and tramps as romantic nonconformists persisted for generations, long after the hoboes and tramps themselves had passed from the scene. It shaped the jurisprudence of Supreme Court Justice William O. Douglas, who took to the road in his youth and whose rulings determine, to this day, cities' options for responding to public disorder.[25]

In other words, this was a subculture that, like the beats and hippies, had its own moral code, lingo, music, and literature.[26] Poets, novelists, and other writers particularly admired the tramp for resisting the lures of a tainted civilization. A good example of the tramp as happy-go-lucky savant may be found in John Steinbeck's *Cannery Row*. This window of life into the World War II-era of Monterey, California, features

"Mack and the boys," a group of tramps who burden their community in numerous ways. They're manipulative alcoholics who sponge off others instead of pursuing steady work. Their home is "the Palace Flophouse and Grill," a former warehouse that they squat in. But Steinbeck portrays Mack and the boys with tremendous affection. Mack and the boys, at one point in the novel, launch a well-intentioned but poorly executed party for Doc, the novel's main character. They destroy his house, but Doc, a man known for taking the long view, does not hold it against them:

> Doc said: "Look at them. There are your true philosophers, I think," he went on, "that Mack and the boys know everything that has ever happened in the world and possibly everything that will happen. I think they survive in this particular world better than other people. In a time when people tear themselves to pieces with ambition and nervousness and covetousness, they are relaxed. All of our so-called successful men are sick men, with bad stomachs, and bad souls, but Mack and the boys are healthy and curiously clean. They can do what they want. They can satisfy their appetites without calling them something else."[27]

The hobos and tramps were laughed at ("'They won't work; they defy my overseers, and they make friends with my dogs'"), and also laughed with.[28] Having a great sense of humor was another quality typically attributed to the premodern homeless. "The characteristic hobo is an optimist who sees the humorous side of many an unpleasant or dangerous situation."[29] See Fred Astaire and Judy Garland's "Couple of Swells" routine in *Easter Parade* and YouTube videos featuring the famous hobo clown Emmett Kelly. For many decades, the hobo served as middle-class American mothers' go-to option for last minute Halloween costumes, requiring not much more than old clothes and something to smear on the face for whiskers. But the hobo costume has fallen out of favor.[30] Political correctness may be one reason but, more generally, we don't view modern homelessness as remotely romantic. The romanticization of homelessness during the late nineteenth and early twentieth century made it easier to laugh at ("Hallelujah I'm a Bum" [1928 song], *My Man Godfrey* [1936 film]). It's hard to laugh at a victim of social injustice, which is the only lens through which modern filmmakers depict the homeless (*Home Alone II*, *The Soloist*, *Time Out of Mind*). A homeless man—Charlie Chaplin's the "Little Tramp" (1915)—was one of the most bankable movie characters toward the latter end of the romantic era.

No one nowadays writes amusing pop songs celebrating life in a tent in San Francisco's Tenderloin or in New York City's Bellevue Men's Shelter. By contrast, what would American folk and country music be without the works of Jimmie Rodgers ("Hobo Bill's Last Ride," "In the Jailhouse Now"), Harry McClintock ("Big Rock Candy Mountain," "Hallelujah, I'm a Bum"), and Woody Guthrie ("Hard Travelin'")? Much of this material trafficked in mythmaking. Some consider it morally suspect. Historian Eric Monkkonen calls literary tributes to the American tramp "patronizing": "To tell those unfairly exploited by a social and economic system that they have benefited is akin to congratulating the victim of a crime for his or her remarkable and expanding experience."[31] Another leading historian of homelessness,

Kenneth Kusmer, agrees: "by excluding any negative content from the description of tramp life, the picturesque image provided a rationalization for neglecting the real problems of the homeless man."[32] The products of hobo/tramp culture made false promises that destroyed families and led to the deaths of many impressionable young men (the tramps and hoboes were disproportionately young).[33] Nashville tourists listening to Grand Ole Opry musicians perform "The Wabash Cannonball" are unknowingly enjoying the early-twentieth-century equivalent of "gangsta rap." Songs and poems promising a vigorous freedom in tramping tended to gloss over the depravity, chronic alcohol dependance, mortal danger, exploitative labor practices, and brutal treatment by police, railroad security, and the more predatory elements of their fellow "knights."[34]

In opposition to Jack London and his ilk, there was a thriving a counter-romantic literature that sought to dissuade American youth from the tramp way of life. Some of these writers were former tramps themselves.[35] In a more sophisticated vein, labor economists criticized poor industrial organization.[36] While the romantics and moralists both emphasized the role that choice played in tramp culture, economists emphasized necessity. Whatever may be the case with wanderlust, too many hit the road simply to find work. Too many men opting too much for casual labor over steady work was, in large measure, a supply problem that called for somehow "decasualizing" the labor market:

> The demand for casual labor is naturally an excessively fluctuating demand. Each employer seeks for help only long enough to help himself out of an emergency. When confronted by some unusual situation he hires extra help to get out of it, and then immediately discharges the help. . . . Employers who complain at the unreliability, incompetence, and indifference of casual laborers would do well to remember that the chances of employment which they offer are as unreliable as the men who accept them, and that the livelihood these men obtain is as insufficient for their needs as the work they perform is insufficient to satisfy the employer.[37]

The economists agreed with the moralists that tramping correlated with bad character. But they argued that poorly arranged economic conditions made men bad, engendering shiftlessness, "drink," and other grievous character defects.[38] Casual laborers were mostly aspiring steady workers who had to settle. The economists were active participants in early-twentieth-century debate over ending homelessness or, as it was expressed at the time, "eliminating the tramp."[39] Addressing homelessness had very little to do with housing at this particular time. Housing reformers were very active during the romantic era of homelessness, but their efforts were not central to the campaign to eliminate the tramp. One concrete recommendation that economists made was unemployment insurance, which would relieve men of the need to travel after losing their job.[40] Thus, in some respects, the New Deal was borne out of debates over how to end homelessness in the early twentieth century.

In the meantime, though, men kept hitting the road, despite its manifest hardships. Record-keeping was erratic and limited only to major cities. Still, the numbers were staggering. One way to count homeless people is through the service systems they use. In the late nineteenth and early twentieth century, police stations were used as shelter. Historian Eric Monkkonen estimates that about 630,000 slept in police stations in 1880, and 615,000 in 1890,[41] and that 10 to 20 percent of all American families had a member who had done so.[42] In our day, the overall US population's more than six times larger but the number of people who experience "sheltered" homelessness annually, is 1.4 million.[43] Social researcher Alice Solenberger considers 40,000 a "conservative" estimate of the denizens of Chicago's lodging house districts in her 1911 study.[44] Sociologist Nels Anderson, writing about a decade later, pegs Chicago's homeless population at 30,000 in good times and 75,000 in hard times.[45] Chicago's homeless population, now, is 5,390.[46] Nationwide, estimates in the early twentieth century ranged from 500,000 to 5 million.[47] Adjusted for population, any of those estimates would dwarf the current count of around 580,000.[48]

Homelessness seems to have been a much more common experience back then. Even leaving aside the many writers who hit the road to write about it, those who had an "experience" of the tramp or hobo lifestyle included Jack Dempsey, Robert Mitchum, and Clark Gable.[49] In a 1940 article, the sociologist Theodore Caplow reckons that the number of people who had experienced transient life ran "into the millions."[50] Some public figures, such as the Greenwich Village-based poet Harry Kemp, Charles Lummis, the onetime head of the Los Angeles Public Library, and Justice Douglas, made their tramp experiences central to their personal brands. In the twenty-first century, there aren't any homeless celebrities or "characters," famous just for their homeless status. Those prominent individuals, such as athletes (the NBA's Jimmy Butler the NFL's Najee Harris) and politicians (US Senator Kyrsten Sinema [D-AZ]) who somehow incorporate an experience with homelessness into their public personas, do so as evidence of adversity overcome or victimhood, never of heroism or defiant nonconformity.

WHERE THEY LIVED

One big reason for why the tramp lifestyle appealed was that living was cheap. In Nels Anderson's canonical 1923 work *The Hobo*, he explains how a man could scrape by on $1 a day (the modern equivalent of $10 to $15) and easily provide for not only his food and recreation but also his housing.[51] In the twenty-first century, homeless single men located in major cities can readily access many necessities such as food, clothing, and even healthcare, but housing is elusive. For a tramp, bum, or hobo in the late nineteenth and early twentieth century, cheap housing was as easy to obtain as cheap food. Some unsheltered homelessness existed, such as in the "jungles" located outside city centers, near railroad yards, but they were far less of a concern than encampments are now.[52] The vast majority of the homeless population found nightly accommodation in the many "Main Stem" neighborhoods near cities' downtowns.[53]

They generally obtained their shelter from for-profit landlords who provided a few different low-quality options renting out at prices ranging from two to twenty-five cents a night. Charles Hoch and Robert Slayton provide an excellent overview of this spectrum of options, from "workingman hotels" to dorm-style set-ups, down to flophouses and the floors of saloons.[54] The cubicle (a.k.a. "cage"-style) hotels, which became so notorious during the postwar Skid Row era of homelessness, at this point occupied a midgrade status. They provided privacy, unlike the sawdust-covered saloon floors and hammocks strewn up in large rooms that were patronized by the poorest of the poor.[55] In the summation of hotel historian Paul Groth, "[1880 to 1930] marked the widest viable range of housing diversity in American urban history."[56]

The variety of extremely low-rent housing options and commercial businesses' lead role in sheltering the poor distinguish that era of housing from our own. We now look almost exclusively to the public and nonprofit sectors to house the homeless. Those sectors also had a role back then, too, through the institutions of the police station, municipal lodging house, mission, and almshouse. Police stations were the first municipal shelter; cop-as-social-worker is not a modern innovation.[57] Police stations were being used as shelters even before the Civil War.[58] By the late nineteenth century, reformers had replaced them[59] with municipal lodging or "wayfarers" houses in larger cities, which sometimes but not always used time limits, bathing requirements, and work tests.[60] Almshouses played an important role in the welfare state in the entire pre-New Deal era, stretching back to colonial times.[61] Missions, generally affiliated with religious organizations, also offered bare-bones temporary lodging in hopes of thereby saving sinners.[62] Reports vary on how preachy the missions were.[63] Public and charitable shelter were not necessarily free. There was often a fee that, if you couldn't meet it, had to be paid off via the woodyard. This deal was resented, as the work was expected to take place during prime hours for searching for real work.[64]

Economic theory would suggest that with so many transient men around seeking temporary accommodations, businesses would turn to providing it, so as to meet that need. In fact, that's exactly what happened. In Chicago, between 1885 and 1915, the number of rooming houses expanded from 492 to 2,424.[65] Low-cost housing proliferated not only because housing standards were lower than they are now but also because of the sheer quantity of homeless men who were around and in the market for it.[66] A landlord who can rent out, for two to five cents a pop, a few dozen hammock slots almost every night of the year has a more viable business model to work with than a landlord who can only rent a few hammock slots on a sporadic basis.

Eventually, Main Stem neighborhoods that were host to large numbers of unskilled workers shrank in concert with the industries that employed them.[67] The West became settled, creating a stable, always-on-the-scene workforce that obviated the need for transient laborers. Mechanization reduced the amount of labor needed.[68] Agriculture accounted for close to half of all jobs in the nation in 1870, but only 17 percent in 1940.[69] Modern transportation systems—public transit and the automobile—allowed for more efficient modes of connecting workers and jobs.[70] ("It is undoubtedly true that nowhere else in the world is there so much ground covered in the blind pursuit of work as there is in these United States," one social reformer had lamented in 1915.)[71] The modern "metro" area, defined by settled commuting patterns, emerged. And the railroad took away, just as surely as, earlier, it had given. Hopping trains had always depended on certain technological conditions that changed through industry innovations, such streamlining, the elimination of boxcars, and fewer refueling stops thanks to dieselization.[72] Hitchhiking never caught on to the degree that freighthopping did. Some have suggested that post-9/11 security restrictions dealt the mercy blow to riding the rails.[73] In retrospect, it's clear that all these trends were underway before the Great Depression, though dispute exists as to when the decline of tramp culture became discernible.[74] Socially, America was settled before the Civil War and after World War II. It was the highly disruptive period in between during which trump culture thrived.

CONCLUSION

To summarize the preceding and anticipate some points that will be developed more fully in the next two chapters, here is how modern homelessness compares with the situation in the late nineteenth and early twentieth centuries. Homeless women and family homelessness were not major problems back then. The hoboes, tramps, and bums were almost completely male and single (a "bachelor subculture").[75] They were also young and "overwhelmingly white."[76] The reasons seem to be southerners in general hit the road at relatively low rates, blacks could not realistically expect employment hundreds of miles from home, and there was strong social discrimination practiced by residents of the next-to-lowest rungs of the social order against those of the absolutely lowest rung.[77] Immigrants were not a large part of the Gilded Age homeless population, nor are they now.[78] The modern homeless don't arrange themselves by social status as did the hoboes, tramps, and bums; their social order is much flatter.

Two constants are substance abuse and public disorder. Substance abuse has been equated with homelessness for as long as poverty has.[79] This creates complications for anyone who wants to blame modern homelessness solely on substance abuse, unless for some reason meth addicts are much more likely to become homeless than chronic alcoholics, who've always been around. Ambivalence and hypocrisy marked the treatment of the premodern homeless. Communities couldn't live with them in a social sense, or without them in an economic sense. The railroads hated hobo trespassers but, at the same time, where would the railroads have been were there no workers to harvest the wheat to ship on railroads?[80] Modern communities are not reliant, economically, on their homeless populations. The modern homeless are by and large considered victims, the premodern homeless were considered heroes. Both boast high rates of disability, but mental disability more so with the modern homeless.

Both populations skew young.[81] Homelessness was more of a common experience in the early twentieth century: a larger proportion of the population seems to have experienced homelessness. At present, we don't celebrate the homeless in song and poetry but we do afford them greater legal protections. We're more legally tolerant of the homeless but less culturally tolerant.

The American economy has become, over time, more rational and organized as a result of changes in both the public and private sectors. Agriculture's share of total employment has shrunk dramatically,[82] which has made the seasonal fluctuations of the job market less pronounced. Modern transportation systems have also reduced the need for transient labor. Employers with a job opening no longer have to wait to fill it until someone came in from hundreds of miles away, and workers no longer need to cross the country in order to find a new job when their last one ends. In the public sector, we have witnessed the rise of the welfare state, which some scholars credit with reducing the mass-scale vagrancy witnessed in early-twentieth-century America.[83] More rational economic organization should mean more social stability and thus less homelessness. And, to some extent, it undoubtedly has. However, as we will see, other changes, such as regarding housing regulations and mental health policy, have served to reduce social stability.

3

The Skid Row Era

Great Depression to 1970s

During the post-World War II era, homelessness takes on a cast more recognizable to modern observers. It becomes structural, responding less to the economy's rhythms. The mobile, working "hoboes" and mobile, nonworking "tramps" both disappear, leaving behind only the immobile, nonworking "bums." America's homeless population was once highly mobile, but that has not been the case for roughly eighty years.

Few participants in the 1980s debate over the "new" homelessness had direct experience with Jack London's "knights of the road." But many knew of "skid row" culture. "Skid row" was the generic term for neighborhoods where place-less men lived in postwar America. The original Skid Row was a Seattle neighborhood used heavily by the logging industry and, thus, a magnet for transient manual laborers.[1] Over time, that proper name morphed into a general category. The normal, major postwar city featured a skid row neighborhood.[2] A skid row neighborhood attracted no more notice than did a central business district, Chinatown, or Little Italy. Skid row neighborhoods were known, most of all, for their concentrations of single-room occupancy (SRO) hotels but also for their missions, bars, liquor stores, centers for day labor opportunities (sometimes termed "slave markets"), barber colleges, blood banks, and academics wandering around trying to make sense of the paradox of a community made up of "disaffiliated men."

THE GREAT DEPRESSION

The Great Depression was a transition period between the romantic and skid row eras of homelessness. Homelessness in America reached extraordinary heights in the Great Depression. "Sleeping rough" censuses in New York City counted 4,044 in 1935 and 5,823 in 1936.[3] The federal government made a fairly serious attempt at a point-in-time homelessness count in January 1933, based on counts done in 809 cities. The number of Americans using homeless services was estimated to be about 370,000, and the total number, including those sleeping outdoors and unsuitable accommodations, was estimated at about 1.2 million.[4] Demand for services surged, particularly shelter.[5] In upstate New York, the Erie County Municipal Lodging House saw about ten times the annual registration in 1933 than it had seen in 1928.[6] Freighthopping, which had declined throughout the 1920s, picked back up.[7] The Southern Pacific Railroad reported 683,457 "trespassers" in 1932, up from 78,099 in 1927.[8]

New groups joined the ranks: youths and families. In any era, which groups make up the homeless population is just as telling as how many there are. According to one widely circulated estimate, 200,000 adolescents were on the road.[9] While few families went "tramping" together between the Civil War and the 1920s, homeless families were a common sight during the Great Depression.[10] Homelessness status often depends on where you sleep. The Great Depression featured a grand experiment in unusual sleeping arrangements. Writes historian Arthur Schlesinger: "With no money left for rent, unemployed men and their entire families began to build shacks where they could find unoccupied land. Along the railroad embankment, beside the garbage incinerator, in the city dumps, there appeared towns of tarpaper and tin, old packing boxes, and old car bodies."[11] One of New York's shelter annexes was a converted pier-shed over East River that hosted 1,724 individuals in one room.[12] Some called for opening up the then largely vacant Empire State Building for use as a public shelter.[13]

Still, transient single adult male workers remained the paradigm.[14] During the Depression, men in their prime working age endured years of unemployment. One of Studs Terkel's interviewees in *Hard Times*, his oral history of the Great Depression, attested that "'Well, I went through the Depression, which took place during the good years of my life. The good physical years, the best mental years. But they were years which made a lot of bums out of good people.'"[15] The migratory worker was place-less because he was anchored to work, not a home. There was no work at his home, so he left it. Compared to modern times, family structure was stabler among families who together fell into homelessness. But many families did dissolve as men abandoned their families under a sometimes-vague promise of seeking work elsewhere.[16]

President Franklin D. Roosevelt responded to the Great Depression with a constitutional revolution. Before the New Deal, social policymaking in America was handled mainly by private charities, states and cities. After the New Deal, every social and economic crisis would force a debate over what the federal government should do about it. The New Deal, more than the later Great Society, made special provision for homeless individuals. New Deal architects saw many flaws in existing state and local relief programs, one of which was how they excluded the transient poor through so-called settlement requirements designed to reserve benefits for locals.[17] It could take years to gain the legal residence requisite for benefit eligibility; some states had been extending the length of residency requirements in response to the uptick in demands for relief.[18] Stringent settlement laws would be struck down by the Supreme Court in *Shapiro v. Thompson* (1969) on the grounds that they violated a constitutional "right to travel." However, the notion that a community may somehow be made responsible for a neighboring community's destitute population remains controversial to this day.[19]

New Dealers argued that the federal government was the only entity in a position to do anything for the increasing numbers of place-less men without settlement.[20] The 1933 Federal Emergency Relief Administration, part of FDR's "first hundred days," set up a federal transient program designed to aid people who had been in their state of residence for less than twelve months.[21] During its brief existence (it lasted until 1935) the transient program served one million individuals.[22] It set up hundreds of transient centers across the nation. Some were basically city shelters; others were camps in rural areas. Assessments of the New Deal's program for transients have been various. Some people claim their lives were saved by them.[23] The transient program eased the strain on local service systems and charities. Some people criticized it for warehousing men out in the woods.[24]

In the grand scheme of the New Deal, the transient program was a sideshow relative to more sweeping changes. But those big changes were influenced by concerns about homelessness. Policy ideas implemented in the 1930s had been developed over previous decades, during which solutions to tramps and transiency were heavily debated. In the early twentieth century, homelessness was considered mainly an unemployment problem rooted in faulty economic organization. Pre-New Deal Progressives did see tramping as morally objectionable but also caused by the unregulated capitalist economy's more exploitative labor practices. The New Deal tried to make the labor market operate in a better-organized manner via stronger unions (the Wagner Act), minimum wage and overtime (Fair Labor Standards Act), and unemployment insurance.

SKID ROW IN PROFILE

The overall effect of the New Deal is difficult to disentangle from the effects of World War II and overall economic growth. During the first few decades of the twentieth century, demand for migratory, casual labor had been declining.[25] It collapsed in the Great Depression and never fully returned. What emerged, post-World War II, was an economic order that was less fluid and more structured. Another important development was advancement in transportation. Subways, automobiles, and paved roads extended the distance between work and home, and in ways affordable to the broader public. Moving ceased to be a logical response to unemployment. The "wandering poor" phenomenon of late-nineteenth-century America reflected the gross inefficiencies of matching employers and workers in a world before modern transportation.[26] Though much of America's transportation infrastructure was built during the early twentieth-century decades, systems' social effects would not be fully felt until the disruptions of the Great Depression and World War II were finally passed.

The skid row era of homelessness lasted from World War II until about 1980. The most striking difference between the inhabitants of main stem neighborhoods in the early twentieth century and inhabitants of skid row neighborhoods, after World War II, was that the latter cohort worked less and was less mobile. Skid rowers were those who never recovered from the Great Depression and those left behind by the prosperity of the post-World War II era. Colm Toibin's 2009 novel, *Brooklyn*, later made into a popular movie, provides a useful glimpse into what skid row-era homelessness looked like. It is set in the 1950s. There is a scene where the young woman protagonist volunteers at a Christmas dinner put on in a parish hall. In reference to a long line of broken men, stooped and visibly intoxicated, the priest in charge of the dinner explains, "They built the tunnels and bridges and the highways. Some of them I only see once a year. God knows what they live on."[27]

The skid row crowd skewed older than the prior era's homeless population[28]; one knowledgeable scholar has likened skid row to a "seedy retirement community."[29] Some observers interpreted skid row's existence as evidence of American families' growing heartlessness toward their aged relatives.[30] At mid-century, the homeless population in America was still comprised mainly of white males.[31] Before modern homelessness emerged around 1980, America's black population endured severe poverty and severe social discrimination. Since the emergence of modern homelessness, America's black population has endured still-considerable poverty but less social discrimination. Anyone familiar with the history of racism in America, but not the history of homelessness, would likely expect homelessness to have been rampant among minority populations under Jim Crow. But the opposite is the case. In the romantic era, homelessness consisted heavily of men traveling for work, and black men simply could not expect the same employment opportunities in strange cities as whites could. Thus, it's understandable that so few black men were tramps and hobos. If transient whites were, often as not, unwelcome presences in many communities, one can scarcely imagine the kind of reception that large masses of transient destitute black men would have received.

The white cast of homelessness in America persisted into the skid row era.[32] To the extent that it makes sense to speak of homelessness as something that happens to someone, it might be said that whites were disproportionately impacted by homelessness until the "modern" era began around 1980. Some scholars have identified black mini-skid rows; black and other minorities did live in SRO hotels located outside the main skid row district.[33] Some one-off studies found that the black share of the skid row population mirrored that of the black population for the city as a whole, but that is still surprising, in light of the extreme poverty and social discrimination to which cities' black populations were subjected.[34] Skid row institutions such as hotels and bars practiced segregation as consistently as institutions in ordinary American society.[35] Pushing into the 1970s, toward the end of the skid row era, black people, like the mentally ill, were appearing in larger numbers on skid row.[36] *Sunshine Hotel* (2001), a documentary about one of the last SROs on the Bowery, features mostly black residents. The subjects of *On the Bowery* (1956) and *How Do You Like the Bowery?* (1960) are mostly white. In photographer

Michael Zettler's 1975 work, *The Bowery*, of the approximately seventy individuals pictured whose race is identifiable, only four are black.

It is not fully clear why homelessness remained so white for so long. Writing in the early 1970s, sociologist Howard Bahr reflects, "In most skid rows, the proportion of blacks is less than the proportionate size of the black population of the city as a whole. Given the fact that skid row men are drawn disproportionately from the lower socioeconomic strata and that blacks are overrepresented among low-income populations in American metropolitan areas, the shortage of blacks on skid row is even more striking."[37] The modern homeless population is disproportionately black.[38] Racism is commonly blamed for modern homelessness.[39] Public opinion surveys demonstrate that Americans have, over the last half century, grown vastly more comfortable with interracial marriage.[40] Claiming that racism explains where modern homelessness came from requires reconciling the ideas that white people have been, more and more, pushing black people into the streets while also, more and more, welcoming them into their families as in-laws. Segregated housing was banned in the 1960s. This opened up many opportunities for the black middle class, many of whom moved to better neighborhoods in the suburbs. "Black flight" destabilized minority neighborhoods. But destabilized neighborhoods have cheap rents. Therefore, neighborhood destabilization can function just as much as a homelessness prevention mechanism as a cause of homelessness. Much "informal" segregation still exists, but as to why that should cause homelessness, when the historical combination of far more powerful formal segregation did not, is unclear. The black population is larger, as a share of the overall population, in Mississippi than in any other state. Mississippi is extremely poor, but it has the lowest homelessness rate of any state. New York's homelessness rate (475 per 100,000) is more than ten times that of Mississippi's (40 per 100,000).[41]

Alcoholism features prominently in every photographic, journalistic, and documentary account of skid row culture. Titles of leading skid row studies include *You Owe Yourself a Drunk*, *Stations of the Lost: The Treatment of Skid Row Alcoholics*, and *Old Men Drunk and Sober*. Many academic articles about skid row were published in alcoholism journals.[42] Writing about skid row without mentioning alcoholism would have been like writing about modern homelessness without mentioning mental illness. In mid-century Minneapolis, more than 40 percent of annual arrests took place in the local skid row district, the Gateway, and of those arrests, more than 90 percent were for drunkenness.[43] In 1958, a sociologist calculated that the per capita liquor store rate in Philadelphia's skid row neighborhood was four times that of the city as a whole.[44]

Men living on skid row probably worked at a lower rate than the hoboes during the romantic era but at a higher rate than the modern homeless population.[45] The railroads were a significant source of skid row residents' jobs. Insofar as the railroads declined, and those jobs weren't replaced, unemployment would have gone up. Restaurants were also major employers.[46] Much of the work was non-steady, unskilled "spot" labor accessed through "slave market" employment agencies.[47] Maladjusted alcoholic men who couldn't maintain a full-time job but were able to work on an ad hoc, off-the-books basis on their "good days."[48] Some have argued that one reason why skid row slums stuck around for as long as they did is because of local economies' need for cheap labor.[49] That might explain why skid rows were tolerated more than encampments are today, since no one views encampments as a valued source of labor, though it's also true that skid rows contained homelessness-related disorder more effectively than encampments do. The members of cities' business elites who oversaw skid rows' decline must not have regarded them as economically essential. There's more than one way an economy can find unskilled laborers when it needs to. Another would be immigration. Skid row's heyday coincided with a historic low of immigration.[50] Many of the off-the-books jobs that immigrants do now were done by skid rowers back in the day. In his important 1963 study, *Skid Row in American Cities*, sociologist Donald Bogue argues that skid row was an "economic liability" for urban America because of the costs in imposed via police and other municipal services and depressed values.[51] Bogue says that "young migrant workers" (black people arriving from the Great Migration and Puerto Ricans) could better meet cities' unskilled labor needs. "[T]he entire skid row labor force could disappear from the economic scene and scarcely be missed."[52]

The cornerstone of the skid row subeconomy was the single-room occupancy hotel. In their most familiar form, these were old buildings—sometimes former factories or warehouses—whose owners had, decades prior, recrafted their interiors into a collection of semi-private "cubicles" or "cages." Typical proportions were 4 × 6, the walls were plywood, and the "ceiling" was chicken wire. An SRO hotel would pack dozens, sometimes hundreds, of men into the same building. For as long as the SROs lasted, prices were kept very low, which required packing in as many units per building as possible and keeping quality very low.[53] Bathrooms were shared and one's sleep was often disturbed by unpleasant smells and noises.

Some scholars believe that homelessness in America hit a historic nadir during the skid row era.[54] This is hard to say for certain due to the absence of quality data and classification issues. A cage hotel resident paying rent on a weekly or monthly basis out of his pension or public assistance has a set-up not unlike that of a supportive housing resident in the twenty-first century. We don't consider the supportive housing resident homeless; was the SRO resident "homeless"? Also, the size of a city's skid row district can't function perfectly as an estimate of its postwar homeless population, because not all SROs were located in skid rows.

But to the extent that homelessness in the postwar period was kept to manageable proportions, much credit must go to the SRO. SRO housing was housing affordable to the poorest of the poor, run by for-profit operators. Investments in publicly-subsidized housing can't get credit for low homelessness during the skid row era, because that's not where the skid rowers lived. Among other reasons, many public housing programs, at least for a while, maintained rigid behavioral standards that skid row types couldn't have met.[55] SRO operators were more understanding about human frailty. Sleeping on the street was rare.[56] Particularly rare seem to have been chronically unsheltered adults—people who sleep outside for years. We have yet to discover a more effective mechanism for preventing poor people from sleeping on the streets than the exploitative for-profit SRO hotel model.

However, there was some sense in which SROs functioned as "welfare housing." This was not a pure free market model. Many who lived in SROs drew modest veterans or railroad pensions, Social Security, or public assistance.[57] In some cases, the local welfare agency sent checks directly to the SRO operator who would then disburse what was left after the rent was paid.[58] Stretching back into the tramp era, some cities operated voucher or "ticket" programs by which taxpayers paid the cost of an SRO stay for someone who couldn't meet it on his own.[59]

Skid row was much more disreputable than the main stem. It attracted many sociologists, journalists, photographers, and documentary filmmakers, but few poets. Every account has some passage like the following: "Skid row represents the bottom, the visible embodiment of the lowest place that one can sink to in our society."[60] Compared to modern public shelters and encampments, skid row was no more effective in moving people out of homelessness. The SRO-dwelling alcoholic was just as socially isolated as the meth-addicted tent dweller today. But skid row burdened non-skid row neighborhoods far less than shelters and encampments burden their host cities. Reasonable people can debate whether skid row was worth saving. But the more interesting question is whether what replaced it is better.

URBAN RENEWAL

One can't understand where modern homelessness came from without understanding the strenuous and ongoing efforts postwar cities devoted to reviving their fortunes.

Skid row was a species of the larger genus "slum." Social reformers had long viewed slums as bad for their residents and the cities host to them. While many slum-clearance programs have been given a bad reputation for classifying as "slum" functional, if old, neighborhoods, if "slum" meant anything, it meant skid row. Skid row had to go as a consequence of urban renewal. By the lights of postwar urbanists, a modern city simply should not allow people to live like that. Writing in 1948, Edmund "Pat" Brown, later governor of California, argues in favor of a combination of public investments in housing and slum clearance, saying, "We do not permit bad and defective meat to be sold because we know that it is dangerous to the community. The same is true of housing. Slums are injurious to the health of the community and must be eliminated."[61]

That skid row districts were often near downtowns placed them even more squarely in urban planners' cross hairs.[62] Skid row was bad for inhabitants and bad for cities. Countless higher and better uses could be imagined for the real estate controlled by the bums and slumlords who exploited them. In the wake of the American victory in World War II, the Great Society, the space program, and so many other accomplishments, confidence ran high that cities could arrange things for the better for skid row and its inhabitants. Certainly, it was assumed, conditions couldn't get any worse.

For a taste of the can-do attitude behind the demolition of skid row, consider the following two passages from the Bogue study mentioned earlier:

> Skid Row is a major barrier to urban renewal. Not only does it tie up square miles of precious land, but it "poisons" a broad surrounding zone for residential renewal. The economic costs in lost opportunities must annually run into many millions of dollars, and are paid by the citizenry at large. Thus from an economic viewpoint, Skid Row must be regarded as a liability to the community, with no necessary or indispensable economic function.

> [P]lans should be made to make Skid Rows unnecessary. From a sociological and psychological point of view it can be done. Economically, it would constitute an effort to stop a large unproductive drain on the municipal economy and free a large tract of valuable land for other use.[63]

Skid row was extensively studied, with much research conducted somehow in conjunction with postwar urban renewal plans.[64] Some accounts were sympathetic, at least in parts; several concluded that it was a depraved community in decline. The inhabitants were old and infirm and no young men were joining them to replenish the ranks, raising expectations that an end to homelessness in its skid row form was in sight. Vacancies in the SRO stock had started to emerge; some hotel owners were pleading to welfare offices to send more clients to prop up their businesses.[65] City planners took heart in such analyses, as it helped support the intellectual foundation of ongoing urban renewal efforts. The notion of a place for placeless men is obviously paradoxical. Over time, cities decided they didn't need to accept the idea of a place for place-less men.

Some predicted that the "dispersion" of skid row denizens would result in more social integration.[66] Skid row was a ghetto. Planners and scholars looked at the fate of those who lived on skid row, and who might live somewhere else if deprived of the option to live there, somewhat like "moving to opportunity" advocates stress the necessity of deconcentrating poverty in the twenty-first century. Skid row represented one of the most intense concentrations of poverty in modern American history.

The decline of skid row and cities' SRO stock happened through sins of commission and omission. Examples of cities whose skid rows were demolished, all or in part, by urban renewal plans include St. Louis, Denver, Philadelphia, Boston, Chicago, San Francisco, Minneapolis, Stockton, and Norfolk, Virginia.[67] The federal government authorized local authorities to grant $5 to single SRO-dwellers displaced by urban renewal.[68] Urban renewal, strictly speaking, did not demolish the major skid row districts in New York and Los Angeles. Los Angeles's skid row is, famously, still around, as a result of a deliberate effort launched to preserve it in some fashion and contain homelessness-related disorder. However, Los Angeles did lose massive amounts of cheap housing through an aggressive code enforcement push in the postwar decades.[69] New York lost some SRO stock via urban renewal on the Upper West Side.[70] As for the Bowery, it was targeted by Robert Moses for urban renewal, but he did not succeed.[71] Urban revitalization killed off the Bowery: redevelopment combined with the liberal use of tax abatement programs.[72] In the 1950s, New York City prohibited construction of new cubicle-style hotels[73] and conversion of existing buildings for that purpose. Such regulations prevented new skid row districts from emerging to replace the old ones that were revitalized away.[74] Some have argued that another contributing factor was the extension of legal protections against eviction to SRO residents.[75] Rental housing from which one can't be easily evicted is higher quality than rental housing from which one can easily be evicted. But it's also housing that's less likely to attract private capital.[76]

Urban renewal efforts left a legacy of vastly improved housing in American cities overall but a much-diminished low-rent housing stock.[77] The history of twentieth-century American housing policy may be summed up in one phrase: better but less affordable. Housing policymakers now spend little time debating how to improve housing quality and a great deal of time debating how to address affordability. That is due in no small part to urban renewal's legacy. Another legacy is encampment culture. All the tent-dwelling chronically unemployed, mentally ill, and/or drug addicted single adults spread throughout public areas would still be concentrated in specialized skid row districts had cities let their SRO stocks be.

Much of skid rows' decline took place during an era of considerable social activism. Multiple civil rights movements were underway, on behalf of racial minorities, women, and the disabled. But few took up the cause of the "Old Men, Drunk and Sober" living on the Bowery. Arguably, they deserved activism more than anyone else, on account of their extreme poverty and "alienation," both of which were top concerns of Great Society planners.[78] And yet, "Few professionals came to the defense of the hotels when urban renewal programs planned and carried out their destruction."[79] Homeless advocacy arrived too late to save skid row, after the damage had already been done.

THE ASYLUM SYSTEM

The mental hospital was another institution critical to the lives of disadvantaged Americans that, circa the 1950s, few people wanted to have much to do with. In surveying homelessness in its premodern varieties, serious mental illness has a "dog that didn't bark" aspect. We have many high-quality studies of the premodern homeless. The researchers who conducted them, unlike modern researchers, did not instinctively assume that the most important fact about the men they studied was their lack of housing. They carefully considered the psychology of the hoboes, bums, and tramps to understand thoroughly who they were and how they wound up in their current state.[80] They did not report elevated rates of schizophrenia. Amid the amazingly rich terminology used to categorize the premodern homeless, there seems to have been no term for "mentally ill homeless." Few mentally ill were served by the Great Depression-era transient program.[81] The romantics even argued that hitting the road was a mark of psychological health, not a disordered mind. Major works about skid row culture devote extensive space to alcoholism but comparatively little space to serious mental illness.

The most sensible explanation for serious mental illness' reduced prominence in the premodern homelessness debate is that the seriously mentally ill who were at risk of being on the streets, back then, were institutionalized. State governments set up "asylums" in the nineteenth century to provide the mentally ill with facilities custom-built for their needs. Mental health advocates, Dorothea Dix most notably, were outraged over the high rates of mental illness among the incarcerated and poorhouse populations of their time. (Many have noted the irony that, in twenty-first-century America, the seriously mentally ill find themselves once again heavily confined to jails and poorhouses.)[82] Asylum programs were expensive. Governments hired some of the leading architects of the day, such as Henry Hobson Richardson and Frederick Clarke Withers, and landscape architect Frederick Law Olmstead, to design asylum buildings and campuses.

Public mental hospitals before deinstitutionalization restored mental stability to many, even without the benefit of modern psychiatric medicine. But their rate of success wasn't sufficient to keep systems from being overwhelmed. By 1940, the institutionalized population was about 190 times larger than it had been in 1840.[83] Over time, the asylums became dumping grounds for problems other than mental illness as we would now conceive of it. Two examples were syphilitics and the elderly with dementia.[84] At the peak of the asylum era, the elderly comprised one-third of the patient census, a function of both the high number of chronic mentally ill but also how mental hospitals had come to function as a "surrogate old age home."[85] Because of the high proportion of patients who could not be treated and had no hope of recovery, mental hospitals became extremely depressing places. Rising censuses pushed down staff-to-patient ratios, compromising the quality of care.[86] States under-invested in mental hospital systems throughout the Depression and World War II years, thus leaving some systems quite the worse for wear around mid-century.[87] The term "snake pit" entered common parlance with the eponymous book (1946) and film (1948) that chronicled novelist Mary Jane Ward's traumatic experience in a New York mental hospital. Journalistic and first-person accounts of mental hospitals dealt blows to their public reputation from which they never recovered.[88] Their reputation among psychiatrists was also low. Asylums were a source of profound embarrassment for the psychiatric profession at a time when it was trying to establish itself as a legitimate medical discipline.[89] Public mental hospitals always provided care. They cared for people no one else would care for. But real doctors treat illnesses and cure them. At real hospitals, people get better and leave. Those who supervised the custodial care of hundreds of senile and chronically psychotic patients provided a vital public service. But they did not appear to be practicing medicine.[90] State government officials were ambivalent about pouring more money into an ineffective system that was already busting their budgets.

The parallels with urban renewal are striking. In the post-World War II era, both skid rows and the asylums faced heavy criticism and lacked strong defenders. In both cases, the perception was that whatever risks a program of radical reform might run, scarcely anyone could imagine conditions getting worse. The advocates of "deinstitutionalization" (as it would eventually become known) claimed that life "in the community" would be far superior to long-term hospitalization. But where was this "community"? Did that term mean something more than "not in a hospital"?[91] As with skid row, a troubling vagueness persisted as to what the new "community"-oriented mental healthcare system would look like ("mental patients could stream forth to take their rightful place in 'the community,' wherever that is.")[92] For many, of course, "the community" would turn out to mean the streets. At present, there are around 37,000 patients in public mental hospitals and an estimated 59,000 unsheltered homeless people with severe mental illness.[93]

During deinstitutionalization's initial phases, not all reformers were committed to a complete dismantling the mental hospital system. Antipsychotics began to come online in the 1950s and some in the mental health community saw them not as providing an alternative to mental hospitals, but as a therapy that would make patients more manageable and therefore allow mental hospitals to function as true hospitals. Symptoms could be controlled and other therapies could then take effect, leading to greater rates of recovery and return to the community, which had always been the goal.[94] Reducing patient censuses could bring down staff-to-patient ratios and ease pressure on the system. Governments began transferring many of the elderly to nursing homes, providing another measure of relief.[95]

But legal and fiscal developments caused momentum to accelerate. Civil commitment laws were changed. In 1967 Governor Ronald Reagan signed into law California's Lanterman–Petris–Short Act. In other states, civil liberties advocates worked through the courts, winning landmark decisions such as *Lessard v. Schmidt* (1972) at the federal district court level and, at the US Supreme Court level, *O'Connor v. Donaldson* (1975). Some lawsuits began as efforts to improve the quality of inpatient care. But the general result was to bar access to inpatient care except for in instances of immediate danger to self or others. The personal freedom of the mentally ill was expanded at the expense of governments' ability to care for and provide treatment to them.

When Medicaid was passed in the 1960s, the federal government wanted to avoid fiscal responsibility for the long-term care of the thousands of patients still held in state mental hospitals. Accordingly, Medicaid reimbursement was denied to "institutions of mental disease"—meaning, mental institutions.[96] States followed the money. With the federal government offering to pick up around half the bill for community-based mental health services, those became the default option, regardless of their clinical appropriateness. Though the institutionalized population had been declining since 1955, the rate of reduction, before Medicaid's passage, had been only a couple percentage points a year. After Medicaid's passage, the annual rate of reduction picked up and had hit double digits by the early 1970s.[97] The inpatient census in traditional public psychiatric hospitals fell by more than 60 percent during the 1970s, or about 230,000.[98] Between the mid-1950s and mid-1970s, though admissions actually increased,[99] the average length of a psychiatric hospitalization fell from 211 days to 38.[100] This all happened after the mental hospitals had returned the easiest-to-release patients to the community and when the baby boomer generation was entering adulthood, when serious mental illness develops.[101] In light of the extraordinary magnitude of the 1970s-era patient census reductions, it is thus probably not a coincidence that in 1980 the modern homelessness debate began. The phrases "die with their rights on" and "falling through the cracks" date back to the 1970s.[102]

The rate of serious mental illness among the homeless population was picking up toward the end of the 1960s.[103] Housing reform and mental health reform intersected as governments sent more and more mentally ill adults into a low-rent housing market whose supply was dwindling. Here's what one man's life looked like in the late 1970s:

> Gerald Kerrigan lived on Manhattan's Upper West Side in 1978. He exhibited odd behavior patterns, such as insisting that his trousers, which he acquired from the Salvation Army or Goodwill, had silver rather than gold zippers. He often stopped on Broadway to look down and examine his zipper to make sure that it was silver. He lived in a 7-by-11-foot room in the Continental Hotel on West 95th Street. The hotel, a place of frequent petty crime and other nuisances, housed 192 people, 92 of whom were former patients in mental health hospitals. A social worker, whose salary was paid for by the city of New York, offered counseling to the Continental Hotel residents. When Kerrigan received his $238.65 SSI check each month, he turned it over to the social worker who took money out to pay the rent, settled the bill that Kerrigan had run up at a local restaurant, and gave him $2.50 a day for spending money.[104]

What we now call supportive housing—subsidized housing for the formerly homeless, accompanied by services—could have emerged out of the old SRO stock had we managed to hold onto it. That would have entailed knitting together income support programs such as SSI, community-based mental health and other social services, and the housing. The old SROs were located in objectively "bad" neighborhoods—skid rows—who exposed formerly institutionalized individuals to temptation and harm. But the buildings would have not faced community opposition, because they were already sited. These were facilities that had housed a troubled, extremely low-income population going back generations. Converting SROs to supportive housing was done in some cases.[105] Unfortunately, though, too many units were lost, leaving governments in the undesirable position of having to build new housing units priced using late twentieth- early-twenty-first-century land, material, and labor costs, and for a troubled population unwelcome in many neighborhoods.

A myth persists that the reason why deinstitutionalization failed was because not enough "community mental health centers" (CMHCs) were built. The plan to use federally-funded CMHCs to replace the traditional state mental hospitals was initiated by President John F. Kennedy. Initially, the plan was 2,000 centers; 754 had been built by 1980.[106] However, it's doubtful that having built the additional 1,246 CMHCs would have made much difference, because those CMHCs that were built didn't replace the mental hospitals. The CMHCs served a different clientele with easier-to-treat maladies and, in some notable cases, didn't function as much of a medical facility but rather a center of political activism.[107] By any measure, mental health services expanded dramatically in the postwar period: the number of mental health professionals (psychiatrists, psychologists, and psychiatric social workers) increased fourteenfold from 1945 until the early 1980s.[108] Spending on mental health services increased more than seventyfold over the course of the second half of the twentieth century.[109] But much of the benefit of these expansions went to people with milder mental disorders, a completely different cohort than the formerly institutionalized, or those who would have been institutionalized in a previous era.

The asylum system was not a hellscape of sadism and oppression. But even if one accepts the "snake pit" accounts as representative of former times, psychiatry is now better qualified to treat serious mental illness, sustained economic growth has made tax bases across the nation more capable of funding psychiatric hospitals, and we have many legal restrictions to prevent deprivation and abuse that weren't in place during the bad old days.[110] And yet, deinstitutionalization continues to this day, following the recommendations of disability rights groups who believe no reduction in hospital beds ever goes far enough.[111] Since 1980, state and county mental hospitals have lost about 100,000 beds.[112]

THE VAGRANCY LAW REGIME

The skid row order was held together by a pull effect of SROs and other businesses catering to destitute single men and a push effect of policing low-level disorder offenses. The premodern homeless were not welcome in most communities. When the "wandering poor" emerged in the post-Civil War era, communities started passing new laws and ramping enforcement of old laws, to regulate them and their behavior.[113] One crucial tool was vagrancy laws. Vagrancy laws made it illegal to *be* a vagrant.[114] Someone who was poor and not working was at risk of being arrested and prosecuted for the crime of vagrancy. Don't want to be arrested on vagrancy charges? Then don't be a vagrant. "Vagrancy law presumed that one's status as a vagrant continued until the vagrant had 'reformed.' Presence on skid row was proof that one had not yet reformed."[115] Vagrancy law targeted the tramp and bum cohorts,[116] less so the hoboes, though in practice it could be difficult to parse who belonged in which of those categories. Vagrancy laws served to deter poor outsiders from communities that did not want to be burdened by large numbers of no-account drifters.

Membership in a social order, such as a family or a community, places informal restrictions on your behavior. If you're not known to be part of any social order, you're also not known to be subject to social restrictions on your behavior.[117] If social restrictions are known or suspected to be unavailing, then legal restrictions will be pursued. Just as the asylum system served to strengthen families, who typically set the civil commitment process in motion, the vagrancy law regime strengthened communities at a time when market capitalism was both increasing prosperity and posing threats to communities' traditional expectations of order and trust. The more strangers there are in a community, the less trust that there will be.

Jack London gives a useful description of how vagrancy laws worked in a chapter entitled "Pinched" in his 1907 book *The Road*. Setting foot in Niagara Falls, New York, early one morning during the summer of 1895, a local policeman confronts London and interrogates him about his housing arrangements. London is unable to answer to the policeman's satisfaction. He's arrested, found guilty through a perfunctory court proceeding, and sentenced to thirty days in the Erie County Penitentiary on a charge of "Tramp."[118] That was the offense: being a tramp.

London's experience was representative. Punishments in the thirty-to-ninety-day range that entailed jail and/or hard labor were standard for a vagrancy conviction.[119] In Woody Guthrie's song "Hard Travelin'," he reports getting "ninety days" for vagrancy. In some cities, you could get charged for vagrancy in some cities if you approached a policeman and asked where the nearest shelter was. If your first offense, the sentence would be waived if you agreed to leave town as soon as possible. You could also be arrested for vagrancy if you showed up more than three times at the same municipal lodging house.[120] In the counter-romantic literature about tramping, the police loom large. Writers trying to dissuade the young from hitting the road would emphasize the likelihood that they would fall afoul of authorities and wind up in jail, sentenced to a few months' incarceration or hard labor. Trespassing on trains was a common offense and the private security forces employed by railroads were sometimes greater presences than municipal police officers. Vagrancy law had enormous flexibility and was deployed not only against bums and tramps but also to keep racial minorities and political radicals in line.[121] Addressing low-level disorder was most certainly considered a responsibility of police, the police insisted they needed maximum discretion to perform that function and governments obliged.

The modern reader will wonder: How was this considered remotely constitutional? A strenuous effort of moral imagination is required to appreciate vagrancy law. Occasionally, critics of modern homelessness policy will call for reviving some element of past eras' approaches, such as mental hospitals, but rarely does anyone call for bringing back vagrancy law. At the time, vagrancy law had three justifications. First, it was rooted in a common law tradition stretching back centuries. Second, it was considered essential to crime prevention. Vagrancy law served as a means of containing disorder so that disorder did not transition into more dire threats to life and property. Preventing crime also required apprehending known criminals, such as mobsters, whose high-priced lawyers helped them exploit loopholes in criminal procedure rules. For better or worse, this was another purpose to which vagrancy law was applied: "an escape hatch to avoid the rigidity imposed by real or imagined defects in criminal law and procedure."[122]

Third, vagrancy law reflected how the public expects police to deal with disorder, and dealing with disorder requires discretion. The concept of police work as "law enforcement" envisions disorder as addressed by legislatures passing laws and then police enforcing them. What the law says certainly matters to police work but, strictly construed, law enforcement does not work well as a response to disorder. Disorderly actions come in too great a variety, and happen too frequently, to be dealt with by simply arresting everyone who commits one. The police made a lot of arrests on skid row and homeless men spent a lot of time jail, quite likely, much more than now. In Howard Bahr's 1973 book, *Skid Row: An Introduction to Disaffiliation*, he cites the example of a man who, in 1965, had been in court almost 280 times on a charge of public intoxication, an offense related to vagrancy, and served, all told, more than sixteen years for those offenses.[123] But accounts of policing under the vagrancy law regime also stress how much discretion was used not to arrest and how arrests were used in tactical ways. Skid row functioned as a containment zone, akin to a red-light district, within which everyone understood your chances of being arrested for certain offenses were far lower than for the same offense committed elsewhere.[124] Verbal warnings or requests to move along carried more authority when officers held in reserve a broader power to arrest than they do now.[125] Low-level arrests were used for de-escalationary purposes, to keep potentially dangerous situations under control. Police exercised considerable leniency under the vagrancy law regime and performed many quasi-social work functions.[126] Writes historian Eric Monkkonen, "While occasionally they arrested tramps for vagrancy, police more often had a supportive relationship with tramps. They lodged them overnight on station house floors or in special lodging rooms, and sometimes provided breakfast, all for no cost or fear of arrests."[127]

The vagueness of vagrancy law—who is a vagrant, what is the crime he is about to commit unless you arrest him for his vagrant status—was, ultimately, what the Supreme Court found unacceptable about it. But it was vague by design.[128] It authorized discretion. If you can trust police to use discretion appropriately, then vagrancy laws were a sensible response to the messiness of public disorder. During the 1960s, police discretion came under close scrutiny. Social mores changed. That vagrancy law was based in centuries of legal tradition no longer seemed like a virtue but, rather, a defect in the eyes of reformers intent on crafting an entirely new social order.

The vagrancy law regime may also be seen as an extension of localism. Communities used it to assert some control over dynamism and the wrenching social change experienced between the Civil War and World War II.[129] Dynamism has always been a major contributing factor to homelessness.[130] "Homelessness seems most prevalent during periods of social change and the disorganization that inevitably follows."[131] In the nineteenth century, anyone without visible means of support came under suspicion because idleness was scorned[132] and, though a responsibility to the poor was recognized, the welfare state was locally oriented. Communities were determined to care only for their own and thus demarcated sharply the border between "their own" and some other community's responsibility. Hence both the settlement laws discussed earlier and vagrancy law.[133] Local welfare programs were, as it happens, sometimes overwhelmed by demands for relief such as during the severe recessions of the late nineteenth century.[134] One of the New Deal's foundational premises was that a community-oriented welfare state could not bear the burden recessions placed on it.

American cities developed the use of vagrancy law to respond to the rise of the wandering poor, when threats to public disorder were often serious. With, perhaps, hundreds of thousands of poor single men traversing the nation in the late nineteenth, early twentieth century,[135] migratory laborers presented a formidable spectacle: "During the prairie wheat harvests, the migration of hobo workers was often so dense that the incoming freights seemed like perches for roosting blackbirds."[136] They were not all happy-go-lucky folk singers. All three of the following statements can be true: (1) migratory laborers were economically necessary for the settling of the West; (2) many migratory laborers were men of low character, who were a bad influence on impressionable area youth; and (3) since they were, almost by definition, strangers, it was impossible to parse the upstanding hoboes from their delinquent and predatory fellow travelers.[137]

Courts and lawyers put an end to the vagrancy law regime. During the post-World War II era, civil liberties lawyers took up cases that might have otherwise been processed as a matter of course, much like Jack London's was, and published law review articles that took aim at the constitutional basis of vagrancy laws as well as laws that served similar purposes such as public drunkenness.[138] *Papachristou et al. v. City of Jacksonville*, a 1972 ruling by the US Supreme Court, put the final nail in the coffin. It struck down the city of Jacksonville's vagrancy ordinance on void-for-vagueness grounds, a violation, in other words, of the Fourteenth Amendment's due process clause. *Papachristou* was unanimous (7 to 0) and was written by William O. Douglas.

Douglas still holds the record as the longest-serving Supreme Court justice in history: thirty-six years. Many of the lawyers who challenged vagrancy laws' constitutionality did not have skid row bums foremost in mind. Often, their plaintiffs were racial minorities, political radicals, and similarly sympathetic figures.[139] But there can be no doubt that, in *Papachristou*, Douglas was thinking of the homeless population.[140] Douglas hailed from the Pacific Northwest and claimed to have gone out tramping and riding the rods (literally) during his youth. In recent high court rulings, such as *Boise v. Martin* (2018), judges have argued that the homeless shouldn't be arrested because they're victims. Douglas argued that the homeless shouldn't be arrested because they're heroes. To him, vagrancy laws stifled the American spirit, what made this nation great. His opinion cited Whitman and Thoreau in explaining the injustice of vagrancy laws. Douglas was writing in 1972, the skid row era. Some hardy souls were yet "riding the rods," but not many.[141] In 1980, Steam Train Maury Graham, probably the last celebrity hobo in America, "estimate[d] that there are fewer than thirty genuine, train-jumping hoboes still traveling across the country."[142] The paradigm was not "Song of the Open Road" but, rather, "Old Men Drunk and Sober" scraping by on the Bowery, and that had been the case since the Great Depression.

Arrests for public drunkenness, vagrancy, and disorderly conduct plummeted between 1960 and 1990.[143] New tools for meeting public complaints about disorder had to be devised. Laws against disorder now must be more specific than in former eras, to avoid being struck down on void for vagueness grounds (Fourteenth Amendment), and behavior-based, not status-based (Eighth Amendment). Regulations on panhandling must be careful not to run afoul of First Amendment's protections for free speech. Street-sleeping and panhandling can still be prohibited, but only under certain conditions. Police discretion is highly restricted by law as well as by cellphone cameras. But demands that police "do something" about public disorder, demands made by the public, remain unrelenting. We will never get police completely out of the lives of homeless individuals until we identify a solution to disorder satisfactory to the public that doesn't rely on the police.

CONCLUSION: AN AMERICAN TRAGEDY

Modern homelessness emerged out of modern liberalism. Modern liberalism nourished extremely ambitious plans during the postwar era that included the idea that society might at some point cease to need a place to put people who don't want to be part of it. In the postwar era, urban planners wrongly conceived of skid row as mainly a physical place when, in fact, it was more accurately understood as a social phenomenon. We learned that public policy can eliminate skid row the physical place, but not the social reality underlying the physical place.[144]

The thread of good government reform's unintended consequences runs throughout the history of urban renewal, vagrancy law, and deinstitutionalization. The tragedy of skid row consists in how the same spirit behind the strong post-World War II economy that reduced homelessness led also to the overreach that demolished skid row and created the current modern homelessness crisis. When governments tightened housing regulations and tried to revitalize old urban areas, they eliminated most of their low-rent housing stock. When governments tried to restrain the abuse of police power, they transformed entire cities into disorder zones. When government tried to do better by the mentally ill, they turned them out onto the streets. Solutions to old problems created new problems.

4

The Modern Era

1980 to Present

In the mid-1970s, New York City almost went bankrupt. Multiple books and studies gave thorough accounts of the causes and effects of New York's fiscal crisis. They discussed crime, the collapse of manufacturing, families fleeing the city, racial tension, arson, property abandonment, the 1977 blackout, drugs, graffiti, dog waste, and fiscal malfeasance. They devoted little attention to homelessness. Flash forward ten years, New York was generally more stable and "homelessness" had become a preeminent topic of public concern. Mario Cuomo highlighted homelessness in his famous speech at the 1984 Democratic National Convention.[1] Celebrities embraced the cause with gusto.[2]

The era of modern homelessness replaced the skid row era around 1980. At that time, Americans began noticing large numbers of extremely poor single adults occupying public spaces during both daytime and nighttime hours. Compared to the traditional skid row crowd, they were younger, they displayed a higher rate of serious mental illness, and they included a number of women soon to become known as "bag ladies." Cities also reported a surge in demand for temporary housing from single mothers. The plights of both the families and single adults were given prominence by the media and a newly organized and assertive homeless advocacy community. Advocates and the media forced into common parlance the term "homeless."

America was at that time enduring a serious recession. Debate raged over whether this "new homelessness" was the result of a temporary economic crisis, or deeper, most structural changes of a social and/or economic character. As the years pushed on, and the newness of the phenomena became more striking, policymakers began to believe that they had a new problem on their hands. There seemed to be more homelessness in the 1980s, based on the increased demand for shelter. But even more indisputable was that the problem had changed character.

SHOULD RONALD REAGAN BE
BLAMED FOR HOMELESSNESS?

Attention turned to the Reagan administration. The coincidence between modern homelessness's emergence and a Republican president's big talk about restructuring the welfare state and deregulating the economy was irresistible to many observers. The idea that Ronald Reagan caused modern homelessness caught on and has never really gone away. Reagan was blamed for homelessness throughout the 1980s, at the time of his passing in 2004, and he has continued to be blamed in recent accounts purporting to take a long view of the street struggles of San Francisco, Los Angeles, and the like.[3]

Modern homelessness, and Reagan's alleged responsibility for it, is closely bound up with the debate over neoliberalism.[4] For progressives who see homelessness as a Reaganist nightmare from which we're trying to awake, history began with the Great Society. The Great Society differed from the New Deal in its forthright commitment to guaranteeing equality of opportunity for all Americans. The Great Society did not respond to an economic emergency. It was premised on abundance. A wealthy modern nation such as the United States can't allow so much injustice and deprivation to persist. Government must mobilize to fight poverty, much as it did to fight Hitler. At the center of this outlook stood a commitment to civil rights for black Americans, but no one ever intended to stop there. Government mobilization on behalf of women and the disabled followed immediately in the wake of the classic Civil Rights movement's successes, and economic injustice, not just social, was always part of the mix. Finally, close to 200 years after the nation began, America finds itself in a position to build a social order of which it can be proud and not ashamed. It was a new founding.

In this narrative, Reagan stands out as something like an Aaron Burr figure, a usurper. He exploited the New Order's fragility and caused it irreparable harm. Reagan strangled social democracy before it had a chance. Reagan began his political career while the War on Poverty was in its infancy; it was still young by the time he had set his sights on national office. He conned the public into viewing big government's growing pains as fatal weaknesses. Still more galling, from progressives' perspective, was how Democrats, beginning with Bill Clinton, embraced Reaganism, out of a sense of envy toward his political success. Reagan's domestic policy was enormously popular, as attested by his electoral success (he won forty-nine states in the 1984 presidential election) and polls registering high levels of dissatisfaction with the welfare state. Everyone seemed to be against "welfare" in the 1980s.[5] Reagan cut income taxes and welfare reform, though not passed until 1996, could only have happened because of Reagan. Reagan initiated the neoliberal era, during which government adopted a more deferential attitude toward private economic activity. Collective responsibility was out and personal responsibility was in. This is at least how the critics of neoliberalism see things.

Throughout the late 1960s and 1970s, crime soared, social unrest was rampant, and once-great cities lost population, commerce, and confidence. When modern homelessness came along, it represented yet more evidence that things had gone off track. But what would it mean to put America back on track? For those on the left, the Great Society was the first time in US history that things really were on track. They saw homelessness as signaling the need for redoubled investment in government. On the right, people wanted less deviant behavior and crime, and less family instability. Reagan came to power riding a wave of discontent over social liberalism. Great Society architects had promised a new dawn of justice and opportunity that did not arrive. Reagan's supporters saw him as pursuing restoration, not usurpation.

To blame Reagan for modern homelessness is to misunderstand the roots of the current crisis. The preceding two chapters showed that, while homelessness may formerly have taken different forms, it has always existed in America. Just because fewer poor, place-less single men lived out of public spaces in the 1960s does not mean that, at that time, everyone had a place in American society. Not only had urban renewal and deinstitutionalization began years before Reagan took office, but debate over their unintended consequences also preceded his inauguration.[6] Moreover, neoliberalism is not an austerity regime. The Great Society *did* lay a baseline for social democracy insofar as spending on means-tested programs grew expansively over subsequent decades.[7] There can always be a debate over whether we should spend more, or spend differently; there cannot be a debate over whether Ronald Reagan and his successors slashed spending, because they did not. Reagan talked a big game about cutting government but, at the end of day, his legacy on retrenchment was modest. Boasts and proposals that never came into effect shouldn't be mistaken for things that actually happened. The year Reagan left office, 1989, during a time of economic expansion, 4.4 percent of the population was on welfare, only a slight dip from the 4.6 percent rate in 1980, a year during which the economy was in recession.[8] Reagan did reduce SSI access. However, those changes were quickly reversed and Supplemental Security Income (SSI) enrollment rebounded throughout the 1980s. There are currently 4.8 million Americans, ages eighteen to sixty-five, now receiving SSI, more than twice as many as during the Reagan years.[9] The program's growth does not seem to have reduced homelessness. The real debate over Reagan and neoliberalism concerns the rate of growth. Reagan's critics believed then and still believe now that if the welfare state's not continuously growing in response to every new challenge, something has gone wrong.

As for homelessness and housing proper, Reagan is commonly accused of ending a golden age in affordable housing by forcing the US Department of Housing and Urban Development 's (HUD) budget to retrench. HUD oversees the main federal subsidized housing programs. Figure 4.1, whose data are drawn from a 2019 report published by the Congressional Research Service, illustrates the growth in terms of subsidized units under HUD's control: public housing, other "project-based" programs, and vouchers.[10]

Federal support for subsidized housing grew during Reagan's years in office. What, then, accounts for claims such as those found in the following passage, from a 2020 *New Yorker* article about San Francisco's homelessness crisis: "Such sights aren't new to the Bay Area, whose homeless population spiked in the eighties, when the Reagan

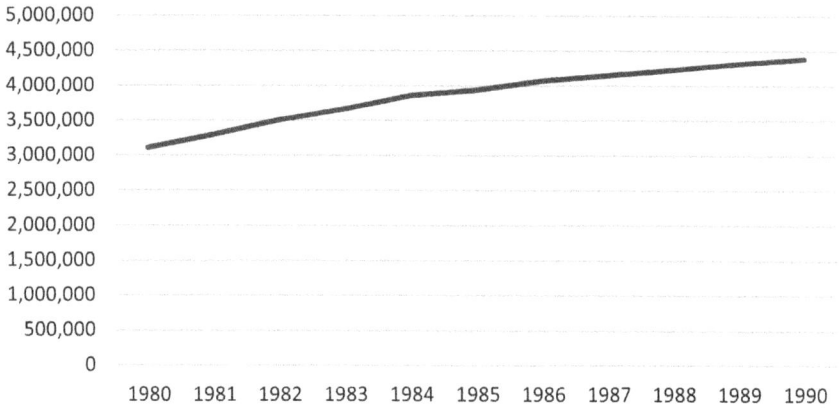

Figure 4.1.   Units in Major Federal Rental Assistance Programs, FY1980–FY1990.

Administration cut the budget of the Department of Housing and Urban Development by 78 percent,"[11] or, similarly, from a 2019 *New Republic* article: "under President Reagan, federal spending on low-income housing plummeted from $32 billion to $7 billion."[12]

The answer, as has been explained by a number of conscientious scholars over the years, lies in the difference between "budget authority" and "budget outlays."[13] Outlays are what the government actually spends; "budget authority" is what it is authorized to spend. Any claim that blames homelessness on Reagan slashing federal housing programs refers to budget authority, not outlays.[14] Objectively, the more important number is how much was actually spent. But for the purposes of partisan debate, the more important number is the reduction in budget authority, because it makes Reagan look worse. Critics can argue, if they like, that Reagan and his successors did not commit enough resources to subsidized housing, because "enough" is a concept based on norms about which people will disagree. But the least that should be done, when Reagan's approach to housing is discussed, is to include both numbers: figures on outlays and figures on budget authority. However, that's rarely done, leaving readers with the impression that after Reagan, the federal government did less to meet housing assistance needs than before he took office.

Major new housing programs were launched during the Reagan era. The Low-Income Housing Tax Credit was enacted as part of the 1986 Tax Reform Act. That $10-billion-a-year program is now the single largest federal affordable housing program.[15] The Stewart B. McKinney Homelessness Assistance Act was signed into law toward the end of the Reagan administration. The programs it created remain, to this day, the most important sources of homelessness funding at the federal level. While one could criticize Reagan for dragging his feet on signing the McKinney Act, one cannot criticize him for not signing it. Moreover, much of the debate over federal support for targeted homelessness assistance programs is, to a degree, symbolic; scholars have cast doubt on how effective federal spending has been in reducing homelessness.[16] Homelessness is a problem shaped greatly by state and local policies and dynamics.

MITCH SNYDER AND THE BIRTH OF
MODERN HOMELESSNESS ADVOCACY

Mitch Snyder forced Reagan's hand on homelessness. Snyder was a member of a group called the Community for Creative Non-Violence (CCNV), originally formed in 1970 to protest the Vietnam War. Snyder joined in 1973, after having been radicalized in prison by the Berrigan brothers. He was serving a three-year sentence for auto theft.[17] Snyder was not the only homeless advocate active in the 1980s but he was the most prominent and most consequential. Martin Sheen played him in a 1986 TV movie (*Samaritan: The Mitch Snyder Story*). No one did more than Snyder to elevate homelessness, which had not been on the media's radar in the 1970s, to an issue of national prominence.

Snyder was media-obsessed to the point of caricature.[18] His father had been in showbiz, and he himself had worked in sales and marketing before becoming a professional activist. In a 1986 *Esquire* profile, one of his former CCNV colleagues said, "I think he should come down and lift up food boxes or go through a dumpster when the television cameras *aren't* around."[19] Snyder favored spectacle and, at times, straightforward hijinks: splashing blood on the US Capitol's steps and the altar of St. Matthew's Cathedral; hunger strikes; letting cockroaches loose in the White House; sleeping out of a carboard box on the mayor of Washington, DC's, front steps; setting up a symbolic graveyard for dead homeless people in Lafayette Park; and ornate funeral processions down Pennsylvania Avenue for unsheltered individuals who froze to death.[20] In the summer of 1982, he organized a "Beggar's Banquet." He persuaded Ted Kennedy, and a couple dozen or so other members of Congress, to host a luncheon in the Rayburn Building made from food gathered from dumpsters.[21] By making DC the stage for his rallies and stunts, Snyder not only made homelessness a national story but also a concern of the federal government. Within a few years, he had succeeded in persuading the federal government to assume responsibility of a policy challenge that not only had never been a federal responsibility before but also had never really been identified as a distinct policy challenge at all.

Snyder was ambivalent about the relevance of evidence to homelessness policymaking. In the 1980s, the most important question was: How large of a problem is homelessness? Everyone had the impression that homelessness had grown enormously and that it was continuing to grow. But no one could be confident as to the hard numbers. The federal government, the only entity in a position to provide a nationwide estimate, would not, on a regular basis, start producing one until the 2000s, and not until 2010 did it become somewhat reliable. Individual cities had some data, but how representative was New York City's experience? One of the best ways to count the size of the homeless population is based on how many people use services like shelters, but some people lived on the street and hardly used any services at all.

During the 1988 presidential debates, Democratic candidate Michael Dukakis cited a figure of 2.5 to 3 million Americans "living on streets and in doorways."[22] That figure, a version of which members of the media cited countless times throughout the 1980s,[23] came from Mitch Snyder, who had no basis for making it. We know this because he admitted as much. Here is the account Snyder gave of his methodology on an episode of *Nightline* in May 1984: "Everybody demanded [a nationwide estimate], everybody said we want a number. . . . We got on the phone, we made lots of calls, we talked to lots of people, and we said, 'Okay, here are some numbers.' They have no meaning, no value."[24] One week after that show, Snyder doubled down. The Reagan administration had come out with an estimate of 250,000 to 350,000 homeless persons nationwide.[25] In a hearing on the study, Congressional Democrats and Snyder dismissed it as a shoddily researched bad faith effort to downplay the scope of the crisis.[26] But when Representative John P. Hiler, a Republican from Indiana, attempted to turn the tables on Snyder by demanding that he explain his own reasons for believing that more than two million Americans were homeless, he responded:

> these numbers are in fact meaningless. We have tried to satisfy your gnawing little minds for a number because we are Americans with Western little minds that have to quantify everything in sight, whether we can or not.

> So, in spite of the fact that we have forced people to disappear into the nooks and crannies of our world, we now come forward and say, "We are going to count you." That is neither fair nor rational nor just. No one should be trying to do it.[27]

As early as September 1980, before Reagan's election, Snyder was testifying to Congress, "How many people in the District of Columbia are homeless? Thousands. How many nationally? Millions. Of that much at last we are certain."[28] In his 1990 book *The Excluded Americans*, William Tucker cites a CCNV fundraising letter that projected eighteen million homeless Americans by 2005.[29] With the benefit of hindsight and better data, we can now say that the Reagan administration numbers, though also assembled through methodologically shaky means, were probably close to the real ones.[30] Snyder's defiant denial of the value of intellectual rigor led to accusations that he was "lying for justice."[31]

It's not obvious that exaggerating a social problem's size helps to solve it. Sometimes, when a problem reaches truly staggering proportions, political will to do anything important about it weakens, since any effort appears futile. As will be discussed in the next chapter, modern homeless advocates pride themselves on their commitment to "evidence-based" policymaking. That represents an implicit rejection of Mitch Snyder's assertion that only morally repugnant people care about a precise estimate of homelessness. And, as much as Snyder protested to the contrary, the numbers did matter to him. CCNV was nothing without the media. Being the source of the two to three million homeless Americans datum gave Snyder crucial credibility as an expert, more than just a merry prankster.

Snyder, who was legendarily high strung, came to a sad end, committing suicide in 1989. But his legacy lives on. Major advocacy groups that carry on Snyder's legacy include the Los Angeles Community Action Network, the New York City Coalition for the Homeless, the San Francisco Coalition for the Homeless, and the National Alliance to End Homelessness. Reporters rely on advocacy groups for story ideas and sources. Their liaison status, between the homeless themselves and reporters and politicians, allows them to foreground the most sympathetic homeless individuals and shunt away cases who are sexually aggressive, violent, embarrassing, and/or offensive. Advocates are invited to serve on blue ribbon task forces and to testify before legislative committees. Politicians, Democrats especially, are expected to meet regularly with advocates and vet their policy proposals with them. The legitimacy of advocates' influence is questionable. They aren't elected to their positions. Their claim to speak for the homeless is based mainly on their having persuaded the media and politicians that they speak for the homeless. Even if we assume that a majority of the homeless are in broad agreement with advocates' agenda, that still fails to establish their legitimacy. Perhaps the broader homeless community might prefer someone else to pursue that same agenda, someone they consider more capable, less corrupt, or just a fresher face. Politicians have to run for reelection, to reestablish their legitimacy, and sometimes against members of their own party in primaries.

THE CAMPAIGN TO END HOMELESSNESS

Advocacy movements that succeed tend to go mainstream. Homeless advocacy has generally shifted from confrontation to diplomacy and from wildly extravagant claims to research and data. If one had to identify a point when homeless advocacy went mainstream, it might have been when George W. Bush's housing secretary, Mel Martinez, gave the keynote address at the 2001 annual meeting of the National Alliance to End Homelessness.[32] One year prior, that group had launched the "campaign to end homelessness."[33] Its central premise was that immediate and unqualified access to permanently subsidized housing is not only the best way to address homelessness, it's the way to end it. This approach, often termed "Housing First," has radical roots but has since risen to become the standard philosophy in homelessness policymaking. Housing First places immediate and unqualified access to permanent housing as the central pillar of homeless policymaking. The history of homelessness policy since 1980 is largely the history of the rise of Housing First.

Since 1980, little has changed, fundamentally, about the nature of the challenge. The nature of homelessness differed more between 1960 and 1980 than it did between 1980 and 2020. But government has modified its response. Up until the Bush years, workfare-style approaches, or programs that took a strong interest in addressing substance abuse and mental illness, held influence in homeless policy circles. Welfare reform gave traditionalism an extra boost, but the local orientation of homeless services also guaranteed its influence. Across the nation, many shelter programs were, in the 1990s and 2000s, and still to this day, run by faith-based groups operating outside the influence of advocacy organizations based out of major cities. Many were and are not dependent on federal funding. But even for those who were so dependent, localism had been respected. The Clinton administration set up the Continuum of Care Program, which was structured to funnel federal grants to hundreds of local organizations who would decide how to distribute the funds to community-based service providers.[34]

That basic structure remains in place, but the federal government has become increasingly less tolerant of solutions to homelessness other than permanently subsidized housing. The Bush administration's executive director of the US Interagency Council on Homelessness (USICH) was Phillip Mangano. Under Mangano, USICH became transformed into a public relations office for the Housing First philosophy. Mangano pushed localities to create ten-year plans to end chronic homelessness based around Housing First.[35] By the summer of 2007, more than three hundred communities had developed some kind of plan to end chronic homelessness.[36] The Obama administration tightened the screws on local Continuum of Care grant recipients, to bring them more in line with the Housing First philosophy.

FROM THE GREAT RECESSION TO COVID-19

The 2010s were the first decade in US history throughout which at least reliable national data on homelessness were available. Though the data remain imperfect, they have helped put to rest a couple questions. We know now that New York City is unique. Even since the Bowery days, New York's homelessness struggles have attracted heavy media attention because it's the nation's media capital. New York had quality data about sheltered homelessness earlier than most cities, so, at the early stages of the modern crisis, anyone interested in an objective basis for making claims about homelessness was tempted to look to New York. In his 1988 book, *Rachel and her Children*, Jonathan Kozol asserts that "New York is unique in many ways but, in homelessness as in high fashion, it gives Americans a preview of the future."[37] That passed as plausible at a time when Mitch Snyder was everyone's source for the magnitude of homelessness in America. But 2020 data show that nationwide, outside New York City, the rate of homelessness is 153 per 100,000. In New York City, the rate of homelessness is 943 per 100,000.[38]

Homelessness data from 2010 to 2020 showcased a "tale of two sets of cities" when it came to homelessness. According to the official HUD numbers, homelessness steadily declined coming out of the Great Recession. But it continued to surge in major cities on the coasts. The data have verified that industrial decline is not a large cause of modern homelessness, though that was commonly suspected to be so during the 1980s.[39] The twenty-first century has been a trying time for many Rust Belt cities: "China Shock"-related job losses; continued flight of the middle class, including the black middle class; the opioid crisis; and Detroit city government declared bankruptcy in 2013. But homelessness was not much part of the "American carnage" saga that propelled Donald Trump to victory in Heartland states. Table 4.1 presents the homelessness rates of all fifty states.

Table 4.1. Per Capita Homelessness Rates, US States, 2019

State	Homeless per 100,000	Ranking
New York	475	1
Hawaii	471	2
Oregon	414	3
California	406	4
Washington	321	5
Massachusetts	282	6
Alaska	269	7
Nevada	265	8
Colorado	191	9
Vermont	174	10
Maine	159	11
New Mexico	157	12
Arizona	157	13
Florida	151	14
Minnesota	150	15
Idaho	148	16
Montana	137	17
Nebraska	129	18
South Dakota	122	19
Tennessee	118	20
Maryland	114	21
Georgia	108	22
New Hampshire	106	23
Oklahoma	105	24
Pennsylvania	104	25
Missouri	103	26
Texas	103	27
Delaware	103	28
Utah	101	29
New Jersey	101	30
Rhode Island	100	31
North Carolina	98	32
Wyoming	97	33
Kentucky	94	34
Arkansas	93	35
South Carolina	90	36
Ohio	90	37
Michigan	87	38
Connecticut	85	39
Indiana	84	40
Kansas	83	41
North Dakota	83	42
Wisconsin	80	43
Illinois	79	44
Iowa	76	45
West Virginia	75	46
Virginia	72	47
Alabama	68	48
Louisiana	65	49
Mississippi	40	50

During the 2010s, homelessness rose 30 percent, 47 percent, 92 percent, and 40 percent in Seattle, New York, Los Angeles, and San Francisco, respectively. In those jurisdictions, the issue has received sustained attention from mayors and other state and local officials. Countless blue-ribbon commissions and task forces have been convened. Spending on homeless services has increased dramatically, in part due to successful ballot initiatives such as Los Angeles's Proposition HHH (2016) and San Francisco's Proposition C (2018). In New York City, the budget for homeless services now exceeds $3 billion. Mayor Bill de Blasio's 15,000-unit supportive housing program, which he introduced in 2015, is not only the largest in city history, it is larger than all prior mayors' efforts combined, and the largest in US history. Prior to the COVID-19 pandemic, homelessness ranked as the number one issue of public concern in major cities and it continues to poll high.[40] It continues to poll high because all the spending, media attention, and high-level priority devoted to homelessness have failed to build public confidence that it's under control.

The COVID-19 pandemic touched off multiple debates over homelessness policy. Early on, many predicted catastrophe, both in terms of COVID's impact and on overall levels of homelessness. Leading scholars estimated that the generally poor health of homeless adults would lead to thousands of deaths.[41] These fears motivated several changes to service systems. Governments transferred homeless single adults who had been in dorm-style congregate shelters into thousands of hotel rooms empty because of the collapse in tourism. The Centers for Disease Control and Prevention (CDC) claimed that dismantling encampments risked spreading the virus. Thus, on the West Coast, governments suspended their encampment "resolution" operations. Cities also increased the direct provision of services and resources to encampments, which they had resisted for years. The CDC also claimed that evictions risked spreading the virus. That led to the imposition of eviction moratoria across the nation.

Thousands of homeless people did not die from COVID-19. It is unclear to what degree policy responses, such as the isolation hotels and eviction moratoria played in preventing catastrophe. But the combined effect of the crisis and election of a Democratic presidential administration have energized the political left. In its COVID relief programs, the federal government allocated tens of billions of dollars toward homelessness and housing assistance.[42] Many hope that the effects of the pandemic, combined with the racial unrest stemming from the May 2020 death of George Floyd, will create conditions for permanent changes to the welfare state, such the establishment of a guaranteed income for families and universal housing choice voucher program. These could have dramatic ramifications for America's homeless population.

CONCLUSION

Table 4.2 breaks the main differences between American homelessness in its three historical eras.

Table 4.2.   The Three Eras of American Homelessness in Profile

	Romantic Era	*Skid Row Era*	*Modern Era*
Mobile?	Yes	No	No
Females?	No	No	Yes
Demographic Profile	Disproportionately White	Disproportionately White	Disproportionately Black
Age	Young	Old	Younger
Mentally Ill?	No	Some	Yes
Substance Abuse?	Yes	Yes	Yes

The next three chapters will discuss what we do about homelessness and why. Not so much why we help the homeless in the first place, but why we do it the way we do it. Which principles shape the ends and operations of homeless services in America? In all eras, governments have faced the question of what to do about place-less men, who are extremely poor and have a tenuous connection to work and family. In our era, policymakers respond that we should reduce the harm associated with place-lessness, show compassion, and work toward social integration. The following section will devote a chapter each to these three ideas of harm reduction, compassion, and social integration.

5

Harm Reduction and Ending Homelessness

The homeless population, a subset of the poor population more generally, makes use of numerous government programs: Supplementary Security Income, Medicaid, cash assistance, and the Supplemental Nutrition Assistance Program, to say nothing of mental hospitals and jails. But these programs were not crafted with the homeless in mind. On their own, they are considered insufficient to meeting the needs of homeless single adults and families. Hence the justification for more specialized forms of support.

The homeless population, for whose benefit the homeless services system is designed, number about 580,000.[1] The US Department of Housing and Urban Development (HUD) maintains that estimate, a sum of the annual or biannual "point in time" (PIT) tallies done by localities. The federal government publishes two other homelessness estimates every year: an annualized count of how many people experienced sheltered homelessness over the prior year, which is also published by HUD,[2] and a count of how many public schoolchildren have experienced homelessness over the prior year, published by the Department of Education (DOE).[3] But the HUD PIT count is what is most often cited. The size of the homeless population will always be indeterminate, due to methodological challenges associated with counting the "unsheltered" population and dispute over who is truly "homeless." Doubled-up families are included in the DOE's count but not HUD's. HUD does not count as homeless adult residents of halfway houses, group homes, mental hospitals, or residential treatment programs. Despite their shortcomings, our homelessness data are now vastly more reliable than what policymakers had at their disposal in the 1980s.

Going back to the nineteenth century, researchers have tried to count and analyze homeless populations via the service systems they use. But many homeless people do not use services, including those we care most about. Thus, we must supplement the information we have from service systems by conducting street surveys. But people who turn down services are also likely to turn down requests to participate in surveys.

Thus, our data inadequacies with homelessness are more of a feature than a bug. If we had no service resistance, we would have better data. But if we had no service resistance, we would have much less homelessness.

SYSTEM DESIGN

Federal, state, and local government, and private charity, share responsibility for America's homeless services system. The federal government spends about $5 billion annually on what are considered "targeted" homeless assistance programs.[4] That sum is modest relative to the multi-trillion-dollar magnitude of the federal budget, though considerable in light of how the homeless population numbers less than 600,000 people. Some cities also spend significant sums on homelessness. New York spends more than $3 billion on homeless services annually, Los Angeles around $1 billion annually, and San Francisco around $1 billion over its two-year budget.[5]

Not every city spends that much on homeless services, though. Broadly speaking, the smaller the community, the less it devotes to homeless services out of its own tax revenues, and the more it relies on the federal government and charities. This may reflect the fact that while, in major metros, the public considers homelessness a crisis, most elsewhere, it's seen as a problem. When homelessness polls high in surveys of public concern, political pressure builds to develop custom-built interventions funded by local taxpayers.

Homeless services mainly consist of housing programs. These come in three basic varieties: shelter, transitional housing, and permanent supportive housing. In broad strokes, they differ in the following ways. Shelter (a.k.a., "emergency shelter") provides short-term housing, basic services, and minimal privacy. Single adults, and even some families, sleep in dorm-style accommodations. Transitional housing offers more privacy, more robust service offerings, and intermediate length stays. Transitional housing providers tend to view their program as one designed to help people rebuild their lives, which offers housing as part of that overall effort. Permanent supportive housing provides a subsidized apartment with no formal time limits. It's "supportive" because the unit comes accompanied with access to dedicated social programs. All three are frequently run by community-based nonprofits who contract with the government.[6]

Other forms of "homeless services" include drop-in centers, outreach, and short-term rental assistance programs. Outreach workers canvass public areas to inform unsheltered individuals of available services and try to persuade them to accept those services. Most of the unsheltered population are already aware of available services and programs and have turned them down countless times. Thus, outreach has a low success rate, but it's far less expensive than housing programs and serves the purpose of showing the non-homeless public that government is doing something about problem. Some outreach programs are operated outside the homeless services system proper, by public transit systems, libraries, and business improvement districts.

Reliance on charities is and has always been substantial.[7] Private charities, many faith-based, have served the homeless since the nineteenth century. Many legacy Catholic Worker organizations started by Dorothy Day, or missions launched during the tramp era, are still in operation.[8] Charities run shelters and many "light-touch" programs such as soup kitchens and clothing, socks, and personal hygiene item distribution efforts. Purely private charities that receive no government funding are not major providers of permanent housing benefits.[9]

The system's extraordinarily fragmented. This frustrates any definitive calculation of the total funding and staff we as a nation devote to serving the homeless. One high-quality study from the 1990s reckoned that at that time there were about 40,000 homeless assistance programs nationwide.[10] Decentralization leads to conflicts between neighboring communities. Public officials in San Francisco sometimes complain that other Bay Area communities under-invest in homelessness, promoting an influx into service-rich San Francisco and placing an unfair fiscal burden on San Francisco taxpayers.[11] In 2019, the mayor of Newark, New Jersey, sued New York City over "exporting" homeless families to his community. At issue was a New York program that offered to pay one year of shelter clients' rent if they moved to Newark.[12] Local politicians in Los Angeles sometimes accuse neighboring communities of illegally policing away their homeless populations.[13] Nothing infuriates advocates so much as suggestions that the homeless "choose" their way of life but advocates will allow that people do exercise some choice over where to be homeless.[14]

As is the case with many safety-net programs, the federal government often increases funding for homeless services during a recession. As noted earlier, the recent pandemic-related recession was no different. Because so many homeless services programs are state- and local-based, they are vulnerable to cuts during a downturn.[15] Unlike the federal government, states, cities, and counties must balance their budgets and can't engage in "counter-cyclical" spending. But, on net, the homeless services system's being state- and local-centered has probably encouraged more funding expansions than cutbacks. Since 2000, the deep-blue political climate of San Francisco, Los Angeles, and New York has facilitated more expansions in homeless services spending than did the more purple national political climate over the same span.

HOUSING FIRST AND HARM REDUCTION

Philosophically, homeless services are not as heterogenous as their decentralized structure may suggest. A philosophy known as Housing First reigns supreme. Housing First's influence extends from shelters located in red rural communities to the bluest big-city outreach program. Housing First has two tenets: permanently subsidized housing is the solution to homelessness and all housing benefits should be provided free of strings, such as sobriety or requirements to participate in services. Proponents of Housing First believe that communities must commit themselves to ending homelessness, and that it is a realistic goal. Housing First is held to be both a moral imperative and an "evidence-based" policy. Because of its reputation for rigor, derived from peer-reviewed studies, Housing First proponents argue that it deserves to be made the organizing principle of homeless services systems. To operate one "wet" shelter program, for street homeless individuals not ready for sobriety, is insufficient. All programs must be brought into line with the overarching Housing First philosophy. The idea is that government should focus on connecting people with permanent housing first, and work on other goals—unemployment, sobriety—later, if at all. Any attempt to focus on those goals first, or concurrently, is counterproductive to the goal of ending homelessness. A program that shows no promise whatsoever at addressing behavioral health and unemployment challenges will keep being funded as long as it's hitting its housing metrics. Excellence in homeless services consists of keeping as many people stably housed for as long as possible.

Since the modern homelessness debate began, advocates have always supported increased investment in affordable housing (a position sometimes referred to as "housing, housing, housing"). But most major government housing programs, such as public housing, Section 8 vouchers, and rent regulation, were developed decades ago for reasons having nothing to do with homelessness. Thus, in setting out to confront modern homelessness, back in the 1980s, advocates had to not only press for more housing but also develop their own homelessness-specific housing agenda. That eventually took shape as Housing First.

When first forced to respond to modern homelessness, cities focused on shelter.[16] One estimate, by HUD, reckoned that shelter beds nationwide increased from 100,000 to 275,000 between 1984 and 1988.[17] Another study estimated that by the mid-1990s, almost 6,000 shelter programs existed nationwide.[18] At the crisis's early stages, shelter attracted attention because temporary housing seemed a logical solution to a temporary crisis, and for political reasons. Advocates have been candid that they felt that they could simply get more from Congress by playing up the emergency nature of the crisis as opposed to demanding more long-term-oriented solutions.[19]

As the years pressed on, though, modern homelessness revealed itself to be more than just a temporary crisis. Government, accordingly, set itself to developing more sophisticated solutions. The first purpose-built homeless services system is sometimes described as having had a "linear" structure.[20] Other terms used to describe the structure of pre-Housing First homeless services include "continuum of care" and "staircase." Cities would offer homeless clients a series of housing options from emergency to transitional to permanent. The thinking was that people needed to be moved off the streets gradually, first to shelter, then to a service-enhanced transitional housing program, and then to permanent housing.[21]

This linear system's development coincided with the debate over welfare reform. In 1994, the Clinton administration released a strategic plan on homelessness that featured an epigraph by the president himself about how "work organizes life."[22] Homeless Americans were portrayed as trapped between the streets, shelter, and unstable housing arrangements. To "break the cycle of homelessness," for many, work was critical.[23] But the "linear" structure of homeless services was seen as appropriate regardless of whether someone's needs had to do with unemployment, substance abuse, or mental illness. It was broadly assumed that the hardest cases would need more support beyond just housing benefits, if for no other reason than to ensure the success of whatever housing intervention they received.[24]

With respect to the mentally ill, the "madness in the streets" crisis[25] had shown that deinstitutionalization's promise of "the open warmth of community concern and capability"[26] was central to deinstitutionalization. More "structured care and residential support" was seen as a necessary correction to the reckless reduction in the psychiatric hospitals' census since the 1960s.[27]

Transitional housing, more than any other model, is associated with the pre-Housing First system. As mentioned, in that service mode, housing benefits are temporary, like shelter, but for a longer-term duration—up to twenty-four months—and more richly enhanced with services. The housing was subordinate to the services designed to get at the root causes of clients' homelessness.[28]

The linear system's day was brief. Housing First, which replaced it, began gathering steam in the 1990s. Sam Tsemberis, a New York-based clinician, came up with Housing First. Tsemberis had experience working with the "service resistant" street population. He argued that policymakers devoted too much effort to needs other than permanent housing. His unsheltered clients said they wanted housing, and yet the system led with offers of help finding a job or rehab. Tsemberis became convinced that homeless people don't need to be made "ready" for housing, they just need to be given housing. Far from reining in deinstitutionalization, Tsemberis, a disciple of the radical psychiatrist R. D. Laing and who claims to not believe in civil commitment, argued it hadn't gone far enough.[29] Tsemberis has asserted that housing is a human right. If something is a right, government should provide it without any preconditions.[30]

Tsemberis has also explained that, more than a housing policy, Housing First is a harm reduction approach.[31] Harm reduction policy seeks to treat the symptoms of social problems rather than their roots. It's most commonly associated with substance abuse treatment. Instead of trying to end drug addiction—an unrealistic goal, according to many—needle exchange programs, methadone clinics, and supervised injection facilities all try to make addiction less harmful to addicts. Homeless services professionals acknowledge that lack of housing is not clients' only problem. But in accordance with Housing First, they believe addressing that problem should take priority over addressing clients' chronic unemployment, untreated mental illness, involvement in criminal activities, and drug addiction. The harm reduction core of Housing First is overlooked, sometimes because of proponents' insistence that it does not mean "Housing Only"[32] and that housing benefits function as a "platform" for human flourishing.[33]

Communities' embrace of Housing First has prompted a major shift of resources away from transitional housing to permanent supportive housing (figure 5.1), and "low barrier"-style interventions more generally. Transitional housing has a paternal-

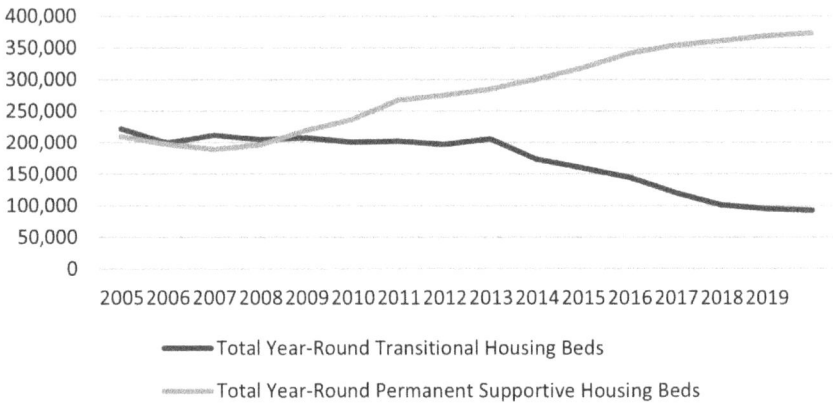

Figure 5.1. Transitional Housing versus Permanent Supportive Housing Units, 2007–2020.

istic reputation associated with what Tsemberis terms the "housing readiness" model. Permanent supportive housing has a slightly different lineage than Housing First but the two models are now considered practically indistinguishable.[34]

Homelessness policymakers in deep blue jurisdictions have been the most enthusiastic about the strategy. As noted, Housing First originated in New York, and California passed a law making it mandatory for state-funded programs.[35] But HUD, a hotbed of support for Housing First, has leveraged communities' dependence on federal funding to implement the policy nationwide. Perfectly competent programs have seen their funding cut, or have been excluded from recent funding expansions, because they favor the workfare-style approach considered acceptable in many anti-poverty policy contexts but considered unacceptable in homeless services. Examples include Community Housing Innovations, the largest provider of homeless services on Long Island,[36] and the New York City-based Doe Fund.[37] Some resistance may be found outside deep blue metros,[38] but every state is purple at least to a degree. Even in red jurisdictions, one finds many progressive Democrats working in certain state and local agencies—libraries, school departments, and certainly social service bureaucracies—just as many conservatives work in police departments in New York and California. HUD support tips the scales to favor Housing First supporters in local homeless services bureaucracies. The Trump administration attempted to weaken Housing First requirements in the HUD Continuum of Care program, the federal government's chief source of general homeless assistance funding. But it was thwarted by advocates and Congress.[39]

In his successful 2020 campaign for the presidency, Joe Biden pledged to "pursue a comprehensive approach to ending homelessness," in part, by enacting the "Ending Homelessness Act" authored by California Representative Maxine Waters.[40] It is more common to hear a politician committing to end homelessness in America than committing to end poverty. This is a legacy of Housing First.

HOUSING FIRST: CONSIDERING THE "EVIDENCE"

Thus, we have, with Housing First, a policy staunchly opposed to attaching strings to aid for the homeless that HUD has implemented, nationwide, by the threat of withholding aid for communities that don't comply with it. Still more curious, we have a harm reduction philosophy dedicated to ending a problem. Housing First proponents have styled themselves "abolitionists."[41] There should not be any two sides to the debate over ending homelessness, which is what their approach, and only their approach, can accomplish. Housing First has been cast as the only morally legitimate position and also the only intellectually legitimate one. An "evidence-based" policy, Housing First has science on its side, whereas alternative approaches are rooted in some unsophisticated mixture of custom, ignorance, and transitional housing services providers' desire to keep their jobs. Not everyone who works in homeless services rejects the value of sobriety requirements and believes in housing as a human right. But few regarded as intellectual authorities do. And as if doing the right and effective thing weren't already enough, Housing First is cheaper than alternative approaches. It will save taxpayers' money. That's at least the case proponents make.

To evaluate claims over the evidence base behind Housing First, let's first take a look at the nationwide point-in-time figures (figure 5.2).

PIT data are presumed to have become more or less accurate around 2010. Since that point, the trend is downward. That would seem to give credence to the idea that Housing First "works": the system organized around Housing First has pushed the numbers down. However, the apparent nationwide decline in homelessness does not prove Housing First's effectiveness for multiple reasons. First, we have no credible data on trends in homelessness throughout the 1980s and 1990s. Certainly, no one was using Housing First during the skid row era, when, according to a number of scholars, homelessness numbers are believed to have been lower than now. Second,

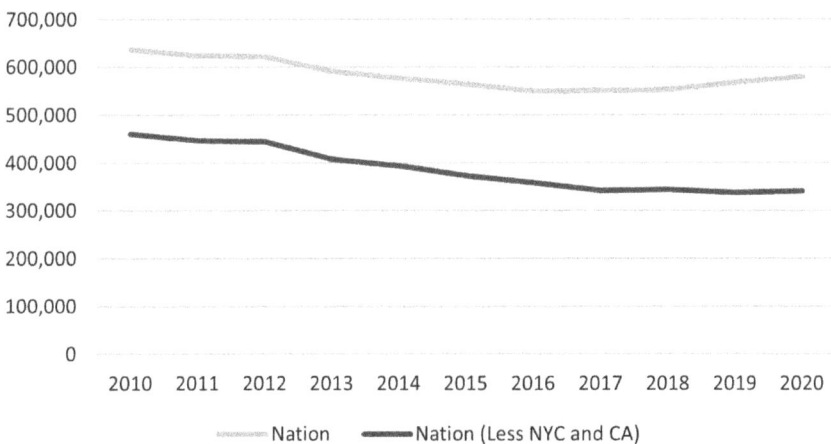

Figure 5.2. Homelessness in America, 2010–2020.

the jurisdictions that have adopted Housing First most enthusiastically have seen their numbers rise significantly. From 2010 to 2020, homelessness rose 47 percent in New York City and 31 percent in California, but declined by 26 percent elsewhere.[42] Third, it's possible that homelessness nationwide didn't decline at all, and the appearance that it did has do with how we define homelessness status. The number of rapid rehousing beds over the 2010s rose by slightly more than 100,000. Rapid rehousing places homeless individuals in private apartments and provides them with temporary rental assistance. When using rapid rehousing, a household is not obviously less homeless than when they're in a transitional housing program. And yet, rapid rehousing program clients aren't officially considered "homeless" in HUD statistics, whereas transitional housing clients are.[43] Were rapid rehousing clients considered homeless, 2010 to 2020, across the nation, would register a 7 percent increase in homelessness as opposed to the official 9 percent decline.

To sort through what is known about Housing First, we must direct our focus away from the national data. Tsemberis founded an organization called Pathways to Housing in 1992. Pathways put its clients, all formerly homeless or at serious risk of homelessness, in subsidized housing units without placing any behavioral expectations on them. Then, Tsemberis began doing studies of his program and published the results in academic journals. He found that the clients placed in Pathways programs tended to stay housed at a higher rate than similar individuals put in more then-standard linear-style housing programs. These studies provided the original basis for Housing First as an "evidence-based practice" that has a legitimacy that alternative approaches do not and, thus, should be a "whole-system orientation,"[44] not simply one program among many.

Housing First analyses measure residential stability over time: how many days someone spends housed over the study length or whether he's still housed at the end.[45] Social science researchers consider the randomized-control trial (RCT) to be the most rigorous test of a policy's effectiveness. An RCT evaluates an intervention by comparing it with another intervention when members of a certain cohort are randomly assigned to each. Depending on the rigor one brings to the definition of "Housing First" and "randomized-control trial," somewhere between four and fifteen RCTs have been done on Housing First.[46] The most famous Housing First RCTs are Sam Tsemberis's Pathways studies and a Canadian study known as At Home/Chez Soi that included five different cities and more than one thousand participants.

Housing First has demonstrated real strength at achieving residential stability, which is to say real strength at addressing homelessness.[47] Residential stability rates, for people placed into a Housing First program, often run in the 70 to 80 percent range over the course of the study that typically lasts a couple years. By contrast, the studies find that people placed into the "usual care" or "treatment first" program stay housed a lower rate, often below 50 percent. In short, people who receive permanent housing without preconditions, even when they have a behavioral health disorder, are likely to hold onto that housing, at least for a while. (Studies of Housing First/permanent supportive housing's outcomes over more than a couple years are rarer, but those that have been done have found lower rates of residential stability than those working with a one-to-two-year timeframe.)[48]

While ordinary Americans may be interested in learning about worthy social service programs, they are especially keen on seeing homelessness decline in their community. When they're informed that Housing First is known to be able to end homelessness, that's what they believe they're being told about it. At the community level, though, Housing First has run into evidentiary trouble. Despite being supposedly embraced by dozens of communities nationwide, proponents have never been able to identify an instance where a community ended homelessness via Housing First. Utah has long been held up as a Housing First success story.[49] But, as a 2015 analysis by economist Kevin Corinth demonstrated, Utah's dramatic reductions in chronic homelessness may mainly be ascribed to methodological changes. It shifted from an annualized to a point-in-time count and modified its definition of "chronic" homeless status.[50]

Given Housing First's respectable showing in the social science literature, and wide application in the real world, why has it not met with more success? One problem is that building housing for the homeless doesn't reduce the homeless population on a one-to-one basis. Multiple units of supportive housing, perhaps as many as ten, must be built to reduce the homeless population by one.[51] Furthermore, another person is always falling into homelessness after someone else's homelessness has been resolved. Any marquee supportive housing initiative will experience a "fadeout" effect, as whatever reduction it manages to achieve only lasts for so long until the numbers start growing again.

In its eagerness to promote Housing First, the federal US Interagency Council on Homelessness developed a definition for "ending" homelessness termed "functional zero." This has been criticized as "Orwellian,"[52] for having as much to do with an evaluation of the capacity of a community's service system, and its conformity to Housing First,[53] as how many homeless people live in that given community. No city would base a claim to having ended murder on an assessment of its police department's capacity, as distinct from the number of recent murders. Communities recognized by USICH as having ended veterans' homelessness were, in 2019, host to more than two thousand homeless veterans.[54]

Far more specious than claims about Housing First's ability to end homelessness are claims about its ability to save taxpayers' money. The most famous journalistic treatment of Housing First came in a 2006 *New Yorker* article by Malcolm Gladwell called "Million Dollar Murray."[55] Gladwell advanced the claim that it's cheaper to end homelessness than manage it. That's because chronically homeless adults are "high utilizers" of expensive services such as jails and mental hospitals when living on the street, but when you rent them an apartment, they cease to burden service systems and taxpayers as much.

This may be true for some people. For a small segment of the "high utilizer" population, a Housing First intervention may shrink government. But restructuring an entire service system around Housing First principles will not save any money.

Let's take these service systems one by one, beginning with criminal justice. Homeless people, particularly the street population, get arrested often, but for minor quality-of-life offenses that don't result in long stays in jail or prison.[56] "Mass incarceration" and the "criminalization of homelessness" are unrelated issues, as the former is driven mainly by long prison sentences imposed to punish serious felonies. Not all Housing First studies have found reduced contact with the criminal justice system.[57] But even when they do, the promise of cost-savings is vain given the high fixed costs of running a jail or prison. Throughout the 2010s, New York's jail system saw its budget swell by one-third while the jail population declined by 40 percent.[58] So-called bail reform reduces the use of pre-trial detention for most offenses. It is a popular idea in progressive circles whose widespread implementation would lead to vast reductions in the jail population and, therefore, also weaken the criminal justice-based cost-savings argument for Housing First.

Psychiatric hospitals also have fixed costs that won't respond to a small reduction in civil commitments coming as a result of a few people receiving a subsidized housing unit. Inpatient psychiatric commitment can run as high as $250,000 per person per year.[59] Claims about Housing First's cost effectiveness have relied heavily on reduced use, for the individuals participating in a study, of mental hospitals. But civil commitment is a tightly regulated process. The eligibility bar, usually dangerousness to self or others, is far too high for the entire seriously mentally ill homeless population to meet. The seriously mentally ill cohort is itself a minority of the nation's homeless population as a whole (120,642 out of 580,466).[60] Million Dollar Murray himself was an alcoholic, not a man with schizophrenia. You can't save costs on a system that someone doesn't use in the first place, either because they avoid it or because they live in a community without much of a mental health system to speak of. Over half of all counties in America have not one psychiatrist.[61]

As for healthcare costs more generally, the hope seems to be that, by housing them, homeless people will be better-positioned to use normal outpatient care and rely less on emergency rooms and other expensive crisis services. Homeless people certainly have bad health.[62] But accepting, for the sake of argument, that housing someone improves their health doesn't mean it would save much money. The longer and healthier someone's life is, the higher their healthcare costs will be.[63] In 2018, the National Academies of Sciences, Engineering, and Medicine defended the view that "housing in general improves health," but also stated, "there is no substantial published evidence as yet to demonstrate that PSH [permanent supportive housing] improves health outcomes or reduces health care costs."[64] Bad health correlates with many other adverse life experiences. Unemployment is bad for one's physical and mental health: is a job healthcare?[65] Poverty correlates with poor health. Is money therefore healthcare? If we allow Medicaid to pay for housing,[66] why not cut out the middleman and allow it to be converted into cash?

Claims that "housing is healthcare" or "housing is treatment" must be matched up against Housing First's sparse record at overcoming behavioral health disorders, such as untreated serious mental illness and drug addiction. That is the conclusion of multiple, thorough surveys of the literature: a 2017 survey published in the *Australian Economic Review*,[67] a 2019 study published by the Trump administration's Council of Economic Advisors (which acknowledged Housing First's record on boosting residential stability),[68] and the 2018 National Academies study.[69] Negligible results on nonhousing-related outcomes has been as consistent, in the Housing First literature, as its strong record on housing outcomes.

Tsemberis has sometimes been candid about Housing First's inability to make much headway with behavioral health disorders.[70] Others, though, cling to rhetoric about housing as a "platform" or "foundation" and keep suggesting that the typical route out of homelessness, via a Housing First intervention, runs straight from housing stability to flourishing.

Employment outcomes are similarly underwhelming. Interest in work has declined markedly since the Clinton era, but never to the point of outright indifference. And rightly so. If government intends to orient all services around Housing First, the philosophy will therefore determine assistance promised for the employable segment of the homeless population. HUD's Family Options Study (2015) used a rigorous design and large sample size to examine a variety of housing interventions for families, who are considered broadly more employable than single adults. Far from encouraging an increased work effort (as platform theory might predict), researchers found that permanent housing subsidies diminished it.[71] Giving homeless people permanent housing gets them out of shelters but reduces their economic independence, as compared with alternative service interventions.

Since the 1960s, a rising share of able-bodied American adults have left the labor force.[72] Some of these "Men Without Work" must certainly be homeless. When one of these cases is placed in permanent housing from the streets or a shelter, from the perspective of homeless services, they are a problem that has been solved. He ceases to appear in the homelessness statistics, though still in the unemployment (or workforce non-participation) statistics. Thus, from the perspective of the "men without work" literature, they are a problem that has yet to be solved. If permanent housing benefits lead to a diminished work effort, fixing his housing problem may actually worsen his unemployment problem.

Shelter is expensive, running, in some jurisdictions, $100 to $200 per bed per night.[73] What's really expensive is quality shelter, enhanced by social services staff and security personnel. Reliance on commercial hotels, common long before the COVID-19 pandemic, is also costly. Since it does not cost more than $36,000 a year to provide a household with a rental subsidy, homeless advocates have long charged that it would be far cheaper to house people than put them in shelters.[74] But it is awkward to compare the cost of a program that will last only a few months or less, such as shelter, jail, or hospitalization, with one that will last for years or, in some cases, the rest of someone's lifetime. Government serves more people through shelter than through permanent housing. On average, nationwide, each shelter bed for single adults serves six clients each year, and each bed for families with children serves 3.5 people per year.[75] Shelter stays are short term whereas housing subsidies can be long term, especially in expensive cities associated with high rates of homelessness. In New York City, the average public housing resident has been in their unit for over two decades.[76] Permanent housing is expensive, too, and any broad expansion of benefits for the homeless population would have to be made available to the low-income population more generally. Estimates of making the Section 8 Housing Choice Voucher Program universal range as high as $100 billion.[77] The homeless services system currently costs a fraction of that, and many shelter programs would still need to be funded even in the event of making vouchers universal.

The peer-reviewed literature on Housing First treats the cost-savings argument with more skepticism than the residential stability argument. The University of Pennsylvania sociologist Dennis Culhane, a prominent progressive homelessness scholar, has warned against "overstating" the cost-savings argument: "in general, the larger the sample (and presumably the more representative of adults who are homeless), the lower the average annual costs of services use."[78] Stefan Kertesz, a physician-researcher based out of Birmingham, Alabama, has challenged the value of distracting from the basic humanitarian case for helping the homeless.[79] Columbia University economist Brendan O'Flaherty is similarly unimpressed with the cost-savings argument.[80]

No politician ever enacted a tax cut in the wake of a massive investment in homeless services spending. Just because a high-utilizer uses tens of thousands of dollars in healthcare services in one year does not mean that those costs will be constant throughout his or her life. A government genuinely interested in maximizing cost-savings would be relentless in targeting only clients on whom it would most likely realize savings. But that kind of targeting is the opposite of a "whole systems" orientation, and it's furthermore unattractive from a humanitarian perspective. Homeless single mothers, for instance, are at low risk of jail and certainly psychiatric hospitalization. They have practically no claim on homeless services agencies if the standard of excellence is how much money can you save.[81]

In noting that San Francisco's homeless services funding increased by 85 percent over a recent ten-year period, while notching a 13 percent increase in overall homelessness, a 2020 *New Yorker* article reflected, "It's puzzling that so much funding did so little."[82] Some conservatives have argued that Housing First's underwhelming real-world outcomes reveal it as a failure. Advocates, though, call for doubling down, arguing that a flood of funding for subsidized housing could succeed where a trickle failed. There may be something to what they say, but that position must be considered to be based in theory or principles, not evidence. "Evidence" should refer to something that actually happened.

HOUSING FIRST: CONSIDERING THE THEORY

Let's turn, then, to theory and principles. Our direction on homelessness policy will always have more to do with principles than "evidence," as defined by social science researchers. Housing First advocates often describe the aim of linear programs as "housing readiness," though that's not always how service providers themselves characterize their work. The real distinction is whether residential stability should be the goal of the program, as it is with Housing First providers, or secondary to primary goals such as economic independence. They're better seen as two different "paradigms" that disagree about ends.[83]

Housing First proponents can fall back on the claim that housing is a human right: this is, in many ways, a more honest argument. Rights-based claims are meaningful only when they impose a specific obligation on government. In the homelessness context, the idea of housing as a human right is invoked not just to defend access to housing, *a la* the 1968 Fair Housing Act, but to call for an entitlement to it. But any need could be framed as a right. Do we have a right to housing in a way that we don't have a right to mobility, healthcare, or income? In a practical sense, launching a new entitlement program to guarantee access to any one of these goods could weaken government's capacity to guarantee any of the others. In a theoretical sense, Americans have, traditionally, resisted the idea that government should provide people with all their basic needs via entitlement programs. When someone loses their job and income, government does not provide them with non-time-limited guaranteed income. It provides them with unemployment insurance and perhaps also job search and training assistance. The equivalent to unemployment insurance, in the homelessness context, would be shelter or perhaps time-limited rental assistance.

Speaking of "rights" helpfully focuses debate on justice, which can be eclipsed by all the utilitarian language about program effectiveness, data, and outcomes. A portion of the homeless population is capable of sobriety, employment, and the formation and maintenance of healthy relationships. Their needs will not be met by a service provider that is formally indifferent to whether its clients are actively using or not, pursuing work or not, and spending all day every day sitting in a dark room by themselves.

Some of the homeless are "purely" economic cases. They need little help beyond shelter, which they will move out of in short order. Others are highly complicated chronic cases. Some are in between. Call them the "middle-class" homeless. They are not well served by a harm reduction approach. For them, harm reduction can be positively harmful. Human beings respond to social pressures and are less likely to give into temptation if they're not exposed to it. Parents who send their kids to "no excuses" charter schools with high discipline standards believe this. Housing advocates who believe in the transformational potential of voucher-enabled moves to the suburbs believe this. Some people overestimate their ability to handle independent living and a degree of supervision could well make the difference between survival and flourishing. Preferences change.[84]

Mimi Silbert is the longtime head of The Delancey Street Foundation, a San Francisco-based service provider with a workfare orientation. She opposed a low-barrier shelter opening near the restaurant her organization runs, out of concern over the influence an influx of active users might have over its clients, many of whom are in recovery.[85] People on parole and probation, a far from insignificant part of the homeless population, risk violating the terms of their community supervision by being placed in a harm reduction setting.[86] One risk with harm reduction is that, by failing to address a problem at its roots, it spread those roots wider and sinks them deeper. Young drug addicts hold more potential for full sobriety than old drug addicts.[87]

To improve lives, government should sometimes structure people's choices using material inducements. Some California progressives are now pushing for greater use of "contingency management" to address the burgeoning drug addiction crisis. Its equivalent in homeless services—using housing benefits to encourage change—receives far less progressive support because it conflicts with the Housing First consensus.[88]

REHABILITATION OR REDISTRIBUTION?

The homeless services system, like most areas of social policy, consists of a mix of efforts to redistribute resources and rehabilitate lives. Rehabilitation entails considerable "overhead": staff to work on repairing lives and facilities in which to do that work. If one truly believes that the only distinction between low- and upper-income populations is their lack of resources, basic redistribution is all that is needed. Permanent housing-oriented solutions to homelessness often use arguments similar to those made by universal basic income (UBI) proponents: cut out all the welfare state's middlemen and just transfer resources to needy people. Some UBI proponents cite Housing First as evidence for their position.[89]

Americans, though, tend not to rest content with the idea of redistribution alone. You can move someone off the streets and into housing, call it a day, and collect evidence on how many times you have done that. That might lead to an "evidence-based" homelessness policy but not a values-based homelessness policy. We will always want to know not only that a social program provides for disadvantaged populations but how much and in what ways it improves their lives. Outside the homelessness context, we see a significant commitment to rehabilitative services across multiple policy areas, such as child welfare (services as an alternative to family separation),[90] domestic violence (services as an alternative to punishment),[91] and criminal justice reform (services as an alternative to incarceration). The opioid crisis has prompted a surge in calls for more investment in rehabilitative services, and not only of a strictly harm reduction variety.

Respect for rehabilitation may be seen in insistence that Housing First does not mean "Housing Only," and the ubiquitous "platform" metaphor for subsidized housing. Much of the work of rehabilitation concerns habits. Homeless people have many bad habits. If an adult member of your family has a drug or alcohol addiction, is chronically unemployed, or involved in criminal activity, you probably want them to change. Though you may be willing to support a person like that, financially, you may also think it prudent to qualify that assistance with evidence of change, provided by them. In our family life, we are accustomed to think that it is sensible, not oppressive, to attach strings to aid.

Some homeless advocates devoted to the "housing, housing, housing" philosophy denounce the "homeless services industrial complex" with as much dudgeon as a Tea Partier.[92] Housing First is not really a small government philosophy. But Housing Firsters have many fair points to make about the low success rate of service interventions, which have been experienced by some temporary housing programs, that try to help the homeless in ways other than subsidized housing. Underneath Housing First's Orwellian rhetoric about "functional zero," the insistence on "not housing only," the deliberate attempts to mislead the public that an end to homeless is just around the bend, the rhetoric about "science," "evidence," and cost savings, lies this sensible idea: it is very difficult to rebuild broken lives, and anyone who tries will fail frequently. Just because a program for the homeless doesn't lead with subsidized housing doesn't make it a good program. Resistance to Housing First can tempt people into promoting mediocre programs or programs that they know very little about, other than the director making himself available for an interview and granting a site visit. Any temporary intervention risks seeing its gains diminish over time. That goes double for the hardest cases. Even well-run programs will often fail. Programs that do succeed often do so based on certain conditions, which limit the ability to scale them. A program that's worked well for sober ex-felons could be destroyed by an influx of mentally ill sex offenders. Conservatives' sympathies for rehabilitative approaches such as transitional housing are noble and rooted in core American values. We should explore alternatives to Housing First—it does not deserve the funding and reputation it now enjoys—while also being humble about what to expect from them.

Redistribution is supposed to be cheaper than rehabilitation and less fraught with conflicts-of-interest on the part of service providers. Housing First has been criticized for perpetuating the social services industrial complex. To a degree, such critics misunderstand the core emphasis that Housing First philosophy places on redistribution over rehabilitation. But whatever critics miss on the plane of theory, they grasp the practical reality of Housing First with unerring accuracy: investing in homeless services will never shrink government, redistribution does not obviate the need for rehabilitation, and Housing First has been used to justify the launch of countless new housing and social programs that employ many people and thus who have a vested interest in their perpetuation. Billion-dollar supportive housing programs have no appreciably "transformational" effect on the social services.[93]

CONCLUSION: MAKING PEACE WITH MANAGING HOMELESSNESS

In public debates, critics of certain policies sometimes charge that "X is no panacea," regardless of whether proponents of policy X claim panacea status for it. Housing First is the rare instance where advocates of a certain policy really do claim that it is a panacea. It's not, though. There's no evidence for the idea that any community can end homelessness by investing enough money in no-strings-attached permanent supportive housing. There's no evidence to support the idea that low-barrier shelters are superior to workfare-style shelters. There's no evidence for the idea that "housing is healthcare" when it comes to our most pressing healthcare challenges such as untreated schizophrenia and substance abuse. Belief in those ideas lacks the certainty of mathematics and the natural sciences. There's no evidence for the idea that every service provider, not just some, must conform to Housing First. The case for Housing First relies much more on theory, and less on evidence and science, than proponents would have the public believe.

There's no shame in theorizing. Economists build theories all the time, to help clarify urgent debates over issues such as immigration where reality is too messy to admit of empirical certainty. Arguments based in claims about human rights are based in theory as well—moral theory. We anchor our values in our moral theory about the way the world should be.

Science-based language has been employed to maintain Housing First's ascendancy as the solely acceptable homelessness policy. But human affairs don't admit of as much certainty as do questions in the physical sciences, mathematics, and medicine. To assert that we *know* how to end homelessness, that a particular policy approach is *certain*, is to delegitimatize alternative opinions. And that is precisely what has happened in the case of Housing First, which is said to be "proven" to be able to end homelessness, even though it has not even managed to make much headway in reducing it. "Evidence-based" rhetoric tries to place homelessness policy outside the realm of ordinary public debate. But we should debate how much we value employment or behavioral health outcomes in social programs as opposed to residential stability.

Housing First has two important lessons to teach: rehabilitative service programs often fail and, while there may be many things subsidized housing can't do, it can keep people housed. Housing First, or something like it, will always have an appeal so long as the challenge is framed as "homelessness." But if the challenge is framed as "unemployment," "untreated serious mental illness," or "drug addiction," it seems less compelling, more like one possible approach among several others. It's eminently arguable that homeless services systems should provide low-barrier options to people not yet ready to "take the next step." It is not true that evidence and, still less, fairness necessitate that the entire system be oriented around Housing First. The federal government should provide local authorities with more flexibility to pursue alternatives to Housing First than they currently enjoy.

Housing First sets the bar too high and too low. It insists on a commitment to "ending homelessness," though that's never been achieved. And it delegitimizes all standards of success other than housing as many people as possible. Government manages many social ills without ending them, some worse than homelessness: child abuse, domestic violence, rape, murder, and so forth. It might be well to reconcile ourselves to the idea of managing homelessness since that's what's going to happen if government doesn't succeed in ending it.

6

Compassion, Con and Pro

Many believe that a dearth of compassion explains why we have homelessness in America.[1] The comedian Louis CK expressed this point in a routine about visiting the Port Authority Bus Terminal, a well-known homelessness hot spot, with a friend to pick up that friend's cousin. The friend's cousin was visiting New York from New Hampshire. When the non-New Yorker comes upon a homeless man sprawled out on the floor, she is aghast and immediately tries to help him. Louis CK and his friend react by instructing her that someone sleeping in squalor in a public place is totally normal:

> "Sir, can we call someone?"
>
> And me and my friend, we're from New York, this is the crazy part, we immediately go to her. We start correcting her behavior like she's doing something wrong.
>
> "Why, is he okay?"
>
> "No, no, he needs you desperately, that's not the point. we just don't do that here. You silly country girl."[2]

In short, what's so hard about doing the compassionate thing? As a policymaking principle, compassion appeals to experts and ordinary Americans alike.

Now, Louis CK's argument could be refuted by pointing to the billions in annual outlays backing America's homeless services system. New York may be a particularly inapposite example of America's lack of compassion for the homeless, because local government there runs the largest homeless services system in the nation. HUD data report that New York City provides 13.5 beds of homeless housing per 1,000 residents, whereas New Hampshire only provides 2.2 beds.[3] But budget data alone can't settle the question of compassion. Paying taxes to fund social services is not an act of compassion, which requires spontaneity. Taxation implies coercion. The taxpayer-funded welfare state is an alternative to charity and, therefore, also in some sense an alternative to compassion.

Welfare state bureaucracies dictate rules meant to determine eligibility and prevent fraud. Such rules protect programs' integrity. But they also can cause stress and hassle in recipients' lives. Even in the case of transactions where eligibility is fairly straightforward—receiving a Social Security disbursement—there's little feeling of compassion. But if putting government in charge of poor relief makes that process feel more impersonal, it also thereby becomes more regular. Paying someone to help poor people creates the risk that their relationship will never be as heartfelt as that between family members and neighbors, while at the same time making it more likely that they'll do something to help them in the first place. In 1884, the prominent social reformer Josephine Shaw Lowell said, "Were the poor to take by force the possessions of the rich, although they might benefit by them, neither of the parties to the transaction would delude themselves with the idea that charity had been bestowed or received."[4] Her point is just as valid when the poor and their supporters vote into power elected representatives constitutionally authorized to raise taxes and redistribute wealth. Redistributing wealth is not really something "we do together." But it may nonetheless benefit the poor and homeless, which raises the question as to how important compassion is at all.

The most purely compassionate homeless services system would be run by private charity and staffed by volunteers. As it happens, volunteer-staffed shelters and soup kitchens run by churches are legion across the nation. But in the cities with the most pressing homelessness challenges, those programs are seen as insufficient. There, the charity-run network of homeless services supplements the formal government system. Government action has more to do with justice and raw power than charity and compassion.[5]

Respect for compassion causes government to rely heavily, for the provision of homeless services, and social services generally, on community nonprofits. These organizations provide a human touch that distant federal bureaucracies can't. It may or may not be more effective to provide services this way. It is certainly, thereby, more aligned with our values and, therefore, more *American*. It's more compassionate, as that term is typically understood. But if we're committed to the community nonprofit model for homeless services, we must confront its limitations. Compassion creates as many problems as it solves.

THE TROUBLE WITH COMPASSION

Most people agree that helping homeless adults and families is the compassionate thing to do. But when pressed, they exhibit uncertainty over which mix of law enforcement, rehabilitative services, and transfer programs they want government to deploy. Compassion points in opposite directions. Families of adult mentally ill individuals believe civil commitment is compassionate. Disability rights groups believe it is sadistic. Former San Diego mayor Kevin Faulconer has criticized California governor Gavin Newsom for not cracking down harder on encampments by charging, "Governor, letting people live on the streets isn't compassion."[6] Homeless adults content to live out of a tent on a sunny California sidewalk disagree. To adjudicate homeless policy disputes requires recourse to a standard other than compassion. Compassion itself settles nothing and can't serve as the basis for coherent policymaking.

Compassion is unreliable; it wavers in its object. One day, a news report out of Los Angeles rivets our attention on a scandal relating to mental hospitals discharging homeless patients directly to skid row.[7] The next day, our attention turns toward famine in Africa, victims of mob violence in India, and/or natural disasters in North America. The homelessness literature is rich with discussions of "compassion fatigue," whereby advocates' unceasing demands for more resources become politically counterproductive.[8] Housing First proponents started claiming that investing in their policy saved money in response to concerns that the public wouldn't support investments based solely on an appeal to compassion.[9]

Even assuming that policymaking should be rooted in our hearts, compassion is not the only emotional response to homelessness. There is also anger. When a commuter passes the same man living in squalor, every day, to and from work, that person might well feel angry at the government that allows that to happen as much as they do compassion toward the homeless man in question. Arguing over what's the angriest solution to homelessness is no more likely to resolve policy disputes than arguing over what's the most compassionate solution.

Sometimes, learning more about a person, group, or social condition deepens our compassion, but not always. It sometimes feels like it's easier to feel unqualifiedly compassionate about people distant from us, who present themselves as abstractions rather than flawed humans. In *Bleak House*, Charles Dickens illustrates this point with Mrs. Jellyby. Her commitment to "telescopic philanthropy" causes her to neglect her own affairs and family to focus on the welfare of Borrioboola-gha, while at the same time being ignorant of the crimes committed there. Even very vulnerable people, the more you learn about them, can be profoundly unsympathetic types. Consider people committed to long-term mental hospitalization due to being found not guilty by reason of insanity of committing a brutal murder, and Class A sex offenders. Both have very poor prospects for economic independence and social integration. Neither are very sympathetic.

In public debates, compassion often functions as a trump card. Partisans portray their position as based on compassion to criticize their opponents as not just factually but also morally wrong.[10] Reasonable people *cannot* disagree about compassion. If public debate is essential to democracy, then there may be something undemocratic about compassion-based policymaking.

The compassionate thing to do for someone might not always be in their long-term best interest. Consider pet ownership, a front-burner issue of homelessness policy in some cities. Traditionally, shelters have not allowed pets and most still do not. But there's growing interest to allow homeless single adults to keep their pets when they enter shelters. This stems from Housing First concern with reducing "barriers" to shelters and compassion. But allowing pets in shelters is a questionable policy. Pets create friction even among the non-homeless population, generally because someone accuses someone else of irresponsibility. By disposition, and as a matter of resources, homeless adults are not great at handling responsibilities. Pets stand to cause more friction among the homeless than non-homeless populations. We should craft homeless services systems in a way that minimizes friction among the clients who use them. Accommodating pet ownership will encourage pet ownership. When someone's allowed into a shelter with his dog, he'll give others the idea that they should get a dog, too. Having a pet hinders mobility: What happens when a homeless adult needs to travel, or go to work? What happens if he doesn't return? Having a pet reduces the number of roommates and landlords available to someone looking to move out of homelessness. A street homeless man, who misguided policymakers encouraged to get a dog, who spends five years with that dog, then, because of an opportunity or crisis, must give up his dog, and is crushed, would have been better off not having gotten the dog in the first place.

COMPASSION AND INCENTIVES

Crafting public policy often entails structuring incentives. The homeless services system must be structured such that people have maximum incentive to move out of homelessness in a rapid and sustainable way. Closely scrutinizing incentives can seem uncompassionate because it requires closely scrutinizing the choices people make. Does anyone choose to be homeless? Many find the question offensive. But homeless people, as humans capable of agency, unquestionably respond to incentives. They gravitate to train stations, busy street corners, subway cars in midtown Manhattan because those areas offer the greatest panhandling opportunities and are near many free or low-cost services and necessities. The street homeless are, in general, profoundly responsive to climate. All things being equal, cities with low January temperatures have higher proportions of sheltered homeless than those with warm wintertime temperatures.[11] Subway lines that stay underground longer attract more homeless people than aboveground lines that let in cold air at every stop.[12] Lower-density Queens, which is the size of Houston, has around the same number of street homeless people as Grand Central Terminal.[13] The higher quality a shelter program is, the more people it will draw in, including from the already-housed population.[14] Interviews with people living homeless in a city that they didn't grow up in reveal that many had considered the service options there in advance of arriving.[15]

However vulnerable the poor may be, they are not so free from agency as to fail to take advantage of benefits made available to them. Jason DeParle's book about welfare reform, *American Dream* (2004), describes the lives of poor single mothers who moved from Chicago to Milwaukee largely because cash welfare benefits were more generous there. And, upon arriving, before beginning their apartment search, the mothers first moved into a homeless shelter, because they'd learned that the local Red Cross would thereby pay their security deposit and first month's rent.[16]

Much of the work social workers do, beyond simply connecting people with programs they're eligible for, boils down to motivation. But what they see as trying to motivate people can seem like hassling people. Homelessness can be exhausting, and weary homeless people don't always want to get up and go. Or they may say they do, but more as an expression of an abstract commitment. The temptation to rest on the safety net is great among this cohort of the underclass who has suffered so much and whose prospects for independence often seem so dim. But while facilitating someone's desire for rest may seem compassionate, it's not necessarily in his or her best interests.

FAITH-BASED ORGANIZATIONS

The COVID-19 pandemic highlighted the homeless services system's reliance on volunteers. Since the virus posed a unique threat to the elderly, and retirees comprise a disproportionate share of volunteers, many programs had to shut down or scale back operations throughout 2020 and 2021.[17] Volunteers serve the homeless out of a sense of compassion and/or religious obligation. They may cite, as inspiration or authority for their actions, Scripture (Hebrews 13:2, Isaiah 58:7–10, Luke 3:11, Luke 9:58, Matthew 25:40), the corporal works of mercy ("Shelter the Homeless"),[18] various artistic figurations of Jesus Christ as a homeless man,[19] and heroes and heroines from the Christian social work tradition. "Social services and care" is the most common use of volunteer hours in America.[20]

Extremely poor and homeless Americans rely on charities for "light touch" benefits and services, such as school supplies and Christmas gifts for children.[21] Membership in a church or girl scout troop may broaden their informal social networks, valuable in itself, even if only temporarily helpful in meeting core demands such as childcare, employment, cash, and affordable housing.[22] For their major wants, they look toward government. This reflects the historic shift, begun by the New Deal, of government's supplanting "organized charity" as the lead provider of social services to the needy.

Debate continues over whether that shift was a mistake.[23] In 1992, Marvin Olasky published *The Tragedy of American Compassion*, a plea for a more charity-directed approach to poverty.[24] In addition to his extensive historical research, Olasky posed as a homeless man to gather evidence for his thesis about the welfare state's inattention to moral concerns. He asked for a Bible at a shelter and was told none were available.[25] Olasky's book had a major influence over federal policymakers. The Clinton, Bush, and Obama administrations all encouraged more faith-based and private provision of public services.[26] Claims continue to be made that we'd have a more effective response to homelessness if the "voluntary sector" had a larger role to play. But it's hard to know for certain whether a charity-led homeless services sector would work better than the one we've got. Data on truly private programs are elusive because they're not obligated to report much. Programs run via contracts with the government will be shaped by the government's priorities. Many large faith-based charities long ago became indistinguishable in their day-to-day poverty work from more secular agencies.[27] A private shelter under no obligation to host violent schizophrenic men has a strong incentive not to do so if it believes it can't do that and serve its other clients. But someone needs to serve violent schizophrenic men. Government is best-positioned to do that, since government has tools of coercion (civil commitment and incarceration) and other forms of leverage unavailable to private groups. During the pre-New Deal organized charity era, government-run asylums cared for violent schizophrenics.

Someone who serves the homeless out of a sense of religious obligation might not hold themselves up to the highest standard of effectiveness. In *The Social Contract* (1762), Rousseau argues that Christians make bad soldiers, because their indifference to death makes them indifferent to victory (IV.8). Churches encourage teenagers to work in soup kitchens and participate in mission trips to impart in them a sense of service. That is, churches organize these activities for the benefit of those providing the services and not only for the benefit of those receiving the services. Addressing homelessness must mean moving people off the street. But distributing clean socks and sandwiches to the street homeless might make street living easier for some people. Certainly, distributing free tents will. Distributing goods to the street homeless could at the same time perpetuate homelessness and fulfill a religious mission.

Marvin Olasky champions colonial-era Christians' ideas about the importance of attending the spiritual, not just material, needs of the poor.[28] The Book of Proverbs contains many injunctions against sloth (6:6–11, 13:4, 19:15, 20:13, 21:25, 24: 30–34) and St. Paul admonishes the "idle and disruptive" in 2 Thessalonians 3:6–16. Some faith-based groups have raised their voices in protest against the moral shallowness of the Housing First consensus.[29] But that's not the case with all groups that identify as faith-based. Others, through their words and actions, endorse secularists' view that serving the poor consists mainly in transferring resources to them and advocating for government to do the same on an even larger scale. Religious liberty has become an important conservative priority in the face of what's viewed as an increasingly assertive secular progressivism. But in the homelessness debate, religious liberty protections can serve the interests of many organizations allied with the progressive left. In its regularly-updated "Housing not Handcuffs" report, the National Law Center on Homelessness and Poverty details multiple instances in which faith-based groups thwarted government efforts to regulate or prohibit their homelessness ministries based on a religious liberty defense.[30] Mitch Snyder, who was ethnically Jewish, was baptized in a Catholic in prison by the radical priest Father Daniel Berrigan. Snyder's organization, the Community for Creative Non-Violence (CCNV), was founded by a priest influenced by Dorothy Day. Throughout its years of high-profile activism, the CCNV's members embraced a philosophy of "Christian anarchy."[31] Glide Memorial Church in San Francisco, a major player on that city's homeless services scene, famously removed the cross from its sanctuary. From an orthodox perspective, progressive religious organizations may seem transparently fraudulent. From a policy and legal point of view, that distinction may be hard to maintain. Probably, conservatives have no practical way to go about expanding the role of faith-based groups that they like and restrict the role of those they don't like.

When faith-based organizations receive public funds to perform social services, the terms of the contract stipulate that that service must be performed on a purely secular basis.[32] However, one area of controversy concerns "service resistance" and shelters run by religious organizations who don't receive government funding. How to move homeless individuals off the street is one of the most vexing practical challenges of homelessness policy. As a legal question, municipal regulations on encampments and sleeping in public places are on firmer ground when the local shelter system provides people with a legitimate alternative to the streets. Street homeless may cite several reasons for declining shelter, one of which is a perceived restriction on their personal freedom. Whatever "proselytizing" a privately-run shelter does is not likely to be particularly aggressive. However, robust respect for religious liberty may well validate someone's insistence that he must be allowed to sleep in a tent in a park because the local shelter has a picture of Jesus on the wall.

TECHNOCRACY VERSUS COMMUNITY ACTION

For as long as homelessness has been around, there has been an industry to supply the goods and services consumed by the homeless population. In the old skid row days, that industry was made up of hotel operators and owners of bars and liquor stores. Now, people who make a living serving homeless adults and children work mainly for nonprofit social service providers funded by the government. Critics deploy the term "social services industrial complex" to suggest that some people perpetuate poverty, homelessness, and other social ills in order to keep a good thing going.[33] Defense contractors have a stake in endless war and homelessness contractors have a stake in endless homelessness. That rhetoric can be exaggerated. The average shelter director would have no idea how to go about ending homelessness if forced to do so at gunpoint. At the same time, it's fatuous to deny that those with a stake in the status quo will resist reform. As Upton Sinclair stated in 1934, "It is difficult to get a man to understand something when his salary depends upon his not understanding it."

In America, the standard way to deliver social services is through government-funded nonprofits. Other common terms for these organizations include "independent nonprofits" and "community-based organizations." When a poor or homeless person has any sort of personal contact with a representative of the welfare state, more often than not, he or she deals not with someone who is employed directly by the government, nor a pure private charity, but rather a nonprofit dependent on government funding.[34] Of the forty thousand homeless service programs estimated to be operating in the mid-1990s, 85 percent were run by nonprofits.[35]

President Lyndon Johnson's War on Poverty laid the foundation of the modern nonprofit-based welfare state. The social policy community, at that time, embraced the concept of "community action," that government should not just redistribute resources to poor people but also give them a say in how to use the resources.[36] War on Poverty planners admired the old ethnic neighborhoods' record on upward mobility and had a "nostalgic" fondness for the localism and community-oriented solutions to social challenges.[37] Many of the planners viewed large bureaucracies as irredeemably corruptive and ineffective.[38] Accordingly, they expanded government grant opportunities. This caused new nonprofit organizations to emerge and persuaded older nonprofits to abandon their traditional reluctance to taking taxpayer money.[39] Throughout the latter decades of the twentieth century, spending on social services continued to grow while a bias against "institutional" modes of service provision continued to harden. Two important examples, both greatly relevant for homelessness, were the deinstitutionalization of the mentally disabled and replacement of public housing projects with voucher and tax credit-oriented modes of subsidized housing. The government-funded nonprofit model was well established as paradigmatic by the time policymakers set themselves to the task of designing a homeless services system in the 1980s. Thus, that's the shape it took.[40] Supportive housing, for example, was an entirely new kind of social program. But projects have been developed with tactics and resources from other nonprofit housing alternatives to public housing, such as the Low-Income Housing Tax Credit.

New life was breathed into the publicly-funded nonprofit model during the "reinventing government" era of the 1990s. Social reformers of a technocratic mindset believed that it was the ideal model to expand accountability and inject a measure of private sector-style dynamism into the provision of public services. The most important example was charter schools, but technocratic attitudes also shaped homeless services. In the 1990s, a task force in New York successfully persuaded the city to spin off most of its government-run shelters to independent nonprofits.[41] The man who led that effort, Andrew Cuomo, went on to serve as HUD secretary under President Clinton (before later becoming governor of New York).

The values of "community action" and "accountability" stand in tension with one another. Long experience with the nonprofit model has shown that meaningful accountability is easier said than done, because it's hard to shut down underperforming programs outside of instances of graft or of gross dysfunction.[42] Homeless services pose three further challenges to accountability. One, technocrats like competition because it makes a virtue out of uncertainty: service providers who believe they might lose their contracts will step it up. Technocrats would run social services more like a business, an idea that goes back to the nineteenth century.[43] But shutting down a program will introduce great disruption into a cohort of very vulnerable people's lives. Policymakers do not relish the thought of making homeless people's lives more uncertain than they already are. It may be difficult to make providers' lives uncertain, while minimizing uncertainty in homeless people's lives. Two, homeless service programs are mostly housing programs, and housing programs are enormously difficult to site. Closing down an underperforming program could mean having to find another neighborhood in which to start a new one. Third, many homeless programs function as informal jobs programs for former clients.[44] They've done so ever since the nineteenth-century missions.[45] Truly to put the screws to underperforming programs would jeopardize many of those jobs, which exist for, substantially, therapeutic reasons. Evaluation and accountability point to the need for more professionalism.[46] We could replace every volunteer and former client with a social worker with a master's degree, but the overall benefit to society might be negligible. Certainly, it would be preposterous to assume that everyone turned out of a job at the shelter would land promptly on their feet in the for-profit economy.

Social service organizations can reknit the social fabric.[47] Even programs that fail to achieve their official ends may nonetheless provide associational benefits, somewhat like mediocre neighborhood schools can do.[48] We at times refer to social programs as "interventions," but they often function as associations. The "intervention," itself, may be less the point than the collective commitment to that intervention.

But acknowledging the shortcomings of technocracy can't turn into an indifference to outcomes and accountability. Without accountability mechanisms, employed along the lines that technocrats suggest, clients' interests will be subverted by the interests of those who work for service providers. New York City Mayor Ed Koch was fond of applying the term "poverty pimp" to leaders of corrupt community nonprofits.[49] Community action spawned many organizations set up to "empower," and provide services in, poor communities wound being run for their leaders' own personal and political benefit.[50] Homeless services has not been immune from corruption scandals, the risk of which will always grow when government ramps up spending on homeless services nonprofits, as it did throughout the 2010s.[51]

Advocacy is heavily political and many organizations straddle the divide between politics and providing services.[52] Running a homeless services organization can be an attractive soft landing for a former government administrator or a local politician or a launchpad for political careers.[53] Provider CEOs manage journalists' access to their programs and clients. In return, journalists quote them and speak highly of their programs. Serving as the head of a major social service nonprofit can afford one a comfortable upper middle-class salary.[54] Even when financial compensation is more modest, another big draw is status. Leaders of major service providers are quoted in major publications, invited to appear on tv and radio programs, serve on task forces, and socialize with prominent politicians and celebrities.[55] Those opportunities might not come their way in another line of work or if homelessness were a much lower-profile issue. Thus, there is a sense in which they benefit from the crisis.

Some providers in major cities are too big, particularly those with a conglomerate character. There are some organizations who appear open to accepting contracts for virtually anything-outreach: job training, permanent supportive housing for people with AIDS, shelters for families, shelters for mentally ill people, and so on. They will defend this by saying they're trying to guard against silos. But the upside, as far as better services for clients, is probably negligible, while it can be extremely complicated trying to exercise oversight over a nonprofit that holds contracts with multiple government agencies. A CEO of a $50 million organization will command a higher salary and more prestige than a CEO who directs a $5 million organization. One massive nonprofit runs a greater risk of developing a bureaucratic character than a network of small- and medium-sized ones. And avoiding bureaucracy was one of the initial goals of this model.

Eliminating really bad programs is easy. Government can contractually require shelter programs to serve three meals a day, specify the proportion of showers to clients, beds per room, and demand a basic level of safety and cleanliness. Determining whether those standards are being met is not a complicated exercise. Government can, and does, institute guardrails to prevent waste, outright embezzlement and fraud, and forestall harm and neglect toward their intended beneficiaries. Any program that fails these requirements would be a bad program. It's much harder to ensure excellence. We must allow that most cities are likely to get mostly mediocre homelessness assistance programs. Excellent programs should be encouraged and expanded, but they will likely be exceptions. We have no example in the history of the welfare state of a community that boasts only excellent social service agencies.

CONCLUSION: ONE CHEER FOR THE SOCIAL SERVICES INDUSTRIAL COMPLEX

Some who invoke homelessness as an indictment of modern American society believe that lack of compassion caused the problem. But, as argued in previous chapters, many elements of the homelessness challenge—ways in which conditions worsened—developed because social conditions improved. We have higher standards for the care of the mentally ill and low-rent housing. We have greater respect for increased personal freedom. People lack stable housing not because of a deliberate scheme to deprive them of it but, rather, because as so often happens, solutions to pressing policy challenges created in their wake new challenges.

Compassion should be appreciated as a question of public administration. We should assess levels of compassion based on how we serve the poor, not just on how much wealth we redistribute to them. Public administration and the how of policymaking was a major theme of compassionate conservativism. Compassionate conservativism was influential during the early George W. Bush presidency before it was consumed by the Iraq War. Though much maligned on both the left and the right,[56] compassionate conservatives understood at least one key insight about the nature of social services: poor people hate dealing with bureaucracies.[57] In the words of Bush speechwriter Michael Gerson, "On complex human challenges like addiction, homelessness, and the moral choices of youth, government bureaucracies are blunt and ineffective instruments. 'Take a number and wait' compassion has little to offer men, women, and children in spiritual and emotional crisis. Sometimes the most urgent human need is for love and concern, and here community and religious institutions—staffed by compassionate and idealistic volunteers—have a comparative advantage."[58] Whether they're aware of it or not, homeless services officials in progressive jurisdictions like Los Angeles and New York live a version of the compassionate conservatives' dream of multiple small and medium-sized nonprofits.

This model will always be open to criticism as being tantamount to a "social services industrial complex." But we have to come to terms with it, because it's better than having everything run directly by government bureaucracies and more realistic than one run by private charities. It should be coupled with appropriate accountability mechanisms. Better accountability requires breaking up conglomerates or preventing them from forming because it's complicated to exercise oversight over one organization with contracts with multiple government agencies. Measure and compare outcomes between service providers who handle similar populations. How safe are their facilities? In the case of temporary housing programs, how rapidly and sustainably are they moving people out of homelessness? Which have the lowest shelter recidivism rates? In the case of permanent housing programs, track client engagement with services and nonhousing-related metrics such as employment. Publish this information publicly so that journalists, politicians, and other watchdogs can use it to inform debate.

7

Homelessness and Social Integration

America began the 2020s a profoundly divided nation. It seems to be an iron law of modern history that every national crisis—war, recession, pandemic—divides us more than unifies us. Homelessness is also a very divisive issue. During the COVID-19 pandemic, New York City, like many other major cities, dispersed its shelter population among hotels emptied out by the tourism collapse. Private hotel rooms provided more protection against COVID than the dorm-style congregate shelters that homeless single adults had been living in. Two of these hotels were located on the Upper West Side: the Lucerne and Belleclaire. After a few hundred homeless single men moved into these facilities, residents noticed an appreciable decline in quality of life. They organized to urge city government to shut the hotels down. But those efforts were, in turn, opposed by a pro-hotel group organized to embrace the homeless men. Homelessness policy compounded the overall anguish of 2020–2021 for Upper West Siders. Neighbor was set against neighbor and the harmony that used to characterize the neighborhood dissolved in a chaos of racism accusations and social media bullying.

The dispute over the Lucerne and Belleclaire was about social integration. Homelessness policy embraces the end of social integration and pursues it using the means of housing programs. The end is understandable, the means are questionable. Integration is a goal or standard in most areas of social policy (mental health, disability services, education, child welfare, criminal justice, etc.). Basic homeless demographics illustrate that lack of social integration is one of the problem's root causes. Members of the sheltered homeless population are five times more likely to be in a one-person household than the US population as a whole.[1] Almost the entire street population is made up of single adults.[2] In the 1980s, sociologist Peter Rossi, one of the first researchers of modern homelessness, reckoned that men without steady work could typically rely on friends and family for four years until they wound up homeless.[3] For families, too, becoming homeless is often an experience of spending down one's social capital.[4]

But housing is a blunt tool to use to bring people together. Americans stopped building public housing decades ago in part because of how it isolated its residents from their broader communities. More recent voucher-oriented rental assistance programs have relocated low-income families to suburban areas, but without registering an impressive record on social integration.[5] And low-income families should be far easier to integrate into ordinary communities than homeless single men with untreated behavioral health disorders. Programs that help people find work and get off drugs are not going to be able to help all homeless single men. But those they do help will be better integrated than those who have stable housing and not much else going for them. Thus, homelessness policymakers must qualify or weaken their now-intense pursuit of getting as many people as possible into stable housing if they want to also maintain a sincere commitment to social integration.

WHY INTEGRATION MATTERS

Homeless people spend too much time around other homeless people. Homelessness is and always has been a condition of place-lessness. The previous chapter, on compassion, explained the rationale behind the community nonprofit-run homeless services system. One criticism of a community-based or locally-based welfare state is that it binds people to places that aren't good for them. Some communities are more abundant in economic opportunity and effective social service programs than others.[6] Integrating the homeless means integrating them into communities that exert positive influence on them. Social circumstances shape individuals, in good ways and bad ways. Criminal justice reformers rely on that premise when they argue for shutting down jails. If an encampment is not as socially toxic as jail, it may not be far off. Relying on positive peer pressure is core to many addiction recovery programs' models.

Social integration theory, in homeless services, draws heavily on ideas derived from mental health, where life "in the community" has been a standard for more than fifty years. The so-called integration mandate established by US Supreme Court's decision in *Olmstead v. L. C.* (1999) requires governments to provide services to the mentally ill within "less restrictive settings." As discussed in an earlier chapter, the original theorists of Housing First were concerned about the quasi-institutional nature homeless services seemed to be taking on back in the 1980s.[7] In its purest form, Housing First considers the best housing for the homeless to be housing for the non-homeless: subsidized apartments located in ordinary apartment buildings, if somehow connected with a social service program.[8] Theoretician-advocates did not deny that many homeless needed services beyond just housing, but they urged cities to decouple social services from housing benefits. That meant not only making participation in services voluntary (the cornerstone Housing First principle) but basing them physically off-site.

Within the context of Housing First research, it's best to see social integration as similar to behavioral health and employment. However effectively low-demand housing can house people, it can't make them members of a community any more than it can restore their mental stability or coax them off heroin.[9] Academic research that argues that subsidized housing *can* affect integration is scarce and, scrutinized appropriately, relies on a fairly watered-down definition of "integration."[10] The case for housing as an instrument of social integration is far weaker than for housing as an instrument of housing stability. You can *hope* that giving people housing will integrate them into their neighborhood, you can support subsidized housing for reasons having nothing to do with social integration, but as far as integration goes, the "evidence" is not really on your side.

If harm reduction reflects a deep pessimism in government's powers, social integration reflects a buoyant optimism. It's startling how much confidence policymakers maintain in integration given government's long track record of failure: busing, deinstitutionalization, dispersal of the homeless population following the demolition of skid row, for a few examples. These efforts suggest that not only are government's integrative initiatives likely not to succeed but they also stand a strong chance of being counterproductive—forcing people apart while, officially, trying to bring them together. Not living in a mental institution shouldn't connote membership in a community.

Addressing mental illness means teaching people how to live as normal of a life as possible and to cope with ordinary social expectations: maintain healthy relationships with people you know, get along with those you don't know, perhaps hold down a part-time job, and manage money, diet, hygiene, and health. Giving someone a private apartment, no questions asked, no expectations imposed, is not likely to integrate them.

It's hard to know, in advance, what housing intervention will work best for someone. When surveyed, the unsheltered homeless will generally express strong preferences for independent living in their own private apartments: the proverbial "room with a key."[11] But there can be no doubt that settings with more supervision, such as residential treatment facilities, are more beneficial for some people who insist they'd be better off living independently.[12] "Generally speaking, there is no clear line between those who have a chance to be self-supporting and those who don't."[13]

THE SITING DILEMMA

Deciding where to put housing for the homeless can be as challenging as identifying funding for it. Often, when money's available, housing programs fail to have much of an effect on overall homelessness because the units come online too slowly.

"NIMBYism" receives much of the blame. Critics accuse NIMBYs of preventing homeless policy from succeeding and thwarting social integration.

Racism plays a smaller role in siting controversies than is commonly assumed. While many siting controversies take shape as a generally white neighborhood opposing a facility likely to house a generally black homeless cohort, majority minority neighborhoods often fail to embrace plans for a new shelter in their midst. If there's anything that unites Americans, at this time of pronounced civil discord, it's that everyone, across all class and racial boundaries, cherishes the power of local land use controls. Wealthy suburban communities of homeowners and poor neighborhoods inhabited mainly by subsidized renters might use their land use authority in different ways. Minority lawmakers demand deeply affordable housing and criticize proposals to build more moderate-income housing in their jurisdictions.[14] But they base that objection on a belief that any new development in their neighborhood should benefit current residents there. That is also the way wealthy suburbanites look at things. Americans anywhere who feel rooted in their community like to know who their neighbors are and who their neighbors are likely to be. Shelter is temporary housing by definition. Shelter residents are just passing through. Additionally, clients of single adult shelter have a high rate of behavioral health disorder, though, unlike residential treatment programs, the goal of shelter is not really to address those problems. Thus, conditions for social integration aren't good for any shelter and their host community.

Nonetheless, modern city governments press on with their plans to integrate the homeless using shelter and other housing-for-the-homeless programs. This is an ambitious social experiment with no precedent in US history. Only in modern times have ordinary residential neighborhoods been expected to accommodate housing facilities for homeless single adults. Before the 1980s, homeless single men were concentrated in skid row districts located close to downtown. The skid row solution worked, for a while at least, because police then had more power to contain disorder and because downtowns can tolerate more disorder than residential neighborhoods. Downtowns are "inhabited," so to speak, by transients: commuters and tourists passing through. Anyone who makes temporary use of a physical space can put up with more public disorder than people who have to literally live with it. Throughout the 2010s, tourism in Los Angeles, New York City, and San Francisco reached historic peaks, as did single adult homelessness. While homelessness-related disorder can hamper tourism and other commercial activity, it can also be kept in check by it.

For their part, homeless policymakers view localistic concerns as unhelpful. Government needs to build housing for the homeless just like it does schools and roads. A larger common good transcends parochial neighborhood concerns. Many policymakers don't even see siting disputes as an instance of rights in conflict but rather as conflicts between proponents of social justice and proponents of neo-redlining.

If a municipal homeless services agency truly has no choice but to build a new facility, the optimal solution is for the community to accept the facility. Experienced leaders of homeless services nonprofits often can rattle off examples of facilities denounced at first but with which everyone eventually made their peace. That does not always happen, though,[15] and in any event, the future might not look like the past. Must cities continually expand the number of shelters and supportive housing facilities indefinitely, as well as halfway houses, supervised injection facilities, methadone clinics, residential treatment facilities for drug addiction, group homes for the mentally ill or developmentally disabled, and drop-in centers? What happens when a city needs to develop all of these at once? A healthy neighborhood can't be comprised only, or even mostly, of social service facilities, and all neighborhoods have a tipping point. Just because a neighborhood can handle one supportive housing building does not mean it can handle multiple supportive housing buildings.

To sort out these disputes, some jurisdictions have developed "fair share" policies that create a formal, principled process to adjudicate siting controversies. The idea that "every neighborhood should do its part" to house the homeless sounds appealing. But it can't be the basis of sound public policy for three reasons. First of all, real estate costs are much lower in poor neighborhoods. Taxpayer dollars can be stretched much farther there and more units can be built, which is, or should be, a hugely consequential consideration for any city facing an affordable housing crisis. Second, fair share clashes with health equity. Low-income communities are often said to be underserved by health services, including behavioral health. For some people, particularly hard cases who need enhanced supervision, appropriate behavioral health treatment requires a residential setting.

Third, fair share clashes with social integration. New York tries to open new shelters in the neighborhood in which families fell into homelessness so that the children can continue to attend the school and the families as a whole benefit from existing community supports.[16] Poor neighborhoods produce far more homelessness than middle-class and wealthy neighborhoods.[17] Thus, it stands to reason that poor neighborhoods should also host more residential programs for homeless people. If not, government becomes formally indifferent to the use of social bonds in relieving homelessness. It's easier to restore social bonds than form new ones.

Progressive policy researchers, keen to evaluate siting from an objective, quantifiable perspective, have studied the effect on poverty values and found in at least some cases that values weren't negatively affected.[18] In other cases, values were found to be negatively affected.[19] But even crediting the no-negative-impact body of research, case studies do not justify blanket declamations such as, "supportive housing benefits communities by improving the safety of neighborhoods, beautifying city blocks with new or rehabilitated properties, and increasing or stabilizing property values over time."[20]

Let's say you own a home on a city block that you're preparing to sell. On the same block, the city recently opened a new mental health shelter. Do you expect that, all things being equal, the new shelter will increase or decrease the number of offers you get on your house? And if you answer "decrease," doesn't that mean that you believe that your house would be worth more if it didn't have a shelter as a neighbor? Policy researchers expect homeowners to believe that shelter expansion is one of the most reliable methods to stabilize and even increase their property values.

Many of the arguments about siting that are based on experience seem to come down to: "the community gets used to it." A shelter or supportive housing facility, once seen as an outrage, becomes tolerated as an inconvenience. However, we don't expect individuals in disadvantaged circumstances to "get used to" their adverse experiences. Would the community be better off with or without the shelter? That question may not solve the siting dilemma but at least it's an honest one.

In normal discussions of city life, we appreciate the wide variety of differences between neighborhoods: poor versus working class versus affluent, or residential versus commercial. And yet, in the debate over siting, all these differences are effaced: shelters and supportive housing facilities are always good things or, at least, no problems whatsoever. A neighborhood comprised largely of single twentysomethings can tolerate more disorder than one comprised of families with children. Some service providers are more effective than others. They certainly serve different populations. A family shelter poses less threat to quality of life than a shelter for single adults. Some service providers will take disorder-related criticism from neighbors seriously, others will blame the government for not giving them more resources for security and programming. Some facilities are larger than others: a two-hundred-bed facility poses a greater risk than a fifteen-bed facility. If a city changes its eligibility criteria say, by, adopting a "coordinated entry" approach by which the hardest cases get placed in supportive housing first, then none of the previous experience with supportive housing is applicable. Supportive housing initiatives are sometimes criticized as too small to reduce homelessness, but their relatively modest scale may preserve their reputations. New York's isolation hotel program, similar in many respects to supportive housing, scaled up rapidly in late spring/early summer 2020 and, as noted earlier, the results in terms of social integration were not encouraging.[21]

Shelter providers who serve single adults are, formally or informally, part of the mental health system. The mental health system has a longstanding reputation for failure. Public officials who, in one policy debate context, castigate the mental health system, in another, direct neighborhood residents to trust in the competence of a single adult shelter provider they know nothing about. This is not consistent.

Homeless adults can make for very bad neighbors. Like when they scream at night.[22] Facilities that house homeless adults can generate enormous volumes of 911 calls, an unwelcome intrusion in quiet neighborhoods.[23] Many people resent the implication that their quality of life is being sacrificed for the sake of someone else's social experiment.[24] To residents of a neighborhood who didn't want a shelter but got one, that building will long symbolize, for them, their status as policymakers' guinea pigs. They will receive daily reminders of their guinea pig status when they walk by, every day, the shelter that city officials placed in their neighborhood to prove an ideological point and not only, or even mainly, for programmatic reasons. That is not a good recipe for social integration.

There's a difference between nighttime needs and daytime needs. Temporary or permanent housing meets people's nighttime needs. Homelessness status is defined by where one sleeps. But many homeless people have nothing to do during the day.

Jane Jacobs's term for homeless adults is the "leisured indigent."[25] They're typically unemployed and not engaged in a committed way in any program or services. Idleness combined with behavioral health disorders can lead to neighborhood disturbances. Thus, siting leads to ongoing "front porch" controversies. Many shelters require clients to be out during the day. Shelter and other programs could offer more in the way of daytime programming but staffing is expensive, many locations don't have appropriate space in which to offer programming, and Housing First philosophy insists that no one be required to participate in anything if they don't want to. No community—low-income, working-class, or affluent—welcomes the prospect of place-less single men loitering around all day long. This was not a problem in the old Bowery days, because the traditional single-room occupancy (SRO) hotels were concentrated on skid row, away from the non-homeless.

Always overlooked in siting debates are the views of the homeless themselves. Advocates insist on maximizing shelter and supportive housing facility placements in "high opportunity" communities like the Upper West Side.[26] By the standard logic of homeless policy debate, if a community group *doesn't* want a shelter in their neighborhood, then it must be true that the shelter clients ardently *do* want it to be there. But why is everyone so sure that the homeless and mentally ill want to be in *that* neighborhood? Robert Hayes is a legendary figure in homeless advocacy circles. Highly active in the early 1980s, he founded the Coalition for the Homeless and led the litigation over the right to shelter in New York. In a candid interview published in 2019, he admits that advocates don't always speak for the homeless:

> After the first court order came down, the municipality got the state government to cede the Keener Building, an abandoned psychiatric hospital under the Triborough Bridge on Wards Island. We, young idealists, thought this was abhorrent: to create a shelter on the grounds of a psychiatric institution, on an island in the middle of the East River, shoving humanity out of sight. And we were ready to try to block that, arguing that the operation was basically a sham: the building was inaccessible, and nobody would go there. But talking to some homeless individuals then living at the Bowery, I learned that those sheltered at the Keener Building were relieved to get away from the pressure and the stress of the hard-living conditions of the Lower East Side. They were welcoming the Keener Building as a refuge, from which they could walk across the bridge from Wards Island right onto Third Street in Manhattan. So sometimes our idealism did not converge with the actual demands of our clients.[27]

WORK AND INTEGRATION

Integration, to be meaningful, must encompass values and habits. Work builds habits in a way that housing does not. You can't form a community out of two groups of people, one of which generally accepts the idea of personal responsibility, the other of which generally believes that any harm they encounter, including being arrested and charged with a serious crime they're guilty of, is the fault of someone else or some distant, oppressive "system." Adult single male residents of a supportive housing facility who find in their midst no job worth doing or pursuing don't see why they shouldn't be free to loiter around outside their building all day and even throughout nighttime hours. Neighborhood residents who do have jobs and need to sleep will find the prospect of loud obscene language, open-air drunkenness, and pot smoking to be out of conformity with their idea of a healthy neighborhood. Communities with high rates of unemployment rates can struggle with social integration because adults who don't have to get up for work every morning often have different ideas about what constitutes a good time from those who do.

Most homeless people do not work, particularly in the sense of full-time on-the-books employment. Off-the-books "spot work" is still around in urban economies.[28] But less of it seems to be available for homeless men, specifically, than in the tramp and skid row eras.[29] Accounts of main stem and skid row neighborhoods noted the existence of employment centers that connected men with day-labor jobs, but there's no equivalent of that institution for encampments.

Unemployment is a significant risk factor for homelessness. Still, many scholars prefer to characterize homeless adults' attachment to the workforce as tenuous but not nonexistent. One 2018 study obtained employment data for more than 160,000 shelter clients in New York City. It found that, annually, on average, 43 percent of adults in families were working in the years prior prior to their initial shelter entrance and 52 percent of single adults were.[30] Another study by the California Policy Lab in 2020 matched government employment and homeless service system records. It found that, of all the clients served by the Los Angeles Homeless Services Authority between 2010 to 2018, three-fourths had been formally employed at some point in their lives before becoming homeless. However, only one-fifth were working around the time they fell into homelessness.[31] The research team also looked at post-homelessness employment data and found that the best predictor of whether someone worked after their experience with homelessness is whether they were working immediately prior to it.[32] That suggests that having a full-time job not only helps keep you out of homelessness while you have it, but even after you've lost it and fallen, temporarily, into homelessness. Re-integration appears to be more promising than integration for the first time. Employment and related therapeutic interventions appear to hold the most promise for those who had previously been on track for a normal, non-homeless life.[33] But more generally, scholars argue, the glass is half full when it comes to the homeless population and employment. A large portion of the homeless population have a legitimate shot at a working-class life if their weak attachment to work can be firmed up.[34]

Some assert that the number of working homeless is growing.[35] Critics invoke this cohort as evidence for (1) the failures of welfare reform and a work-oriented safety net overly oriented toward work, and (2) the "just folks" thesis about how homeless people don't differ from non-homeless people. But longitudinal data aren't available. Our best information on homelessness and employment comes from one-off studies and surveys that don't study the same kind of samples and ask different questions. Communities in California have been feeling more pressure to accommodate "safe parking" programs, some of which accommodate working adults and families. But that's not the case in the rest of the country. It's fair to claim that there are too many working homeless in America. It's more speculative to assert that their ranks have grown of late.

Though housing can't directly lead to social integration, perhaps it could do so indirectly, by facilitating employment. People without stable housing lead disorganized lives. They can't easily find and keep employment. Theoretically, stabilizing a household's unstable housing situation could boost their employment rates. Previously tenuous attachments to work could strengthen. There are examples of Westernized countries with a more expansive welfare state than America's but whose workforce participation is comparable or even superior.[36] Reasonable as this theory sounds, it does not conform to the American experience. About 40 percent of households subsidized by US Department of Housing and Urban Development (HUD) are able-bodied. About 20 percent of them haven't worked in the past three years and, at any given time, about 60 percent are employed.[37] If we assume that, before receiving their subsidy, they weren't working steadily, then experience suggests that a rental subsidy is not quite the launchpad advocates claim. If we assume they were working steadily before receiving the subsidy, and aren't now, the evidence is even more damning. About half of those employed aren't working full-time. In sum, per HUD, "Federal, state, and local efforts to promote self-sufficiency among HUD-assisted households and individuals experiencing homelessness have shown mixed results in earnings and employment outcomes for participants. . . . Stable, affordable housing, which can be obtained through use of housing assistance, can be a platform for securing employment, but for many individuals eligible for housing assistance or experiencing homelessness, housing assistance alone is likely to be insufficient for achieving economic independence."[38] Subsidized housing should not be framed as a workforce development program. Whatever may be Europe's experience with social democracy, America's experience with subsidized housing has been that it leads to more unemployment and underemployment.

We should always care about employment and homelessness because work integrates people more effectively than housing alone does. Work puts people in a position where they can contribute to others' well-being and minimize the degree that they burden their families. Zoom out to the neighborhood level. Families inordinately burdened by too many dependents can become unstable. Unstable families create unstable neighborhoods. The more that non-disabled adults work, the less instability in neighborhoods and families we will have. Of course, many of the homeless are disabled. But the case of the disabled illustrates work's integrative value even more clearly than the non-disabled, because it highlights why it's worth doing even when the economic justification is not powerfully compelling. Work helps the mentally ill and drug addicted recover because it gives them something to recover *for*.[39] (The therapeutic and integrative potential of work is an idea that is taken more seriously in mental health policy circles than in homeless policy circles.)[40] Defending the benefit of work for the homeless population must mean defending the benefit of menial work. Some mentally ill individuals view art therapy as infantilizing and a mundane job as preferable, cognizant of the fact that most ordinary adults work for a living and treat music and art as hobbies.[41] A mentally disabled man who works part-time stuffing envelopes for a marketing firm, in all likelihood, never goes out for drinks with his firm's CEO nor regularly attends dinner parties at his colleagues homes and may well feel uncomfortable if somehow pressed to participate in those activities. But if he's showing up, meeting his responsibilities, he is far more socially integrated than a formerly homeless man who spends most of every day in his supportive housing unit with the shades drawn.

SHIFLESSNESS

The homeless population, throughout history, has always included people who place a high value on personal freedom and distance from normal human relationships. These could be termed "nothing left to lose" types, or votaries of "the uncommitted life."[42] They may not have anything clinically wrong with them. They just don't fit or function well in ordinary society. Social expectations that most people find merely inconvenient they consider deal-breakers. Relationships that sociologists may characterize as rich in social capital they deem oppressive. Homelessness and destitution feel to them, if not like absolute freedom, still freer than their available alternatives. Consider the following passage from Donald Bogue's 1963 study of skid row:

> A certain proportion of workingmen have left their home communities for personal reasons and settled here in order to get away from social situations which they found intolerable or as a substitute for living in a desirable situation from which they have been expelled. Family trouble, a major disappointment or sorrow, acute maladjustment to a given job or other responsibility, and other psychological and personal problems may produce the unsettled condition in which they find themselves. Not infrequently persons in such a plight want to go where they cannot easily be found, or where they can be anonymous and no one will ask questions or quiz them about their past successes or failures.[43]

Housing First advocates claim that the homeless' ability to live on the streets proves their preparedness for independent life in the community.[44] Living on the street demonstrates toughness and a certain resourcefulness but not necessarily the basic capacity for civility and other social skills requisite to a normal life among the nonhomeless. Life on the street normalizes many behaviors that hinder people from functioning in normal society. Because the streets aren't safe, a prudent man trusts no one and might even carry a weapon. Those are habits that might make him seem like a paranoid delusional in a non-homeless context. The day-to-day experience of being a member of the middle class is not at all one of unrestricted independence. Normal communities set expectations and impose obligations that must be respected by any member of that community. Accounts of the impressively entrepreneurial hustle of scavengers prove less than they purport to.[45] There may be a connection between the qualities that allows someone to survive on the streets and the qualities that caused him to wind up on the street in the first place.

For lack of a better word, some homeless adults are shiftless. They do not have a serious mental illness or incapacitating substance abuse disorder. They are not registered sex offenders. And yet, they are unmotivated, they somehow reach their thirties without a career or prospects of a career, thus becoming a burden on others. Their outlook on life is suffused with excuses, resentment, and grievances. Many of us have had someone like this in our family. A shiftless person from a poor family is more likely to wind up homeless than a shiftless person from a wealthy family. His shiftlessness is still a problem, though.

Shiftlessness is probably a smaller factor than drug addiction, mental illness, and unaffordable housing in causing homelessness. It's surely smaller than all of these combined. But it may yet be significant. Shiftlessness could easily contribute 5 to 10 percent to the problem. Governments regularly claim victory for homelessness reductions of less than 5 to 10 percent. Whenever trying to attribute the homelessness crisis to any cause (drugs, housing), it must pass the test of history. Shiftlessness passes this test. The workforce participation rate of non-disabled adults has declined in recent decades.[46] Quite possibly, YouTube and iPhones have contributed to homelessness by having reduced the cost of entertainment down to zero and making idle hours more tolerable. The homeless population reads less than they used to. In the 1920s, Nels Anderson observed, "The homeless man is an extensive reader. . . . The tramp employs his leisure to read everything that comes his way. If he is walking along the railroad track, he picks up the papers that are thrown from the trains; he reads the castoff magazines. If he is in the city, he hunts out some quiet corner where he may read."[47] In the twenty-first century, homeless people spend enormous amount of time in libraries but they're not doing much reading there.[48]

Shiftlessness can be rooted in pride. An official at HUD wrote recently "most people experiencing homelessness are working or wish to do so."[49] Reflected in that "wish to do so" clause may be unrealistic standards. Someone with a modest education and no substantial prior work experience is not going to be qualified for many jobs. To work, he may have to swallow his pride. That's not a step everyone's willing to take. Shiftlessness can be hard to understand for people who are themselves quite hardworking. They imagine that, were their income and standard of living to plummet abruptly, they'd spare no effort to climb back up. But the fact of the matter is that homeless adults do not always stir themselves to escape their reduced circumstances. Giving them housing could provide them with the stability they need to push into the working class, or it might allow them to rest. One economist, writing in 1919, remarked on the curious phenomenon of the "increase in labor turnover which frequently accompanies a sharp increase in wages":

> When any one's income exceeds his standard of living his incentive to work is removed. He has nothing to work for . . . one whose standard of living rises no higher

than satisfying his stomach with "something that will fill up" or who has no abhor-
rence for the crowding of the tenement, is happy when he has a bottle and some
cigarettes, and is content with the clothes that come from the second-hand store, has a
standard of living quickly attained. He will see no reason for working as long as he has
some money in his pockets. "Why should I take a job? I'm not broke," is an expression
that is familiar to employment office managers."[50]

If getting a raise can incline some people with low standards of living to reduce their
work effort, it should come as no surprise that receiving subsidized housing can,
as well.

For some homeless people, integration requires motivation. Often, what's described as paternalism is really an attempt to encourage motivation. Living a hard life
can stifle motivation. You've been lied to countless times by social workers. Betrayed
by supposed friends. Maybe you no longer even trust yourself. But there's no doing
without motivation. Motivated people get more out of every system, including government bureaucracies. Housing alone won't do much to stimulate motivation and
for some people it may even dampen it.

AGAINST LIVED EXPERIENCE

Social integration concerns have always affected the how of social service provision.
We should go about helping the poor in a way that doesn't lead to resentment and
ill will. Voluntarism, a core tenet of the pre-New Deal "organized charity" era, was
touted partly for its social integration value. Practices such as "friendly visiting"
with charity recipients in their homes gained a reputation for being intrusive and
paternalistic,[51] but, for many at the time, they represented a sincere commitment to
efface social boundaries.[52]

Trying to help poor people sometimes pushes them away. A favored modern
response to the welfare state's dis-integrative tendencies is the emphasis on "lived
experience." Policy should be made *with* homeless people, not just on their behalf.
Homeless people are regularly recruited to serve on boards and speak on panels.[53]

"Lived experience" is a more problematic concept than it at first seems. To begin
with, only certain homeless adults' lived experience tends to count. Someone who,
while homeless, fatally stabbed another person and is receiving psychological services
from the criminal justice system to make him fit to stand trial will not be asked to
speak on a panel. Nor is a single mother working three jobs. It's the moderately functional types, with time on their hands, who tend to speak for the "lived experience"
of, by implication, all homeless adults. Lived experience injects a strain of identity
politics into the homelessness debate. When someone's encouraged to craft an identity—a source of pride—around their homelessness status, that may well dampen
their ambition for exiting homelessness. It would be better to encourage homeless
people to develop a sense of pride in something other than the wisdom they've derived from their experience with homelessness. Consulting the "lived experience" of

homeless people to better suit systems to their needs often seems to have less of an effect on the systems in question than the people consulted.

"Lived experience" is a more valid concept in the case of mental illness, where "peer support" counselors are very common. It is more meaningful to speak of the "experience" of psychosis than that of the "experience" of homelessness, because "homelessness" could mean numerous things. Becoming a licensed peer support counselor can be a milestone in a mentally ill person's path to recovery, a source of pride, and a source of income. It's logical to recruit the services of a formerly homeless veteran to facilitate another veteran's path out of homelessness. It's logical for people further along in recovery from drug or alcohol addiction to help along those only at the beginning stages. But too much emphasis on peer support works against the goal of social integration. Formerly homeless and mentally ill people should aspire to surround themselves with people without any experience of homelessness or mental illness. That would be more likely to happen if they acquire and maintain a part-time menial job than going to work at the service provider that they used to be a client at. Working as a peer makes you a professional mentally ill person, a professional homeless person.

How much do homeless policymakers truly care about what homeless people think? The test would have to be whether any policy has been changed, against the wishes of public officials, at the urging of homeless peers. The lessons imparted by homeless peers tend to mainly be that they want more benefits, especially housing benefits, with as few preconditions as possible. But that's Housing First, which leading policymakers are already committed to, based on their belief in harm reduction and housing as a human right. If peers with lived experience are selected and cultivated simply so as to give further support to the Housing First consensus, the whole exercise is dishonest.

Lessons derived from "lived experience" tend to teach either things we already know or are contradictory. Homeless people demand that shelters be made safer but also criticize shelters for restricting clients' personal freedom. People who experience homelessness also experience many other forms of adversity: parents and relatives who are addicted to drugs; assault, robbery, and rape; having to attend bad schools throughout one's childhood, and so forth. The issue about "lived experience" is not whether we should work to reduce the incidence of adversity in the lives of low-income Americans. The issue is, rather, whether our failure to do so has to do with our failure to listen to the victims of that adversity. An alternative explanation for that failure is that we disagree about solutions as well as measures of success. As it happens, victims of crime, failing schools, and homelessness themselves often disagree about solutions. In his valuable 2021 book, *San Fransicko*, Michael Shellenberger interviews a number of former homeless addicts, and parents of homeless addicts, who reject the Housing First/harm reduction philosophy favored by progressives that is supposedly uniquely rooted in "lived experience."[54]

One source of "lived experience" too rarely consulted, for purposes of crafting a more effective homeless services system, is that of families. Families are quite influential in the mental health context through groups such as the National Alliance on Mental Illness. They play no role in the crafting of homelessness policy. This is unfortunate. Families could explain to homeless policymakers what programs and reforms could have helped them better manage their homeless relative and, thus, may have prevented their descent to the streets. Relative to current norms, policymakers should spend less time listening to homeless people talk about their lived experience and more time listening to their families.

CONCLUSION: HOMELESSNESS AND SOCIAL CAPITAL

The spectacle of modern homelessness, to many observers, attests to the social disintegration of modern America.[55] Do these men have no families? Where did they come from? Is there no community that will take them back and care for them? Homeless people report that they have no friends at a much higher rate than nonhomeless people do.[56] In a recent study of faith-based organizations' responses to homelessness, researchers for the Baylor Institute for Studies of Religion quote one such Portland, Oregon-based group as saying, "People don't become homeless when they run out of money, at least not right away. They become homeless when they run out of relationships."[57] Stronger social cohesiveness probably accounts for the low levels of homelessness among otherwise poor immigrant cohorts.[58] Thus, among the many other reasons for why we should work to reknit civil society's frayed fabric is, we might thereby reduce homelessness.

That said, caution must be exercised when trying to apply concepts drawn from the social capital debate to homelessness. In the conventional social capital debate, we don't think of adults as facing a choice between no social bonds and bad social bonds. Sadly, those may be the only two realistic options homeless adults face at certain times in their lives. The lower down the income scale one descends, the more ambivalent social bonds tend to become. The "wrong crowd" looms larger in poor neighborhoods, and certainly on the streets, than it does among better-off adults and families, for whom social capital is more of a question of thriving or quality of life. High school dropouts should not join gangs, not even if they're lonely. Former drug addicts should stay away from their old crowd, among whom they're certain to encounter triggers that will lead to relapses.[59] As unsustainable as the single-parent family model may be, domestic violence victims should focus on staying single instead of reuniting with their abusers. In unstable families, new fathers fail to commit to their children because their friends lure them into crime and drugs.[60] Most child abuse and sexual violence (against adults and children) is perpetrated by people who are not strangers to their victims.[61] Homeless-on-homeless crime is widespread in encampments and shelters. Ideally, in low-income communities, social connections would operate like "shock absorbers,"[62] but a more accurate metaphor might be "crabpots."[63] One reason for the underwhelming outcomes of the Moving to Opportunity program, which gave vouchers to families to allow them to move to the suburbs, is that families retained strong ties to their old neighborhoods.[64] To com-pletely neutralize the risk of bad social bonds, voucher relocation programs would have to operate more like the witness protection program, but it's unclear how much demand there would be for that.

Frontline providers of "second chances" are families and communities. We should be careful about how much we expect stable families to do, in the way of "second chances," for their unstable neighbors and relations. The mother of the woman who was abused by a man recently released from prison: How does she feel about encountering him on the subway or at the bodega? The adult sister of the recovering opioid addict who once stole from her to buy drugs: Will she consider letting him live with her and her family, and if so, under what conditions? Undoubtedly, some working-class families are stronger by virtue of having distanced themselves from their hard case relations. After decades of "black flight," low-income neighborhoods are desperate to hang on to as much of the working class as they have left. Looser social bonds might be a condition of neighborhood stability.

With respect to social capital and the homeless and poor populations, government can play a handmaiden role. It can set up programs that give families an objective way to assess whether someone has changed. Housing alone can't attest whether someone has changed. Employment can. Menial jobs may lack strong psychologi-cal and financial rewards, while still providing the social benefit of giving a sign of stability to neighbors and family members. Menial jobs can also strengthen social bonds by creating a sense of gratitude on the part of children on whose behalf they're performed. Someone who regularly attends AA is more likely to be taken back in by formerly-alienated family members than someone who expects everyone to take their word that they've got everything under control. High-quality daytime programs, for the mentally ill, may also provide a measure of objective validation. To send these kinds of signals, programs must be at least somewhat selective. A program in which anyone can participate doesn't tell you that much about those who participate in it.

8

All Our Kin

The Challenge of Homeless Families

The debate over family homelessness is closely connected with family policy debate, more generally, and the legacy of welfare reform. Welfare reform, enacted in 1996, was a rare counterrevolution in social policy. Since the 1960s, American norms have grown increasingly liberal and since the New Deal, the welfare state has tended to grow. But during the welfare reform debate of the early-1990s, public opinion displayed *more* concern over bourgeois norms around work and marriage than it had twenty to twenty-five years prior. And while welfare reform did not enact a net reduction in government spending, it did enact the only restructuring of a major federal safety net program in US history.

During the welfare reform debate, Senator Daniel Patrick Moynihan famously invoked family homelessness as a bellwether of deep poverty in America. He predicted that welfare reform would prove every bit as catastrophic, for families, as deinstitutionalization had been for the mentally ill, with "half a million children on the streets of New York City in ten years' time, and we will wonder where they came from. We will say, 'Why are these children sleeping on grates? Why are they being picked up in the morning frozen? Why are they scrambling? Why are they horrible to each other, a menace to all, most importantly to themselves?'"[1]

Deep poverty has remained of interest to anyone debating welfare reform's legacy. At the time, some welfare reformers considered an increase in deep poverty a risk they were willing to run if it meant weakening the culture of dependency more generally and over the long term.[2] But sober analyses have suggested that the bottom didn't fall out. Deep poverty either increased less than doomsayers' predictions back in the 1990s or perhaps didn't increase at all.[3] The workforce participation rate among poor single mothers rose and child poverty rates declined.[4] More welfare recipients live in a family with a member who works than before reform.[5] Single-female-headed families boast a lower poverty rate now than before welfare reform.[6] Some voiced concern that more single mothers in the workforce would create a crisis in child supervision.[7] But that's hard to square with several other improvements concurrent with welfare reform's phase-in: the urban crime decline, the successes of the K–12 reform movement, and the decline in teen pregnancies.[8] Children placed in foster care rose slightly in welfare reform's immediate aftermath then dropped steadily throughout the 2000s.[9] Relative to overall "dependency," it bears mentioning that, viewing as a collective cash welfare, food stamps, and social security disability income payments, a greater share of the population now depends on those programs than before welfare reform (20.9 percent versus 16 percent), but a lower share derives more than half of their total income from them (4.1 percent versus 5.2 percent).[10]

Family homelessness itself first emerged, in a major way, in the early 1980s—before welfare reform. Whether welfare reform increased family homelessness is hard to settle definitively, because the US Department of Housing and Urban Development (HUD) only has data since 2007. According to HUD data, since 2007, family homelessness, both overall and of the unsheltered version of interest to Senator Moynihan, has trended downward. Conceivably, there could have been a surge, just after welfare reform but uncaptured by the HUD data. However, that seems unlikely, given the generally positive news on poverty during the 1997 to 2007 period and the lack of any other major antipoverty initiatives around 2007 to arrest and reverse the speculative post-welfare reform spike in family homelessness. The unsheltered figures may not be perfectly reliable, especially in the early years represented in figure 8.1, but these are the only official data available for homeless families.

Before the welfare reform debate, advocates and journalists under their influence were predicting a vast increase in unsheltered families as one of the "new" homelessness's defining features.[11] But like the idea of deindustrialization as a major cause of homelessness, better data that were unavailable in the 1980s have challenged that idea. Traditionally, the entire notion of a homeless family was almost a contradic-

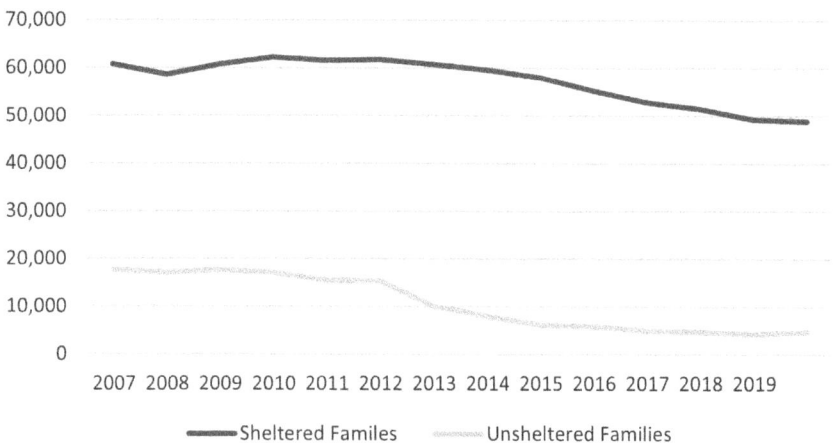

Figure 8.1.   Family Homelessness, 2007–2020.

tion in terms. "Unattached" or "disaffiliated" men, on the road or on skid row, were socially defined by not being part of a family. Families did not live on skid row.[12] Over recent decades, the once-fairly-young single adult male homeless population has trended older, but the single mother homeless cohort, who constitute most of the family homelessness challenge, has remained young.[13] There's much more of a sense of hope for what social service systems can accomplish for young adults than for older adults. The "chronically homeless" share of sheltered homeless single adults is about three times that of the rate among sheltered adult heads of homeless (21 percent versus 7 percent).[14]

But homeless families are still hard cases because of the children. Though no one can seriously claim, now, that welfare reform was as disastrous as deinstitutionalization, that family homelessness exists at all raises questions about the state of equal opportunity in America. Robert Hayes asserted back in 1987, "children have a right to a sense of permanence."[15] The case for investing in social programs for children is always more compelling than the case for investing in social programs for adults. But with respect to many programs, such as housing, it's impossible to invest in children and not in adults. The same program will have different effects and not, in both cases, necessarily positive effects. This "dual clientele" dilemma, which can be found in any debate involving families (immigration, child welfare, child support enforcement) frustrated welfare reformers for many years.[16]

The welfare reform era now appears to be ending. Guaranteed income-style programs such as an expanded child tax credit and family allowance are gaining traction. So, too, are proposals for a "right to housing" enacted through a universal housing choice voucher program. Layered onto traditional progressive preoccupations over welfare reform's mistakes have been centrist and conservative concerns over a declining birth rate and calls for a domestic policy more attentive to all families' needs and wants.

UNSHELTERED VERSUS SHELTERED
FAMILY HOMELESSNESS

Ordinary Americans conceive of homelessness as single adults living on the streets. The public perception is not inaccurate: unsheltered family homelessness happens, but it's rare.[17] According to HUD point-in-time estimates, there are about 4,800 unsheltered homeless family units (9 percent of total homeless family units), including 8,900 children under eighteen (also 9 percent of the total).[18] Adults without children comprise 70 percent of the total homeless population and 92 percent of the total unsheltered population. HUD data do not tell us much about the circumstances of people in unsheltered families. About 3,000 people in unsheltered families are considered chronic cases: people whose homelessness is long term and somehow stemming from a disability. As with all matters relating to unsheltered homelessness,

California plays an outsized role, accounting for more than one-third of the total. HUD data report about 6,100 people living in unsheltered families in California. No other state has more than 1,900. Only three other states report more than 1,000 people living in unsheltered families.[19] Homeless families are comparably "invisible" both because there are fewer of them than single adults but also because both the government-based and informal, friends- and family-based safety nets respond more forthrightly than they do with single adults.

Why aren't there more families on the street? The research provides no clear answers. One explanation is child welfare laws.[20] Certainly, low-income mothers place a high value on motherhood[21] and will sometimes take extraordinary measures to avoid the attention of loathed "Jane Crow" child welfare workers. At the same time, child welfare agencies have a reputation for laxity even when faced with evidence of imminent danger.[22] If a parent is living out of a tent in a temperate climate, and does not have a behavioral health disorder and their child shows no signs of being undernourished or abused, would child welfare agencies intervene there more aggressively than do when faced with reports of physical harm in a case of people with housing?

Public shelters give housing-unstable families options. Family shelters are nicer than single adult shelters, both because of their formal design—they offer more privacy—and because homeless single mothers are less disturbing to be around than homeless single adults. Any homeless woman with untreated schizophrenia, violent tendencies, and/or a raging drug addiction, if she has children, has likely lost them and would thus be cared for by the single adult system, not the family system.[23] Families are, and always have been, more tolerant of their adult female relatives.[24] Single adult males are a much larger part of the overall homelessness problem (ca. 285,000 people) than families with children (ca. 172,000 people) and single adult females (ca. 120,000 people).[25] Some surveys have found higher rates of mental illness among homeless single women than homeless single men (though not necessarily substance abuse).[26] That evidence could suggest that single women have to become truly unmanageable before they and their family part ways, whereas too much mooching is enough to sever ties between families and single men.

THE SINGLE-PARENT FAMILY CHALLENGE

There are about 54,000 homeless families in America.[27] Since the origins of the modern crisis, homeless families have, overwhelmingly, been headed by single mothers.[28] In its 2018 Annual Homelessness Assessment Report, HUD notes that 77 percent of all families with children in a shelter were headed by a single parent, while only 16 percent of all families with children in the nation were single parent headed and 39 percent of families under the poverty line.[29] Some surveys and systems have placed the rate near or even above 90 percent.[30] For families, single parent status is an enormous risk factor for homelessness, even more so than mental illness is for single adults. In no city does the rate of serious mental illness among homeless single adults reach 90 percent. The data may be skewed by shelter eligibility practices and capacity. Insofar as family homelessness is mostly homelessness in shelters, and some family shelters don't admit men, that might serve to reduce the rate of two-parent family homelessness.[31] But that wouldn't apply in the case of New York City, which has a large shelter system that accommodates all families and even grants them a right to shelter.

Family homelessness's correlation with the single parent family crisis marks it as a distinctive "modern" problem. Family homelessness was bad in the Great Depression, but homeless families were overwhelmingly intact.[32] From 1960 to 1980, the number of single-mother-headed families in America doubled, then increased by another two-thirds by 2010, and since then has stayed flat.[33] Around the time of the Great Recession, unmarried births hit 40 percent of all births and has since held steady.[34] Before the 1960s, the figure was 5 percent. Among black Americans, around 70 percent of all births are to unmarried women.[35]

We'd have less housing instability in America had we more family stability. At the same time, as is the case with assessing any "risk factor" for homelessness, other factors, housing most notably, must be taken into consideration. Seventy percent of children in Detroit live in a single-parent family, while only 40 percent of children in New York City do.[36] And yet, HUD reports that there are only about 170 homeless families in Detroit, compared with more than seventy times as many—about 13,200—homeless families in New York City.[37] A poor two-parent family in New York is much less likely to wind up homeless than a poor single-parent family. But both would be at far less risk of homelessness if they lived in Detroit. Whether they would be better-off in every way would be another question.

The link between single-parent headed households and family homelessness undermines the "poor man's Brady Bunch" reinterpretation of modern family instability.[38] In the American "single parent family," there's typically a father or male somehow in the picture, and a network of adult female relative and friends who express loyalty or at least affection towards the children. Some have argued for seeing these "random family" arrangements as an alternative to the nuclear family more than a corruption of it. But one test of resiliency it patently fails is preventing family homelessness, which wasn't a major social challenge sixty years ago. Single mothers wind up homeless at high rates because they have trouble holding down full-time employment. Another reason is the poorly defined obligations and commitments within their social networks. If a young woman has three children by two fathers, which of those two grandmothers should house her and her children if she is evicted? If a young mother has provided childcare for her cousin, also a young mother, does that relieve her of the responsibility to put up her cousin or create an expectation for doing so? Low-income families have less resources to share but, then, that's also the case with much of the immigrant population, past and present, whose tolerance for doubling up is well known. Government shelter programs help simplify matters for random families. With so much intergenerational homelessness, by this point, staying in a shelter has been normalized in many neighborhoods.

DOMESTIC VIOLENCE

Many homeless women have experienced domestic violence.[39] Of our nation's total stock of shelters and other temporary housing beds for the homeless, 12 percent are dedicated for domestic violence purposes.[40] The feminist movement built much of this stock.[41] Back in the 1960s, a woman who didn't have access to a shelter and had no other option but to stick with her abuser would not have been classified as "homeless." As the social services and criminal justice systems became more responsive to domestic violence, family homelessness grew.[42] Thus, to an extent, increased family homelessness is a consequence of social progress. More family homelessness means fewer women sticking with men who beat them.

Systems draw a distinction between domestic violence as an adverse experience common in the lives of homeless women and as a direct cause of homelessness itself. In the 2010s, while close to one-third of all families with children entering New York's shelter system each month were headed by an adult with a history of domestic violence, only 10 percent faced an "ongoing domestic violence threat."[43] It is not clear how often homeless women are fleeing abusers upon whom they were dependent for their housing or some other economic reason. Economic anxiety does come up in the "Why she stayed" literature.[44] One 2002 survey of women living in a domestic violence shelter reported that, of those who had returned to an abuser, about half had done so for reasons of "economic need."[45] But the men in the lives of low-income women are themselves often unemployed and housing unstable, more likely to be guests than hosts in a doubled-up situation. Indeed, the economic theory of modern family instability, most closely associated with William Julius Wilson, holds that it's because more men can't provide that single-parent families have proliferated. Research published by the National Institute of Justice has found that women with unemployed partners were far more likely to be victims of domestic violence than women whose partners had steady jobs.[46]

Domestic violence victims are not perfectly served by the permanent housing-oriented philosophy of addressing homelessness. When a woman flees an abuser to a shelter, she has an immediate need for safety and perhaps also psychological services. Signing her up for a housing choice voucher would address neither of those needs and could well make her a target for an abuser who, himself. might be in need of permanent housing. For such scenarios, transitional housing, which provides services and housing over a medium-term duration, would be most appropriate.[47] Under the influence of Housing First philosophy, cities have been under-investing in transitional housing for years. Surely some women stay too long with a man who is no good for them because they're worried that severing all relations would send *him* into homelessness. As the recent debate over the child tax credit expansion has once again demonstrated, focusing on "the children" is one of the most politically compelling ways to go about growing the welfare state. Single men are less sympathetic. Expanding permanent subsidized housing, for the sake of the children, especially when coupled with an increased child tax credit or family assistance grant, would benefit many homeless women but, if not done carefully, risks attracting more housing unstable abusers.

DOUBLING UP: SOLUTION OR CAUSE?

The Department of Education considers doubled-up families homeless. HUD does not, though it does characterize people living doubled up as "precariously housed."[48] Doubling up is commonly portrayed as a step along the way to homelessness. That is true for many but not everyone. Certainly, doubling up is an extremely common experience among low-income families.[49] Single-parent-headed families are disproportionately likely to double up and to wind up in shelters.[50] Not all doubling up is equally harmful. Discussion of doubling up and sharing housing don't always clarify which party is host and which is guest, and other distinctions such as kin versus nonkin and varying motivations and levels of tolerances between groups. Ethnic groups vary considerably in their propensity to double up.[51] For example, a 2016 report about homelessness in the New York City public school system reported that, while twice as many black students were in shelters than in doubled up situations, in every other ethnic cohort, the doubled-up share was larger than the sheltered share.[52] While that certainly reflects, in part, lack of access to stable, permanent housing among black households in New York, there's also considerable poverty among Hispanic and Asian cohorts in New York.[53] In America, the rate of children doubling up has been rising but mainly because of more kids living with their grandparents.[54] While 15 percent of children live "doubled up," only half do so as guests and the vast majority of them live with grandparents. Only 0.3 percent live doubled up as guests with a nonrelative, a percentage that has ticked down over recent decades.[55]

Scholars point out that, since the rate of sharing housing decreases the richer the household is, that must mean most people would prefer not to do it. Crowded living conditions have always raised concerns about public health (including during the COVID-19 pandemic) and sexual abuse. Nineteenth-century reformers believed that bad housing led to immorality through girls and young women being forced to share apartments with boarders and other males.[56] To a degree, these concerns persist. But though grandparents can meddle,[57] if so much of it is multigenerational living, it's not clear how harmful doubling up is. Reporting on crisis levels of homelessness among school children is a case in point, since three-fourths of all the children counted as having experienced homelessness over the school year were doubled up.[58] Most families enter shelters from doubled-up situations,[59] but that's not to say that most doubled-up families are doomed to someday enter shelter. Potential positives of doubling up include reduced rental expenses for the guest and perhaps also the host (taking in boarders happens more than people think), access to childcare assistance, and, to the extent doubling up reduces social isolation, it may enhance mental health.[60] The easiest way to reduce doubling up would be to invest massively in family shelter, but that would only be sensible if, generally, being in shelter is better than being doubled up.

For most people, the doubling up experience is closer to being stably housed than living in a shelter and certainly than living on the streets. We should consider how much we want to normalize shelter use, as an alternative to doubling up, since shelter normalization is a certain consequence of investing in it. The Department of Education reports that homeless school children generally perform lower than other children considered "economically disadvantaged."[61] But housing instability is a spectrum. Doubled-up kids cycle through fewer schools per year than kids living in shelter and have better attendance rates.[62] Shelter families may be in some ways qualitatively different than doubled-up families. Families in shelter could well have a higher rate of emotionally-disturbed teenagers than doubled up families, since that's one reason why doubling up doesn't always work out for families. Doubled-up schoolchildren would therefore likely have higher rates of academic performance than sheltered schoolchildren.

Those who call for including the doubled up in the homeless population expand the notion of what it means to "experience" homelessness beyond the point of usefulness. In the words of one researcher,

> homelessness is not a homogenous experience for children and it can be challenging to make generalized statements about the impact of "homelessness" on children because "homelessness" is not the same thing for all those who experience it . . . it seems easier to discern a poverty-related effect in studies of homeless and low-income children than a homelessness-specific effect. . . . When viewed in the context of a much broader range of adversities, it is apparent that *homelessness is but one of many stressors that children living in poverty all too frequently encounter.*[63]

Research on homelessness and crime also provides evidence of qualitative differences. The doubled-up population is much less at risk of being victimized than the sheltered and unsheltered homeless populations.[64]

Housing is not only a major household expense, it's a fixed one. It can't be cut back like spending on food and transportation, and certainly non-necessities such as entertainment. The fixed nature of housing costs has led some to argue that it makes them uniquely deserving of government assistance. But the "fixed" nature of housing also makes it easier to share. It's certainly easier than sharing income. When a relative of ours faces unemployment, we might give them a cash injection, but we're less likely to set them up with an ongoing stream of payments lasting two to three months. We will more readily consider giving them a place to stay for two to three months. Doubling up is a "fix it first"-style solution to homelessness, a way to work with what we've got. Average family size has been in decline for decades.[65] The above-discussed increase in doubling up notwithstanding, levels of crowding in the United States are at historic lows.[66]

Maybe, instead of citing statistics on doubling up as evidence for a broader homelessness crisis that merits increased investment in affordable housing, we could explore ways to make doubling up more tolerable. Maybe we could even encourage more of it, by addressing the disincentives toward sharing housing baked into certain major safety net programs, such as subsidized housing and food stamps, that allocate benefits based on household size.[67] Other programs have explored ways of renting whole houses, then subletting rooms to homeless single adults.[68] Two significant obstacles to more sharing, that will have to be addressed, are occupancy codes that prohibit doubling up and landlord resistance.[69] On a smaller scale, government could make sharing more tolerable by providing recreational opportunities such as restaurant and Uber vouchers and rec center memberships to doubled-up families. In his history of homelessness in New York City, Baruch College's Thomas Main describes how a resourceful social worker once stabilized a tense double-up scenario by securing a cable tv subscription that settled down some truculent grandchildren.[70]

CONCLUSION: ON VIRTUE FATIGUE

Family homelessness developed before welfare reform and does not seem to have been greatly exacerbated by it. It has, however, persisted, much like the single-parent family challenge with which it's closely connected. Policymakers feel defeatist over the prospects of restoring the two-parent family. In other social policy contexts, Americans have displayed near limitless zeal for changing values and behavior. Examples include critical race theory, public education campaigns against dropping out of school, D.A.R.E., campaigns to reduce the stigma of mental illness, and dog-curbing laws. Even when such hearts-and-minds initiatives don't work, they keep going, justified as the right thing to do. Similar pushes to reduce unmarried births have been tried, found ineffective, and led to diminished confidence in whether they're even the right thing to do. If homeless advocates around the year 2000 had to reckon with "compassion fatigue," conservatives and centrists have of late come down with "virtue fatigue" with respect to the single-parent family.

We appear to be entering a third era in the debate over unstable families. Concerns were first raised, in an important way, with the publication of Daniel Patrick Moynihan's 1965 report "The Negro Family: The Case for National Action." Progressives challenged the idea that changing family structure merited any specific policy response, and, through the welfare rights movement, proceeded to complete the transformation of public assistance from a widows' pension program to relief for never-married young mothers. Throughout the 1970s and 1980s, though, public disenchantment grew with entitlements for able-bodied adults, even if they had children at home. That led to welfare reform, which tempered dependency but had little effect on illegitimacy. The welfare reform consensus held for a remarkably long period of time. The Trump administration pushed to advance welfare reform further by expanding work requirements beyond cash assistance programs. Now, though, welfare reform is under siege, as universal basic income, until recently considered something out of social science fiction, has entered mainstream family policy debate in a big way. It has done so through the expansion of the child tax credit and its conversion, under the Biden administration, into a monthly allowance for families. Though, at present, the child tax credit's expansion appears to have been only temporary, it has given a permanent boost to the idea of universal basic income.

Deep poverty families in or at risk of homelessness were featured more prominently in the welfare reform debate in the 1980s and 1990s than the current family policy debate about the child tax credit and family allowances. Progressives have led efforts to institute a basic income, but support has been offered by some conservatives and many centrists who in another era would have been ardent welfare reformers. During the welfare reform debate, many scoffed at conservatives who alleged that poor single mothers had more children to get more cash assistance. Now, family assistance grant proponents on the right hope to encourage larger families via more cash assistance. For conservatives and centrists, the inner-city single mother, who stood at the center of the welfare reform debate, has been partially eclipsed by stressed out two-parent families who would like the option of having one member stay at home or work less. Progressive proponents of more generous benefits for families very much still have the case of deep poverty in mind and include among them some who never accepted welfare reform.

One core premise of welfare reform was that parents who work set a better example for children than parents who don't. Therefore, public policy should reduce dependency and increase work participation, and that goes also for single mothers if they're the only parent around. Ideally, public policy should reduce the rate of single-parent families. But if it can't do that, government must still take a position on whether it's important if children are raised thinking work is something normal adults do. Welfare reform was about social integration. Poor single-parent families living in inner city neighborhoods presented the spectacle of a class apart, wholly unintegrated into the currents of mainstream American society. Hence why, in the 1990s, promoting work for unmarried mothers was the socially conservative position.

More recently, though, social conservatives who stake out a pro-family position have become more ambivalent about work. They do not want public policy, broadly speaking, to favor the two-working-parents model over the one-working-parent model. As noted earlier, increased work participation among mothers has long been held as evidence of welfare reform's success, but some pro-family conservatives reject boosting work participation among mothers as a valid policy goal. They would be happy to see more women stay home to raise children and for government to support them in this. But whatever may be the case with the middle and upper classes, when low-income single mothers stay home, the government takes the place of a father. In the 1980s, CBS aired a program called "Crisis in Black America," which featured a man named Timothy McSeed who had fathered six children by four women. He justified his nonsupport of these children by saying, "the majority of the mothers are on welfare, and—welfare gives them a stipend for the month. See, what I'm not doing, the government does."[71]

By affirming the value of work for poor single mothers, government promotes social integration for those mothers, reduces the risk of children growing up without the example of a parent who works, and avoids endorsing the lifestyle of Timothy McSeed. Expanding subsidized housing to address homelessness, among other reasons, stands at the top of progressives' domestic policy wish list. Subsidized housing programs, such as vouchers, have a long record of leading to increased unemployment and underemployment. Subsidized housing reduces the need for income. Subsidized housing coupled with a child allowance will reduce the need for income, and thus the need to work, still more. Welfare reform tried to do something about unstable families. Expanding benefits may solve a different problem than welfare reform—reducing stress levels for the middle-class—but it won't solve the problem of unstable families and may well even exacerbate it.

9

You Can't Catch Schizophrenia from the Streets

Mental illness is one of the homeless population's most notable features. Debate exists, though, as to whether homelessness leads to mental illness or vice versa. Addressing mental instability, on the one hand, and housing instability, on the other, are not unrelated goals. But how should a program be evaluated if it succeeds with respect to housing instability but achieves nothing with respect to mental stability?

Many advocates for the homeless prefer to see mental illness as an effect of homelessness. Maximizing support for more subsidized housing is their main strategic goal, and they fear that any interest in nonhousing-related aspects of homelessness will reduce support. They point out that most of the homeless population does not have a serious mental illness and that most seriously mentally ill Americans have housing.[1] These claims are fair enough but misleading.

The US Department of Housing and Urban Development (HUD) data report a rate of about 25 percent of serious mental illness for homeless adults (sheltered and unsheltered). That is likely a conservative estimate, given that part of the estimate is based on volunteers asking the street homeless if they have a mental illness. Many mentally ill individuals do not believe they have a mental illness. Evidence derived from the methodologically limited HUD data has been supplemented, over the years, by one-off studies in which social science professionals took a homeless cohort in some city or cities and closely assessed the extent and severity of psychiatric impairment.[2] Many have found a rate higher than 25 percent.

Studying the homeless carefully raises several of the same challenges as counting them. The easiest approach is to locate them through the services they use. However, many homeless adults do not use services. Different shelters and "service settings" where researchers may come into contact with potential study participants can attract different clientele. The street population, among whom rates of behavioral health disorders run the highest, can be particularly footless and disinclined to participate in an evaluation of their psychiatric impairment. Scrupulous researchers strive to identify a group that is representative of the homeless population in the larger community, but no study is perfect. When it comes the link between behavioral health and homelessness, we don't know for certain, we can only estimate, and our knowledge is unlikely to deepen anytime soon.

Those caveats aside, it seems fair to say that 25 to 33 percent of the adult homeless population is somehow functionally impaired by serious mental illness.[3] Those rates would run generally lower for adults who are heads of homeless families, generally higher for single adults sleeping in shelter, and higher still for single adults living on the street. A community comprised of individuals where behavioral health disorders ran at one-third of the population or higher, such as an encampment, can't be described as being just like any other community save for the fact that no one has housing.

History helps bring the current challenge into focus. During the main stem and skid row eras, psychosis did not define homelessness in the popular imagination. Drunkenness, yes, shiftlessness, absolutely, but not schizophrenia. Social work has always relied on social science.[4] As discussed earlier, early-twentieth-century social researchers closely observed the behavior and psychology of homelessness men, and they were less convinced that lack of housing defined homeless adults. Thus, they were even more motivated to attend to psychological factors than modern researchers, but their studies said very little about schizophrenia.

The deinstitutionalization of the mentally ill left many Americans who, formerly, would have been committed to a long-term mental hospital to live on the streets. State asylums were in continual expansion mode from the nineteenth century up until the 1950s, a period that encompasses the entire tramp era and about half of the skid row era. The asylum system was a blunt approach to mental healthcare. Not everyone with a mental disorder needs inpatient treatment but, before deinstitutionalization, that's more or less all that government had on offer. The asylum system did, though, keep people housed. Daily encounters with mentally ill street homeless are a distinctive experience of modern urban life. The bag lady phenomenon is entirely driven by deinstitutionalization. Almost no women occupied the ranks of the single adult homeless before the 1980s.

Toward the end of the skid row era, as deinstitutionalization ramped up, more mentally ill began to be noticed on the Bowery and similar neighborhoods. During the runup to the emergence of homelessness in 1980, deinstitutionalization moved at an especially rapid rate. The state hospital census peaked at 559,000 in the mid-1950s and now stands at around 40,000. Of that total reduction, about 45 percent, a drop of about 230,000 patients, happened in the 1970s.[5] During the early stages of deinstitutionalization, hospital directors focused on placing out into the community people who had families to return to and elderly adults with dementia. The 1970s-era releases concentrated on harder cases less likely to have a family to take them in.[6] This explains why deinstitutionalization contributed to homelessness in the 1970s but not the late 1950s, when it first began.

The best argument *against* the link between mental illness and homelessness is that public mental health systems are dysfunctional everywhere in America, but rates of homelessness vary considerably. That Detroit's rate of homelessness is lower than San Francisco's reflects more about those cities' housing markets than the quality of their respective mental health systems. Housing always matters. But, as was discussed in the previous chapter about unstable families, certain characteristics place an individual or family at greater risk of homelessness even if low-rent housing is scarce, and one such factor is mental illness. In the 1970s, large numbers of former mental hospital patients were discharged to skid row.[7] Had cities taken steps to preserve their very low-rent housing stock in skid row districts, those neighborhoods would, up to a point, resemble modern encampments. We would have for-profit single-room occupancy (SRO) operators reliant on social security income (SSI) payments just as nonprofit permanent supportive housing operators on the scene are now. The homeless problem would have been different, and maybe we wouldn't have even called it "homelessness," but it still would have been a serious social problem.

If 25 to 33 percent of homeless adults have a serious mental illness, this implies that *most* of the homeless are *not* mentally ill. But 25 to 33 percent still seems high. The seriously mentally ill homeless may not be most of the homeless, but they surely comprise most of the hardest cases. Perhaps the public exaggerates the share of serious mental illness among the homeless population as a whole. But the public tends to come in contact with the least functional cases. If you're talking about person who is a purely down-on-his-luck case, who sleeps in a shelter but works at a full-time job all day long, then that is someone who the public is unlikely to come in contact with and is also likely to be less concerned about. The system is also less concerned about that person. The public is confused about many things about homelessness. Many members of the public, in the big blue cities where homelessness is worst, believe that homelessness emerged because of catastrophic cuts to the safety net enacted under President Reagan. This theory is false, but advocates don't go out of their way to disabuse people of it.

Advocates have been open about how they developed the term "homeless" for reasons of political advantage.[8] When talking about how much money supportive housing saves, advocates play up how often homeless adults use expensive mental hospitals. But given how strict civil commitment criteria now are, only someone with a very serious mental illness would use a mental hospital. If hospitalization is an all-too-common experience among the homeless population, then serious mental illness must, too, be a common experience among them. However, in other contexts, when homeless advocates are talking about stigma or the degree to which the homeless are just like the non-homeless, they downplay mental illness.

UNTREATED SERIOUS MENTAL ILLNESS

The government defines a "serious mental illness" based on how much a mental disorder impairs someone's ability to function in normal society. A mental disorder that prevents someone from performing basic self-care and hygiene, holding down a job, and maintaining relationships qualifies as "serious." At least as far as government definitions go, "seriousness" is not assessed based on a diagnosis, though, in practice, most individuals considered "seriously" mentally ill have schizophrenia, bipolar disorder, or major depressive disorder.[9] Around 5 percent of the adult population has a serious mental illness.[10] The federal Substance Abuse and Mental Health Services Administration reckons that about one-third of all seriously mentally ill adults, 4.5 million people, receive no treatment every year.[11]

Mental illness causes homelessness when people with untreated schizophrenia become hard to live with. They keep odd hours, behave erratically, disturbingly even, express themselves in obscene and politically incorrect language,[12] and can't be trusted to be left alone, for their sake and others'. They abuse drugs and alcohol at high rates and exercise bad judgment about the company they keep. They can be violent toward loved ones, caregivers, and random strangers. Most were once housed, though, and lived with their families. At some point after the onset of their illness, they became unmanageable. They left, so as to be free from restrictions their family tried to impose on them, likely for their own benefit, or they had to be asked to leave for the sake of the others in their family. There are also economic reasons why mentally ill people become homeless. Few have full-time employment because of their disorder and, thus, no income. Some lose their government benefits because they refuse to submit to the application process due to the suspicion that there is some sort of conspiracy behind it.[13] Social workers find mentally ill people hard to serve for reasons similar to why their families find them hard to live with. "Leaving serious mental illness untreated can cause bizarre behavior that makes living with families untenable and homelessness inevitable."[14]

You can't catch schizophrenia from the streets like you can many other harmful, infectious diseases. But to say that homelessness causes mental illness or substance abuse could mean, in effect, that it causes or contributes to disorders that are going untreated. Treatment is of pivotal importance. The difference between an untreated serious mental illness and a treated serious mental illness can be larger than the difference between a serious mental illness and a mild mental illness. Treated bipolar disorder can almost seem like a different illness than untreated bipolar disorder. Most people on the street are unlikely to receive treatment so long as they stay on the street.

But we must think clearly about barriers to treatment and how homelessness erects or strengthens them. Advocates often speak of scenarios such as people losing their medication when the government callously dismantles the encampment in which they're living. That scenario, and others like it, implies that the unsheltered mentally ill are trying to access or stay in treatment but flawed policy thwarts them. It is not safe to assume that all people on the street are strongly motivated to pursue treatment. Many mentally ill people don't like the side effects of medication or simply don't believe that they are truly mentally ill. Homelessness could certainly thwart treatment by encouraging substance abuse. Perhaps in some cases homelessness causes substance abuse, not vice versa, because it brings someone into contact with the broader homeless population among whom drug addiction is extremely common.

FAMILIES AND THE MENTALLY ILL

To say that mentally ill people are hard to live with means, often, they have trouble living with their families. One 2011 study suggested that close to half of all adults with schizophrenia lived with their families or loved ones.[15] Progressives see the growth of the welfare state as having been a tremendous boon to the American family. Whereas problems such as unemployment and disability were once thrust on families alone, social insurance programs transferred much of those burdens to society more broadly. The opposite happened with mental illness. Prior to deinstitution-alization, families were not assumed to be responsible for their adult schizophrenic relatives. Indeed, as the late dean of mental health policy history Gerald Grob once explained, they were often the party that initiated institutionalization:

> In practice commitment was an informal process that involved human decisions rather than strictly legal ones. The decision to commit was largely made by the family of the mentally ill person. . . . The decision to commit was normally undertaken with a great deal of reluctance. Indeed, most families did everything within their power to find alternative means of dealing with mentally disordered members. The final decision generally came after prolonged tensions had created a crisis, and forced a choice between institutionalization and destruction of the family unit.[16]

Now, though, families of mentally ill adult relatives bear a heavy burden. Having to care for a mentally ill relative can destroy a family: estranging parents and children, breaking up marriages, draining resources, ruining careers, and destabilizing relationships with neighbors.

It is interesting to reflect on the fact that prior to the 1960s, when families were much stabler than now, the default solution to dealing with a mentally ill relative was to place them in an institution.[17] In modern social policy debates, conservatives often focus on the risk that looking too often to the government to respond to problems that were once managed within the context of civil society will "crowd out" the prerogatives, and eventually the vitality, of the family and other private institutions. But for a parent of a child with schizophrenia, crowding out is the least of their concerns. What they're up against isn't overreach but cruel indifference from government policymakers. The history of mental illness policy teaches that sometimes strong families require strong government institutions.

Deference to families became legally impossible in the wake of the 1960s' civil rights revolution, when disabled groups, including the mentally disabled, cast the mentally ill in the role of an unjustly oppressed minority group.[18] Working both through the courts and state legislatures, mental health advocates expanded civil liberties for the mentally ill with the result that it became very difficult to institutionalize people against their will unless they posed an immediate threat to themselves or others. Families have borne much of the brunt of weakened civil commitment laws. Memoirs of dealing with a seriously mentally ill relative, such as Pete Earley's *Crazy*, or "When My Crazy Father Actually Lost His Mind," a longform

2012 article in the *New York Times Magazine*, provide wrenching detail about how hard it is to help someone who is blessed enough to have family members devoted to getting them the care they need, but whose psychosis is not (yet) sufficiently violent to merit inpatient commitment.[19] In civil commitment proceedings, the Supreme Court (*Heller v. Doe*) has allowed party status for families of the mentally retarded but not families of the mentally ill.[20]

SUBSTANCE ABUSE

Attempts to assess the rate of substance abuse among the homeless population has traditionally raised many of the same problems as attempts to assess the rate of mental illness. In a study in New York's shelter system in the early 1990s, a urinalysis showed drugs in two-thirds of the single adult population, though only 48 percent self-reported that they had used drugs in the past year, and 29 percent of the families population, though only 18 percent self-reported that they had used drugs in the past year.[21] The official HUD statistics reckon the number of homeless people afflicted with "chronic substance abuse" to be about 100,000, which is close the number of seriously mentally ill homeless, per HUD (those are overlapping, not exclusive, cohorts).[22]

Thus, it's likely that 25 to 33 percent of homeless adults have a functionally impairing substance abuse disorder. Around 25 to 33 percent of the non-homeless population do not have an incapacitating problem with drugs or alcohol. The federal government estimates that among the teenager and adult population, about 5 percent has an "alcohol use disorder" and 3 percent an "illicit drug use disorder."[23] The rates are highest for young adults (ages eighteen through twenty-five at 9 percent alcohol-use disorder and 8 percent illicit drug-use disorder). Rates of substance abuse disorders vary between jurisdictions but not to a degree or way that would account for variations in homelessness between jurisdictions.[24]

Debate over substance abuse and homelessness follows the same tracks as debates about the other leading risk factors, such as mental illness and single-parent families. In a 2019 interview with the *Los Angeles Times*, the head of the Los Angeles Homeless Services Authority pushed back on the idea of a strong connection between behavioral health disorders and homelessness by asserting, "Most people with mental illness are housed. The vast majority of people with serious substance abuse issues are housed. They're using their substances in their bedrooms and in their living rooms and you're not watching it."[25] Balanced out against that argument are all the used needles and other drug paraphernalia littering streets in West Coast cities overwhelmed with the encampment scourge. Any parent who has ever had to do a sweep of a local park for needles before letting their kid play in it will naturally posit a strong connection between drug abuse and homelessness.[26] That same parent is not likely to be comforted by the thought that, however many people are doing drugs in shared public spaces near them, far more are doing drugs in private locations out of their sight. An addiction to drugs and alcohol sucks up limited resources that could be put toward rent, makes people violent toward romantic partners and other loved ones, leads to involvement in the criminal justice system, develops harmful social bonds with other addicts, and makes people unemployable.

Encampments are known as places to go to buy and use drugs. They concentrate addiction, geographically, and may also encourage more of it among members of the broader population who might otherwise find it difficult to locate a community of users. Sociologists described skid row was a place where, though perhaps not literally everyone was an alcoholic, alcoholics felt more at home there than non-alcoholics.[27] Accommodating encampments means accommodating communities in which meth and opioid addiction are normalized behaviors.

But is the reason why certain cities have full-blown homeless crises, more than just problems, because they have uniquely bad drug addiction challenges? Many communities have bad drug problems but not encampment crises. Rural New Hampshire and West Virginia have not been, of late, overrun with encampments as have cities in California. In their 2020 book, *Deaths of Despair*, Anne Case and Angus Deaton don't mention homelessness.[28] In his 2019 book, *Dignity*, Chris Arnade makes a couple stray references to homelessness but never discusses it in depth and doesn't present one photograph of a tent.[29] Though Sam Quinones does explore homelessness in his more recent book *The Least of Us* (2021), he makes only a couple brief references in *Dreamland* (2015).[30]

To say that modern homelessness is a substance abuse problem would have to mean that the rate of substance abuse is much higher now than it was in the past. Mentally ill adults abuse drugs and alcohol well above those of non-mentally ill adults.[31] So, perhaps the mere presence of the mentally ill, themselves, in the ranks of homeless adults in such large numbers, boosts the overall rate of substance abuse among the homeless population. But America has always grappled with substance abuse. Our focus on the connection between modern homelessness and drug addiction (crack was the concern in the 1980s, meth and opioids are now) can cause us to overlook how bad alcoholism was in former eras. In 1965, public drunkenness charges accounted for almost two out of the six million arrests nationwide.[32] Yes, that figure indicates how much more authority police had back then to arrest people for public drunkenness, but it must also reflect the serious extent of problem drinking going on. "There is nothing that quite prepares you to sit down in the gutter with a man who has vomited his last three meals onto his overcoat, possibly pissed himself several times, and talk about the state of the world."[33]

Alcoholism typically kills gradually, whereas fatal drug overdoses can take place almost immediately after using.[34] Drugs are illegal, or they were for a long time and still are in many places. Alcohol is not. Someone involved with drugs is more likely to run into trouble with the cops. Thus, to the extent that arrests and incarceration contribute to homelessness, and they are more the result of drug use than alcohol use, drugs could contribute to homelessness more than alcohol. But historically, homeless adults have always been heavily involved with the criminal justice system. They were arrested for slightly different offenses, but they were still arrested in large numbers.

In addition to arrests for public drunkenness, vagrancy laws used to be constitutional and widely enforced.[35] Skid row neighborhoods' reputation for disorderliness matched that of modern encampments. Data from 2019 showed that the Tenderloin, in San Francisco, was host to 40 percent of the city's street population, and that is also where around 55 percent of the city's drug arrests took place.[36] In 1950, Philadelphia's skid row accounted for one-third of all arrests but with only a total of 3,000.[37]

It is true that the second half of the twentieth century did witness the normalization of illegal drug use among the middle class.[38] Or, perhaps the difference may lie less in trends in underlying substance abuse than changes in how we respond, similar to the case of domestic violence. Whether or not domestic violence has increased over time, more family homelessness came as a result of building large numbers of battered women shelters in the 1970s and 1980s. The deinstitutionalization of the mentally ill is an even more obvious example of how our response to a certain problem, more than a growth in the problem itself, led to modern homelessness. But while our response to substance abuse has changed since the 1970s, those changes are nowhere near as dramatic as deinstitutionalization. When the skid row SRO hotels shut down, substance abuse-related homelessness became a different kind of problem, but that points to how homelessness is a housing challenge. If nothing had changed with respect to housing over the last fifty years, and skid rows were still with us, those neighborhoods would now have the reputation of drug-ravaged communities, much as encampments do.

Access to subsidized housing is the goal of most homelessness policy. Stable housing is a condition of recovery. No clinician would prefer to work with someone, on their addiction and/or their psychiatric challenges, with them living in an encampment rather than in stable housing. Giving permanent housing to someone in an unstable housing situation will often reduce the stress in his or her life. But "less stressed out" is far from the only standard for mental health. Another would be sobriety. The path from stable housing to sobriety is far from straightforward. Drug addiction certainly exacerbates serious mental illness. Giving a mentally ill drug addict permanent housing can facilitate their addiction. In his 2011 book, *Homelessness, Housing, and Mental Illness*, sociologist Russell K. Schutt notes that "Providing independent housing for homeless persons struggling with addictions can lead to exacerbation rather than resolution of the substance abuse problem."[39] Someone who is less stressed out because he has stable housing, but also more deeply engaged in pursuing addiction, is not on net a more mentally stable individual. Subsidized housing allows people to make their poverty more bearable. It provides relief and reduces harm. Mentally ill people and drug addicts need something to recover *for*. Subsidized housing doesn't provide someone something to recover *for*.

More than one path exists into chronic drug and alcohol addiction. Most people nowadays with substance abuse disorders are housed; during the skid row era, most alcoholics did not live on skid row.[40] Perhaps casual users would have remained casual users or aged out of substance abuse had they not wound up on the streets. At the same time, putting someone in permanent housing has not been shown to be an effective way to help him overcome his addiction. One traditional solution, made famous by Alcoholics Anonymous (AA), is to connect people who want recovery with people in recovery. AA has not "ended" alcoholism and this model does not do much to help people who policymakers want to help but themselves don't want to be helped. But the lesson to draw from AA's persistent appeal is that government should do all it can to facilitate the formation of communities centered around the shared goals of sobriety and true recovery. That could be done through housing programs.

IS HOUSING HEALTHCARE?

"Housing is Healthcare" is a slogan commonly heard voiced in the homelessness debate. Its premise taps into a housing policymaking tradition that stretches back to the tenement reformers of the late nineteenth century. Government has always hoped to improve lives by improving housing. In a February 2019 hearing of the United States House Committee on Financial Services, Representative Katie Porter likened giving housing to the homeless via a "Housing First permanent supportive housing approach" to treating breast cancer.[41] In a February 2020 tweet, California governor Gavin Newsom asserted that "Doctors should be able to write prescriptions for housing the same way they do for insulin or antibiotics."

But framing housing as healthcare is conceptually complicated. Poor-quality housing that exposes occupants to lead paint or creates respiratory problems harms health in a far more direct way than overly expensive housing. Tenement reformers were concerned mainly with poor-quality housing; contemporary housing reformers are concerned mainly with overly expensive housing. Affordability challenges may be said to be related to health challenges, but in substantially the same way as poverty and unemployment are. Arguing that "Housing is Healthcare" proves too much, in the same way that claiming that "childcare is infrastructure" does.[42] If everything is healthcare, then nothing is. The famous Oregon Medicaid Experiment questioned the degree to which subsidized health insurance improved health outcomes for low-income populations. Should we expect subsidized housing to improve health outcomes more than subsidized health insurance?

There is some evidence, derived from largescale voucher experiments and else-where, that when people who don't have stable housing receive it, certain physical health measures are improved, such as relating to AIDS and diabetes.[43] But in the homelessness debate, the health questions we're most interested in are behavioral health questions: substance abuse and untreated serious mental illness. The mentally ill homeless often need housing but also more targeted interventions. Subsidized housing is not a targeted intervention. It should be situated within a broader pro-gram of mental health reform. Some studies of permanent supportive housing have found that residents tend to die at a remarkably high rate. That would seem to undermine the notion that housing functions like "healthcare" in the way that term is normally understood.[44]

Let's say you have an adult family member who is mentally ill, addicted to heroin, and difficult to get along with. His situation could well be described as housing unstable, but how high on your list of priorities would you place giving him his own private apartment for the rest of his life? Upon receipt of that apartment, he might immediately overcome his addiction, but the risk seems at least equal that he might pursue it more enthusiastically, having become unencumbered by intrusive relatives trying to pry into his personal affairs. Much like cash, the effect of housing is too uncertain to be called healthcare.

CONCLUSION: HOW MENTAL HEALTH REFORM CAN REDUCE HOMELESSNESS

Across all fields of public policy, many favor "going upstream" or taking a "preventative" approach to social problems. You invest in pre-K so you don't have to invest in jails. Because mental illness causes homelessness for many people, mental health reform would be a way to pursue an "upstream" solution to modern homelessness. More funding, in the case of worthy programs, may be helpful. But in the United States, mental health services already receive considerable fiscal support from Medicare, Medicaid, private insurance, state governments, and other sources. Over the last half of the twentieth century, spending rose from only $1 billion to $85 billion (in 2001 dollars).[45] That expansion took place during the era of deinstitutionalization and amid the emergence of modern homelessness. A 2013 analysis done by President Obama's Office of Management and Budget reckoned that, at that time, federal funding for mental health stood at about $150 billion.[46] If funding alone were the difficulty, we would expect more effectiveness from New York City and California's systems.[47] New York and California spend significantly on mental healthcare both because of the basic strength of their tax bases and their progressive political cast. And yet, given the crisis on the city streets of California and the subways of New York, and the reputations of Los Angeles County Jail and Rikers Island as two of the largest mental health facilities in the nation, plainly, a lot of mental health reform remains for New York and California, along with practically all other jurisdictions across the nation.

Mental health reform should be guided by two principles: supporting families' efforts to care for their mentally ill adult relatives and supervision. Permanent housing is not a top priority for parents of a mentally ill adult child living with them. He has housing. They might well place more emphasis on meaningful day activities, such as can be provided through a clubhouse program or supported employment. They might emphasize reducing barriers to their access to their child's health information. The latter must be pursued through reform of the federal Health Insurance Portability and Accountability Act. They also need readier access to hospitalization and outpatient civil commitment programs. Parents often cannot keep their child stable by themselves but, with the appropriate supports, they could prevent him from winding up on the streets.

Supervision is crucial for those without strong family and social networks. Supervision means responsible adults in your life looking out for you, advocating for you when necessary, but more basically monitoring levels of mental stability and preventing you from "falling through the cracks." Certainly, a mental hospital can provide supervision. But so can assisted outpatient treatment programs, and, for those involved in the criminal justice, probation-style diversion programs. The main barrier to expanding supervision is opposition from civil liberties groups.

Civil liberties groups' position is that expanding personal freedom is simply the right thing to do. Homeless policymakers' position is that it improves outcomes. Those are different arguments and the second is far less convincing in the case of mentally ill adults. Even leaving aside considerations about insight and the frequently erratic judgment of someone with untreated schizophrenia, people's preferences change.[48] If restricting people's freedom is always counterproductive, and leads homeless adults to withdraw, decompensate, and more strongly attach themselves in street living, why have assisted outpatient treatment programs, such as New York's Kendra's Law, produced such effective outcomes, including with respect to homelessness? Assisted outpatient treatment's claim to being an "evidence-based" approach is at least as strong as that of Housing First, and yet it's rarely mentioned or explored in the homelessness policy context. More basically, the mentally ill need structure in their lives, as opposed to absolute deference toward their caprices and urges, because all of us need structure in our lives. This point is emphasized by the economists Abhijit Banerjee and Esther Duflo in their 2011 book, *Poor Economics*, in their argument that what distinguishes life in developed versus non-developed countries is how many decisions are made for people who live in the former: "it is easy, too easy, to sermonize about the dangers of paternalism and the need to take responsibility for our own lives, from the comfort of our couch in our safe and sanitary home. Aren't we, those who live in the rich world, the constant beneficiaries of a paternalism now too thoroughly embedded into the system that we hardly notice it?"[49] The goal is integration. In the post-deinstitutionalization community-based context, we want people with mental disabilities to, as much as possible, live lives that resemble those of people without mental disabilities. Non-disabled adults with families and jobs are expected to not engage in destructive behavior, face consequences when they do, and face, on a daily basis, constant demands on their time.

How we try to solve a social problem depends on how we frame it. The same man could be defined as a mentally ill man who happens to be homeless or as a homeless man who happens to have a mental illness. In the former framing, the standard of success is mental stability. In the latter framing, the standard of success is residential stability. Certain ideas have more legitimacy in the mental health context than they do in the homelessness context. Families are accorded more influence over mental health policy than homelessness policy. Mental health policymakers place much more emphasis on the therapeutic value of employment, even if part-time and/or supported. Homelessness policymakers are not opposed to the idea of boosting the employment rate among the homeless population but they don't see themselves as in any way failures if they make no progress on that front. Homelessness policymakers tend to disparage the concept of a "Continuum of Care" as paternalistic and corrupt, or, at best, only give it lip service. In mainstream mental health circles, by contrast, the concept of a Continuum of Care of services and programs is taken much more seriously.

Homelessness policymakers minimize the mental health dimension of homelessness so as to avoid qualifying the idea of homelessness as a housing problem and, thereby, undermine support for more subsidized housing. But mental health reformers view as unhelpful arguments that deemphasize the connection between mental illness and homelessness since, from their perspective, the high rate of serious mental illness among the homeless is Exhibit A for why reform is urgently needed. With a more effective mental health system, such as one that provides more support to families caring for mentally ill adult children, we would have less homelessness and particularly less of the disturbing, chronic variety. Most mentally ill people are housed, but some of them are going to lose their housing someday. Overwhelmingly, the mentally ill street population once had housing. Anyone who lived with their family had housing. Mental health reform would help maintain stability of the mentally ill who already have housing.

10

Police Work and Social Work

For many Americans, the term "homelessness" connotes public disorder. They've never been assaulted by the panhandler who approaches them every day during their morning commute. Nor do they enjoy being approached. They moreover can't grasp why more can't be done to address this lose-lose situation, which is neither good for them nor the panhandler whose life never seems to improve.

Public disorder is more difficult to address than serious crime. In her 1990 book, *Out of Bedlam*, Ann Braden Johnson describes an incident wherein a mentally ill man went around smelling the hair of every woman on a crowded subway platform one morning in New York. He was arrested after one of these women turned out to be an undercover cop. Subsequent investigation by the district attorney's office determined, "convinced he was allergic to hairspray, he had systematically sniffed the head of each woman on the platform in order to determine which ones had used hairspray so he could stand elsewhere."[1] A civilized society does not impose long-term prison sentences for sniffing hair (according to Johnson, the man was harmless). But a civilized society also protects women against having their hair sniffed by mentally ill strangers. Can problems such as this one be solved by increased investment in social services? Perhaps, but not always. The social services work best by helping people who want to be helped. Many homeless adults don't want to be helped or have a highly selective concept of the type of help they're willing to accept. The social safety net doesn't catch them, and thus they become the responsibility of the criminal justice system, in its capacity as the safety net below the safety net. When systems built around voluntary compliance fail to help someone who needs help, he becomes the responsibility of system built around involuntary compliance. In "The Death of the Hired Man," Robert Frost says, "'Home is the place where, when you have to go there, / They have to take you in.'" Jails and prisons *have* to take people in a way that shelters and day programs don't.

Many homeless people have serious problems but commit lots of unserious crimes. When a mentally ill man assaults several individuals with a knife, some fatally, the government response is straightforward: arrest him and hold him without bail. When a homeless man is arrested for an offense less serious than murder but still serious enough to merit incarceration, such as breaking into a car, he may be placed in a probation-style program, which allows him to live in the community if he complies with treatment. But many low-level offenses merit neither pretrial detention nor prison. At the same time, we pass laws to prohibit certain kinds of nonviolent behavior for a reason, and the social order depends on enforcing those laws.

The criminal justice system has acquired an electric-fence-like reputation in progressive circles. *Any* contact is seen as harmful, be it a prison sentence, a brief stay in jail, a booking, or merely a brief conversation with a patrol officer, because who knows what direction an encounter like that might take? The "defund the police" and de-incarceration movements both rely on the electric fence premise. The fewer encounters homeless people have with police, courts, and jails, the better it will be for them. When contact can't be avoided, they should be diverted away from the criminal justice system instead of drawn more deeply into it. Diversion redirects homeless adults from the criminal justice system to the social services, whose professionals, allegedly, know best how to meet the needs of homeless adults. This outlook is flawed, though. Criminal justice professionals have expertise that social services professionals lack and we need their involvement in the design of systems to repair broken lives.

DISORDER AND CIVIC HEALTH

San Francisco has many natural advantages—its fog, its harbor views, its forty-eight hills and rolling vistas (so conducive to car chase scenes), and its refreshing climate. San Francisco is also renowned for its architecture. The 1906 earthquake prompted a building boom at just the moment when the Beaux Arts school was hitting its stride. Architectural historian Henry Hope Reed called San Francisco's City Hall "the most magnificent interior in America" and the Civic Center's arrangement of the War Memorial Veterans Building, War Memorial Opera House, and City Hall "The greatest architectural ensemble in America."[2] San Francisco has maintained a commitment to classical architecture, as shown, for example, by the neo-Beaux Arts façade of the San Francisco Public Library, to ensure that, at least in the Civic Center area, new buildings conform to the set pieces around them. Wealth from the tech and tourism industries has kept up San Francisco's historic department store district along Market Street. Also, you've got the financial district's Art Deco office buildings and the Golden Gate Bridge.

Going on long strolls to enjoy architecture is an attraction on offer in only a handful of American cities. Street homelessness does real harm to such cities. People should not urinate anywhere in public. But when they do so directly on a work of inspiring architecture, that is really depressing. Grand public architecture "dignif[ies] the ordinary lives of ordinary people"[3] and is the distinctive pride of healthy cities. Spectacular train stations are rare in suburbs, even rich ones. Some urbanists have argued that street homelessness poses no serious threat to public spaces and may even benefit them by imparting an earthiness to an otherwise sterile, Disney-like milieu.[4] They further assert that the street homeless need access to public spaces more than the non-homeless because the latter have options.

The non-homeless avoid public spaces overrun by homeless single adults. While the non-homeless may have "options" for where to pass their idle hours, they don't have options for where to do so *as a community*. It's a sign of civic health when office workers opt to eat lunch in a shared public space, such as a park, instead of at their desk. Public spaces aren't genuinely shared if they've been converted into someone's private accommodations. To walk through an open-air drug market is to feel like an intruder. In low-income neighborhoods, the right of youths to congregate outside bodegas comes directly into conflict with right of old ladies to be free from thick clouds of marijuana smoke. Orderly public spaces are a cause of community life, because without them people live more of their lives in private. A city that allows its public spaces to become inhospitable to everyone but homeless adults can't sincerely claim to consider those spaces essential in a civic sense.[5] Beaux Arts-era planners had built spaces they hoped the democratic public would be proud to call its own but would still meet or even exceed the high aesthetic bar standardized by aristocratic Europe. By contrast, some modern urbanists evaluate public spaces' design based on the standard of how accommodating they are to the street homeless population.[6]

Some cities and neighborhoods have more to lose from disorder than others. In the average small- or medium-sized city's downtown, storefront retail not recovered since suburban malls put the local department store out of business forty years ago. Retail in some major cities has managed to hang on, but fears of a "retail apocalypse" have continued to run high as more and more commercial activity gravitates toward online platforms, a trend intensified by the pandemic.[7] Brick-and-mortar retail enlivens the streetscape. Its viability is more of a quality-of-life concern than an economic development one. City leaders want to help brick-and-mortar retailers, but they are often at a loss as to how: Commercial rent control? Cutting taxes and regulations? So many of the threats to local retail are far beyond the ability of municipal government to address. But many local retailers are clear that municipal government could help them by doing more to curb homelessness-related disorder.[8]

Another group affected by homelessness-related street disorder are municipal employees who work in public spaces. During the COVID-19 pandemic, New York City had a problem with unsheltered homeless people taking over entire subway cars. Throughout the pandemic, government expected transit workers to continue to supervise and clean subway cars. These "frontline workers," otherwise heralded for their commitment and sacrifice (more than 150 died from COVID), objected to the surge in homelessness on the subways. The city eventually responded, to a degree, by deploying more police officers, but they did so over the objections of progressive advocates. West Coast cities have seriously debated whether police should be involved at all in encampment clean-up operations. Some of the strongest supporters of police involvement are the sanitation workers who would otherwise have to go it alone, putting their hands on the personal property of volatile encampment dwellers.⁹

CRIME VERSUS DISORDER

Since World War II, homelessness and serious crime have moved on separate tracks, sometimes diverging, sometimes converging. During the "urban crisis" era of the 1970s, there was enormous concern about escalating crime but not as much about homelessness. *Dirty Harry* (1971), *The New Centurions* (1972), *Midnight Cowboy* (1969), and *Death Wish* (1974): these films depicted urban America as a hellscape, but homelessness was not part of the picture. The current debate over "modern" homelessness began around when President Reagan took office. Between then and the mid-1990s crack epidemic era, violent crime surged. In response, calls to reduce homelessness-related disorder and violent crime surged. The convergence of the two challenges gave plausibility to "broken windows" policing advocates' claims that addressing disorder would help bring down crime. Broken windows was implemented, along with a few other new policing tactics, and violent crime declined during the 1990s and 2000s.

But in the 2010s, homelessness and crime trends diverged in major cities. Violent crime stayed flat or kept dropping in San Francisco, Seattle, New York City, and Los Angeles while homelessness surged. Other cities that gained national notoriety for crime spikes, such as Baltimore, St. Louis, and Chicago, did not experience surging homelessness.

The connection between disorder and crime thus, once again, became confounded. Cities concerned about murders weren't concerned about homelessness. Cities concerned about homelessness weren't concerned about murders.

The relationship between a city's overall crime rate and its rate of homelessness is complicated. Gang culture and its attendant cycles of retributive violence surely drive the murder rate far more than levels of single adult homelessness. Progressives, for their part, conflate crime and disorder issues by mixing rhetoric over the "criminalization of homelessness" and "mass incarceration." Those are distinct issues. Enforcement of quality-of-life ordinances does not send large numbers of people to prison. States sentence people to prison mainly for offenses like murder, rape, assault, burglary, and robbery.¹⁰ The most direct routes to reducing the number of people in prison are either reducing the number of major violent and property offenses committed or limiting the use of imprisonment for major violent and property offenses.

Sometimes, people push back against the idea that homeless individuals are criminally-active by invoking the concept of "crimes of survival." This can be a fuzzy concept. Normally, what is implied by the term is an offense made necessary by a poor person's circumstances, the paradigm being theft. But when someone

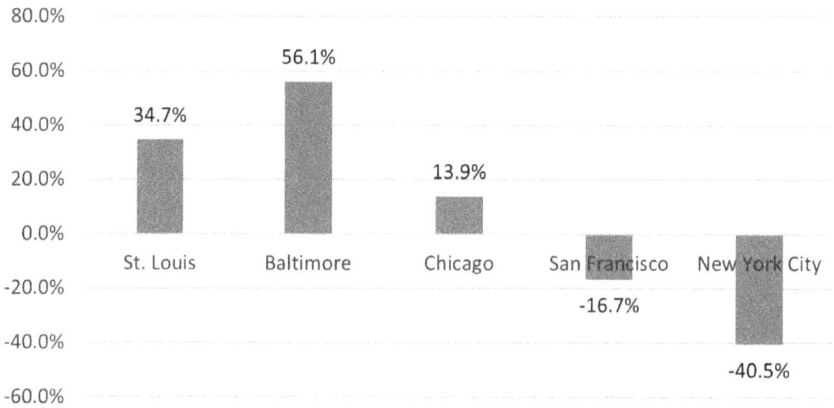

Figure 10.1.   Change in Murders, Selected Cities, 2010–2019.

Figure 10.2.   Change in Homelessness, Selected Cities, 2010–2019.

with a substance abuse disorder steals liquor, or steals something to sell for money to buy drugs with, they are reducing their chances of "survival" by feeding an addiction certain to shorten their life. Urban-based private charities make available an abundance of resources, such as free food, hygiene products, and clothing, to the street homeless population. In cities where such resources are less abundant, it would probably not be too difficult or costly to set up programs for their provision. The law allows cities to ramp up their enforcement of street-sleeping regulation in proportion to how much shelter they make available as an alternative to the streets. Perhaps cities could ramp up their enforcement against shoplifting from local retailers in proportion to the amount of free food, hygiene products, and clothing made available to the local street population.

CRIMINALIZATION AND VICTIMIZATION

Referring to any public safety practice as "criminalizing" homelessness means to characterize that practice as unconstitutional. Per the Supreme Court's rulings of the 1960s, someone can be arrested for their conduct (something they did), not their status (who they are). But prohibiting homeless adults from performing certain physical functions in public, such as sleeping or relieving themselves, comes close to criminalizing their status and homelessness itself. Courts have been receptive to those arguments but, at the same time, have upheld sit-lie ordinances and encampment regulations so long as they are not blanket, citywide bans and cities have made other options available.

America, in the twenty-first century, does not impose long-term prison sentences for panhandling or public urination. Honest scholars concede that point but nonetheless assert that public safety responses to homelessness are still motivated by insidious "regulating the poor" intentions and are moreover counterproductive because they keep people homeless.[11] But there are many reasons why people stay homeless. The longer someone stays on the street, the likelier it is that they will rack up arrests. But that doesn't mean that it's the arrests that are keeping them from leaving the street. A reduction in low-level enforcement in New York City over the last decade did not contribute to any meaningful reduction in single adult homelessness.[12] (Not that the preceding era's *increase* in low-level arrests reduced homelessness, either.) Claims that the "criminalization of homelessness" is on the rise are often based on research that counts the number of cities that have recently passed laws to regulate street disorder.[13] But hard data on how often those laws are enforced are elusive. San Francisco voters passed a sit-lie ordinance in 2010 but enforcement fell off dramatically over subsequent years.[14] We don't have very good data on misdemeanor arrests generally speaking, much less misdemeanor arrests of homeless people. It's easiest to speak of very long-term historical trends. We can say with confidence that arrests for low-level offenses have been common, especially for homeless populations, throughout US history. When street homelessness increases, the disorder attendant on street homelessness increases, as well, and that could lead to more arrests for disorder-related offenses.[15] But that would not necessarily indicate a higher overall rate of "criminalization" going on. As explained in an earlier chapter, police have never faced more limits on their discretion than at present. Back in the skid row era, there was no need for encampment regulations because people didn't live in tents and cops moreover had stronger tools at their disposal than sit-lie ordinances.

Housing advocates, because they see homelessness mainly as a housing problem, tend to downplay nonhousing-related reasons for people's homelessness. But they make an exception for incarceration. We hear more from advocates about how many substance abusers and mentally ill people have housing than we do from them about how many of the hundreds of thousands of people released each year from prison avoid winding up on the streets. An uptick in releases from jails and prisons does not necessarily lead to an increase in sheltered homelessness.[16] Still, incarceration is, undoubtedly, a risk factor.[17] In New York, state prisons send three to four thousand ex-offenders directly to city shelters every year.[18] Having committed a crime serious enough to merit prison could be evidence of antisocial tendencies that are also serious enough to weaken bonds with friends and family and reduce one's couch-surfing opportunities, thereby placing one at risk of homelessness. Different studies of incarceration as a risk factor for homelessness have come to different conclusions, as is the case with studies of other risk factors. A 2008 paper surveyed the literature and reckoned that around 20 percent of the single adult male homeless population had been incarcerated at some point in their lives.[19] If that is accurate, the experience of incarceration would be less important as a "risk factor" than mental illness and substance abuse. Because when we speak of the rate of serious mental illness and substance abuse among the homeless population, we're speaking of active disorders. It's easier to understand how an active behavioral health disorder causes someone to be homeless than how a brief jail stay two years ago did.

Debate about the link between incarceration and homelessness tends to center around why government isn't doing more to provide stable housing to ex-offenders. It does not make sense to give everyone released from prison a subsidized private apartment in which they can live for their rest of their lives. Time-limited programs with service supports, such as transitional housing, make a great deal of sense. Transitional housing provides an option for ex-felons between emergency shelter and permanent subsidized housing. As for people just out from a brief stay in jail, it's not clear government has any specific obligation with respect to their housing options.

Homeless people are victimized at a very high rate.[20] According to one recent survey of the literature, compared with the general population, homeless adults are assaulted eleven times more often, robbed twelve times more often, and stolen from more than twenty times as often.[21] Talking about the high rates of victimization among the homeless population can lead in a couple directions. One is to suggest that the main reason why they get robbed and assaulted so much is because they don't have stable housing. Surely, there's something to that. It's hard to understand the street homeless population's firm insistence that shelters are too dangerous to sleep in. The notion that someone would be safer on the streets than in a shelter is supported neither by common sense nor academic research about homelessness victimization.[22] But lack of housing alone can't account for why certain homeless cohorts appear to face more victimization than others. Experiences with incarceration, substance abuse, and mental illness—all common among homeless adults—heighten the risk of victimization.[23] Substance abuse and mental illness place one at greater risk of both offending and being the victim of crime.[24] Someone with a substance abuse disorder and/or a serious mental illness, and is homeless, runs an even greater risk of predation than someone without those afflictions.

Often left out of discussions of the victimization of homeless people is how much of it is perpetrated by other homeless people. The street homeless always say they won't go into shelters because the shelters are unsafe. But shelter entry is often tightly regulated. Thus, only shelter clients—homeless adults—are in a position to perpetrate crimes against shelter clients. On the streets, as well, the homeless population is very socially isolated, and so high rates of victimization point toward other homeless people. The menace of "jackrollers" who preyed on intoxicated members of the premodern homeless was endlessly discussed in accounts of tramp and skid row culture.[25] One 2014 survey of more than five hundred homeless individuals found that, of the roughly half who had been a victim of a violent attack while homeless, about one-third had been victimized by another homeless individual.[26] One study from the 1980s using arrest data in from Austin, Texas, tried to deflect fears that the homeless are dangerous by showing that much of their criminal activity is concentrated among themselves.[27] Another study from 2010, of victimization and homelessness, found that "in most instances the vast majority of the respondents reported their victimization by another homeless individual."[28] Even speaking of predators and victims as if they're two separate groups may not be accurate, as people may move constantly between being the victim and doing the victimizing.[29]

We could drastically reduce any role that "criminalization" plays in exacerbating homelessness by never arresting homeless people for any charge. But one risk that policy would run would be increasing the rate of "homeless-on-homeless" crime.[30] The high rates at which homeless adults victimize one another should refute any conception of encampments as socially rewarding communities strengthened by habits of mutual aid and bonds developed through a sense of shared adversity. Homeless people steal from and assault each other with disturbing frequency. Homeless people, especially when living on the street, have very significant public safety needs. Homeless people's public safety needs cannot be addressed without relying on the police to arrest other homeless people. Arresting and incarcerating someone for assaulting or robbing someone else might do much to reduce the local homelessness rate, but it would benefit that man's victim.

CLIMATE AND CROWDS

Police are not the only means used by cities to keep homelessness-related disorder in check. Even more important are climate and crowds. Cities' levels of unsheltered homelessness are related to the warmth of local temperatures in January. New York has a high rate of homelessness, but less than 10 percent of its homeless population lives in the streets. New York is temperate three season of the year. However, tent cities don't mushroom all throughout Manhattan between April and October. New York City government has long discouraged encampments, even under the recent era of progressive leadership. But in some ways that policy is enabled by the climate, which keeps unsheltered homelessness at low rates. Encampments can therefore be dismantled without the discouraging whack-a-mole problem places like Seattle and San Francisco face. Cold winters help keep street disorder in check without authorities having to rely on expensive and forceful public safety methods.

Crowds curb disorder, too, through the imposition of "internalized norms of street etiquette."[31] Dense city neighborhoods provide "eyes on the street," which, as Jane Jacobs explained, keep people safe through local self-government. Jacobs was active before the modern homelessness crisis but her thinking inspired many people who have been involved in dealing with that crisis such as policing expert George Kelling and Dan Biederman, the influential creator of business improvement districts in New York.

Much disorder can be addressed at the community level, either by cops or local actors, simply through people exercising their judgment based on knowledge of community conditions and standards. Police are less likely to shoot dead a mentally ill man behaving erratically if his neighbors don't call 911 on him in the first place, because they've known him since he was a child and understand that he's harmless. Officers that do respond to any call placed might themselves know him to be harmless if they have deep familiarity with his neighborhood. Two men are drinking in public. One remains sitting on a stoop and his bottle is covered with a paper bag. The other is up and about, making no attempt to conceal his vodka bottle. These are not the same crime. From the perspective of an informed beat officer, the brown bag user is observing a community norm whereas the other man is not. Unsheltered homeless people are themselves sometimes responsive to community norms, such as by avoiding public spaces in the daytime that they occupy at night.[32]

Localistic, community-based solutions to disorder require deference to local actors' discretion about when to enforce the law and when to not. Many civil rights lawyers doubt that cops, in particular, can be trusted to use discretion appropriately. Letting some people but not others bend the rules sounds to them like a recipe for discrimination. Who gets to decide how many panhandlers are too many? Justice requires universal rules. Civil rights lawyers' abstract philosophies have been devastating for public order, as explained by James Q. Wilson, one of the architects of broken windows policing:

> Courts are institutions whose special competence lies in the discernment and application of rights. This means that to the extent courts decide matters, the drift of policy will tend to be toward liberty and away from community. The court will, typically, hear a case brought by (or on behalf of) an *individual* beggar, sleeper, or solicitor. Such an individual rarely constitutes much of a threat to anyone, and so the claims of communal order often seem, in the particular case, to be suspect or overdrawn. But the effects on a community of *many* individuals taking advantage of the rights granted to *an* individual (or often, as the court sees it, an abstract, depersonalized individual) are often qualitatively different from the effects of a single person. A public space—a bus stop, a market square, a subway entrance—is more than the sum of its human parts; it is a complex pattern of interactions that can become dramatically more threatening as the scale and frequency of those interactions increase. As the number of unconventional behaviors increases arithmetically, the number of worrisome behaviors increases geometrically.[33]

Judges and public interest lawyers are some of the most powerful homeless poli-cymakers on the scene today. Communities in Idaho, when they pass municipal ordinances regulating sleeping in public, must gain the approval of the Ninth Circuit Court of Appeals, based in San Francisco. Any Central Valley community that begins to move on encampments should expect a threatening letter from Los Angeles-based civil liberties groups. Courts directed the development of New York City's sprawling shelter system across over two decades. Both judges and police are parts of the crimi-nal justice system. Critics of "criminalization" claim that the cops' role in solving social challenges should be much more diminished, because that's not their area of competence. But those same critics allow judges wide latitude to shape homelessness policy. In reality, judges know very little about what homeless people are like and how homeless services systems work, whereas patrol officers have extensive experi-ence with those matters. Somewhere between 10 and 20 percent of all police calls are mental health related.[34]

PUBLIC DISORDER: DISPERSAL OR CONTAINMENT?

By far the most vexing homelessness-related disorder challenges cities now face are encampments. Homeless encampments, host to hundreds of individuals, have been encountered all up and down the West Coast. It's hard for a city to house its way out of its encampment dilemma. Even when officials embrace and pursue that goal over the long term, they must respond, in the short term, to pressing, practical questions about encampment conditions.

Three basic approaches to encampments exist:

1. Encampments are normal communities that, like any normal community, deserve city services such as sewage and trash removal.
2. Encampments are not normal communities and should not be treated as such, but they should be formally sanctioned and regulated, or at least informally tolerated as a necessary evil.
3. Encampments should not be tolerated.

Number 3 is the most sensible approach, though it is easiest to implement in cities where homelessness is a problem, but not yet a crisis. Two real-world examples of its implementation would be votes taken in Denver and Austin to restrict sleeping in public places in 2019 and 2021, respectively. If ever there were a social problem best addressed through prevention, it's unsheltered homelessness. No American city has ever brought unsheltered homelessness permanently under control after first allowing it to get out of control. Encampments create "agglomeration" effects that cause unsheltered homelessness to increase. It's easier to be the two thousand and first street homeless person in a city than the first one. Individuals experienced in unsheltered living can provide guidance to those newer to the experience as to how to obtain street drugs, avoid the cops, obtain food and other resources for free, and so on. By essentially the same principle, immigrant communities in US cities reduce the cost of immigration for their newly-arrived kin.[35] The unsheltered homeless attest that "There's safety in numbers."[36] Twenty homeless people scattered throughout a city, living and sleeping in obscurity and alone, are less of a public nuisance than a twenty-person encampment established in a high-profile location. Unsheltered homeless individuals gravitate toward high-profile locations because those areas afford better access to transit and other public services, and a greater feeling of safety.

Number 1 is not a constructive approach. During the COVID-19 pandemic, cities took some reluctant steps toward endorsing number 1, for fear that breaking up encampments and failing to provide health and social services onsite would spread the virus. Charitable groups that distribute tents and provisions to the street homeless implicitly endorse the idea that living in an encampment can be made normal. Someone might be inclined toward supporting encampments if they believe in a right to housing—if government doesn't give people the housing to which they're entitled, then they should be allowed to sleep in public[37]—or the idea that the only important difference between the homeless and non-homeless populations is lack of access to permanent housing.[38] But though the "desire for community" allegedly prompts some encampments to form,[39] no healthy community can be comprised mainly of single adults who are addicted to drugs, seriously mentally ill, and/or chronically unemployed.

Number 2 was the approach cities took between World War II and 1980. Different rules applied inside the Bowery and other skid row districts than outside them. When cities demolished their skid row districts, they dispersed their homeless populations throughout their cities. Living on skid row certainly brought one into contact with police, though less so than when skid rowers strayed out into ordinary commercial or residential neighborhoods.[40] Skid rows kept separate the homeless and non-homeless populations. Urban renewal has led to more contact between the homeless and non-homeless populations. This has led to many non-homeless people calling the police to *do something* about homelessness-related disorder.

Some argue for reviving skid row through a "containment zone" approach. This would be like zoning for public spaces.[41] Containment zones have, in a way, been endorsed by federal courts, who have found it constitutional for cities to enforce anti-public-sleeping regulations or sit-lie ordinances in certain neighborhoods but not every neighborhood in a city. Los Angeles's Skid Row and San Francisco's Tenderloin neighborhoods have often been said to function as containment zones.[42]

But a "containment zone" approach is hard to implement in the twenty-first-century context. However well containment zones worked during the skid row era, times have changed. The modern single-adult homeless population has more women among it than did the skid row crowd, raising concerns about rape. There are more seriously mentally ill homeless now. We are more concerned about racial segregation now than in the postwar period, and the homeless population is now far more disproportionately black. Critics call containment zones "redlining."[43] Public safety

policy toward street homelessness is not simply a question of deciding how much
public urination a city should "contain." Government cannot content itself with a
policy of "containment" toward assault and robbery. An egalitarian conception of
justice would mandate taking those crimes seriously regardless of whether the victim
is homeless or non-homeless. We should reflect on what it means that so many drug
arrests take place in and around encampments. It means widespread exploitation of
the homeless: drug dealers making money off of their suffering. The street homeless
are often said to be "the most vulnerable members of society." Do we care about pro-
tecting the most vulnerable among us from predators? Lack of restitution for crime
victims was one of the hallmarks of Jim Crow.[44]

Containment doesn't work if it doesn't contain the problem. Street homelessness
has spread beyond the borders of both Los Angeles's Skid Row and San Francisco's
Tenderloin. Those neighborhoods seem more often to seed and nurture disorder
than to contain it. Los Angeles's Skid Row is estimated to comprise less than 10
percent of Los Angeles County's homeless population.[45] According to one estimate
from the late 1980s, Skid Row was then host to close to half of Los Angeles County's
total homeless population.[46] It can be difficult to secure and maintain buy-in for the
containment zone idea from local residents and businesses, for whom containment
seems sometimes hard to distinguish from indifference. Here's an account of an
encampment that was allowed to develop in Minneapolis, 2020: "As time went on,
some residents felt abandoned by the government and frustrated that the bulk of care
duties were falling on untrained volunteers. Encampment safety concerns grew too,
with at least three incidents of sexual assault taking place between June 26 and July
5, one person threatened with a knife, and several overdoses."[47]

In homelessness, like all other social policy challenges, preventing a problem from
turning into a crisis is more attractive than trying to attack a crisis after it has already
come to fruition. Cities in America who don't now face homelessness crises at the
level of New York and San Francisco should do everything they can to avoid those
cities' fates. They should keep encampments as small as possible. Dispersing encampments is far from ideal but preferable to allowing a "containment zone" to emerge and
certainly better than an attitude of complete laissez-faire. Large encampments have a
tendency to get larger. Cities should pay especially close attention to how many young
people they're attracting (a.k.a. "crusties").[48] Homelessness and many of the behaviors
associated with it can be eventually aged out of. But if street living is accommodated,
then young people will be encouraged down a path they may not be able to leave.
Youth homelessness is not inevitable. Young people did not live on skid row.

Cracking down on deviant street behavior will not end homelessness. It may well,
though, improve civic life for non-homeless residents and local businesses. Cities
with decrepit downtowns are bereft of civic pride. You've got two cities, both of
which have had a homelessness problem since the 1980s. Neither seems remotely
close to "ending" homelessness. But one city does a better job of regulating disorder
in their downtown. The other, due to a combination of lack of political will and an
emboldened activist community, does not. It is better to have a city with an endless

homeless problem but a downtown you can take some pride in than a city with an endless homeless problem and a downtown that is a disgrace.

CONCLUSION: POLICE WORK AND SOCIAL WORK

In 1895, Josiah Flynt, a top authority on tramp culture, asserted, "The best places in the United States in which to study tramps are the jails."[49] We have never known a time in modern American history without homelessness, and we've never known a time when cops and jails did not play a large role in the lives of homeless men. Dealing with homelessness falls to both public safety and social service agencies, though how they should divvy up responsibilities remains in question. Conservatives don't like the idea of cops performing social work functions because it sounds soft. Progressives don't like the idea of cops performing social work functions because it sounds harsh. "Defund" advocates and critics of the "criminalization of homelessness" want to entrust more responsibility to the social services and less to cops. But absent of a program for dramatic reform, that would fail, because cops wouldn't be as involved in the lives of the homeless were the social services more effective. Just as conservatives have a tendency to back into touting mediocre rehabilitative programs when they criticize Housing First, progressives have a tendency to back into touting social workers as miracle workers when they criticize the police presence in the lives of homeless people. Reform, in the case of social services, must mean something other than just increasing funding. Increasing funding may simply allow social workers to spend more time helping the more functional cases not at risk of homelessness. Many mental health professionals have no contact with people with untreated schizophrenia. Cops in certain city neighborhoods deal with people with untreated schizophrenia multiple times a shift.

We should avoid looking at police work and social work as an either/or proposition. Police-like public safety personnel are found all throughout the social services, in welfare centers, mental hospital wards, public libraries heavily patronized by homeless people, and also in public schools. Social work can sometimes entail finding people somewhere to sleep who don't have one because they're homeless. Social work entails siting and running homeless shelters. Some people will never accept living near a shelter because its presence does not accord with their conception of a healthy neighborhood. Other non-homeless households at least claim to be open to the idea if the organization is competent and responsive to neighborhood concerns. Being responsive to neighborhood concerns sometimes requires police. At present, many in homeless policymaking circles are calling for both an aggressive expansion in homeless housing facilities and also less "criminalization," which can only mean less contact between police and the homeless population. Neighborhoods are going to be even more resistant to shelters than they already are if told that they can't expect police intervention to deal with shelter-related disorder because the risks of "criminalization" are too great.

With respect to some social problems related to homelessness, we should *increase* the use of the criminal justice system, due to the unique leverage it can bring to bear. One example is probation-style diversion programs. Judges, lawyers, and personnel who run mental health courts and drug courts have years of experience using the threat of imprisonment as a way to stabilize unstable individuals. Expanding the use of such programs requires a willingness to put people in prison, at least sometimes, when they fail to comply with the terms of their release.

We should be sure to grant police, prosecutors, and correctional officers a seat at the table in contemplating mental health reform. Having been entrusted with social problems other agencies failed to solve, public safety agencies have built up extensive expertise with challenges such as untreated schizophrenia. In de-escalation training programs, cities bring in social workers to teach cops about mental illness. It might be more fruitful to have police and jail personnel give lectures to social workers about what it's like to work with people with untreated schizophrenia and violent tendencies. One far-reaching reform would be to authorize public safety agencies to bill mental health agencies for all the time they spend having to manage people with untreated serious mental illness.

11

Housing, Housing, Housing

The best argument against seeing homelessness as a housing problem is a political one. When housing is all that anyone debates, nothing winds up getting done about public disorder, drug addiction, and untreated mental illness. Housing First philosophy holds that those other challenges can't be addressed until enough housing is secured for the homeless population. But enough housing never gets secured. Thus, anyone demanding a solution to disorder and drug addiction are, in effect, being told to wait for a utopia that will never arrive.

Clearly, homelessness is not *only* a housing problem. Rents are high in New York City, but does that mean there must be close to 80,000 homeless people, as opposed to 30,000? Over the course of the 2010s, Los Angeles and New York City both experienced surging homelessness whereas other communities in their same region, and thus subject to the same housing market pressures, did not see the same surge.[1] The vacancy rate in 1921 in NYC was .15 percent.[2] Though it certainly had a problem, at that time, with "place-less" tramps, that problem was of a much different character than the one facing the city today. Other points in New York City history have seen a contraction in the vacancy rate but no concurrent rise in the homelessness rate.[3] Throughout the 2010s, nationwide, the number of severely cost-burdened renters ticked up slightly and the number of very low-rent units declined. Those factors would seem to project a general increase in homelessness nationwide. Per official US Department of Housing and Urban Development (HUD) data, though, homelessness declined or was flat.[4]

Still, though, homelessness is a housing problem. In the latter decades of the twentieth century, the low-rent housing market changed in ways that are every bit as essential to understand, if we're to grasp the modern crisis, as changes to family structure, public safety policy and law, and mental health policy. People live in tents, train stations, and shelters set up in the 1980s because all the cheap housing in skid row districts was demolished. Communities with dire shortages of low-rent housing face an elevated risk of homelessness. Such communities are more common in twenty-first-century America than they were in past eras.

The academic literature is well stocked with studies showing that high rents drive homelessness rates in communities and fairly sparse in studies claiming that those two factors have nothing to do with one another.[5] Sussing out the relation between homelessness and high rents is both complicated and simple. HUD provides community-level data of homelessness but for each "Continuum of Care"—that is, the local funding mechanism through which HUD delivers homelessness assistance grants. Often, a Continuum of Care's borders conform to that of a natural community, whose rents are reported by the Census Bureau, but not always. A simpler way to look at the matter is to sort communities based on their rent levels. The Census Bureau's American Community Survey program lists 940 metro areas. Table 11.1 shows the results of sorting them by median gross rent. Nearly every one of the top twenty-five metro areas, based on median gross rent, are in regions known for their homeless challenges: Southern California, the Bay Area, New York, and Hawaii.[6] That is probably not a coincidence.

Look at it this way. Deinstitutionalization left mental health systems in shambles all across the nation, but homelessness is not a crisis everywhere. Deinstitution-

Table 11.1. Top Twenty-Five Metro Areas in the United States, by Median Gross Rent

Metro	Median Gross Rent
San Jose-Sunnyvale-Santa Clara, CA	$2,249
San Francisco-Oakland-Berkeley, CA	$1,905
Oxnard-Thousand Oaks-Ventura, CA	$1,776
Urban Honolulu, HI	$1,745
Santa Cruz-Watsonville, CA	$1,717
Napa, CA	$1,700
Washington-Arlington-Alexandria, DC-VA-MD-WV	$1,690
San Diego-Chula Vista-Carlsbad, CA	$1,658
Santa Maria-Santa Barbara, CA	$1,643
Key West, FL	$1,627
Santa Rosa-Petaluma, CA	$1,621
Edwards, CO	$1,594
Vallejo, CA	$1,592
Los Angeles-Long Beach-Anaheim, CA	$1,545
Kahului-Wailuku-Lahaina, HI	$1,510
Bridgeport-Stamford-Norwalk, CT	$1,499
Salinas, CA	$1,495
Boulder, CO	$1,495
Seattle-Tacoma-Bellevue, WA	$1,492
San Luis Obispo-Paso Robles, CA	$1,476
Boston-Cambridge-Newton, MA-NH	$1,475
Vineyard Haven, MA	$1,459
New York-Newark-Jersey City, NY-NJ-PA	$1,439
California-Lexington Park, MD	$1,398
Heber, UT	$1,397

alization can help explain why homelessness is different now than in the 1960s. It cannot explain why homelessness, now, runs higher in some cities than others. Both these statements can be true: (1) mental health reform is essential to addressing modern homelessness, and (2) deinstitutionalization alone can't explain where modern homelessness came from.

"Housing, housing, housing" has been homeless advocates' rallying cry for decades.[7] Like all rallying cries, though, complications arise when government tries to translate it into real-world policies. Much of America's housing policy infrastructure was developed prior to the modern homelessness crisis and/or without the homeless population directly in mind. This chapter will examine the intersection between the homelessness crisis and housing policy debates more generally. Major questions and themes it will look at include quality versus affordability, shelter versus permanent housing, project versus tenant-based subsidies, evictions, landlords, the promise of private market development, immigrants, and gentrification. Overall, the chapter will explain why, even though homelessness is a housing problem, housing-oriented solutions have met with such underwhelming results recently.

HOUSING STANDARDS AND THE AMERICAN DREAM

Housing nowadays is a lot nicer than it used to be. Far fewer Americans live in housing that's physically defective, bereft of basic utilities and amenities, or overcrowded than was the case in the past.[8] Plumbing would be one obvious metric: close to half of all units lacked complete plumbing in 1940; now, that figure is around 1 percent.[9] "Severely deficient housing," as measured by the Census' American Housing Survey, stood at around 3 percent in the early 1990s and has since declined to about 1 percent. HUD keeps an annual scorecard on "worst case housing," and of the households who fall into that category, about 95 percent do so on the basis of unaffordability, not quality.[10] Housing standards in the United States stack up favorably against elsewhere: "Americans are better housed than most other people in rich countries."[11] General economic growth has enriched tens of millions of American households. When people have more money, they'll spend more on housing and related amenities, access to which private industry has expanded via innovations in areas such as heating and cooling systems, indoor plumbing, food management, lighting, and telecommunications. Smaller families have meant less crowding.

It's hard to say exactly how much credit government should get for expanding Americans' access to decent, affordable housing. Disgraceful public housing programs pushed down quality standards in the latter decades of the twentieth century. During the same period, cities lost much of their low-rent stock through abandonment, sale, or demolition. Government failed to stop that process and, in some cases, actively participated in it. Housing regulations make it illegal to build and operate certain very low-quality forms of rental housing. Just like labor law prohibits workers from agreeing to work under dangerous conditions, housing regulations limit the kind of cheap housing poor people can rent. Some cities destroyed their cheap rental stock through urban renewal or the aggressive enforcement of the local housing code.[12] In others, the process was more indirect. Housing regulations were applied prospectively, and old buildings out of conformity with new laws were allowed to stay in business on a grandfathered-in basis.[13] But if those buildings were torn down or rehabbed and converted for another purpose other than to house the poor, they could not be replaced by new units built exactly like them.

Housing standards reflect our belief in the American Dream. As middle-class housing standards have risen, tolerance for low-quality housing has collapsed. President Franklin D. Roosevelt memorably described the goal of housing policy as decent, affordable housing for all. In America, "decency" is defined by what the middle class has. Much social progress in America has had the following structure: the middle class gets something, then expectation grows that the lower classes should have it, as well. (In Charles Dickens's novels, no one questions a social order in which certain goods are enjoyed by some classes but not others.) Federal home ownership assistance programs have pushed up housing standards and even for those who don't directly benefit from them. Many progressives pour scorn on the home mortgage tax deduction and mortgage insurance because of those programs' regressive tilt.[14] But to the extent that those programs have allowed the middle class to consume more housing, they've pushed up housing standards for the nation as a whole. Had the middle class remained confined to cramped apartments built in the late nineteenth century, raising housing standards for the lower classes would have seemed less urgent.

Low-quality housing is easier to tolerate, both for a tenant and for society as a whole, if it's presumed to be temporary. It certainly was temporary in the romantic era: the tramps and hobos lodged in cheap boarding houses during the winter as they awaited spring and another round of seasonal employment. Intergenerational poverty qualifies our belief in the American Dream and its application to housing standards. If we believe that, in whatever housing we allow, some people might stay a long time and never move to something better, we will want higher standards than if we assume they'll soon be moving on and up.

To a degree, it seems a simple matter of social integration to assert that the poor deserve quality housing just as surely as the middle and upper classes. But the more expansive our definition of housing quality becomes, the less that housing policy alone can do about it. Traditional standards of housing quality include physical upkeep, amenities, and rate of crowding. Since any unit's rent is also determined by external factors such as access to jobs and transportation, neighborhood safety and the schools, these have become relevant to housing policy debates, as well. Awkwardness arises, though, when different households define "quality" differently. Should policymakers intervene when a family makes the "wrong choice," such as opting for a recently-rehabbed unit in a bad neighborhood instead of a shabby one in a good neighborhood? Some might be more willing to put up with a longer commute and more distance from their friends and family if it means better schools for their kids. Others might value family over schools. Homeless policymakers may define a "high-quality" shelter experience as one that provides not just a bed and food ("three hots and a cot") but access to social services. Some of the street homeless themselves, by contrast, view the presence of social workers as creating a lower-quality housing experience than living in a tent on a sidewalk.

Government began involving itself in the housing market in the late nineteenth century. But during the tramp and skid row eras, reformers concerned themselves little with the housing needs of destitute single men. City planners' vagueness as to where the "bums" would live in post-urban renewal future was one of the cardinal sins of omission that led to the current crisis. But why should those planners have worried? It had never been a problem before, finding housing for destitute single men. Flash forward to present times, and the conventional wisdom holds that the only way destitute single men can find housing is through extravagantly expensive government programs targeted, with surgical precision, at the cases of greatest need.

Having run up the score so far on housing standards, we might consider the benefit of letting them dip somewhat, or at least not forcing them to rise still higher. If we incentivize more shared housing, we might increase crowding and thus, by one standard measure, reduce overall housing quality. But we might also thereby reduce homelessness. Truly to absorb the lessons of the past over the reckless demolition of skid row, government should positively affirm the existence of whatever cheap, low-quality housing remains in cities. Such a "fix it first" approach to housing the homeless and those at risk of homelessness tends to be eclipsed by debates over how to build new housing. Two examples of at-risk low-quality housing are three-quarters housing in New York City and board and care facilities in California.

Three-quarters housing facilities are illegal boarding houses. They're run by private landlords and serve extremely poor single men, many of whom are ex-offenders and/or addicts. City government cracked down on them in response to critical reports by the *New York Times* and the John Jay College of Criminal Justice's Prisoner Reentry Institute.[15] Hundreds of individuals were relocated to city housing programs. That shift may or may not have substantially improved those men's lives. It definitely increased the burden on already beleaguered government housing systems. Parallels with the old single-room occupancy (SRO) model are striking. As dismal as conditions in three-quarter housing may be, some men prefer to pay to stay in them over free lodging in one of New York's public shelters. Another attraction appears to be "peer support." The John Jay researchers, though in many ways critical of the housing model, conceded that "tenants almost unanimously express their preference to live in a Three-Quarter House, rather than in a shelter or on the street. Some tenants appreciated the social support they received in their houses from housemates with similar backgrounds or life experiences."[16]

Board and care homes are group homes for mentally ill adults. They are legal, generally run by small "mom and pop" operators, and provide care (meals, laundry, and cleaning) though not much in the way of social services. Board and cares serve a population at great risk of homelessness, but they have been largely left out of California's surge in homelessness funding throughout the 2010s. Many have closed. One April 2019 report found that Los Angeles County lost about 15 percent of its board and care beds over the prior three years.[17] Most blame is placed on inadequate reimbursement rates from state government. Governor Gavin Newsom, to his credit, has recently attempted to take steps to address the reimbursement problem and stabilize the board and care system. Board and cares are shabbier than new, custom-built permanent supportive housing projects, but the latter cost hundreds of thousands per unit to build in California, and programs take forever to get off the ground.[18]

The parallels with deinstitutionalization are also striking. Cities are still losing very low-quality housing for single adults, and they're still losing inpatient psychiatric beds. Demand for housing for destitute single men exists in proportion to the number of destitute single men in a given community. When there are enough destitute single men around, who have at least some income, some provider will step forward to meet their housing needs. The cases of three-quarters housing and board and care homes differ from each other and the old SRO hotels in certain important ways. But they pose similar questions regarding client autonomy, making the great the enemy of the adequate, and whether we want to learn from the mistakes of the past or repeat them. The soundest course would be for cities to work with the stock they have, because they'll miss it when it's gone.

THE ETERNAL RECURRENCE OF SHELTER

In former times, the daily rhythms of single adult homeless men's lives centered around SROs. Now, they center around shelters.[19] In the 1980s, government brought online tens of thousands of shelter beds, after having lost tens of thousands of SRO units in the previous decades. Shelters' social service offerings are on average more robust than SROs were, and because they are run by the government or nonprofits, shelters exploit the poor less than the private landlord-run SRO model did. But it's not clear how much any of that matters to the street homeless.[20] If the bottom-line consideration is how effectively does a housing model keep people from sleeping on the street, SROs seem vastly superior to shelters. Urban policymakers dealt with many grave challenges in the 1960s, but tent cities were not one of them.

Shelters have few strong defenders. The homeless view shelters as crowded, dangerous, noisy, and restrictive. The non-homeless view them as outrageously expensive, unwelcome presences in neighborhoods and unsuccessful at addressing street homelessness. Shelter spending fatigue naturally prompts the question: Why not just redirect spending on shelter—temporary housing—to permanent housing? Denunciations of shelter are often heard during campaign season, when candidates for city office introduce themselves to voters as the first person ever to consider using permanent housing to address homelessness. However, what they find, upon taking office, is that, not only can they not afford to neglect shelter, they likely need to expand it. When Mayor Bill de Blasio took office in early 2013, he imposed a shelter moratorium, trusting that his new rental subsidy programs would suffice. But in response to public outcry over continually swelling homelessness, de Blasio announced plans in 2017 to build ninety new shelters. Los Angeles voters passed Proposition HHH, a $1.2 billion bond program in November 2016. The first of the projected ten thousand units did not open until December 2019; over that three-year span, homelessness in Los Angeles grew 16 percent.[21] Outraged at the slow pace of development, in the spring of 2021, US. District Court judge David Carter ordered the City of Los Angeles to provide shelter to everyone on Skid Row by the next fall.[22] (This order was later overturned by an Appeals Court, but the underlying lawsuit is ongoing.)

The very concept of shelter is fraught with contradictions. It needs to be nice enough to attract people in off the street, but dorm-style living is not inappropriate for housing that's supposed to be temporary and needs to be brought online rapidly to respond to a crisis. Investing in shelter improvements quickly turns into a problem of diminishing returns in part because it's impossible to please everyone. Hiring more security personnel makes some people feel safer but deters others, and the same principle applies for hiring more social workers.

At least three points may be made on behalf of shelter. First, most people only need temporary housing, just like most unemployed only need temporary income support after losing their job. Second, for some temporary housing problems, the cleanest solution is a shelter bed somehow controlled by the public sector. Sometimes, government just needs a place to put people, a place to take in those who have nowhere to go ("indoor relief"). Third, shelter is a very efficient way to benefit lots of needy people because beds have a high turnover. As noted earlier, shelter beds for both families and single adults serve multiple clients per year.[23] Permanent housing turns over at a lower rate, particularly in tight rental markets.[24]

SUBSIDIZED HOUSING: THE PROJECT-BASED APPROACH

Permanent housing benefits in America operate on a two-tier system. Government provides home ownership assistance for the middle classes (and above) and rental assistance for lower income households. Rental assistance comes in two forms. Through "project-based" subsidy programs, government builds (or requires or incentivizes to be built) units that rent on a below-market basis. "Tenant-based" subsidy programs defray the cost of a unit rented on the open market. The standard example of "project-based" subsidies would be public housing. The standard example of "tenant-based" subsidies is a Section 8 voucher.

Project- and tenant-based rental assistance programs have different attractions. Vouchers require no large up-front capital costs, don't lead to siting headaches, don't have the stigma of public housing, and are considered better for social integration.[25] The many advantages of voucher-based programs have caused them to supplant project-based forms of housing subsidies over recent decades. However, project-based subsidies retain a strong appeal in homelessness circles. Not only do they increase the stock of low-rent housing (a voucher can only be used on a unit that the private market makes available), they are a more appropriate mode of support for individuals that are low-functioning, not just low-income. When policymakers say that they intend to end homelessness through housing, they usually mean that they intend to build new permanent supportive housing units to house the chronically homeless. The chronically homeless are the hardest cases: those who have been homeless for a long time or on multiple occasions and who have some kind of a disability meaning, often, a mental disability. Housing First theory, in its purest form, stresses personal autonomy and the value of housing mentally ill homeless people in normal apartments just like everyone else. However, chronically homeless individuals can't be helped, exclusively and at scale, with a straightforward voucher approach. Navigating the low-rent market and dealing with landlords is hard even for someone without a mental disability. Most people believe our obligation to the chronic street homeless extends beyond handing them a voucher and wishing them the best.

As was emphasized in the previous discussion about shelter, sometimes, government needs a place to put people. When that place doesn't exist, government has to build it, which takes time. The project based-focus of housing-for-the-homeless programs helps explain the treadmill-like aspect of efforts by California communities to house their way out of homelessness. If homelessness in a city runs high, that probably means that new construction is expensive. Rental streams pay for construction projects. People in or at risk of homelessness have extremely low-incomes and can't pay much in rent. Thus, if new construction is expensive, that will limit what the government can do to house extremely low-income populations just as surely as it limits what for-profit developers could do on that front. "For-profit or nonprofit, building a building is building a building."[26] Cities' street crises will continue to grind on so long as their homelessness policies center around project-based permanent supportive housing.

SUBSIDIZED HOUSING: THE VOUCHER APPROACH

The high cost of permanent housing for the homeless leads to scarcity. When there's not enough housing to go around, government has to decide who gets it: the literally homeless, or those at risk of homelessness, meaning the low-income population more broadly? Providing housing units only to the literally homeless is unattractive. If only they have access to subsidized housing, some low-income individuals will be tempted to declare themselves homeless to move up in the queue. Since sleeping on the streets or in shelters are adverse experiences, many find it offensive to suggest that those who expose themselves to homelessness are somehow trying to scam the system. But what if the "experience" of homelessness only entailed a two-to-three-hour wait in a welfare office while a case worker processed and fulfilled your request for permanent housing? What if it was a shelter stay of two to three nights? Anyone responsible for a social services budget will be interested in managing levels of demand, which is to say they'll be concerned about moral hazard.

One way to eliminate the risk of moral hazard related to homelessness would be to make housing assistance an entitlement, available to the entire low-income population. At the top of housing advocates' wish list is establishing an entitlement for federal housing choice vouchers.[27] Medicaid and food stamps are entitlements: everyone who qualifies for them gets them. By contrast, people who qualify for vouchers, based on their earning an income of less than 50 percent of the median income in their metro area, often get placed on a waiting list. The number of vouchers in circulation depends on annual appropriations. An estimated four to five times as many Americans qualify for vouchers as receive them.[28] Across the nation, local waiting lists for vouchers number in the thousands, and many have for years been closed to new applicants. Vouchers allow households to rent a basic apartment at the cost of 30 percent of their income.

Cost estimates for making vouchers an entitlement—also known as a universal housing choice voucher program—reach as high as $100 billion a year. This would be one of the very largest safety net programs in America. A universal housing choice voucher program would benefit the more functional members of the homeless population. Many beneficiaries would be already-housed individuals who would get a permanent break on their rent and insurance against eviction from their current unit. In the current program, about one-quarter of voucher recipients lease in place.[29] Even if government handed a voucher to every schizophrenic drug addict now living on the street, it is doubtful that government could easily locate enough studio apartments owned by private landlords willing to rent to street homeless schizophrenic drug addicts. Even now, perhaps one-third of voucher holders can't find an apartment to rent.[30]

Proponents of universal housing choice vouchers claim that it would reduce homelessness, a pledge many would view skeptically, given cities' recent track record on trying to house their way out of homelessness. However, some policy solutions don't work in a linear fashion. Even the most incompetent government would have trouble spending $100 billion on subsidized housing without having some effect on homelessness.

But though making a housing an entitlement may reduce homelessness, it may also lead to more unemployment and underemployment. Any benefit program reduces the need for income, and thus the need to work. Multiple studies have found reduced work effort to be a side effect of rental subsidy programs, including the "Family Options Study," which specifically looked at the benefit of vouchers for homeless families.[31] A 2019 analysis found that only about half of nondisabled nonelderly, non-full-time student voucher holders had earned income.[32] The most optimistic interpretation of the research on rental subsidies and work effort would be to say that any subsidy-induced reduction will be only temporary and fade into a neutral effect over the long term.[33] But, broadly, low income households need to put forth a more than neutral work effort to be elevated above their current socioeconomic status.

The motivation to work to earn income may be further undermined when government gives people more income, as has happened with Congress's recent expansion and restructuring of the child tax credit. If employment is valuable for social integration, then reducing homelessness via a universal housing choice voucher program may well reduce social integration.

Simply reducing a low-income family's housing costs does not benefit children in a robust way. Stable housing in a "distressed" neighborhood, the most typical situation voucher households find themselves in, still exposes children to poor schools and questionable influences.[34] For a long time, the hope was that vouchers would prove a more successful rental assistance model than public housing. Public housing concentrated poverty but if rental assistance were attached to the tenant, not the unit, it could be used anywhere. Insofar as better neighborhoods make for better adults and children, a voucher-facilitated massive relocation from bad neighborhoods to good neighborhoods could disrupt intergenerational poverty. One high-profile study, the Moving to Opportunity program, found some evidence that voucher-facilitated relocations to better neighborhoods can benefit children, but the move needs to happen when the kids are young (under thirteen).[35] That interpretation of "neighborhood effects" would justify a targeted voucher program but not a universal one that would benefit families with older children, single adults, or one which allowed voucher recipients to lease in place. Many low-income Americans prefer to live near where they grew up and their network of extended friends and family. The schools are better in the suburbs but employment opportunities for workers with modest skills and educational attainment aren't more abundant and may even be worse, given that public transportation options are more meagre than in the city.

Vouchers can provide a sense of relief and flexibility.[36] Vouchers enable poor single mothers who'd like to move from a shabby unit in a working-class neighborhood to a nicer unit in a poor neighborhood, or vice versa, to do so. Families who move from a situation of housing instability to stability, or from a high-crime neighborhood to a low-crime one, experience a reduction of stress in their lives.[37] Rarely, though, do proponents of a housing entitlement leave it at "relief" but, rather, layer on claims about upward mobility that vouchers alone cannot achieve. Many of the shortcomings associated with the traditional non-universal housing choice voucher program would be exacerbated by making it universal: finding willing landlords, finding units outside troubled neighborhoods, and avoiding reductions in work effort. Reductions in homelessness would be largest among the non-chronic population, not the street population of greatest concern to the public.

LEARNING TO LIVE WITH LANDLORDS

It is customary to hold residential landlords in low repute. Back during a rent strike in Newark during the 1960s, famous progressive activist Tom Hayden asserted, "The real cause of poverty is that the landlord fleeces the tenant so much that the tenant doesn't have enough money to get out of poverty."[38] In his 2016 work, *Evicted*, sociologist Matthew Desmond advanced a more sophisticated version of this critique by arguing that landlords take advantage of how in poor neighborhoods, compared to elsewhere in their same metro, property values are much lower whereas rents are only somewhat lower.[39] At the same time, other accounts of landlord life stress the precarity of a business model reliant on rent payments from sporadically or never-employed tenants.[40] In fact, some base their argument for a voucher entitlement on the premise that the low-rent property business won't pencil out without one.[41]

Progressive housing policymakers can't live with landlords, but nor can they live without them. Progressives' best shot at significantly expanding affordable housing, in the near term, would be through vouchers. In theory, enacting a voucher entitlement could create, overnight, as many as 8 million new affordable housing units.[42] But though expanding vouchers is more practical than expanding public housing or other project-based subsidy programs, it yet faces two serious practical obstacles. HUD does not allow vouchers to be used on a $25,000 a month rental in the Hamptons. A payment standard is set at a given community's "Fair Market Rent": that's how much HUD believes it would cost a low-income household to affordably rent an apartment of average quality. The promise of a universal housing choice voucher program thus rests on how many private apartments at or below fair market rent, in decent physical conditions and in good neighborhoods, exist that are vacant and could be rented to voucher holders if everyone eligible for a voucher had one. Careful studies have questioned how many rental units check all those boxes: perhaps a few hundred thousand, nationwide. They probably do not number in the millions.[43] Suburban communities with low crime and good schools are not known for their overabundance of moderately priced rental apartments. In fact, many are not even known for their rental stock at all. They're communities of homeowners. If the vast majority of poor households that receive a voucher rent in place in the same cheap-but-troubled neighborhood in which they're now living, the program stands no chance whatsoever in improving those households' lives the way that many proponents predict.

The second obstacle is landlord participation. At present, many landlords don't participate in the voucher program because they don't want to submit to its administrative requirements, physical inspections of their properties, they think they can get more in rent from a non-subsidized tenant, and/or they believe voucher holders make for bad tenants. As noted earlier, under the current program, around one-third of voucher holders can't find a unit; the utilization rate is lower still in tight housing markets like New York.

Landlords want to rent to people who pay their rent on time, don't engage in criminal activity, and are responsible property stewards. To select tenants based upon who they think will be a good tenant, they rely on formal means such as criminal background and credit checks but also their judgment, or "gut feeling."[44] Housing policymakers and advocates who want to expand access to affordable housing believe landlords' judgment over tenant selection must be regulated to prevent discrimination. "Source of income discrimination" laws prohibit landlords from not renting to voucher holders based only on the fact that part of the rent is paid by a voucher.

Such laws would be one way to compel landlords to participate in a universal housing choice voucher program. But exactly how successful compulsion-type approaches
would succeed in expanding landlord participation is uncertain.[45]

Notwithstanding Desmond's claims about how housing the poor presents a spectacular business opportunity, many people do not consider it to be an attractive way
to make a living. You must involve yourself far more in people's lives than, say, an
owner of a bodega or liquor store in a poor neighborhood, you will never shake the
reputation of being an exploitative slumlord, and your revenue source is volatile. We
cannot require people to make a living by providing housing to poor people. We can
do more to restrict landlords' freedom not rent to tenants they don't want to, but if
we take that too far, we will restrict the number of people who want to be in the low-
rent housing industry. We shouldn't force people out of that industry, and discourage
others from entering it at a time in which we'd like to increase the overall supply of
low-rent apartments. Current owners could abandon their properties, convert them
into moderate or even "luxury" housing, or sell them to someone who wants to do
something with the properties other than house poor people.

If landlords lose control over the front door, they will still expect control over the
back door—meaning, the authority to evict when tenants they believed would work
out did not. Even more than homelessness, interest in making housing an entitlement stems from concern over eviction. Desmond's *Evicted* pushed the issue to the
top of the progressive housing agenda. Much of the rhetoric around eviction comes
down to the indignity of the experience: anti-eviction websites feature sidewalks
strewn with belongings. In an August 2019 article about "the New American Homeless," a *New Republic* reporter quoted a low-income housing advocate describing
eviction as "the civil equivalent of capital punishment."[46] During the COVID-19
pandemic, a blurry mix of public health and economic justifications kept eviction
moratoria in place across the nation.

Evictions are often cited as a cause of homelessness but they might be better
understood as a cause of housing instability.[47] US jurisdictions with the highest eviction rates are concentrated in Southern states with a low cost of living and modest
homelessness challenges.[48] Over the course of his two terms in office, New York's
mayor, Bill de Blasio, invested heavily in anti-eviction legal services. In a May 2020
testimony before the city council, de Blasio's social services chief, Steven Banks, said
that local anti-eviction initiatives had led to "evictions by marshals dropping by 41
percent since 2013, while evictions are up all across the country."[49] Between 2013
and 2020, homelessness rose 22 percent in New York City and declined 5 percent
elsewhere in the nation (going by the official HUD estimates).

Evictions create vacancies in the low-rent housing stock. If another poor family,
themselves at risk of homelessness, moves into a newly-vacated unit due to an eviction, the impact on the community's rate of housing stability is essentially a wash.
Eviction does not only affect the individual or family that's evicted, it also affects their
neighbors, but not always in a negative way. If a landlord does not want a tenant in a
certain unit, there is a chance that others in the same building don't appreciate their

presence, either: "No one relishes the prospect of evicting failed households from housing developments. The process surely does not solve the family's problem. But like many another practical public act which falls short of the ideal program of the philosopher king, it does at least remove the threat to others in the development."[50]

Low-rent landlords value the power to evict. As stated in a 2018 report published by HUD, "[w]hen landlords are operating at the fringes of financial stability, they cannot afford to house tenants indeterminately in arrears."[51] When government extended eviction protections to SRO tenants, some building owners left the low-rent housing business. A tightly-regulated system of eviction protections would protect currently-housed households against losing their apartments. But it may also prevent them from gaining access to that apartment in the first place. One could even consider an argument in favor of making it easier to evict problem tenants in order to incentivize more landlord participation in a vastly expanded voucher program. We rely heavily on private landlords to house the poor not because of some abstract commitment to neoliberalism but for practical reasons. The prospects seem dim of building millions of new public housing units anytime soon. Any advocate serious about making a dent in homelessness via affordable housing must rely on private landlords. A "fix it first" approach to affordable housing must rely on private landlords.

YIMBYISM'S PROMISE

Poor people have to live somewhere. Back in the days of the tenements, it was economically viable to build new housing for the poor.[52] But since the advent of modern housing regulations, housing built for the poor has required some sort of public subsidy.[53] Housing reformers have always understood the tension between quality and affordability. Boosting housing quality has a paternalistic thrust insofar as it risks forcing poor people to spend more on housing than they necessarily would have chosen to.[54] But, reformers reason, some housing is simply abhorrent, government must take action, and, eventually, adjustments in the broader market will deal with any initial disruptions caused by the new regulatory regime.

One important adjustment reformers have in mind is "filtering." Filtering happens when housing built for the middle or upper classes is abandoned by them, thus declining in cost, and probably also quality, down to within reach of the poor. Filtering, a part of the natural growth cycle of cities, is a concept rooted in simple economic logic and experience.[55] Countless examples exist of housing units currently occupied by households poorer than the households for which those units were built.[56] Members of the "Yes in My Backyard," or "YIMBY," movement argue for reducing regulations on housing supply to promote more private market development and induce filtering.[57]

The question, for present purposes, is not whether filtering happens or whether more private market development is a good idea but how much cities should look to private market development to help address homelessness. Filtering's effect must reach quite far down the income spectrum to reach households who are homeless or at risk of homelessness. But it must not exert so much downward pressure on rents to convince landlords of low-rent properties that their properties are no longer economically viable as low-rent properties.[58] Thus, filtering's effect must be calibrated, as well as broad and strong. Filtering, at a scale large enough to meaningfully affect rents for the extremely low income, might depend on neighborhood deterioration.[59] Many people, when they imagine filtering, may think of apartments in buildings in need of a paint job or with old-fashioned fixtures, but a more realistic conception might be apartments in a dangerous neighborhood with bad schools. When middle-class households move to better neighborhoods, they free up units in their old neighborhoods but also accelerate their destabilization. Middle-class flight is a cause of neighborhood decline, not just an effect of it. Certainly, any filtering-oriented response to homelessness would take time, though that is not a strong criticism since subsidized housing for the homeless programs also proceed at a notoriously slow pace.

Both progressive housing advocates and YIMBYs agree that homelessness is a housing problem and count themselves critics of prevailing norms in land use regulation. But the two groups have a tendency to talk past one another. The land use restrictions advocates dislike most are those that make it difficult to site new shelters and supportive housing projects. YIMBYs want weaker land use restrictions over private market development. Progressive Democrats sometimes express an openness to more market rate development, but not in lieu of more directly subsidized housing. The housing and homeless advocacy communities do not believe the private market can play a meaningful role in housing the poor. They criticize filtering as "trickle-down housing."[60] Local politicians prefer project-based subsidized housing because it's a more targeted response to unaffordable housing and has a strong "ribbon-cutting" appeal.

Everyone agrees that the rent is too damn high but it's hard to get people to agree on solutions. Private market development and subsidized programs present different strengths. Subsidized housing will remain a cornerstone of homelessness and local housing policy for the foreseeable future. It's expensive and has a weak recent track record in addressing homelessness. But, in its defense, the benefit is highly targeted. Supportive housing programs don't help many people, but everyone they do help has profound needs.

A strict YIMBY approach would bring online more units and at minimal cost to government. None of the new units would be affordable to anyone at risk of homelessness, much less anyone who's part of the current homeless population. But YIMBYism could be framed as a way to go on the defensive against rising rents, such as by arresting the "filtering up" process of, in tight markets, owners rehabbing old units to appeal to higher-income households.[61] YIMBYism could serve as a homelessness prevention strategy, a way to keep Austin from turning into San Francisco. We should not overpromise with respect to private market development and homelessness. The history of homelessness policymaking is already littered with enough broken promises. To re-emphasize, there may be other reasons to reconsider land use regulations other than as a way to reduce homelessness, such as making life easier for moderate-income households, economic development, and the value of having housing unit growth keep pace with job growth in a community.

GENTRIFICATION AND IMMIGRATION

Filtering's potential depends on demand-side considerations. Two important demand-side considerations are gentrification and immigration. Neither gentrifiers nor immigrants are themselves at great risk of homelessness. But both groups compete for scarce low-rent units with people who are at risk of homelessness.

Gentrifiers' capacity and needs differ from "native" low-income renters in ways that place upward pressure on rents. Even when gentrifiers are, technically, low or moderate income themselves, they can bid up local rents by having recourse to family support.[62] And their needs differ. Upwardly mobile single college graduates can be rent burdened without it being a pressing social problem in a way that single mothers cannot. Having to devote half your income to the rent is more sustainable if you don't have to support two to three children on the remaining half. Researchers have struggled to quantify how much "displacement" gentrification caused, which would also make its effect on homelessness hard to evaluate.[63] True gentrification in the sense of a neighborhood being thoroughly transformed from low-income to moderate-income is a relatively rare phenomenon nationwide.[64] But it may have contributed to homelessness in crisis cities such as New York.[65]

Gentrification's pressure on housing markets could ease in coming years due to demographic decline. America has fewer future college graduates in the pipeline, with a big drop expected toward the end of the 2020s.[66] This has caused, thus far, more consternation in higher education than urban policy circles, though both areas will be affected. Additionally, the millennial generation was slower than past generations to make the shift from renter to homeowner, but that may be changing.[67] If a larger proportion of upper-middle-class adults become homeowners, demand for rental apartments in cities will run lower in coming years than it has in the recent past.

Immigration is less likely to decline. To be clear, immigrants themselves do not now, and never have, made up a large share of the homelessness population, Emma Lazarus's "New Colossus" notwithstanding ("Send these, the homeless, tempest-tost to me, I lift my lamp beside the golden door!"). That was just as true in the tramp and skid row eras as it is now.[68] The immigrant experience qualifies the idea of homelessness as a purely economic problem. Immigrant poverty exceeds that of natives.[69] Two explanations for why there aren't more homeless immigrants, despite their being so poor, could be immigrants' stable family structures[70] and exit.[71] When a native-born individual from Brooklyn falls on hard times, in Brooklyn, he is not as likely to move somewhere else as an immigrant recently arrived from elsewhere when he falls on hard times.

Immigrants are attracted to places with strong economies and help those places grow by increasing the labor supply and buying things from vendors looking for consumers. But talking about overall economic growth explains little, with respect to immigration's effect on homelessness, because homelessness concerns how communities grow, not whether they grow. One thing that immigrants buy (or rent) is housing. Some have cited increased demand for housing as one of immigration's positive economic effects.[72] Increasing rents may be a sign that neighborhood conditions are improving, perhaps for reasons relating to why more immigrants are moving in. But that scenario still might lead to increased homelessness, if some can't keep pace.[73] The low-rent housing market is notoriously lacking in dynamism: when more poor people come to a city looking for units renting at around $800 a month, supply of such units does not automatically materialize. High housing prices of the sort likely to cause homelessness can, of course, be a deterrent to immigration.[74]

Many people concerned with the welfare of homeless adults emphasize the extreme fragility of modern American labor markets. Low-skill immigration exerts a negative effect on employment and earnings for low-skill natives.[75] The low-skill native population overlaps with the adult homeless population. Immigrants almost certainly take jobs that homeless men, or men at risk of homelessness, could do. But just how large an effect that is depends on how "substitutable" immigrants and homeless men are. A native with chronic schizophrenia may be able to work under some conditions, but not as a full-time construction or landscape worker. Thus, the immigrant who does that job does the man with schizophrenia no particular harm. Ex-offenders, though, might be a different case, as well as men in the early stages of recovery from a substance abuse disorder. As once expressed by Steven A. Camarota of the Center for Immigration Studies, "politically[,] employers would say, well, look, we've got to try to do more to rehabilitate prisoners and to get people off drugs. Oh, wait, we've got immigrants to do this work; why do I care?"[76] If it's reasonable to suspect, even if you can't quantify it, that immigrants crowd out job opportunities at the very lowest rungs of the labor market, then it's reasonable to suspect, even if you can't quantify it, that immigration contributes to homelessness.

A city could argue that without immigration the tax base won't grow, leaving government incapable of funding homelessness programs. But government-funded homelessness programs aren't terribly effective. What really helps is preventing homelessness from arising in the first place. If immigrants arrive in hot housing markets and make them hotter, they thereby exacerbate housing shortages in the low-rent stock.

CONCLUSION: HOMELESSNESS AND URBANISM

Tent cities in California are often denounced for their "third world" conditions. However, homelessness could just as well be seen as a "first world problem." At crisis levels, homelessness is an offshoot of urban success. Unhealthy cities may have some vagrancy-related challenges, but they don't have homelessness crises on the scale of Los Angeles, San Francisco, and New York. Detroit does not have a more functional behavioral health system, or a lower rate of single-parent households, than New York and San Francisco. It does however boast cheaper housing and fewer opportunities to make extraordinary incomes. New York boasts more than 25,000 income millionaire households.[77] Were they all to leave tomorrow, rents would decline, but one might wonder what a city would look like from which thousands of millionaires fled and whether homelessness might not be its most pressing problem. The surest way for a city to keep housing costs down is to fail.

A city should not be judged only by its homelessness rate. But accepting the importance of reducing homelessness, what is a standard of urban success that could accommodate that goal? One answer would be a model that squares with the earlier discussion of "fix it first." Boarding houses, board and care homes, crowded apartments: these don't conform easily to urbanists' conception of what a city needs to be successful, but low-quality housing is cheap housing. If we're going to learn from the past, we should be wary of keeping up the pressure on housing standards and by some measures, such as crowding, we might even countenance declines in quality. Expanding supply, on its own, should help a city prevent a homeless crisis from arising. But regulations pertaining to quality, not just supply, should be examined.

Working with the rental stock we've got will require working the people who own it. There is no practical near-term way to significantly expand affordable housing without relying on landlords. Just to maintain the low-rent stock we have will require carefulness as to how we regulate landlords' business practices. We don't want, even in a modest way, a repeat of the skid row era during which thousands of irreplaceable low-rent units were removed from the stock. Low-quality housing helps reduce homelessness.

12

Conclusion

What might a new direction on homelessness look like? No one big recommendation quite fits. Our solutions to the problem should reflect the underlying diversity obscured by the abstraction "homelessness." Throughout the preceding discussion, multiple policy suggestions were made as they emerged naturally from the analysis. To recap:

- Share more housing. Do it via community-based programs set up to connect roommates and make doubled-up situations more sustainable for families, and by addressing sharing disincentives baked into safety net programs.
- Set up programs that can objectively validate, for families, whether their adult relative has truly changed.
- Ease up on Housing First requirements in federal programs. That will allow communities to invest in models in which they're now under-investing, such as transitional housing. Vulnerable populations that are well served by transitional housing include ex-offenders and victims of domestic violence.
- Consult the "lived experience" of homeless people less. Consult the lived experience of families of homeless people more.
- Make peace with the social services industrial complex but hold it accountable for outcomes.
- Match any commitment to social integration with a commitment to employment and behavioral health programs. Only those kinds of programs, not housing, can truly integrate homeless adults into ordinary society.
- Take a "fix it first" approach to affordable housing: redouble efforts to work with the current stock, even if low-quality, and the private landlords who own that stock.
- Prevent homelessness crises from emerging by easing up on housing regulations both with respect to supply and to quality.

- Reform the mental health care system to help families keep their mentally ill relatives stable and exercise more supervision over those with untreated serious mental illness.
- Don't frame police work and social work as either/or.

And, in conclusion, here are three final suggestions.

CLEAN UP YOUR LANGUAGE

Give the "ending homelessness" talk a rest. Defining one's position as dedicated to "ending homelessness" amounts to suggesting that anyone with a different position is pro-homelessness. Some people may believe they know how to end homelessness, but no one truly knows how to do it. Homelessness policy questions should not be considered more settled than any other question of poverty or social policy.

Cease speaking of subsidized housing as a "platform." The platform theory of subsidized housing has been studied about as thoroughly and carefully as any policy topic over the last thirty years. We can state with considerable confidence that subsidized housing does not function as a platform with respect to employment, addiction, or mental stability. "Platform" seems especially inapplicable for the homeless and near-homeless populations whose problems are complex. "Relief" is a better term than "platform." Relief is the old-fashioned word for cash welfare. It gets closer to what housing assistance can reliably achieve. Subsidized housing provides people with a sense of relief. It does not radically improve their lives.

Talk less about housing. Even accepting the value of subsidized housing for at least some members of the homeless population, there is no realistic path for cities to house their way out of homelessness anytime soon. Where will these hundreds of thousands of units go? Which landlords will accept these vouchers? In the meantime, something needs to be done about street disorder. Robert Marbut, the former executive director of the US Interagency Council on Homelessness, is fond of asking, "What can you do today, tomorrow, and in the next week, not three years from now?"[1] This is a reasonable question to ask about homelessness policy. It does not reject the idea of investing in permanent housing. But it does point toward less emphasis on that solution than we have at present.

DISBAND HOMELESS SERVICES SYSTEMS

The earlier list of policy suggestions was premised on the idea that homeless services, in the future, will retain more or less the same structure as it has now. Another reform to consider would be to completely restructure the system.

"Homeless services" is just as artificial of a concept as "homelessness." Agencies and programs devoted to addressing homelessness exist at all levels of government and across the nation. They were set up to demonstrate governments' commitment to dealing with homelessness and to relieve other agencies of having to deal with it. The second goal was not achieved. Other agencies—police, schools, transit systems, sanitation, libraries, and so on—are constantly preoccupied with homelessness-related challenges. Standalone agencies and programs have outlived their symbolic justification.

We don't need standalone homeless service systems. Existing systems could be dismantled and their resources disbursed among other social service agencies. Meeting social challenges sometimes requires programs with a residential component. That certainly goes for mental illness and substance abuse. The criminal justice system uses residential programs for reentry and probation purposes. Schools deal with homeless students. All of the systems that serve these populations could simply be responsible for their respective populations' housing needs using the resources currently controlled by standalone homeless services agencies.

The unrelenting focus on subsidized housing now found throughout the homeless policymaking community may simply be inevitable, given how the challenge was framed decades ago. Perhaps asking why homeless policymakers don't care more about employment and behavioral health might be asking the wrong question. A better question might be: Do we need homeless policymakers at all?

STOP BREAKING PROMISES

When a new program to end or dramatically reduce homelessness launches, the politicians backing it may have convinced themselves that "this time it will be different." But if they don't deliver in a way that's appreciable to the homeless and low-income population, and public more broadly, their program will leave a legacy of mistrust. Advocates and politicians' colleagues may understand them to be making the best of a bad hand and, thus, if programs don't prove transformative, they deserve only so much blame. But outside that circle of colleagues, on the street, in shelters, on the subway, and in poor and working-class neighborhoods, failure doesn't translate as "'A' for effort."

For any homeless individual who placed hopes in a new policy initiative that underwhelmed, failure can translate as betrayal. We shouldn't betray people if we want to motivate them to overcome homelessness. That challenge is hard enough: the implicit tax effect of losing access to entitlement programs; the explicit tax of child support payments; the scarcity of decently paying jobs with a sense of dignity available to people without much education, skills, or work experience; and/or being made a target for victimization based on the fact that you work and have money.[2] How can backsliding when people hit the second and third rungs of the socioeconomic ladder be prevented? In the near-term, moving up the economic ladder may well make people feel more stressed and less free. When should people be told to expect that? A sense of betrayal can be debilitating to motivation. It validates the street wisdom that there is no point in trying. When the path out of homelessness gets framed as choosing foolishness over prudence, many will take a pass. So, one standard of success in homeless policymaking could be fewer homeless people made fools of by policymakers who claim to be devoted to helping them.

Notes

Chapter 1. "Homelessness": An Elusive Concept

1. Celia Dugger, "Conversations/Nancy Wackstein; Memo to Democrats: Housing Won't Solve Homelessness," *New York Times*, July 12, 1992.

2. On the origins of the term "homelessness," see Richard W. White Jr., *Rude Awakenings: What the Homeless Crisis Tells Us* (San Francisco: ICS Press, 1992): ch. 9; Robert C. Ellickson, "Controlling Chronic Misconduct in City Spaces: Of Panhandlers, Skid Rows, and Public-Space Zoning," *The Yale Law Journal* 105 (1996): 1192–93 and 1214; Brendan O'Flaherty, *Making Room: The Economics of Homelessness* (Cambridge: Harvard University Press, 1996): 9–11; Kim Hopper, *Reckoning with Homelessness* (Ithaca: Cornell University Press, 2003), 7 and 15; Forrest Stuart, *Down, Out, and Under Arrest: Policing and Everyday Life in Skid Row* (Chicago: University of Chicago Press, 2018), 49; Marian Moser Jones, "Creating a Science of Homelessness During the Reagan Era," *The Milbank Quarterly* 93, no. 1 (2015): 148–49.

3. James D. Wright, *Address Unknown: The Homeless in America* (New York: Aldine de Gruyter, 1989), 29.

4. Donna Wilson Kirchheimer, "Sheltering the Homeless in New York City: Expansion in an Era of Government Contraction," *Political Science Quarterly* 104, no. 4 (Winter 1989–1990): 618.

5. Source: author calculation based on data derived from HUD's Continuum of Care program: https://www.hudexchange.info/resource/3031/pit-and-hic-data-since-2007/.

6. Merrill Perlman, "2020 AP Stylebook Changes: Person-First Language, and the Great 'Pled' Debate," *Columbia Journalism Review*, May 6, 2020; Alissa Walker and Emma Alpern, "The Language Around Homelessness Is Finally Changing," curbed.com, June 11, 2020.

7. Jonathan Kozol, *Rachel and her Children: Homeless Families in America* (New York: Crown, 1988), 1–26.

8. Michael B. Katz, *The Undeserving Poor: America's Enduring Confrontation with Poverty* (New York: Oxford University Press, 2013), 233.

9. Quoted in Kenneth L. Kusmer, *Down and Out, on the Road: The Homeless in American History* (New York: Oxford University Press, 2002), 4.

10. Greg Berman and John Feinblatt, *Good Courts: The Case for Problem-Solving Justice* (New York: New Press, 2005).

11. Katz, *The Undeserving Poor*, 241; Roger Starr, *America's Housing Challenge: What it is and How to Meet it* (New York: Hill & Wang, 1977), 88–89.

12. Source: author calculation based on data derived from HUD's Continuum of Care program: https://www.hudexchange.info/resource/3031/pit-and-hic-data-since-2007/.

13. ProPublica, Right to Fail: https://www.propublica.org/series/right-to-fail.

14. Amam Z. Saleh, Paul S. Appelbaum, Xiaoyu Liu, T. Scott Stroup, and Melanie Wall, "Deaths of People with Mental Illness during Interactions with Law Enforcement," *International Journal of Law and Psychiatry* 58 (May–June 2018): table 2.

15. Michael D. Tanner, *The Inclusive Economy: How to Bring Wealth to America's Poor* (Washington DC: Cato Institute, 2018), 1.

16. Charles Dickens, *Dombey and Son* (New York: Oxford University Press, 2008 [orig. 1848]), chapters 48 and 49; Evelyn Waugh, *Brideshead Revisited* (New York: Little, Brown and Company, 2012 [orig. 1945]), chapter II.5, "Epilogue"; G. K. Chesterton, *St. Francis of Assisi* (New York: Doubleday, Doran & Company, 1924), 85, 113, and 213.

Chapter 2. The Romantic Era (Post-Civil War to the 1920s)

1. Howard M. Bahr, *Skid Row: An Introduction to Disaffiliation* (New York: Oxford University Press, 1973), chapter 2.

2. Stefan G. Kertesz, et al., "Permanent Supportive Housing for Homeless People—Reframing the Debate," *New England Journal of Medicine* 375 (December 1, 2016): 2115.

3. The technical term was "riding the rods"—as in, from Hank Snow's version of "Wabash Cannonball": "She's a mighty rushin' engine, you can hear them hobos call / As they ride the rods and the brake beams on the Wabash Cannonball." The "rods" in question were machinery under a train's carriage. Sequestering oneself under a train's carriage on the rods was a second-best option to boarding an empty box car.

4. Roger Bruns, *Knights of the Road: A Hobo History* (New York: Methuen, 1980), 15; Kenneth L. Kusmer, *Down and Out, on the Road: The Homeless in American History* (New York: Oxford University Press, 2002), 102–4.

5. Mark Wyman, *Hoboes: Bindlestiffs, Fruit Tramps, and the Harvesting of the West* (New York: Hill & Wang, 2010).

6. Bruns, *Knights of the Road*, 13, 129–31; Eric H. Monkkonen, "Introduction," in *Walking to Work: Tramps in America, 1790–1935*, edited by Eric H. Monkonnen (Lincoln: University of Nebraska Press, 1984), 14; Nels Anderson, "Book Review: The Demolition of Skid Row by Ronald J. Miller," *Social Forces* 62, no. 4 (June 1984): 1119–21; Charles Hoch and Robert A. Slayton, *New Homeless and Old: Community and the Skid Row Hotel* (Philadelphia: Temple University Press, 1989), 39

7. Robert Hunter, *Poverty* (New York: The MacMillan Company, 1905), chapter 3; Kusmer, *Down and Out*, 125; Don D. Lescohier, *The Labor Market* (New York: The Macmillan Company, 1919), 49; Harry Kemp, "The Lure of the Tramp," *Independent* 70 (June 8, 1911): 1270–71.

8. Hoch and Slayton, *New Homeless and Old*, chapters 2 and 3; Bruns, *Knights of the Road*, 19, 184–85; John C. Schneider, "Tramping Workers, 1890–1920," in *Walking to Work: Tramps in America, 1790–1935*, edited by Eric H. Monkonnen (Lincoln: University of Nebraska Press, 1984), 225; Kusmer, *Down and Out*, 149.

9. Amos Warner, *American Charities: A Study in Philanthropy and Economics* (New York: Thomas Y. Crowell & Company, 1894), chapter 9; Alice Solenberger, *One Thousand Homeless Men: A Study of Original Records* (New York: Charities Publication Committee, 1911); Nels Anderson, *The Hobo: The Sociology of the Homeless Man* (Chicago: The University of Chicago Press, 1923): 87ff. discusses meaning of "homeless" in various writers.

10. Josiah Flynt, *Tramping with Tramps* (New York: The Century Co., 1901), 392–98; Bruns, *Knights of the Road*, 200–204; Anderson 1923, chapters 6 and 7; Matt Stopera, "61 Things I Learned At The National Hobo Convention," *Buzz Feed News*, August 21, 2012.

11. Hoch and Slayton, *New Homeless and Old*, chapter 3.

12. Lawrence Stessin, "That Vanishing American: The Hobo," *New York Times Magazine*, August 18, 1940.

13. Hoch and Slayton, *New Homeless and Old*, 44.

14. Clark C. Spence, "Knights of the Tie and Rail: Tramps and Hoboes in the West," *Western Historical Quarterly* 2, no. 1 (January 1971): 4–19; Bruns, *Knights of the Road*, 11, 78, and 83.

15. Eric Foner, *Free Soil, Free Labor, Free Men: The Ideology of the Republican Party before the Civil War* (New York: Oxford University Press, 1970); Judith N. Shklar, *American Citizenship* (Cambridge, MA: Harvard University Press, 1991).

16. Michael B. Katz, *The Undeserving Poor: America's Enduring Confrontation with Poverty* (New York: Oxford University Press, 2013), 234.

17. Mokkonnen, "Introduction," 4–5; Anderson, *The Hobo*, 12–13; Solenberger, *One Thousand Homeless Men*, 9; Alice Sparberg Alexiou, *Devil's Mile: The Rich, Gritty History of the Bowery* (New York: St. Martin's Press, 2018), 204.

18. Kevin Corinth and David S. Lucas, "When Warm and Cold Don't Mix: The Implications of Climate for the Determinants of Homelessness," *Journal of Housing Economics* 41 (2018): 45–56.

19. William Kennedy, *Ironweed* (New York: Penguin, 1983); Kusmer, *Down and Out*, 10; Anderson, *The Hobo*, 96–97 and 117–21.

20. Anderson, *The Hobo*, chapter 9.

21. Peter Speek, "The Psychology of Floating Workers," *Annals of the American Academy of Political and Social Science* 69 (January 1917): 50–57; Lescohier, *The Labor Market*, chapter 13; Hoch and Slayton, *New Homeless and Old*, chapter 3; Schneider, "Tramping Workers, 1890–1920," 218–20; Anderson, *The Hobo*, chapter 4 and 5.

22. Studs Terkel, *Hard Times: An Oral History of the Great Depression* (New York: The New Press, 2000 [Orig. 1970]), 38; Hoch and Slayton, *New Homeless and Old*, chapter 3; Schneider, "Tramping Workers, 1890–1920," 218; Kusmer, *Down and Out*, 158; Frances A. Kellor, *Out of Work: A Study of Unemployment* (New York: G. P. Putnam's Sons, 1915), 16–17.

23. Anderson, *The Hobo*, 82–85.

24. Kusmer, *Down and Out*, 9

25. William O. Douglas, *Go East Young Man: The Early Years; The Autobiography of William O. Douglas* (New York: Random House, 1974), chapter 6.

26. Kusmer, *Down and Out*, chapter 9.

27. John Steinbeck, *Cannery Row* (New York: Penguin, 2002 [Orig. 1945]), chapter 23.

28. The quote is from O. Henry's "Whistling Dick's Christmas Stocking" published in *Roads of Destiny* (New York: Doubleday, Page & Company, 1918), 272.

29. Anderson, *The Hobo*, 211.

30. Sara Dorn, "JetBlue Worker Slammed for 'Racist' Homeless Person Halloween Costume," *New York Post*, November 2, 2019.

31. Monkkonen, "Introduction," 4.

32. Kusmer, *Down and Out*, 183.

33. "Most tramps were between twenty and forty years old, and because there is no evidence of a changing age structure, we can infer that most tramped only for a portion of their adult lives." Monkkonen, "Introduction," 14.

34. Kusmer, *Down and Out*, 41.

35. Flynt, *Tramping with Tramps*; A–No.1, *The Curse of Tramp Life* (Cambridge Springs, PA: The A–No.1 Publishing Co., 1912); Jim Tully, *Beggars of Life* (New York: A. & C. Boni, 1924); Bruns, *Knights of the Road*, 90–91.

36. Anderson *The Hobo*, 64.

37. Lescohier *The Labor Market*, 63.

38. Lescohier *The Labor Market*, 63, 107, and 116.

39. Kusmer, *Down and Out*, 57, 79, and 93; Edmond Kelly, *The Elimination of the Tramp* (New York: G. P. Putnam's Sons, 1908).

40. Kellor, *Out of Work*; Lescohier, *The Labor Market*.

41. Monkkonen, "Introduction," 8.

42. Kusmer, *Down and Out*, 6.

43. US Department of Housing and Urban Development, "The 2018 Annual Homeless Assessment Report (AHAR) to Congress; Part 2: Estimates of Homelessness in the United States," September 2020. https://www.huduser.gov/portal/sites/default/files/pdf/2018-AHAR-Part-2.pdf.

44. Solenberger, *One Thousand Homeless Men*, 9.

45. Anderson, *The Hobo*, 3.

46. US Department of Housing and Urban Development, "2020 CoC Homeless Populations and Subpopulations Report-IL-510: Chicago CoC," December 15, 2020. https://files.hudexchange.info/reports/published/CoC_PopSub_CoC_IL-510-2020_IL_2020.pdf.

47. Frank Charles Laubach, *Why There Are Vagrants: A Study* (New York: Columbia University, 1916); Kelly, *The Elimination of the Tramp*; Speek "The Psychology of Floating Workers."

48. US Department of Housing and Urban Development, "HUD 2020 Continuum of Care Homeless Assistance Programs Homeless Populations and Subpopulations," December 15, 2020. https://files.hudexchange.info/reports/published/CoC_PopSub_Natl TerrDC_2020.pdf.

49. Bruns, *Knights of the Road*, 16.

50. Theodore Caplow, "Transiency as a Cultural Pattern," *American Sociological Review* 5, no. 5 (October 1940): 731.

51. Anderson, *The Hobo*, chapter 4; Kusmer, *Down and Out*, chapter 8 shows that Chicago's situation was representative.

52. Anderson, *The Hobo*, chapter 2; Bruns, *Knights of the Road*, 16.

53. Kusmer, *Down and Out*, 9, 135–36; Kemp, "The Lure of the Tramp"; Bruns, *Knights of the Road*, 19–20; Schneider, "Tramping Workers, 1890–1920," 224–25, Hoch and Slayton, *New Homeless and Old*, 29 and 92–93.

54. Hoch and Slayton, *New Homeless and Old*, chapters 2 and 3.

55. Kellor, *Out of Work*, 8–9, chapter 12; Hoch and Slayton, *New Homeless and Old*, 43 and 51; George Orwell, *Down and Out in Paris and London* (New York: Penguin, 2001 [Orig. 1933]), chapter 37.

56. Paul Erling Groth, *Living Downtown: The History of Residential Hotels in the United States* (Berkeley: University of California Press, 1994), x.

57. Michael B. Katz, "Poorhouses and the Origins of the Public Old Age Home," *The Milbank Memorial Fund Quarterly* 62, no. 1 (Winter 1984), 110–40; Hoch and Slayton, *New Homeless and Old*, chapter 3

58. Kusmer, *Down and Out*, 24.

59. Kusmer, *Down and Out*, 111–12.

60. Kellor, *Out of Work*, chapter 12; Schneider, "Tramping Workers, 1890–1920," 222; Kusmer, *Down and Out*, 55–56, 74–79, and 94–95; Hoch and Slayton, *New Homeless and Old*, chapter 3; Bruns, *Knights of the Road*, 89.

61. David Rothman, "The First Shelters: The Contemporary Relevance of the Almshouse," In *On Being Homeless: Historical Perspectives*, edited by Rick Beard, 10–19 (New York: Museum of the City of New York), 1987.

62. Schneider, "Tramping Workers, 1890–1920," 222–23; Hoch and Slayton, *New Homeless and Old*, chapter 3.

63. Kusmer, *Down and Out*, 88–90; Kellor, *Out of Work*, 9, chapter 12; Hoch and Slayton, *New Homeless and Old*, 103.

64. Kellor, *Out of Work*, chapter 12; for more on work tests, see Kusmer, *Down and Out*, 69–70, Hoch and Slayton, *New Homeless and Old*, chapter 3

65. Hoch and Slayton, *New Homeless and Old*, 16.

66. "The presence of so many highly transient men living outside of private households ultimately led to a small revolution in urban housing between 1880 and 1910." Schneider, "Tramping Workers, 1890–1920," 221.

67. Hoch and Slayton, *New Homeless and Old*, 89.

68. Bruns, *Knights of the Road*, 23–24 and 185–90; Kusmer, *Down and Out*, 126 and 224; Anderson, "Book Review: The Demolition of Skid Row by Ronald J. Miller"; Hoch and Slayton, *New Homeless and Old*, chapters 3 and 5.

69. Robert J. Gordon, *The Rise and Fall of American Growth: The U.S. Standard of Living since the Civil War* (Princeton: Princeton University Press, 2017), 53.

70. Monkkonen, "Introduction," 7–8; Bruns, *Knights of the Road*, 23–24 and 189–90.

71. Kellor, *Out of Work*, 17.

72. Bruns, *Knights of the Road*, 197; Lawrence Stessin, "That Vanishing American: The Hobo," *New York Times Magazine*, August 18, 1940; Kusmer, *Down and Out*, 39–40 and 72.

73. Matt Stopera, "61 Things I Learned at the National Hobo Convention," *Buzz Feed News*, August 21, 2012. https://www.buzzfeed.com/mjs538/things-i-learned-at-the-national -hobo-convention.

74. Stessin, "That Vanishing American: The Hobo"; Anderson, "Book Review: The Demolition of Skid Row by Ronald J. Miller."

75. Monkkonen, "Introduction," 14; Kusmer, *Down and Out*, 10.

76. Schneider, "Tramping Workers, 1890–1920," 215 and 226; Kusmer, *Down and Out*, 106–7, 113–14; Hoch and Slayton, *New Homeless and Old*, chapter 3.

77. Hoch and Slayton, *New Homeless and Old*, 29–32; Eric H. Monkkonen, "Regional Dimensions of Tramping, North and South, 1880–1910," In *Walking to Work: Tramps in America, 1790–1935*, edited by Eric H. Monkonnen, 196–201.

78. Hoch and Slayton, *New Homeless and Old*, chapter 3; Monkonnen, "Introduction."

79. Josiah Flynt, "How Men Become Tramps," *Century Magazine* 50 (October 1895): 941–45; Laubach, *Why There Are Vagrants*; Bruns, *Knights of the Road*, 70–71.

80. Bruns, *Knights of the Road*, 58.

81. Schneider, "Tramping Workers, 1890–1920," 214–15; Kusmer, *Down and Out*, 117–18; Bruns, *Knights of the Road*, 143.

82. Monkkonen, "Introduction," 3.

83. Schneider, "Tramping Workers, 1890–1920," 228; Monkkonen, "Introduction," 3.

Chapter 3. The Skid Row Era (Great Depression to 1970s)

1. There is some dispute over the etymology of "Skid Row." See Nels Anderson, "Book Review: The Demolition of Skid Row by Ronald J. Miller," *Social Forces* 62, no. 4 (June 1984): 1119–21.

2. A list of many postwar Skid Rows may be found in Donald Bogue, *Skid Row in American Cities*, Community and Family Study Center, University of Chicago, 1963.

3. Kim Hopper, "The Public Response to Homelessness in New York City: The Last Hundred Years," in *On Being Homeless: Historical Perspectives*, edited by Rick Beard (New York: Museum of the City of New York, 1987), 96.

4. Joan M. Crouse, *The Homeless Transient in the Great Depression: New York State, 1929–1941* (Albany: State University Press of New York Press, 1986), 48.

5. Kusmer, *Down and Out*, 103 (graph 6.4) and 194–98; Hoch and Slayton, *New Homeless and Old*, 74–79.

6. Joan M. Crouse, "The Remembered Men: Transient Camps in New York State, 1933–1935," *New York History* 71, no. 1 (January 1990): 71.

7. Kusmer, *Down and Out*, 193.

8. Grace Abbott, *From Relief to Social Security: The Development of the New Public Welfare Services and their Administration* (Chicago: The University of Chicago Press, 1941), 50.

9. Theodore Caplow, "Transiency as a Cultural Pattern," *American Sociological Review* 5, no. 5 (October 1940): 732.

10. Monkkonen, "Introduction," 5; Terkel, *Hard Times*, 14–15.

11. Arthur Schlesinger, *The Crisis of the Old Order, 1919–1933* (New York: Houghton Mifflin, 1957), 171. See also 3, 167–68, 250, and 259; T. H. Watkins, *The Great Depression: America in the 1930s* (Boston: Little, Brown and Company, 1993), 61; Terkel, *Hard Times*, 50; Kusmer, *Down and Out*, 201–2 and 221.

12. Ella Howard, *Homeless: Poverty and Place in Urban America* (Philadelphia: University of Pennsylvania Press, 2013), 69; Hopper, *Reckoning with Homelessness*, 42.

13. Hopper, *Reckoning with Homelessness*, 43.

14. Schlesinger, *The Crisis of the Old Order*, 251.

15. Terkel, *Hard Times*, 438.

16. Howard, *Homeless*, 67.

17. Abbott, *From Relief to Social Security*, 49–68; Kusmer, *Down and Out*, 25, 194–95, and 210.

18. Crouse, *The Homeless Transient in the Great Depression*, 48.

19. Bogue, *Skid Row*, chapter 9; Maura Dolan, "Homeless People from Other Cities Moving to San Francisco for Hotel Rooms, Mayor Says," *Los Angeles Times*, April 29, 2020. https://www.latimes.com/homeless-housing/story/2020-04-29/san-francisco-coronavirus-ho tel-rooms-homeless-people-from-other-cities.

20. Howard, *Homeless*, chapter 2.

21. Crouse, "The Remembered Men: Transient Camps in New York State, 1933–1935," 74.

22. Kusmer, *Down and Out*, 210–20.

23. Terkel, *Hard Times*, 33–34.

24. Caplow, "Transiency as a Cultural Pattern," 734.

25. Stephen Metraux, "Waiting for the Wrecking Ball: Skid Row in Postindustrial Philadelphia," *Journal of Urban History* 25 no. 5 (July 1999): 695.

26. Michael B. Katz, *In the Shadow of the Poorhouse: A Social History of Welfare in America* (New York: Basic Books, 1986), 5.

27. Colm Toibin, *Brooklyn: A Novel* (New York: Scribner, 2009), 87–88.

28. Kusmer, *Down and Out*, 225 and 241.

29. Kim Hopper, "CityViews: The Long View on New York's Homeless Problem," *City Limits*, February 6, 2017. https://citylimits.org/2017/02/06/cityviews-the-long-view-on-new-yorks-homeless-problem/.

30. Bogue, *Skid* Row, 52.

31. Kusmer, *Down and Out*, 154 and 241; Kirsten Moore Sheeley, et al., "The Making of a Crisis: A History of Homelessness in Los Angeles," UCLA Luskin Center for History and Policy, January 2021, 23, 36–38. https://luskincenter.history.ucla.edu/wp-content/uploads/sites/66/2021/01/LCHP-The-Making-of-A-Crisis-Report.pdf.

32. Hoch and Slayton, *New Homeless and Old*, chapters 3 and 5, 97–98; Hopper, "The Public Response to Homelessness in New York City: The Last Hundred Years," 97.

33. Kusmer, *Down and Out*, 233; Bogue, *Skid Row*, 106; Joan Hatch Shapiro, *Communities of the Alone* (New York: Association Press, 1971).

34. Howard, *Homeless*, 164.

35. Howard, *Homeless*, 164–65; Bogue, *Skid Row*, chapter 11.

36. David Levinson, "The Etiology of Skid Rows in the United States," *International Journal of Social Psychiatry* 20, nos. 1–2 (April 1974): 29.

37. Howard M. Bahr, *Skid Row: An Introduction to Disaffiliation* (New York: Oxford University Press, 1973), 105.

38. US Department of Housing and Urban Development, "HUD 2020 Continuum of Care Homeless Assistance Programs Homeless Populations and Subpopulations," December 15, 2020. https://files.hudexchange.info/reports/published/CoC_PopSub_Natl TerrDC_2020.pdf.

39. "LA Alliance for Human Rights, et al. v. City of Los Angeles, et al.," United States District Court, Central District of California, Case 2:20-cv-02291-DOC-KES, Document 277, April 20, 2021; Jugal K. Patel, Tim Arango, Anjali Singhvi, and Jon Huang, "Black, Homeless, and Burdened by LA's Legacy of Racism," *New York Times*, December 22, 2019.

40. Source: Lane Kenworthy, June 2020 https://lanekenworthy.net/key-facts/#whites-embrace-of-african-americans.

41. Source: Author calculation based on 2019 American Community Survey and HUD figures.

42. Francis E. Feeney, Dorothee F. Mindlin, Verna H. Minear, and Eleanor E. Short. "The Challenge of the Skid Row Alcoholic," *Quarterly Journal of Studies on Alcohol* 16, no. 4 (1955): 645–67; James F. Rooney, "Group Processes among Skid Row Winos: A Reevaluation of the Undersocialization Hypothesis," *Quarterly Journal of Studies on Alcohol* 22, no. 3 (1961): 444–60.

43. James Eli Shiffer, *The King of Skid Row: John Bacich and the Twilight Years of Old Minneapolis* (Minneapolis: University of Minnesota Press, 2016), 79.

44. Steve Metraux, "Digging Up Vine Street in Search of Old Skid Row," hiddencityphila.org, April 26, 2017. https://hiddencityphila.org/2017/04/digging-up-vine-street-in-search-of-old-skid-row/.

45. Nels Anderson, "Book Review: The Demolition of Skid Row by Ronald J. Miller," *Social Forces* 62, no. 4 (June 1984): 1119–21.

46. Bahr, *Skid Row*, chapter 4.

47. Roger Bruns, *Knights of the Road: A Hobo History* (New York: Methuen, 1980), 204; Bogue, *Skid Row*, 55–56, 469, and 489–90.

48. Christopher Jencks, *The Homeless* (Cambridge: Harvard University Press, 1994), 53.

49. Barrett A. Lee, "The Disappearance of Skid Row: Some Ecological Evidence," *Urban Affairs Quarterly* 16, no. 1 (September 1980): 81–107; Nicole Stelle Garnett, "Relocating Disorder," *Virginia Law Review* 91, no. 5 (September 2005): 1118; Metraux, "Waiting for the Wrecking Ball: Skid Row in Postindustrial Philadelphia"; Bogue, *Skid Row*, chapter 6.

50. National Academies of Sciences, Engineering, and Medicine, "The Economic and Fiscal Consequences of Immigration," 2016, table 2.1. https://d279m997dpfwgl.cloudfront.net/wp/2016/09/0922_immigrant-economics-full-report.pdf.

51. Like "high-utilizers" today, Skid Row residents were often described as an expensive burden on government: Shapiro, *Communities of the Alone*, 17.

52. Bogue, *Skid Row*, 476.

53. Metraux, "Digging Up Vine Street in Search of Old Skid Row." https://hiddencityphila.org/2017/04/digging-up-vine-street-in-search-of-old-skid-row/.

54. Kusmer, *Down and Out*, 6 and 225–26; Hoch and Slayton, *New Homeless and Old*, chapter 5; Shapiro, *Communities of the Alone*, 150.

55. Nicholas Dagen Bloom, *Public Housing that Worked: New York in the Twentieth Century* (Philadelphia: University of Pennsylvania Press, 2008), appendix B; Schwartz, *Housing Policy in the United States*, 147.

56. Kim Hopper, *Reckoning with Homelessness* (Ithaca: Cornell University Press, 2003), 45; Peter Rossi, *Without Shelter: Homelessness in the 1980s* (New York: Priority Press Publications, 1989), 13 and 19; Metraux, "Digging Up Vine Street In Search Of Old Skid Row." https://hiddencityphila.org/2017/04/digging-up-vine-street-in-search-of-old-skid-row/.

57. Harvey Siegal and James Inciardi, "The Demise of Skid Row," *Society* 19, no. 1 (1982): 39–45; Kusmer, *Down and Out*, 227; Bogue, *Skid Row*, 2; Metraux, "Waiting for the Wrecking Ball: Skid Row in Postindustrial Philadelphia."

58. Shapiro, *Communities of the Alone*, 39–42.

59. Bogue, *Skid Row*, 54–55; Hoch and Slayton, *New Homeless and Old*, 102 and 104.

60. Siegal and Inciardi, "The Demise of Skid Row," 39.

61. Conor Dougherty, *Golden Gates: The Fight for Housing—and Democracy—in America's Most Prosperous City* (New York: Penguin Press, 2020), 65; Ethan Rarick, *California Rising: The Life and Times of Pat Brown* (Berkeley: University of California Press, 2005), 398.

62. Siegal and Inciardi, "The Demise of Skid Row," 40; Hoch and Slayton, *New Homeless and Old*, chapter 6.

63. Bogue, *Skid Row*, 477 and 496. See, more generally, "Chapter 23 Conclusion: Skid Row can be Eliminated: Views of the Research Director."

64. Peter H. Rossi, "Troubling Families: Family Homelessness in America," *American Behavioral Scientist* 37, no. 3 (January 1994): 343–44; Marian Moser Jones, "Creating a Science of Homelessness During the Reagan Era," *The Milbank Quarterly* 93, no. 1 (2015): 145–46.

65. Bogue, *Skid Row*, 478.

66. Bahr, *Skid Row*, 37–38.

67. Dorothy Gazzolo, ed., "Skid Row Gives Renewalists Rough, Tough Relocation Problems," *Journal of Housing* 18 no. 8 (August–September 1961): 327–39; Ronald Vander Kooi, "The Main Stem: Skid Row Revisited," *Society* 10 (September–October 1973): 64–71; Richard M. Smith, "Skid Row: An Overview for Geographers," *Journal of Geography* 78, no. 1 (January 1979): 7–12; Meredith Minkler and Beverly Ovrebo, "SRO's: The Vanishing Hotels for Low-Income Elders," *Generations: Journal of the American Society on Aging* 9, no. 3 (Spring 1985): 40–42; US Senate, Special Committee on Aging, "Single Room Occupancy: A Need for National Concern," 1978; Lee, "The Disappearance of Skid Row: Some Ecological Evidence"; Metraux, "Waiting for the Wrecking Ball: Skid Row in Postindustrial Philadelphia"; Gary Kamiya, "Don't Call Them Bums: Hobos once Filled the South of Market," *San Francisco Chronicle*, July 26, 2019. https://www.sfchronicle.com/chronicle_vault/article/Don-t-call-them-bums-Hobos-once-filled-the-14185808.php?psid=9hkpU.

68. Paul Erling Groth, *Living Downtown: The History of Residential Hotels in the United States* (Berkeley: University of California Press, 1994), 282–83.

69. Gilda Haas and Allan David Heskin, "Community Struggles in Los Angeles," *International Journal of Urban and Regional Research* 5 no. 4 (December 1981): 555.

70. Shapiro, *Communities of the Alone*, "Appendix."

71. Howard, *Homeless*, chapter 4.

72. Brian J. Sullivan and Jonathan Burke, "Single-Room Occupancy Housing in New York City: The Origins and Dimensions of a Crisis," *CUNY Law Review* 17, no. 1 (Winter 2013): 122–23.

73. Brendan O'Flaherty, *Making Room: The Economics of Homelessness* (Cambridge: Harvard University Press, 1996), 175–77.

74. Jencks, *The Homeless*, 72–74.

75. John Tierney "Save the Flophouses," *New York Times*, January 14, 1996; David Isay, Stacy Abramson, and Harvey Wang, *Flophouse: Life on the Bowery* (New York: Random House, 2000), 74; O'Flaherty, *Making Room*, 188–90.

76. Estimates range as to exactly how many SRO units were lost due in part to difficulties defining precisely which buildings qualify as the kind of "single room occupancy hotels" that were housing people who would otherwise have been in shelters or on the streets. Some claim the figure tops one million while others believe one to two hundred thousand is a more realistic estimate. Desmond, *Evicted*, 394; Jencks, *The Homeless*, 61–64.

77. John M. Quigley and Steven Raphael, "Is Housing Unaffordable? Why Isn't It More Affordable?" *Journal of Economic Perspectives* 18, no. 1 (Winter 2004): 191–214.

78. Daniel P. Moynihan, *Maximum Feasible Misunderstanding: Community Action in the War on Poverty* (New York: The Free Press, 1969).

79. Hoch and Slayton, *New Homeless and Old*, 155.

80. Peter Speek, "The Psychology of Floating Workers," *Annals of the American Academy of Political and Social Science* 69 (January 1917): 50–57; Anderson, *The Hobo*, chapters 5 and 9.

81. Elizabeth Wickenden, "Reminiscences of the Program for Transients and Homeless in the Thirties," in *On Being Homeless: Historical Perspectives*, edited by Rick Beard (New York: Museum of the City of New York, 1987), 83.

82. Gerald N. Grob, *The Mad Among Us: A History of the Care of America's Mentally Ill* (New York: The Free Press, 1994), "Prologue."

83. Council of State Governments, "The Mental Health Programs of the Forty–Eight States: A Report to the Governors' Conference" (1950), 29.

84. Grob, *The Mad Among Us*, chapter 5.

85. Grob, *The Mad Among Us*, 116–24.

86. Grob, *The Mad Among Us*, chapter 7.

87. Gerald N. Grob, *From Asylum to Community: Mental Health Policy in Modern America* (Princeton: Princeton University Press, 1991), 8 and chapter 4.

88. Nellie Bly, *Ten Days in a Madhouse* (New York: Ian L. Munro, 1887); Albert Deutsch, *Shame of the States* (New York: Harcourt, Brace, 1948); Albert Q. Maisel, "Bedlam: Most US Mental Hospitals Are a Shame and a Disgrace," *Life*, May 6, 1946. Clifford W. Beers, *A Mind that Found Itself: An Autobiography* (New York: Longmans, Green, & Co., 1908).

89. Edward Shorter, *A History of Psychiatry: From the Era of the Asylum to the Age of Prozac* (New York: John Wiley & Sons, 1997), 65–68; Grob, *From Asylum to Community*, chapters 6 and 7.

90. Grob, *The Mad Among Us*, chapters 5 and 6.

91. Jeffrey L. Geller, "Defining the Meaning of 'in the Community,'" *Hospital and Community Psychiatry* 42, no. 12 (1991): 1197; Jeffrey L. Geller, "American 'Community' Psychiatry," *The Lancet Supplement* 356 (December 2000): 40.

92. Ann Braden Johnson, *Out of Bedlam: The Truth about Deinstitutionalization* (New York: Basic Books, 1990), xxii.

93. US Department of Housing and Urban Development, "HUD 2020 Continuum of Care Homeless Assistance Programs Homeless Populations and Subpopulations," December 15, 2020. https://files.hudexchange.info/reports/published/CoC_PopSub_Natl TerrDC_2020.pdf; National Association of State Mental Health Program Directors, "Trend in Psychiatric Inpatient Capacity, United States and Each State, 1970 to 2014," Assessment #10, August 2017, Table 1. https://www.nasmhpd.org/sites/default/files/TAC.Paper_.10 .Psychiatric Inpatient Capacity_Final.pdf.

94. Morton M. Hunt, *Mental Hospital* (New York: Pyramid Books, 1962); Susan Sheehan, *Is There No Place on Earth for Me?* (New York: Houghton Mifflin Harcourt, 1982), 10–11.

95. Grob, *The Mad Among Us*, 290.

96. Stephen Eide and Carolyn D. Gorman, "Medicaid's IMD Exclusion: The Case for Repeal" (Manhattan Institute for Policy Research, February 2021). https://media4.manhattan-institute.org/sites/default/files/medicaids-imd-exclusion-case-repeal-SE.pdf.

97. Edward D. Berkowitz and Larry DeWitt, *The Other Welfare: Supplemental Security Income and US Social Policy* (New York: Cornell University Press, 2013), 105.

98. National Association of State Mental Health Program Directors, "Trend in Psychiatric Inpatient Capacity, United States and Each State, 1970 to 2014," table 9. https://www .nasmhpd.org/sites/default/files/TAC.Paper_.10.Psychiatric Inpatient Capacity_Final.pdf.

99. Grob, *From Asylum to Community*, 260.

100. Johnson, *Out of Bedlam*, 130.

101. Grob, *The Mad Among Us*, 295.

102. Darold Treffert, "Dying with Their Rights On," *American Journal of Psychiatry* 130, no. 9 (September 1973): 1041; Steven P. Segal, Jim Baumohl, and Elsie Johnson, "Falling

through the Cracks: Mental Disorder and Social Margin in a Young Vagrant Population," *Social Problems* 24, no. 3 (February 1977): 387–400.

103. Robert L. Spitzer, George Cohen, J. David Miller, and Jean Endicott, "The Psychiatric Status of 100 Men on Skid Row," *The International Journal of Social Psychiatry* 15, no. 3 (Summer 1969): 230–34; Richard G. Frank and Sherry A. Glied, *Better but not Well: Mental Health Policy in the United States since 1950* (Baltimore: Johns Hopkins University Press, 2006), chapter 7 and table 7.6.

104. Berkowitz and DeWitt, *The Other Welfare*, 107.

105. Ted Houghton, "A Description and History of The New York/New York Agreement to House Homeless Mentally Ill Individuals," Corporation for Supportive Housing, May 2001; Rael Jean Isaac and Virginia C. Armat, *Madness in the Streets: How Psychiatry and the Law Abandoned the Mentally Ill* (New York: Free Press, 1990), 292–94; Shapiro, *Communities of the Alone*; Carol L. M. Caton, *The Open Door: Homelessness and Severe Mental Illness in the Era of Community Treatment* (New York: Oxford University Press, 2017), chapter 6.

106. Grob, *The Mad Among Us*, 262.

107. Grob, *From Asylum to Community*, chapter 10; E. Fuller Torrey, *Nowhere to Go: The Tragic Odyssey of the Homeless Mentally Ill* (New York: Harper & Row, 1988), chapters 5–7; Isaac and Aramt, *Madness in the Streets* chapters 3 and 4; Comptroller General of the United States, "Returning the Mentally Disabled to the Community: Government Needs to Do More," 1977, 73. https://www.gao.gov/assets/hrd-76-152.pdf.

108. Torey, *Nowhere to Go*, 164.

109. Frank and Glied, *Better but not Well*, chapter 4 and table 4.1.

110. D. J. Jaffe, *Insane Consequences: How the Mental Health Industry Fails the Mentally Ill* (Amherst, NY: Prometheus Books, 2017), chapter 14.

111. Jaffe, *Insane Consequences*, 147–48.

112. National Association of State Mental Health Program Directors, "Trend in Psychiatric Inpatient Capacity, United States and Each State, 1970 to 2014," table 9. https://www.nasmhpd .org/sites/default/files/TAC.Paper_.10.Psychiatric%20Inpatient%20Capacity_Final.pdf.

113. Bruns, *Knights of the Road*, 49–54.

114. Forrest W. Lacey, "Vagrancy and Other Crimes of Personal Condition," *Harvard Law Review* 66, no. 7 (May 1953): 1203–26.

115. Risa Goluboff, *Vagrant Nation: Police Power, Constitutional Change, and the Making of the 1960s* (New York: Oxford University Press, 2016), 84.

116. Mark Wyman, *Hoboes: Bindlestiffs, Fruit Tramps, and the Harvesting of the West* (New York: Hill and Wang, 2010), 39 and 265–66; George L. Kelling and Catherine M. Coles, *Fixing Broken Windows: Restoring Order and Reducing Crime in our Communities* (New York: Martin Kessler Books, 1996), 50–51; Kusmer, *Down and Out*, 53.

117. Bahr, *Skid Row*, 41–42.

118. Richard W. Etulian, "Introduction," in *Jack London on the Road: The Tramp Diary, and other Hobo Writing*s, edited by Richard W. Etulain (Logan: Utah State University Press, 1979), 4.

119. "Dirty days is der price," in "Whistling Dick's Christmas Stocking, in O. Henry, *Roads of Destiny*, 261; Bruns, *Knights of the Road*, 81; Kusmer, *Down and Out*, 54; Studs Terkel, *Hard Times: an Oral History of the Great Depression* (New York: The New Press, 2000 [orig. 1970]), 40–42; James P. Spradley, *You Owe Yourself a Drunk: An Ethnography of Urban Nomads* (Prospect Heights, Il: Waveland Press, 2000 [orig. 1970]), 26.

120. Kellor, *Out of Work*, 421–22.

121. Goluboff, *Vagrant Nation.*

122. Caleb Foote, "Vagrancy-Type Law and Its Administration," *University of Pennsylvania Law Review* 104, no. 5 (March 1956): 649.

123. Bahr, *Skid Row*, 228.

124. Robert C. Ellickson, "Controlling Chronic Misconduct in City Spaces: Of Panhandlers, Skid Rows, and Public-Space Zoning," *The Yale Law Journal* 105 (1996): 1208–9; Bogue, *Skid Row*, 62 and chapter 2.

125. Ellickson, "Controlling Chronic Misconduct in City Spaces: Of Panhandlers, Skid Rows, and Public-Space Zoning," 1201.

126. Egon Bittner, "The Police on Skid-Row: A Study of Peace Keeping," *American Sociological Review* 32, no. 5 (October 1967): 702 and 709; Bogue, *Skid Row*, 433–34.

127. Eric H. Monkkonnen, "Regional Dimensions of Tramping, North and South, 1880—1910," in *Walking to Work: Tramps in America, 1790–1935*, edited by Eric H. Monkonnen (Lincoln: University of Nebraska Press, 1984), 193.

128. Goluboff, *Vagrant Nation*, 73, 188, and 343.

129. Kusmer, *Down and Out*, 8.

130. "Although tramps and vagrants were considered deviants by many, it is my thesis that they were in fact the natural result of a virtually unregulated capitalist economy in transition from an agricultural system to an urban industrial one." Kenneth L. Kusmer, "The Underclass in Historical Perspective: Tramps and Vagrants in Urban America, 1870—1930," in *On Being Homeless: Historical Perspectives*, edited by Rick Beard (New York: Museum of the City of New York 1987), 21.

131. Bahr, *Skid Row*, 18; Caplow, "Transiency as a Cultural Pattern," 731.

132. Kusmer, *Down and Out*, 19, 47, and 176–77.

133. Benjamin Soskis, "Both More and No More: The Historical Split between Charity and Philanthropy," Hudson Institute October 2014. https://www.hudson.org/research/10723-both-more-and-no-more-the-historical-split-between-charity-and-philanthropy.

134. Bruns, *Knights of the Road*, 28.

135. Edmond Kelly, *The Elimination of the Tramp* (New York: G. P. Putnam's Sons, 1908).

136. Bruns, *Knights of the Road*, 131.

137. Hamlin Garland, *A Son of the Middle Border* (New York: The Macmillan Company, 1928), 174–75; Kusmer, *Down and Out*, 40–42, 57–58, and 110–11; Bruns, *Knights of the Road*, 48.

138. Kelling and Coles, *Fixing Broken Windows*, chapter 2.

139. Goluboff, *Vagrant Nation.*

140. Goluboff, *Vagrant Nation*, 228 and 324.

141. Douglas A. Harper, *Good Company* (Chicago: University of Chicago Press, 1982).

142. Bruns, *Knights of the Road*, 4–5.

143. Rossi, "Troubling families: family homelessness in America," 347–48.

144. James Burnham, *Suicide of the West: An Essay on the Meaning and Destiny of Liberalism* (New York: Encounter Books, 2014 [orig. 1964]), 110–13.

Chapter 4. The Modern Era (1980 to Present)

1. Mario M. Cuomo, "1984 Democratic National Convention Keynote Address," July 16, 1984, San Francisco, CA, https://www.americanrhetoric.com/speeches/mariocuomo1984dnc.htm.

2. Dennis McDougal, "Comic Relief will Give Aid to the Homeless in US," *Los Angeles Times*, January 15, 1986.

3. Kevin Fagan, "Ronald Reagan / 1911–2004 / Amid Tributes, Activists Lament Reagan's Failure on Homelessness," *San Francisco Chronicle*, June 10, 2004, https://www.sfchronicle.com/politics/article/RONALD-REAGAN-1911-2004-Amid-tributes-2750499.php#photo-2188953; Myles Miller, "A Christmas Day Vigil in Grand Central Remembers the Plights of the Homeless," ny1.com, December 25, 2018, https://www.ny1.com/nyc/all-boroughs/news/2018/12/25/the-doe-fund-honors-mamma-doe-homeless-people-struggling-in-nyc-grand-central-vigil; Ed Leibowitz, "Reinventing Skid Row," *Politico*, March 5, 2014, https://www.politico.com/magazine/story/2014/03/los-angeles-skid-row-reinvention-104266/.

4. Eric Hobsbawm, *The Age of Extremes: A History of the World, 1914–1991* (New York: Pantheon Books, 1994), 10, 337, and 406.

5. David T. Ellwood, *Poor Support: Poverty in the American Family* (New York: Basic Books, 1988), 4 and 41.

6. US Senate, Special Committee on Aging. "Single Room Occupancy: A Need for National Concern," 1978.

7. Robert Rector and Vijay Menon, "Understanding the Hidden $1.1 Trillion Welfare System and How to Reform It," Heritage Foundation, April 5, 2018, https://www.heritage.org/sites/default/files/2018-04/BG3294.pdf; Scott W. Allard, *Out of Reach: Place, Poverty, and the New American Welfare State* (New Haven, CT: Yale University Press, 2009), 88–89.

8. US Department of Health and Human Services, "Welfare Indicators and Risk Factors Nineteenth Report to Congress 2020," February 8, 2021, table 7, https://aspe.hhs.gov/sites/default/files/private/pdf/265031/welfare-indicators-and-risk-factors-19th-report.pdf.

9. US Department of Health and Human Services, "Welfare Indicators and Risk Factors Nineteenth Report to Congress 2020," table 10, indicator 3, https://aspe.hhs.gov/sites/default/files/private/pdf/265031/welfare-indicators-and-risk-factors-19th-report.pdf.

10. Figure 4.1's data are drawn from table 16 in Maggie McCarty, Katie Jones, and Libby Perl, "Overview of Federal Housing Assistance Programs and Policy," Congressional Research Service, March 27, 2019, https://crsreports.congress.gov/product/pdf/RL/RL34591; For another source that documents reliance on housing assistance over recent decades, see Council of Economic Advisers, "Expanding Work Requirements in Non-Cash Welfare Programs," July 2018, figures 2a and 2b, https://trumpwhitehouse.archives.gov/wp-content/uploads/2018/07/Expanding-Work-Requirements-in-Non-Cash-Welfare-Programs.pdf.

11. Nathan Heller, "A Window onto an American Nightmare," *New Yorker*, June 1, 2020, https://www.newyorker.com/magazine/2020/06/01/a-window-onto-an-american-nightmare.

12. Brian Goldstone, "The New American Homeless," *New Republic*, August 21, 2019, https://newrepublic.com/article/154618/new-american-homeless-housing-insecurity-richest-cities.

13. Alex F. Schwartz, *Housing Policy in the United States*, fourth edition (New York: Routledge, 2021) Kindle Edition, chapter 2, esp. figure 2.10; Christopher Jencks, *The Homeless* (Cambridge: Harvard University Press, 1994), chapter 9; William Tucker, *The Excluded Americans: Homelessness and Housing Policies* (Washington, DC: Regnery Gateway 1990), chapter 1.

14. New York City Commission on the Homeless, "The Way Home: A New Direction in Social Policy," February 1992, chapter 4; Marian Moser Jones, "Creating a Science of Homelessness During the Reagan Era," *The Milbank Quarterly* 93, no. 1 (2015): 166.

15. Schwartz, *Housing Policy in the United States*, 7 and 118; Joint Committee on Taxation, "Estimates of Federal Tax Expenditures for Fiscal Years 2020–2024," November 5, 2020, https://www.jct.gov/publications/2020/jcx-23-20/.

16. David S. Lucas, "The Impact of Federal Homelessness Funding on Homelessness," *Southern Economic Journal* 84, no. 2 (October 2017): 548–76.

17. Gwenda Blair, "Saint Mitch," *Esquire*, December 1, 1986, https://classic.esquire.com/article/1986/12/1/saint-mitch.

18. Victoria Rader, *Signal Through the Flames: Mitch Snyder and America's Homeless* (Kansas City, MO: Sheed & Ward, 1986), 42.

19. Blair, "Saint Mitch."

20. Blair, "Saint Mitch"; Rader, *Signal Through the Flames*, 130–32 and 150.

21. Cynthia J. Bogard, *Seasons Such as These: How Homelessness Took Shape in America* (New York: Aldine de Gruyter, 2003), 51–52; Rader, *Signal Through the Flames*, 161–67.

22. "Presidential Debate in Winston-Salem, North Carolina," September 25, 1988, transcript at https://www.presidency.ucsb.edu/documents/presidential-debate-winston-salem-north-carolina.

23. Martin Wooster, "The Homeless Issue: An Adman's Dream," *Reason*, July 1987, https://reason.com/1987/07/01/the-homeless-issue-an-admans-d/?print=.

24. Richard W. White Jr., *Rude Awakenings: What the Homeless Crisis Tells Us* (San Francisco: ICS Press, 1992), 3.

25. US Department of Housing and Urban Development, "A Report to the Secretary on the Homeless and Emergency Shelters," April 23, 1984, 18.

26. US Congress, "Joint Hearing Before the Subcommittee on Housing and Community Development of the Committee on Banking, Finance and Urban Affairs and the Subcommittee on Manpower and Housing of the Committee on Government Operations, House of Representatives, Ninety-Eight Congress, Second Session, May 24, 1984," 2, 7, and 9.

27. US Congress, "Joint Hearing Before the Subcommittee on Housing and Community Development of the Committee on Banking, Finance and Urban Affairs and the Subcommittee on Manpower and Housing of the Committee on Government Operations, House of Representatives, Ninety-Eight Congress, Second Session, May 24, 1984," 32.

28. US Congress, "Problems in Urban Centers: Oversight Hearings Before Committee on the District of Columbia, House of Representatives, Ninety-Sixth Congress, Second Session on Problems in Urban Centers, Washington, DC, and the Federal Government Role, June 25, 26, 27, July 23, 24, 30, and September 30, 1980," 638.

29. Tucker, *The Excluded Americans*, 35.

30. Could the confusion be chalked up to the difference between an annualized estimate of how many experienced homelessness over the course of a year versus how many were homeless at a given time? An estimate of two to three million homeless people on an annualized basis would be in the ballpark of our more accurate twenty-first-century figures. But an annualized figure is a more complicated concept to explain. It requires more qualifications. Probably, when most Americans heard two to three million, they assumed that that meant the number of homeless people at the time the statement was made. The 1984 HUD estimate was definitely a point-in-time estimate. The CCNV estimate, when repeated in the press, was typically expressed as a point-in-time estimate ("'Desperate situation' for two million across winter, reported USA Today in late 1982 Carol Stevens, "Families: New Breed of Street People," *USA Today*, December 15, 1982) "there may be as many as 2.5 million citizens without a place to live, homeless for the holidays," Rone Tempest, "Millions Hit Bottom in the Streets," *Los*

Angeles Times, December 26, 1982) and that also is how Snyder himself represented it. See, for example, this December 1982 statement of his before Congress: "Between 2 million and 3 million Americans right now are down and out; they are criss-crossing this country looking for work, begging for jobs. They are living in their cars and tents. They are living in abandoned buildings (US Congress, "Homelessness in America: Hearing Before the Subcommittee on Housing and Community Development of the Committee on Banking, Finance, and Urban Affairs, House of Representatives, Ninety-seventh Congress, Second Session, December 15, 1982," 16–17; Rader, *Signal Through the Flames*, viii and 144.

31. White, *Rude Awakenings*, chapter 1.

32. Mel Martinez, "Taking on the Problem That 'Cannot Be Solved,'" US Department of Housing and Urban Development, Secretary [Mel] Martinez's Speeches and Testimony, July 20, 2001, https://archives.hud.gov/remarks/martinez/speeches/homelessness.cfm.

33. National Alliance to End Homelessness, "A Plan, Not a Dream: How to End Homelessness in Ten Years," 2000, https://b.3cdn.net/naeh/b970364c18809d1e0c_aum6bnzb4.pdf.

34. Ester Fuchs and William McAllister, "The Continuum of Care: A Report on the New Federal Policy to Address Homelessness," US Department of Housing and Urban Development, December 1996.

35. Thomas J. Main, *Homelessness in New York City: Policymaking from Koch to de Blasio* (New York: New York University Press, 2017), 144–47; Douglas McGray, "The Abolitionist," *The Atlantic*, June 2004, https://www.theatlantic.com/magazine/archive/2004/06/the-abolitionist/302969/; Libby Perl, et al., "Homelessness: Targeted Federal Programs," Congressional Research Service, October 18, 2018, 21–23, https://sgp.fas.org/crs/misc/RL30442.pdf; US Interagency Council on Homelessness, "US Interagency Council on Homelessness Historical Overview," December 2016, https://www.usich.gov/resources/uploads/asset_library/USICH_History_2016.pdf.

36. US Department of Health and Human Services, Substance Abuse and Mental Health Services Administration, "A Treatment Improvement Protocol: Behavioral Health Services for People Who Are Homeless (TIP 55)," 2013, 15, https://store.samhsa.gov/sites/default/files/d7/priv/sma13-4734.pdf; For an example, see Bring LA Home Blue Ribbon Panel, "Bring Los Angeles Home: The Campaign to End Homelessness," 2006.

37. Jonathan Kozol, *Rachel and her Children: Homeless Families in America* (New York: Crown, 1988), 18.

38. US Department of Housing and Urban Development, "HUD 2020 Continuum of Care Homeless Assistance Programs Homeless Populations and Subpopulations," December 15, 2020, https://files.hudexchange.info/reports/published/CoC_PopSub_Natl-TerrDC_2020.pdf; US Department of Housing and Urban Development, "HUD 2020 Continuum of Care Homeless Assistance Programs Homeless Populations and Subpopulations, NY-600 New York City CoC," December 15, 2020, https://files.hudexchange.info/reports/published/CoC_PopSub_CoC_NY-600-2020_NY_2020.pdf.

39. Kusmer, *Down and Out*, 240; Kozol, *Rachel and her Children*, 6–11.

40. "New York City Mayor Gets Worst Grades on Corruption, Quinnipiac University Poll Finds; 96% Say Homelessness Is Serious Problem," Quinnipiac University, March 1, 2017, https://poll.qu.edu/poll-results/; Benjamin Oreskes, Doug Smith, and David Lauter, "95% of Voters Say Homelessness is LA's Biggest Problem, Times Poll Finds. 'You Can't Escape It,'" *Los Angeles Times*, November 14, 2019, https://www.latimes.com/california/story/2019-11-14/homeless-housing-poll-opinion; San Francisco Chamber of Commerce, "Public Safety, Homelessness and Affordability Are Biggest Issues in 2018 SF Chamber Poll," Press Release,

February 2, 2018; "Across the Entire State, WA Voters Rank Homelessness as the No. 1 Issue Lawmakers Must Address," crosscut.com, January 9, 2020, https://crosscut.com/2020/01 /across-entire-state-wa-voters-rank-homelessness-no-1-issue-lawmakers-must-address; Public Policy Institute of California, "Californians & Their Government: PPIC Statewide Survey," October 2020. https://www.ppic.org/wp-content/uploads/ppic-statewide-survey-californians -and-their-government-october-2020.pdf.

41. Dennis Culhane, Dan Treglia, Ken Steif, Randall Kuhn, and Thomas Byrne, "Estimated Emergency and Observational/Quarantine Capacity Need for the US Homeless Population Related to COVID-19 Exposure by County; Projected Hospitalizations, Intensive Care Units and Mortality," March 27, 2020, 6. https://endhomelessness.org/wp-content /uploads/2020/03/COVID-paper_clean-636pm.pdf.

42. "Congressional Leaders Agree to Coronavirus Response Package with Funding for Homelessness and Housing," National Low-Income Housing Coalition, March 25, 2020, https://nlihc.org/resource/congressional-leaders-agree-coronavirus-response-package-funding -homelessness-and-housing; "President Biden Signs American Rescue Plan Act with Nearly $50 Billion in Housing and Homelessness Assistance," National Low-Income Housing Coalition, March 15, 2021, https://nlihc.org/resource/president-biden-signs-american-rescue-plan -act-nearly-50-billion-housing-and-homelessness.

Chapter 5. Harm Reduction and Ending Homelessness

1. US Department of Housing and Urban Development, "HUD 2020 Continuum of Care Homeless Assistance Programs Homeless Populations and Subpopulations," December 15, 2020, https://files.hudexchange.info/reports/published/CoC_PopSub_NatlTerrDC _2020.pdf.

2. US Department of Housing and Urban Development, "The 2018 Annual Homeless Assessment Report (AHAR) to Congress; Part 2: Estimates of Homelessness in the United States," September 2020, https://www.huduser.gov/portal/sites/default/files/pdf/2018 -AHAR-Part-2.pdf.

3. National Center for Homeless Education, "Federal Data Summary, School Years 2015–2016 Through 2017–2018, Education for Homeless Children and Youth," January 2020, https://nche.ed.gov/wp-content/uploads/2020/01/Federal-Data-Summary-SY-15.16 -to-17.18-Published-1.30.2020.pdf.

4. Perl, et al., "Homelessness: Targeted Federal Programs," https://sgp.fas.org/crs/misc /RL30442.pdf.

5. New York City Comptroller, "FY 2022 Agency Watch List: Homeless Services Provider Agencies," March 2021, 2, https://comptroller.nyc.gov/wp-content/uploads/docu ments/Watch_List_Homeless_Services.pdf; Kevin Fagan, "Newsom Talks Homeless Policy at Encampment Sweep in Mission," *San Francisco Chronicle*, August 21, 2021, https:// www.sfchronicle.com/politics/article/Newsom-grabs-a-broom-and-talks-homeless-policy -at-16417072.php.

6. Due to the decentralized nature of service systems, and twists and turns in the debate over the years, it is hard to be precise when describing different models of housing for the homeless. "Supported housing" used to mean private rental apartments leased by a service provider on behalf of a client. The subsidy was "tenant-based" and though services were made available 24/7, they were based offsite so as to avoid any "institutional" dimension to the

housing. Now, that model is more typically called "scatter-site" supportive housing. Originally, "supportive housing" was the project-based mode of subsidized housing for the chronic homeless—custom-built affordable housing for the homeless that offers 24/7 services onsite. Project-based supportive housing is now sometimes called "congregate," though, unlike in dorm-style shelters, people have their own private rooms. Transitional housing is "supportive," in the sense that it's housing with services, but it's time-limited. "Supportive housing" is understood to be non-time-limited subsidized housing. Higher quality "shelter" programs that serve families and provide them with private accommodations are more like transitional housing programs but they're still called "shelter." For discussions that parse the differences between shelters and transitional housing, see Peter H. Rossi, "The American Homeless Family Shelter 'System,'" *Social Service Review* 69, no. 1 (March 1995): 86–107; US Interagency Council on Homelessness, "Homelessness: Programs and the People They Serve: Findings of the National Survey of Homeless Assistance Providers and Clients," September 1999, chapter 14; on permanent supportive housing models, see Carol L. M. Caton, *The Open Door: Homelessness and Severe Mental Illness in the Era of Community Treatment* (New York: Oxford University Press, 2017), chapter 6.

7. For more on charities' contribution, past and present, see US Interagency Council on Homelessness, "Homelessness: Programs and the People They Serve: Findings of the National Survey of Homeless Assistance Providers and Clients," September 1999, chapter 14, https://www.huduser.gov/portal/publications/homeless/homeless_tech.html; and Byron Johnson, William H. Wubbenhorst, and Alfreda Alvarez, "Assessing the Faith-Based Response to Homelessness in America: Findings from Eleven Cities," Program on Prosocial Behavior, Baylor Institute for Studies of Religion, February 1, 2017, http://www.baylorisr.org/wp-content/uploads/ISR-Homeless-FINAL-01092017-web.pdf.

8. See Citygate Network website, "About," https://www.citygatenetwork.org/agrm/Citygate_Network_About.asp; The Catholic Worker Movement website, "Directory," https://www.catholicworker.org/communities/directory-picker.html; Jason Storbakken, *Bowery Mission: Grit and Grace on Manhattan's Oldest Street* (Walden: Plough Publishing House, 2019).

9. US Interagency Council on Homelessness, "Homelessness: Programs and the People They Serve: Findings of the National Survey of Homeless Assistance Providers and Clients," chapter 14, https://www.huduser.gov/portal/publications/homeless/homeless_tech.html.

10. Martha Burt, et al., "Homelessness: Programs and the People They Serve: Findings of the National Survey of Homeless Assistance Providers and Clients, Summary Report," Urban Institute, December 1999, https://www.urban.org/sites/default/files/publication/66286/310291-Homelessness-Programs-and-the-People-They-Serve-Findings-of-the-National-Survey-of-Homeless-Assistance-Providers-and-Clients.PDF.

11. Heather Knight, "A View of Progress," *San Francisco Chronicle*, June 28, 2018, https://www.sfchronicle.com/news/article/SF-homelessness-chief-Thrilled-with-13031080.php.

12. Joe Anuta and David Giambusso, "Newark Mayor Sues Progressive Ally de Blasio for Exporting Homeless," *Politico*, December 2, 2019, https://www.politico.com/states/new-york/albany/story/2019/12/02/newark-mayor-sues-progressive-ally-de-blasio-for-exporting-homeless-1230258.

13. Elijah Chiland, "Councilmembers Say Other Cities Sending Homeless Residents to LA," *Curbed*, June 5, 2019, https://la.curbed.com/2019/6/5/18654438/homelessness-los-angeles-other-cities-enforcement.

14. Juan Williams, "Homeless Choose to Be, Reagan Says," *Washington Post*, February 1, 1984, https://www.washingtonpost.com/archive/politics/1984/02/01/homeless-choose-to-be -reagan-says/781996b6-ab3b-499b-96ea-38155d1c5127/.

15. Mosi Secret, "Clock Ticks for a Key Homeless Program," *New York Times*, May 31, 2011, https://www.nytimes.com/2011/06/01/nyregion/new-york-city-close-to-ending-key -housing-program.html.

16. Linda Weinreb and Peter H. Rossi, "The American Homeless Family Shelter 'System,'" *Social Service Review* 69, no. 1 (March 1995): 86–107; Nancy K. Kaufman, "State Government's Response to Homelessness: The Massachusetts Experience, 1983–1990," *New England Journal of Public Policy* 8, no. 1 (1992): 471–82.

17. US Department of Housing and Urban Development, "The 1988 National Survey of Shelters for the Homeless," March 1989, exhibit 1, https://www.huduser.gov/portal /Publications/pdf/HUD–5356.pdf.

18. US Interagency Council on Homelessness, "Homelessness: Programs and the People They Serve: Findings of the National Survey of Homeless Assistance Providers and Clients," September 1999, chapter 14, https://www.huduser.gov/portal/publications/home less/homeless_tech.html.

19. Maria Foscarinis, "Beyond Homelessness," *Saint Louis University Public Law Review* 12, no. 1 (1993): 48–50 and 56–7.

20. Stefan G. Kertesz, et al., "Housing First for Homeless Persons with Active Addiction: Are We Overreaching?" *The Milbank Quarterly* 87, no. 2 (June 2009): 495–534, https://www .ncbi.nlm.nih.gov/pmc/articles/PMC2881444/.

21. US Interagency Council on Homelessness, "Priority: Home! The Federal Plan to Break the Cycle of Homelessness," 1994, 73–75 (digitized by Google), https://books .google.com/books?id=eSfC-UbC-yoC&printsec=frontcover&source=gbs_ge_summary_r &cad=0#v=onepage&q&f=false; US Department of Housing and Urban Development, "Notice of Funding Availability for Continuum of Care Homeless Assistance; Funding Availability," Federal Register 61, no. 52 (March 15, 1996): 10866–77, https://www.govinfo .gov/content/pkg/FR-1996-03-15/pdf/96-6396.pdf.

22. US Interagency Council on Homelessness, "Priority: Home! The Federal Plan to Break the Cycle of Homelessness," iii.

23. Shannon E. Couzens, "Priority: Home! A True Priority? An Analysis of the Federal Plan to Break the Cycle of Homelessness," *Journal of Social Distress and the Homeless* 6, no. 4 (1997): 275–82.

24. New York City Commission on the Homeless, "The Way Home: A New Direction in Social Policy," February 1992, 13, 32, 39–41, 55, and 59; Thomas J. Main, *Homelessness in New York City: Policymaking from Koch to de Blasio* (New York: New York University Press, 2017), chapter 3; US Interagency Council on Homelessness, "Priority: Home!" 20–21, 37, 55–56, 94–96, and 111–13; Marvin Olasky, *The Tragedy of American Compassion* (Wheaton, IL: Crossway Books, 2008 [orig. 1992]), 210; Peter H. Rossi "The American Homeless Family Shelter 'System,'" *Social Service Review* 69, no. 1 (March, 1995): 86–107; Alice S. Baum and Donald W. Burnes, *A Nation in Denial: The Truth about Homelessness* (Boulder, CO: Westview Press, 1993), chapter 8.

25. Rael Jean Isaac and Virginia C. Armat, *Madness in the Streets: How Psychiatry and the Law Abandoned the Mentally Ill* (New York: Free Press, 1990).

26. President John F. Kennedy, "Special Message to the Congress on Mental Illness and Mental Retardation," February 5, 1963, https://www.presidency.ucsb.edu/documents/special-message-the-congress-mental-illness-and-mental-retardation.

27. Jack Tsai, Alvin S. Mares, and Robert A. Rosenheck, "A Multi-Site Comparison of Supported Housing for Chronically Homeless Adults: 'Housing First' Versus 'Residential Treatment First,'" *Psychological Services* 7, no. 4 (November 2010), 220.

28. "Most [Linear Residential Treatment] housing providers regard themselves as treatment providers rather than as landlords," Sam Tsemberis. "From Streets to Homes: An Innovative Approach to Supported Housing for Homeless Adults with Psychiatric Disabilities," *Journal of Community Psychology* 27, no. 2 (March 1999), 227; "The residential program is seen as primarily a clinical modality designed to treat mentally ill individuals rather than a home for those who live there." Priscilla Ridgway and Anthony M. Zipple, "The Paradigm Shift in Residential Services: From the Linear Continuum to Supported Housing Approaches," *Psychosocial Rehabilitation Journal* 13, no. 4 (April 1990): 17; "Practitioners' goals for project-based transitional housing . . . extend beyond housing stability to adult well-being and aspects of family self-sufficiency." Daniel Gubits, et al., "Family Options Study: Short-Term Impacts of Housing and Services Interventions for Homeless Families," US Department of Housing and Urban Development, Office of Policy Development and Research, July 2015, xxi, https://www.huduser.gov/portal/sites/default/files/pdf/FamilyOptionsStudy_final.pdf.

29. Main, *Homelessness in New York City*, 60.

30. Sam Tsemberis and Sara Asmussen, "From Streets to Homes: The Pathways to Housing Consumer Preference Supported Housing Model," *Alcoholism Treatment Quarterly* 17, nos. 1–2 (1999): 113–14 and 127.

31. Deborah Padgett, Benjamin Henwood, and Sam Tsemberis, *Housing First: Ending Homelessness, Transforming Systems, and Changing Lives* (New York: Oxford University Press, 2015).

32. Batko Samantha, et al., "Open Letter to Secretary Ben Carson, Joe Grogan and Robert Marbut," March 18, 2020, https://endhomelessness.org/wp-content/uploads/2020/03/Homelessness-Researcher-Letter.pdf.

33. Sara K. Rankin, "Punishing Homelessness." *New Criminal Law Review: An International and Interdisciplinary Journal* 22, no. 1 (Winter 2019), 131; Sam Tsemberis, Leyla Gulcur, and Maria Nakae, "Housing First, Consumer Choice, and Harm Reduction for Homeless Individuals with a Dual Diagnosis," *American Journal of Public Health* 94, no. 4 (May 2004): 652 and 655; National Alliance to End Homelessness, Fact Sheet, April 2016, http://endhomelessness.org/wp-content/uploads/2016/04/housing-first-fact-sheet.pdf; Gubits, "Family Options Study: 3-Year Impacts of Housing and Services Interventions for Homeless Families," xx and 101, https://www.huduser.gov/portal/sites/default/files/pdf/Family-Options-Study-Full-Report.pdf; US Interagency Council on Homelessness, "The Evidence Behind Approaches that Drive an End to Homelessness," September 2019, 4, https://www.usich.gov/resources/uploads/asset_library/Evidence-Behind-Approaches-That-End-Homelessness-Brief-2019.pdf; US Interagency Council on Homelessness, "Home, Together: The Federal Strategic Plan to Prevent and End Homelessness," July 2018, 23, https://www.usich.gov/resources/uploads/asset_library/Home-Together-Federal-Strategic-Plan-to-Prevent-and-End-Homelessness.pdf; National Academies, "Permanent Supportive Housing," 4, 13, 41, and 50; US Department of Housing and Urban Development, "Fiscal Year 2020 Annual Performance Report," January 15, 2021, 8, https://www.hud.gov/sites/dfiles/CFO/documents/HUD_FY20_Annual_Performance_Report_1-15-21.pdf.

34. Richard Cho, "Four Clarifications About Housing First," usich.gov, June 18, 2014, https://www.usich.gov/news/four-clarifications-about-housing-first; Ted Houghton, "A Description and History of The New York/New York Agreement to House Homeless Mentally Ill Individuals," Corporation for Supportive Housing, May 2001.

35. California Senate Bill No. 1380, Chapter 847, September 29, 2016, https://leginfo.legislature.ca.gov/faces/billNavClient.xhtml?bill_id=201520160SB1380.

36. Community Housing Innovations, Executive Director's Message, 2017–2018 Annual Report, http://www.communityhousing.org/wp-content/uploads/2018/08/CHI-2017-18-Annual-Report-FINAL-1.pdf.

37. "New Priority Means Fewer Beds in City Shelters," Editorial, *New York Times*, May 17, 2016; Laura Nahimas, "HUD Slashes Funding for Some New York City Homeless Shelters," *Politico*, May 9, 2016, https://www.politico.com/states/new-york/city-hall/story/2016/05/hud-slashes-funding-for-some-new-york-city-homeless-shelters-101531.

38. US Department of Housing and Urban Development, "Letter to The Honorable Darrell Issa." August 9, 2017; Mitch Perry, "Ted Yoho Urges Ben Carson to Reverse Obama-Era 'Housing First,' Reinstate Homeless Shelter Funds," floridapolitics.com, June 19, 2017, https://floridapolitics.com/archives/240348-ted-yoho-calls-ben-carson-revise-hud-housing-first-approach-homelessness/; Johnson, Wubbenhorst, and Alvarez, "Assessing the Faith-Based Response to Homelessness in America: Findings from Eleven Cities."

39. National Alliance to End Homelessness, et al., "Letter to Reps. Collins, Price, Reed, and Diaz-Balart," December 3, 2019, https://cdn.theatlantic.com/assets/media/files/los_for_2018_coc_nofa_in_thud_appropriations.pdf; Kriston Capps, "Trump's Plan to Criminalize Homelessness Is Taking Shape," CityLab, December 17, 2019, https://www.bloomberg.com/news/articles/2019-12-17/how-trump-is-criminalizing-homelessness; US Congress, 116th Congress of the United States, "Further Consolidated Appropriations Act, 2020," (HR 1865), 458, https://www.congress.gov/116/bills/hr1865/BILLS-116hr1865enr.pdf.

40. "The Biden Plan for Investing in Our Communities through Housing," Joe Biden website, https://joebiden.com/housing/.

41. Douglas McGray, "The Abolitionist," *The Atlantic*, June 2004, https://www.theatlantic.com/magazine/archive/2004/06/the-abolitionist/302969/.

42. Source: author calculation based on data derived from HUD's Continuum of Care program: https://www.hudexchange.info/resource/3031/pit-and-hic-data-since-2007/.

43. Council of Economic Advisers, "The State of Homelessness in America," September 2019, 26–29.

44. Cho, "'Four Clarifications About Housing First'; US Interagency Council on Homelessness, 'Deploy Housing First Systemwide,'" August 15, 2018, https://www.usich.gov/solutions/housing/housing-first/; Padgett, Henwood, and Tsemberis, *Housing First*, 2015; US Interagency Council on Homelessness, "The Evidence Behind Approaches that Drive an End to Homelessness," September 2019, 4, https://www.usich.gov/resources/uploads/asset_library/Evidence-Behind-Approaches-That-End-Homelessness-Brief-2019.pdf.

45. Sam Tsemberis, Douglas Kent, and Christy Respress, "Housing Stability and Recovery Among Chronically Homeless Persons with Co-Occurring Disorders in Washington, DC," *American Journal of Public Health* 102, no. 1 (January 2012): 13–16, is an example of a study that looks at number of people still housed at the end of the study; Robert Rosenheck, et al., "Cost-Effectiveness of Supported Housing for Homeless Persons with Mental Illnes," *Archives*

of General Psychiatry 60, no. 9 (September 2003): 940–51, is an example of a study that uses "days housed" measure; see also National Academies, Permanent Supportive Housing, 40, 41, 49, 68, and 84–85.

46. Angela Ly and Eric Latimer, "Housing First Impact on Costs and Associated Costs Offsets: A Review of the Literature," *Canadian Journal of Psychiatry* 60, no. 11 (November 2015): 475–87, https://www.ncbi.nlm.nih.gov/pmc/articles/PMC4679128/; Stefan G. Kertesz and Guy Johnson, "Housing First: Lessons from the United States and Challenges for Australia," *Australian Economic Review* 50, no. 2 (May 2017): 220–28.

47. Surveys of this literature may be found in Padgett, Henwood, and Tsemberis, *Housing First*; Brendan O'Flaherty, "Homelessness Research: A Guide for Economists (and Friends)," *Journal of Housing Economics* 44 (2019): 1–25; Kertesz and Johnson, "Housing First: Lessons from the United States and Challenges for Australia."

48. Jill S. Roncarati, et al., "Housing Boston's Chronically Homeless Unsheltered Population 14 Years Later." *Medical Care* 59 (April 2021): S170–S174.

49. Michael Hobbes, "Why America Can't Solve Homelessness," Huffpost.com, May 15, 2019; Matthew Doherty, "What I Learned About Housing First from Lloyd Pendleton," end homelessness.org, May 6, 2019, https://endhomelessness.org/what-i-learned-about-housing -first-from-lloyd-pendleton/.

50. Kevin C. Corinth, "On Utah's 91% Decrease in Chronic Homelessness," American Enterprise Institute, March 2016, https://www.aei.org/wp-content/uploads/2016/03/Utah -Homelessness.pdf.

51. Thomas Byrne, Jamison D. Fargo, Ann Elizabeth Montgomery, Ellen Munley and Dennis P. Culhane, "The Relationship Between Community Investment in Permanent Supportive Housing and Chronic Homelessness," *Social Service Review* 88, no. 2 (June 2014): 234–63; Kevin Corinth, "The Impact of Permanent Supportive Housing on Homeless Populations," *Journal of Housing Economics* 35 (March 2017): 69–84.

52. Barbara Duffield, "Are We Creating Chronic Homelessness? The Past, Present, and Future of Federal Homelessness Policy," Institute for Children, Poverty, and Homelessness, October 2016, 3, https://www.icphusa.org/reports/are-we-creating-chronic-homelessness-the -past-present-and-future-of-federal-homelessness-policy/.

53. US Interagency Council on Homelessness, "What Does Ending Homelessness Mean?" June 4, 2018, https://www.usich.gov/goals/what-does-ending-homelessness-mean/.

54. Stephen Eide, "Housing First and Homelessness: The Rhetoric and the Reality," Manhattan Institute for Policy Research, April 2020, Figure 6, https://media4.manhattan -institute.org/sites/default/files/housing-first-and-homelessness-SE.pdf.

55. Malcolm Gladwell, "Million-Dollar Murray," *New Yorker*, February 5, 2006, https:// www.newyorker.com/magazine/2006/02/13/million-dollar-murray.

56. Issa Kohler-Hausmann, *Misdemeanorland: Criminal Courts and Social Control in an Age of Broken Windows Policing* (Princeton: Princeton University Press, 2018); Gale Holland and Christine Zhang, "Huge Increase in Arrests of Homeless in LA—But Mostly for Minor Offenses," *Los Angeles Times*, February 4, 2018, https://www.latimes.com/local/politics/la-me -homeless-arrests-20180204-story.html.

57. Maria C. Raven, Matthew J. Niedzwiecki and Margot Kushel, "A Randomized Trial of Permanent Supportive Housing for Chronically Homeless Persons with High Use of Publicly Funded Services," *Health Services Research* 55, no. S2 (October 2020): 797–806, https://on linelibrary.wiley.com/doi/full/10.1111/1475-6773.13553.

58. New York City Comptroller, "NYC Department of Correction FYs 2009–19 Operating Expenditures, Jail Population, Cost Per Incarcerated Person, Staffing Ratios, Performance Measure Outcomes, and Overtime," December 6, 2019, https://comptroller.nyc.gov/reports /nyc-department-of-correction/.

59. National Association of State Mental Health Program Directors, "Trend in Psychiatric Inpatient Capacity, United States and Each State, 1970 to 2014," Assessment #10, August 2017, 11, https://www.nasmhpd.org/sites/default/files/TAC.Paper_.10.Psychiatric Inpatient Capacity_Final.pdf.

60. US Department of Housing and Urban Development, "HUD 2020 Continuum of Care Homeless Assistance Programs Homeless Populations and Subpopulations," December 15, 2020, https://files.hudexchange.info/reports/published/CoC_PopSub_Natl TerrDC_2020.pdf.

61. Angela J. Beck, Cory Page, Jessica Buche, Danielle Rittman, and Maria Gaiser, "Estimating the Distribution of the US Psychiatric Subspecialist Workforce," University of Michigan School of Public Health Workforce Research Center, December 2018, https:// behavioralhealthworkforce.org/wp-content/uploads/2019/02/Y3-FA2-P2-Psych-Sub_Full -Report-FINAL2.19.2019.pdf.

62. Travis P. Baggett, et al., "Mortality Among Homeless Adults in Boston: Shifts in Causes of Death Over a 15–Year Period," *JAMA Internal Medicine* 173, no. 3 (February 2013): 189–95, https://www.ncbi.nlm.nih.gov/pmc/articles/PMC3713619/.

63. Wei Sun, Anthony Webb, and Natalia Zhivan, "Does Staying Healthy Reduce Your Lifetime Health Care Costs?" Center for Retirement Research at Boston College, May 2010, https://crr.bc.edu/wp-content/uploads/2010/05/IB_10-8.pdf.

64. National Academies, "Permanent Supportive Housing," 4; Kertesz and Johnson, "Housing First: Lessons from the United States and Challenges for Australia," at 223: "Randomised trials have typically found no or minimal benefit for standard health measures."

65. Peter Cove, *Poor No More: Rethinking Dependency and the War on Poverty* (New York: Routledge 2017), chapters 4 and 6.

66. Joshua Bamberger, "Reducing Homelessness by Embracing Housing as a Medicaid Benefit," *JAMA Internal Medicine* 176, no. 8 (August 2016): 1051–52.

67. Kertesz and Johnson, "Housing First: Lessons from the United States and Challenges for Australia."

68. Council of Economic Advisers, "The State of Homelessness in America," September 2019, 24.

69. National Academies of Sciences, Engineering, and Medicine, "Permanent Supportive Housing: Evaluating the Evidence for Improving Health Outcomes Among People Experiencing Chronic Homelessness," 2018, esp. chapter 9.

70. Padgett, Henwood, and Tsemberis, *Housing First*, chapter 4.

71. Gubits, "Family Options Study: 3-Year Impacts of Housing and Services Interventions for Homeless Families," exhibit 3–12; pp. 41–44.

72. Nicholas Eberstadt, *Men Without Work: America's Invisible Crisis* (West Conshohocken, PA: Templeton Press, 2016).

73. Kevin Fagan, "Bay Area Homelessness: 89 Answers to Your Questions," *San Francisco Chronicle*, July 28, 2019, https://projects.sfchronicle.com/sf-homeless/homeless-questions/; Office of New York City Mayor Bill de Blasio, "Mayor's Management Report," September 2019, 197, https://www1.nyc.gov/assets/operations/downloads/pdf/mmr2019/2019_mmr.pdf.

74. Robert Hayes, "Litigating on Behalf of Shelter for the Poor," *Harvard Civil Rights-Civil Liberties Law Review* 22 (1987): 91–92; Office of New York State Senator Liz Krueger, "Home Stability Support Bill Moves Out of Senate Social Services Committee," Press Release, March 5, 2019, https://www.nysenate.gov/newsroom/press-releases/liz-krueger/home-stability-support-bill-moves-out-senate-social-services.

75. US Department of Housing and Urban Development, "The 2017 Annual Homeless Assessment Report (AHAR) to Congress, Part 2: Estimates of Homelessness in the United States," October 2018, 2–15 and 3–17, https://www.hudexchange.info/resource/5769/2017-ahar-part-2-estimates-of-homelessness-in-the-us/.

76. New York City Housing Authority, "NYCHA 2020 Fact Sheet," March 2020, https://www1.nyc.gov/assets/nycha/downloads/pdf/NYCHA-Fact-Sheet_2020_Final.pdf.

77. Alan Mallach, *The Divided City: Poverty and Prosperity in Urban America* (Washington, DC: Island Press, 2018), 268; Mary K. Cunningham, "It's Time to Reinforce the Housing Safety Net by Adopting Universal Vouchers for Low-Income Renters," Urban Institute, April 7, 2020, https://www.urban.org/urban-wire/its-time-reinforce-housing-safety-net-adopting-universal-vouchers-low-income-renters.

78. Dennis P. Culhane, "The Costs of Homelessness: A Perspective from the United States." *European Journal of Homelessness* 2 (December 2008):105, https://www.feantsaresearch.org/download/article-45447406638645867364.pdf.

79. Stefan G. Kertesz, et al., "Permanent Supportive Housing for Homeless People—Reframing the Debate," *New England Journal of Medicine* 375 (December 1, 2016): 2115–17.

80. O'Flaherty, "Homelessness Research: A Guide for Economists (and Friends)," 3.

81. Kelly M. Doran, Elizabeth J. Misa, and Nirav R. Shah, "Housing as Health Care—New York's Boundary-Crossing Experiment," *New England Journal of Medicine* 369, no. 25 (2013): 2375–76; Kertesz and Johnson: "Housing First: Lessons from the United States," 224.

82. Nathan Heller, "A Window onto an American Nightmare," *New Yorker*, June 1, 2020, https://www.newyorker.com/magazine/2020/06/01/a-window-onto-an-american-nightmare.

83. Ridgway and Zipple, "The Paradigm Shift"; Kertesz, "Housing First for Homeless Persons with Active Addiction"; Victoria Stanhope and Kerry Dunn, "The Curious Case of Housing First: The Limits of Evidence Based Policy," *International Journal of Law and Psychiatry* 34, no. 4 (July/August 2011): 275–82.

84. Russell K. Schutt with Stephen M. Goldfinger, *Homelessness, Housing, and Mental Illness* (Cambridge, MA: Harvard University Press, 2011).

85. Heller, "A Window onto an American Nightmare."

86. Barry Campbell, "Testimony of the Fortune Society, Presented by Barry Campbell," New York City Council Committee on General Welfare, March 15, 2016.

87. Sally Satel, "Happy Birthday, Methadone!" *Washington Monthly*, November/December 2014.

88. Sydney Johnson, "SF Could Expand Program that Pays Drug Users to Stay Clean," *San Francisco Examiner*, September 7, 2021, https://www.sfexaminer.com/news/sf-could-expand-program-that-pays-drug-users-to-stay-clean/.

89. Guy Standing, *Basic Income: A Guide for the Open-Minded* (New Haven: Yale University Press, 2017), 81.

90. Richard J. Gelles, "Creating an Effective Child Welfare System," in *Urban Policy Frontiers* (Manhattan Institute for Policy Research 2017), chapter 3, https://media4.manhattan-institute.org/sites/default/files/MI_Urban_Policy_Frontiers_2017.pdf.

91. Leigh Goodmark, *Decriminalizing Domestic Violence: A Balanced Policy Approach to Intimate Partner Violence* (Berkeley: University of California Press, 2018).

92. Craig Willse, *The Value of Homelessness: Managing Surplus Life in the United States* (Minneapolis: University of Minnesota Press, 2015); Denis Slattery, "Queens Assemblyman Calls Out Cuomo over Donations from Homeless Shelter Providers Amid Homeless Crisis," *New York Daily News*, July 28, 2019; "The Business of Homelessness: Financial and Human Costs of the Shelter-Industrial Complex," Picture the Homeless Research Committee, 2018.

93. Padgett, Henwood, and Tsemberis, *Housing First*, 2015.

Chapter 6. Compassion, Con and Pro

1. Jason Storbakken, "The pain of homelessness: A plea for New York City to deal compassionately with people in deep need," *New York Daily News*, November 7, 2019, https://www.nydailynews.com/opinion/ny-oped-on-the-bowery-14-decades-of-lives-transformed-20191107-vzjt3na7wzgpzg6yetdxm5dery-story.html; Nita Lelyveld, "How to un-harden our hearts toward homeless people," *Los Angeles Times*, January 25, 2020, https://www.latimes.com/california/story/2020-01-25/homeless-solutions-los-angeles-providing-aid.

2. Louis CK, "Homeless Guy at Port Authority Bus Terminal," drpenfeild, excerpt from *Louie*, Season 1, Episode 3, posted May 20, 2014, YouTube video, 3:01, https://www.youtube.com/watch?v=hmr-NRCbnus.

3. Author calculation based on "HUD 2020 Continuum of Care Homeless Assistance Programs Housing Inventory Count Report, State: New Hampshire," U.S. Department of Housing and Urban Development, January 13, 2021 (https://files.hudexchange.info/reports/published/CoC_HIC_State_NH_2020.pdf) and U.S. Department of Housing and Urban Development, "HUD 2020 Continuum of Care Homeless Assistance Programs Housing Inventory Count Report, CoC Number: NY-600," January 13, 2021 (https://files.hudexchange.info/reports/published/CoC_HIC_CoC_NY-600-2020_NY_2020.pdf).

4. Josephine Shaw Lowell, *Public Relief and Private Charity* (New York: G. P. Putnam's Sons, 1884), 88.

5. On the traditional debate between justice and charity as it has shaped the American welfare state, see Benjamin Soskis, "Both More and No More: The Historical Split between Charity and Philanthropy," Hudson Institute October 2014, https://www.hudson.org/research/10723-both-more-and-no-more-the-historical-split-between-charity-and-philanthropy.

6. Libby Denkmann, "Can A Republican Be Governor Again in California? Kevin Faulconer Will Try to Carve Arnold-esque Path," Laist.com, February 2, 2021, https://laist.com/news/former-san-diego-mayor-kevin-faulconer-will-try-to-carve-arnold-esque-path-to-governorship.

7. Cbsnews.com, "Dumped on Skid Row," May 17, 2007, https://www.cbsnews.com/news/dumped-on-skid-row/.

8. Nancy A. Millich, "Compassion Fatigue and the First Amendment: Are the Homeless Constitutional Castaways?" *UC Davis Law Review* 27, no. 2 (1994): 275–81; Ellen Goodman, "Compassion Fatigue," *Washington Post*, February 3, 1990.

9. "Cost-benefit analysis may be the new compassion in our communities." Phillip Mangano, quoted in Erik Eckholm, "New Campaign Shows Progress for Homeless," *New York Times*, June 7 2006, https://www.nytimes.com/2006/06/07/us/07homeless.html.

10. William J. Voegeli, *The Pity Party: A Mean-spirited Diatribe against Liberal Compassion* (New York: Broadside Books, 2014).

11. Brent D. Mast, "Measuring Homelessness and Resources to Combat Homelessness with PIT and HIC Data," *Cityscape: A Journal of Policy Development and Research* 22, no. 1 (2020): 215–26, https://www.huduser.gov/portal/periodicals/cityscpe/vol22num1/ch7.pdf.

12. Annie Correal, "In Deepest Cold, a Subway Car Becomes the Shelter of Last Resort," *New York Times*, January 8, 2018.

13. Metropolitan Transportation Authority, "Safety Committee Meeting Materials," July 2019, 13, http://web.mta.info/mta/news/books/pdf/190724_0800_Safety.pdf; New York City Department of Homeless Services. "NYC HOPE 2019 Results," n.d., 5, https://www1.nyc.gov/assets/dhs/downloads/pdf/hope-2019-results.pdf.

14. Brendan O'Flaherty, *City Economics* (Cambridge: Harvard University Press, 2005), 434–35.

15. Rachel Aviv, "Netherland," *New Yorker*, December 3, 2012, https://www.newyorker.com/magazine/2012/12/10/netherland; Steve Lopez, "They Come from Around US to Live Homeless on Hollywood's Streets. How Much More Can We Take?" *Los Angeles Times*, November 17 2019; US Interagency Council on Homelessness, "Homelessness: Programs and the People They Serve: Findings of the National Survey of Homeless Assistance Providers and Clients," September 1999, chapter 4, https://www.huduser.gov/portal/publications/homeless/homeless_tech.html.

16. Jason DeParle, *American Dream: Three Women, Ten Kids, and a Nation's Drive to End Welfare* (New York: Viking 2004), 6–7, 58–61, and 198.

17. Jay Willis, "Who Will Run the Soup Kitchens?" *Atlantic*, March 20, 2020, https://www.theatlantic.com/family/archive/2020/03/the-coronaviruss-impact-on-homeless-services/608467/; Barbara Poppe and associates for the Coalition on Homelessness and Housing in Ohio, "Double Jeopardy: The Coronavirus & Homelessness in Ohio," March 24, 2020, figure 5, https://cohhio.org/wp-content/uploads/2020/03/DoubleJeopardy-web.pdf.

18. United States Conference of Catholic Bishops, "The Corporal Works of Mercy," web page, http://www.usccb.org/beliefs-and-teachings/how-we-teach/new-evangelization/jubilee-of-mercy/the-corporal-works-of-mercy.cfm.

19. G. K. Chesterton, *The Thing* (London: Sheed & Ward, 1946), chapter 35, "The Spirit of Christmas." https://www.sculpturebytps.com/portfolio_page/homeless-jesus/.

20. Urban Institute, "The Nonprofit Sector in Brief 2019," June 4, 2020, https://nccs.urban.org/publication/nonprofit-sector-brief-2019#the-nonprofit-sector-in-brief-2019.

21. Kathryn J. Edin and H. Luke Shaefer, *$2.00 a Day: Living on Almost Nothing in America* (Boston, MA: Houghton Mifflin Harcourt, 2015), 101–5; Lauren Sandler, *This is All I Got: A New Mother's Search for Home* (New York: Random House, 2020), 189; Scott W. Allard, *Out of Reach: Place, Poverty, and the New American Welfare State* (New Haven: Yale University Press, 2009), 126.

22. Nikita Stewart, *Troop 6000: The Girl Scout Troop that Began in a Shelter and Inspired the World* (New York: Ballantine Books, 2020).

23. For defenses of the private-oriented pre-New Deal welfare state, see David T. Beito, *From Mutual Aid to the Welfare State: Fraternal Societies and Social Services, 1890–1967* (Chapel Hill: University of North Carolina Press, 2000) and Howard Husock, *Who Killed Civil Society?: The Rise of Big Government and Decline of Bourgeois Norms* (New York: Encounter Books, 2019).

24. Marvin Olasky, *The Tragedy of American Compassion* (Wheaton, IL: Crossway Books, 2008 [orig. 1992]).

25. Olasky, *The Tragedy of American Compassion*, chapter 12.

26. Olivier Zunz, *Philanthropy in America: A History* (Princeton: Princeton University Press, 2012), chapter 8; Steven Rathgeb Smith, "Social Services," In *The State of Nonprofit America*, edited by Lester M. Salamon, 192–228 (Washington, DC: Brookings Institution Press, 2012).

27. Brian C. Anderson, "How Catholic Charities Lost Its Soul," *City Journal*, Winter 2000.

28. Olasky, *The Tragedy of Compassion*, chapter 1, https://www.city-journal.org/html/how-catholic-charities-lost-its-soul-12150.html.

29. Byron Johnson, William H. Wubbenhorst, and Alfreda Alvarez, "Assessing the Faith-Based Response to Homelessness in America: Findings from Eleven Cities," Program on Prosocial Behavior, Baylor Institute for Studies of Religion, February 1, 2017, http://www.baylorisr.org/wp-content/uploads/ISR-Homeless-FINAL-01092017-web.pdf.

30. The National Law Center on Homelessness and Poverty, "Housing Not Handcuffs: A Litigation Manual," 2018; The National Law Center on Homelessness and Poverty, "Housing Not Handcuffs 2019: Ending the Criminalization of Homelessness in US Cities," December 2019, https://homelesslaw.org/wp-content/uploads/2018/10/Housing-Not-Handcuffs-Litigation-Manual.pdf.

31. Victoria Rader, *Signal Through the Flames: Mitch Snyder and America's Homeless* (Kansas City, MO: Sheed & Ward, 1986), 44, 49, 123, and 253.

32. Scott W. Allard, *Out of Reach Place, Poverty, and the New American Welfare State* (New Haven & London Yale University Press, 2009), 122.

33. Daniel Stid, "Dismantling the Social Services Industrial Complex," *Washington Post*, April 25, 2012, https://www.washingtonpost.com/national/on-innovations/dismantling-the-social-services-industrial-complex/2012/04/25/gIQAuTcMhT_story.html?utm_term=.1d75d46c087f.

34. Allard, *Out of Reach*; Steven Rathgeb Smith and Michael Lipsky, *Nonprofits for Hire: The Welfare State in the Age of Contracting* (Cambridge: Harvard University Press, 1995); Zunz, *Philanthropy in America*, chapter 8.

35. US Interagency Council on Homelessness, "Homelessness: Programs and the People They Serve: Findings of the National Survey of Homeless Assistance Providers and Clients," September 1999, chapter 14, https://www.huduser.gov/portal/publications/homeless/homeless_tech.html.

36. Peter Marris and Martin Rein, *Dilemmas of social reform: poverty and community action in the United States*, second edition (London: Routledge and Kegan Paul, 1972); Daniel P. Moynihan, *Maximum Feasible Misunderstanding; community action in the war on poverty* (New York, Free Press, 1969).

37. James T. Patterson, *America's Struggle Against Poverty, 1900–1980* (Harvard University Press, 1981), 24–25.

38. Patterson, *America's Struggle Against Poverty, 1900–1980*, 138.

39. Michael B. Katz, *In the Shadow of the Poorhouse: A Social History of Welfare in America* (New York: Basic Books, 1986), 263; Allard, *Out of Reach*, 21–24; Smith and Lipsky, *Nonprofits for Hire*, chapter 3.

40. Smith and Lipsky, *Nonprofits for Hire*, 63–64; Donna Wilson Kirchheimer, "Sheltering the Homeless in New York City: Expansion in an Era of Government Contraction," *Political Science Quarterly* 104, no. 4 (Winter 1989–90): 607–23.

41. New York City Commission on the Homeless, "The Way Home: A New Direction in Social Policy," February 1992; Thomas J. Main, *Homelessness in New York City: Policymaking from Koch to de Blasio* (New York: New York University Press, 2017), 109–12.

42. ". . . in practice losing contracts is still relatively rare." Smith "Social Services," 211.

43. Roy Lubove, *The Professional Altruist: The Emergence of Social Work as a Career, 1880–1930* (Cambridge: Harvard University Press, 1965), chapter 1.

44. US Interagency Council on Homelessness, "Successfully Connecting People Affected by Opioid Use to Housing: Central City Concern in Portland, Oregon," March 2017, 3, https://www.usich.gov/resources/uploads/asset_library/case-study-central-city-concern-march-2017.pdf.

45. See the character Pee Wee Packer in William Kennedy's *Ironweed* (New York: Penguin, 1983); Nels Anderson, *The Hobo: The Sociology of the Homeless Man* (Chicago: The University of Chicago Press, 1923): chapter 17.

46. Steven Rathgeb Smith, "Social Services," in The State of Nonprofit America, Ed. Lester M Salamon (Washington, DC: Brookings Institution Press, 2012), 207.

47. Andrew Doran, "A Modern Mendicant," *First Things*, April 2020, https://www.firstthings.com/article/2020/04/a-modern-mendicant.

48. Greg Berman and Aubrey Fox, "Lessons from the Battle over D.A.R.E.: The Complicated Relationship between Research and Practice," Bureau of Justice Assistance, 2009, https://www.courtinnovation.org/sites/default/files/DARE.pdf; Sarah Halpern-Meekin, *Social Poverty: Low-income Parents and the Struggle for Family and Community Ties* (New York: New York University Press, 2019).

49. The term may have been invented by Saul Alinsky. Patterson, *America's Struggle Against Poverty, 1900–1980*, 144.

50. This is the theme of Tom Wolfe's "Mau-Mauing the Flak Catchers." See also Peter Cove, *Poor No More: Rethinking Dependency and the War on Poverty* (New York: Routledge 2017), chapter 1.

51. Carl Campanile "Bronx Homeless Services Provider Faces State Criminal Probe," *New York Post*, October 5, 2020, https://nypost.com/2020/10/05/bronx-homeless-services-provider-faces-state-criminal-probe/.

52. Jennifer E. Mosley, "From Skid Row to the Statehouse," in *Nonprofits and Advocacy: Engaging Community and Government in an Era of Retrenchment*, edited by Robert J. Pekkanen, Steven Rathgeb Smith, and Yutaka Tsujinaka, 107–34 (Baltimore: Johns Hopkins University Press, 2014).

53. Christopher Legras, "California's Homeless are Fodder for an Insatiable Bureaucracy," allaspectreport.com, December 14, 2020, https://allaspectreport.com/2020/12/14/californias-homeless-are-fodder-for-an-insatiable-bureaucracy/; Laura Nahmias, "Christine Quinn to head nonprofit for homeless women," *Politico*, September 17, 2015, https://www.politico.com/states/new-york/city-hall/story/2015/09/christine-quinn-to-head-nonprofit-for-homeless-women-000000.

54. Legras, "California's Homeless are Fodder for an Insatiable Bureaucracy."

55. Fan Zhong, "Richard Gere and Alec Baldwin Care About the Homeless," *W Magazine*, November 18, 2015, https://www.wmagazine.com/story/richard-gere-alec-baldwin-artwalk-ny.

56. C. Bradley Thompson, "The Decline and Fall of American Conservatism," The Objective Standard, August 20, 2006, https://theobjectivestandard.com/2006/08/decline-fall-american-conservatism/.

57. Lisa Hoffman and Brian Coffey, "Dignity and Indignation: How People Experiencing Homelessness View Services and Providers," *The Social Science Journal* 45, no. 2 (2008): 207–22.

58. Michael J. Gerson, *Heroic Conservatism: Why Republicans Need to Embrace America's Ideals (And Why They Deserve to Fail If They Don't)* (New York: HarperOne, 2007), 168; Steven M. Teles, "The Eternal Return of Compassionate Conservatism," *National Affairs*, Fall 2009, https://www.nationalaffairs.com/publications/detail/the-eternal-return-of-compassionate-conservatism.

Chapter 7. Homelessness and Social Integration

1. US Department of Housing and Urban Development, "The 2017 Annual Homeless Assessment Report (AHAR) to Congress, Part 2: Estimates of Homelessness in the United States," October 2018, 1–11, https://www.hudexchange.info/resource/5769/2017-ahar-part-2-estimates-of-homelessness-in-the-us/.

2. US Department of Housing and Urban Development, "HUD 2020 Continuum of Care Homeless Assistance Programs Homeless Populations and Subpopulations," December 15, 2020, https://files.hudexchange.info/reports/published/CoC_PopSub_Natl TerrDC_2020.pdf.

3. Richard C. Tessler and Deborah L. Dennis, "A Synthesis of NIMH-Funded Research Concerning Persons who are Homeless and Mentally Ill," National Institute of Mental Health, February 9, 1989, 46.

4. Debra J. Rog, C. Scott Holupka, and Lisa C. Patton, "Characteristics and Dynamics of Homeless Families with Children," US Department of Health and Human Services, Office of the Assistant Secretary for Planning and Evaluation, 2007, 2–6 and 2–7, https://aspe.hhs.gov/sites/default/files/private/pdf/75331/report.pdf.

5. Xavier de Souza Briggs, Susan J. Popkin, and John Goering, *Moving to Opportunity: The Story of an American Experiment to Fight Ghetto Poverty* (New York: Oxford University Press, 2010, Kindle Edition), chapter 6.

6. Allard, *Out of Reach*; Henry Olsen, "A New Homestead Act—To Jump Start the U.S. Economy," National Interest, December 15, 2015, https://nationalinterest.org/feature/new-homestead-act%E2%80%94-jumpstart-the-us-economy-14618.

7. Priscilla Ridgway and Anthony M. Zipple, "The Paradigm Shift in Residential Services: From the Linear Continuum to Supported Housing Approaches," *Psychosocial Rehabilitation Journal* 13, no. 4 (April 1990): 11–31.

8. Geoffrey Nelson and Timothy MacLeod, "The Evolution of Housing for People with Serious Mental Illness," in *Housing, Citizenship, and Communities for People with Serious Mental Illness: Theory, Research, Practice, and Policy Perspectives,* edited by John Sylvestre, Geoffrey Nelson, and Tim Aubry (New York: Oxford University Press, 2017), 3, 22.

9. Jack Tsai, Alvin S. Mares, and Robert A. Rosenheck, "Does Housing Chronically Homeless Adults Lead to Social Integration?" *Psychiatric Services* 63, no. 5 (May 2012): 427–34, https://ps.psychiatryonline.org/doi/pdf/10.1176/appi.ps.201100047; Deborah Quilgars and Nicholas Pleace, "Housing First and Social Integration: A Realistic Aim?" *Social Inclusion* 4, no. 4 (2016): 5–15, doi:10.17645/si.v4i4.672; Tom Baker and Joshua Evans, "'Housing First' and the Changing Terrains of Homeless Governance," *Geography Compass* 10, Issue 1 (2016): 25–41; Jack Tsai and Robert A. Rosenheck, "Considering Alternatives to the Housing First Model," *European Journal of Homelessness* 6, no. 2 (December 2012): 201–8, https://www.feantsaresearch.org/download/ejh6_2_resp_housingfirst55412642448344839392.pdf; Kim

Hopper, "The Counter-Reformation That Failed? A Commentary on the Mixed Legacy of Supported Housing." *Psychiatric Services* 63, no. 5 (2012): 461–63.

10. Leyla Gulcur, Sam Tsemberis, Ana Stefancic, and Ronni M. Greenwood, "Community Integration of Adults with Psychiatric Disabilities and Histories of Homelessness," *Community Mental Health Journal* 43, no. 3 (June 2007): 211–28; National Academies of Sciences, Engineering, and Medicine, "Permanent Supportive Housing: Evaluating the Evidence for Improving Health Outcomes Among People Experiencing Chronic Homelessness," 2018, 51–53.

11. Dirk Richter and Holger Hoffmann, "Preference for Independent Housing of Persons with Mental Disorders: Systematic Review and Meta-Analysis," *Administration and Policy in Mental Health and Mental Health Services Research* 44, no. 6 (2017): 817–23.

12. Ellen E. Lee, et al., "Comparison of Schizophrenia Outpatients in Residential Care Facilities with Those Living with Someone: Study of Mental and Physical Health, Cognitive Functioning, And Biomarkers of Aging," *Psychiatry Research* 275 (May 2019): 162–68, https://escholarship.org/content/qt9kt7529c/qt9kt7529c.pdf?t=qejeqy; Russell K. Schutt with Stephen M. Goldfinger, *Homelessness, Housing, and Mental Illness* (Cambridge, MA: Harvard University Press, 2011).

13. Michael Jindra, "Inside the Safety Net," *Hedgehog Review*, Fall 2014; Marvin Olasky, *The Tragedy of American Compassion* (Wheaton, IL: Crossway Books, 2008 [orig. 1992]), 44–45.

14. Gothamist, "Is East New York The Next Bushwick?," July 23, 2014, https://gothamist.com/news/is-east-new-york-the-next-bushwick; Will Bredderman, "Council's Land Use Committee Approves 'Astoria Cove' Mega-Project," *Observer*, November 12, 2014, https://observer.com/2014/11/councils-land-use-committee-approves-astoria-cove-mega-project/#ixzz3gdjiNmt5.

15. Peter Jamison, "DC Housed the Homeless in Upscale Apartments. It Hasn't Gone as Planned," *Washington Post*, April 16, 2019.

16. Office of New York City Mayor Bill de Blasio. "Turning the Tide on Homelessness in New York City," February 2017, 93, https://www1.nyc.gov/assets/dhs/downloads/pdf/turning-the-tide-on-homelessness.pdf.

17. New York City Independent Budget Office, "The Rising Number of Homeless Families in NYC, 2002–2012," November 2014, https://ibo.nyc.ny.us/iboreports/2014dhs.pdf; Jarrett Murphy, "Data Drop: Which NYC Neighborhoods Host the Most Homeless-Shelter Beds?" *City Limits*, September 10, 2019, https://citylimits.org/2019/09/10/data-drop-which-nyc-neighborhoods-host-the-most-homeless-shelter-beds/.

18. Vicki Been, Ingrid Gould Ellen, Michael Gedal, and Ioan Voicu, "The Impact of Supportive Housing on Surrounding Neighborhoods," Furman Center for Real Estate & Urban Policy, Working Paper 2008–2006, October 2008, https://furmancenter.org/files/publications/A3ImpactofSHonNeighborhoods_000.pdf.

19. New York City Independent Budget Office, "Close to Home: Does Proximity to a Homeless Shelter Affect Residential Property Values in Manhattan?" September 2019, https://ibo.nyc.ny.us/iboreports/close-to-home-does-proximity-to-a-homeless-shelter-affect-residential-property-values-in-manhattan-2019.pdf.

20. Los Angeles County Chief Executive Office, "Approved Strategies to Combat Homelessness," February 2016, 92, https://homeless.lacounty.gov/wp-content/uploads/2017/01/HI-Report-Approved2.pdf.

21. Jason Curtis Anderson, "A Lucerne for Every Neighborhood," janesdefenders.nyc, May 2021, https://www.janesdefenders.nyc/essays/a-lucerne-for-every-neighborhood.

22. Heather Knight, "Poop. Needles. Rats. Homeless Camp Pushes SF Neighborhood to the Edge," *San Francisco Chronicle*, June 24, 2018, https://www.sfchronicle.com/news/article /Neighbors-disgusted-over-despair-on-block-hit-13015964.php.

23. Venice Neighborhood Council, Public Health and Safety Committee, "Special Report: LAPD Calls for Service by Venice Homeless Service Providers," February 9, 2021, https:// www.venicenc.org/ncfiles/viewCommitteeFile/12775.

24. Seth Barron, *The Last Days of New York: A Reporter's True Tale* (New York: Humanix, 2021), 239.

25. Jane Jacobs, *The Death and Life of Great American Cities* (New York: Vintage Books, 1992) [orig. 1961]), 100–102 and 154.

26. "United for Housing: from the Ground Up 2021," New York Housing Conference, December 14, 2020, 8 and 46, https://thenyhc.org/2020/12/14/united-for-housing-releases -report/.

27. Lluís Alexandre Casanovas Blanco, "A Cut Above the Streets: Robert M. Hayes, Co-Founder of Coalition for the Homeless, in Conversation with Lluis Alexandre Casanovas Blanco," Archinect.com, May 1, 2019, https://archinect.com/features/article/150133042/a-cut -above-the-streets-robert-m-hayes-co-founder-of-coalition-for-the-homeless-in-conversation -with-llu-s-alexandre-casanovas-blanco.

28. Sudhir Alladi Venkatesh, *Off the Books: The Underground Economy of The Urban Poor* (Cambridge: Harvard University Press, 2006); Matthew Desmond, *Evicted: Poverty and Profit in the American City* (New York: Crown Publishers, 2016), chapter 10.

29. Christopher Jencks, *The Homeless* (Cambridge: Harvard University Press, 1994), 53; Kim Hopper, "The Public Response to Homelessness in New York City: The Last Hundred Years," in *On Being Homeless: Historical Perspectives*, edited by Rick Beard (New York: Museum of the City of New York, 1987), 90.

30. Stephen Metraux, Jamison Fargo, Nick Eng, and Dennis P. Culhane, "Employment and Earnings Trajectories During Two Decades Among Adults in New York City Homeless Shelters," *Cityscape: A Journal of Policy Development and Research* 20 no. 2 (2018): 173–202, https://www.huduser.gov/portal/periodicals/cityscpe/vol20num2/ch11.pdf.

31. Till von Wachter, Geoffrey Schnorr, and Nefara Riesch, "Employment and Earnings Among LA County Residents Experiencing Homelessness," California Policy Lab, February 2020, figure 1, https://www.capolicylab.org/wp-content/uploads/2020/02/Employment -Among-the-Homeless-in-Los-Angeles.pdf.

32. Wachter, Schnorr and Riesch "Employment and Earnings Among LA County Residents Experiencing Homelessness," 14.

33. Joanne Bretherton and Nicholas Pleace, "Is Work an Answer to Homelessness? Evaluating an Employment Programme for Homeless Adults," *European Journal of Homelessness* 13, no. 1 (2019): 57–81, https://www.feantsaresearch.org/public/user/Observatory/2019/EJH /EJH_13_1/Feantsa-2019_13-1_Article-3.pdf.

34. For more research on employment rates among the homeless population, see "Homelessness: Programs and the People They Serve: Findings of the National Survey of Homeless Assistance Providers and Clients," US Interagency Council on the Homeless, chapter 5, https://www.huduser.gov/portal/publications/homeless/homeless_tech.html; New York City Commission on the Homeless, "The Way Home: A New Direction in Social Policy," February 1992, table 7; Rog, Holupka and Patton, "Characteristics and Dynamics of Homeless Families with Children," 2–5 and 2–6.

35. Brian Goldstone, "The New American Homeless," *New Republic*, August 21, 2019, https://newrepublic.com/article/154618/new-american-homeless-housing-insecurity-richest-cities.

36. Lane Kenworthy, *Social Democratic Capitalism* (New York: Oxford University Press, 2019).

37. US Department of Housing and Urban Development, "Housing and Employment," Evidence Matters, Summer/Fall 2018, 2, https://www.huduser.gov/portal/sites/default/files/pdf/EM-Newsletter-summer-fall-2018.pdf.

38. US Department of Housing and Urban Development, "Housing and Employment," 8.

39. Scott Wetzler, "Defeating Dependency: Work First," American Enterprise Institute, September 2018, https://www.aei.org/wp-content/uploads/2018/09/Defeating-Dependency.pdf.

40. Rael Jean Isaac and Virginia C. Armat, *Madness in the Streets: How Psychiatry and the Law Abandoned the Mentally Ill* (New York: Free Press, 1990), 289.

41. Bliss Forbush, *The Sheppard & Enoch Pratt Hospital 1853–1970, A History* (Philadelphia: J. B. Lippincott Company, 1971), 133; Mary Flannery and Mark Glickman, *Fountain House: Portraits of Lives Reclaimed from Mental Illness* (Center City, MN: Hazelden, 1996), especially chapter 1.

42. Egon Bittner, "The Police on Skid-Row: A Study of Peace Keeping," *American Sociological Review* 32, no. 5 (October 1967): 706; "Freedom may seem a funny word to use in connection with these men, but there certainly is a perverse sense of freedom that pervades this street. Once you've reached bottom what the hell can you say or do to make it worse?" Michael D. Zettler, *The Bowery* (New York: Drake Publishers, 1975), vii.

43. Donald Bogue, *Skid Row in American Cities*, Community and Family Study Center, University of Chicago, 1963, 58.

44. Sam Tsemberis, Leyla Gulcur, and Maria Nakae, "Housing First, Consumer Choice, and Harm Reduction for Homeless Individuals with a Dual Diagnosis," *American Journal of Public Health* 94, no. 4 (May 2004): 652.

45. Teresa Gowan, *Hobos, Hustlers, and Backsliders: Homeless in San Francisco* (Minneapolis: University of Minnesota Press, 2010), chapter 5. For a critical take on homeless entrepreneurialism, see Steven Boone, "Designer Shades, Quiet Hustle: The Entrepreneurs of the New York City homeless shelter," *Politico*, May 12, 2011, https://www.politico.com/states/new-york/city-hall/story/2011/05/designer-shades-quiet-hustle-the-entrepreneurs-of-the-new-york-city-homeless-shelter-067223.

46. Nicholas Eberstadt, *Men Without Work: America's Invisible Crisis* (West Conshohocken, PA: Templeton Press, 2016).

47. Nels Anderson, *The Hobo: The Sociology of the Homeless Man* (Chicago: The University of Chicago Press, 1923), 185.

48. Stephen Eide, "Disorder in the Stacks," *City Journal*, Spring 2019.

49. US Department of Housing and Urban Development, "Housing and Employment," 3.

50. Don D. Lescohier, *The Labor Market* (New York: The Macmillan Company, 1919), 94–95; See also Erving Goffman, *Asylums: Essays on the Social Situation of Mental Patients and Other Inmates* (Garden City: Anchor Books, 1961), 183–84.

51. Konrad Bercovici, *Crimes of Charity* (New York: A. A. Knopf, 1917).

52. Howard Husock, "How the Agency Saved My Father," *City Journal*, Spring 1999, https://www.city-journal.org/html/how-agency-saved-my-father-12151.html; Benjamin Sos-

kis, "Both More and No More: The Historical Split between Charity and Philanthropy," Hudson Institute, October 2014, https://www.hudson.org/research/10723-both-more-and -no-more-the-historical-split-between-charity-and-philanthropy; Roy Lubove, *The Professional Altruist: The Emergence of Social Work as a Career, 1880–1930* (Cambridge: Harvard University Press, 1965), 13–14.

53. Los Angeles City Councilmember Mike Bonin, "Mike Proposes New Commission Composed of People Who Are or Have Been Homeless," Press, Release. September 4, 2019, https://11thdistrict.com/news/mike-proposes-new-commission-composed-of-people-who -are-or-have-been-homeless/; New York City Continuum of Care, "Governance Charter of the New York City Continuum of Care," May 22, 2020, II.C, https://www1.nyc.gov/assets /nycccoc/downloads/pdf/Governance%20Charter_Final_Adopted%205.22.20.pdf.

54. Michael Shellenberger, *San Fransicko: Why Progressives Ruin Cities* (New York: Harper, 2021). See especially 150.

55. Myron Magnet, *The Dream and the Nightmare: The Sixties' Legacy to the Underclass* (New York: William Morrow and Company, 1993), 108.

56. Tessler and Dennis, "A Synthesis of NIMH-Funded Research Concerning Persons who are Homeless and Mentally Ill," table 3.

57. Byron Johnson, William H. Wubbenhorst, and Alfreda Alvarez, "Assessing the Faith-Based Response to Homelessness in America: Findings from Eleven Cities," Program on Prosocial Behavior, Baylor Institute for Studies of Religion, February 1, 2017, 21, http://www .baylorisr.org/wp-content/uploads/ISR-Homeless-FINAL-01092017-web.pdf.

58. Will Sarvis, "The Homelessness Muddle Revisited," *The Urban Lawyer* 49, no. 2 (Spring 2017): 328–29.

59. Jason DeParle, *American Dream: Three Women, Ten Kids, and a Nation's Drive to End Welfare* (New York: Viking, 2004), 203.

60. Kathryn Edin and Maria Kefalas, *Promises I Can Keep: Why Poor Women put Motherhood before Marriage* (Berkeley: University of California Press, 2005), chapter 3.

61. Sharon G. Smith, et al., "The National Intimate Partner and Sexual Violence Survey (NISVS): 2010–2012 State Report," National Center for Injury Prevention and Control, Centers for Disease Control and Prevention, April 2017, table 3.3, https://www.cdc.gov /violenceprevention/pdf/NISVS-StateReportBook.pdf; US Department of Health and Human Services, Administration for Children and Families. "Child Maltreatment 2019." 2021, tables 3–12 and 4–4, https://www.acf.hhs.gov/sites/default/files/documents /cb/cm2019.pdf.

62. David Brooks, "The Nuclear Family Was a Mistake," *The Atlantic*, March 2020, https:// www.theatlantic.com/magazine/archive/2020/03/the-nuclear-family-was-a-mistake/605536/.

63. DeParle, *American Dream*, 79, see also 46; Edin and Kefalas, *Promises I Can Keep*, 101–2 and 149; Barrett A. Lee, and Christopher J. Schreck, "Danger on the Streets: Marginality and Victimization Among Homeless People," *American Behavioral Scientist* 48, no. 8 (April 2005): 1060–61.

64. See discussion of "the weakness of strong ties" in Xavier de Souza Briggs, Susan J. Popkin, and John Goering, *Moving to Opportunity: The Story of an American Experiment to Fight Ghetto Poverty* (New York: Oxford University Press, 2010 Kindle Edition), chapter 6.

Chapter 8. All Our Kin: The Challenge of Homeless Families

1. US Congress. "Congressional Record: Proceedings and Debates of the 104th Congress, First Session," 141, no. 137, September 6, 1995, S 12682, https://www.govinfo.gov/content/pkg/CREC-1995-09-06/pdf/CREC-1995-09-06-senate.pdf.

2. Ron Haskins, *Work over Welfare: The Inside Story of the 1996 Welfare Reform Law* (Washington, DC: Brookings Institution Press, 2006), 29–30, 178, and 256.

3. Scott Winship, "Poverty After Welfare Reform," Manhattan Institute for Policy Research, August 2016, https://media4.manhattan-institute.org/sites/default/files/R-SW-0816.pdf.

4. Thomas Gabe, "Welfare, Work, and Poverty Status of Female-Headed Families with Children: 1987–2013," Congressional Research Service, November 21, 2014, figures 11 and 16; Haskins, *Work over Welfare*, chapter 15, https://crsreports.congress.gov/product/pdf/R/R41917/18.

5. US Department of Health and Human Services, "Welfare Indicators and Risk Factors Nineteenth Report to Congress 2020," February 8, 2021, table 5, indicator 2, https://aspe.hhs.gov/sites/default/files/private/pdf/265031/welfare-indicators-and-risk-factors-19th-report.pdf.

6. US Department of Health and Human Services, "Welfare Indicators and Risk Factors Nineteenth Report to Congress 2020," February 8, 2021, table 18, indicator 8, https://aspe.hhs.gov/sites/default/files/private/pdf/265031/welfare-indicators-and-risk-factors-19th-report.pdf.

7. DeParle, *American Dream*, 113.

8. US Department of Health and Human Services, "Welfare Indicators and Risk Factors Nineteenth Report to Congress 2020," table 21 and indicator 10.

9. Child Trends, https://greenbook-waysandmeans.house.gov/sites/greenbook.waysandmeans.house.gov/files/2012/CW%20Table11-4_FC-Entering_Served_Exiting_Incare_82-11%20RM-ES.pdf.

10. US Department of Health and Human Services, "Welfare Indicators and Risk Factors Nineteenth Report to Congress 2020," table 1 and indicator 1.

11. Carol Stevens, "Families: new breed of street people, *USA Today*, December 15, 1982; Rone Tempest, "Millions Hit Bottom in the Streets," *Los Angeles Times*, December 26, 1982

12. Linda Weinreb and Peter H. Rossi, "The American Homeless Family Shelter 'System,'" *Social Service Review* 69, no. 1 (March 1995): 89.

13. Dennis P. Culhane, Stephen Metraux, Thomas Byrne, Magdi Stino, and Jay Bainbridge, "The Age Structure of Contemporary Homelessness: Evidence and Implications for Public Policy," *Analyses of Social Issues and Public Policy* 13, no. 1 (December 2013): 228–44.

14. US Department of Housing and Urban Development, "The 2018 Annual Homeless Assessment Report (AHAR) to Congress; Part 2: Estimates of Homelessness in the United States," September 2020, 3–7, https://www.huduser.gov/portal/sites/default/files/pdf/2018-AHAR-Part-2.pdf.

15. Robert Hayes, "Litigating on Behalf of Shelter for the Poor," *Harvard Civil Rights-Civil Liberties Law Review* 22 (1987): 90.

16. R. Kent Weaver, *Ending Welfare as We Know It* (Washington, DC: Brookings Institution Press, 2000), 45–48.

17. Kathryn Edin and Maria Kefalas, *Promises I Can Keep: Why Poor Women put Motherhood before Marriage* (Berkeley: University of California Press, 2005), 182; Sarah Ravani, "Theo Homeless at Age 7," *San Francisco Chronicle*, July 29, 2020, https://www.sfchronicle.com/projects/2020/theo/.

18. US Department of Housing and Urban Development, "HUD 2020 Continuum of Care Homeless Assistance Programs Homeless Populations and Subpopulations," December 15, 2020, https://files.hudexchange.info/reports/published/CoC_PopSub_Natl TerrDC_2020.pdf.

19. Source: HUD, "2020 AHAR: Part 1—PIT Estimates of Homelessness in the US," March 2021, https://www.huduser.gov/portal/datasets/ahar/2020-ahar-part-1-pit-estimates -of-homelessness-in-the-us.html.

20. O'Flaherty, "Homelessness Research: A Guide for Economists (and Friends)," 22.

21. Edin and Kefalas, *Promises I Can Keep*.

22. Dennis Saffran "Massacre of the Innocents," *City Journal*, Winter 2018, https://www .city-journal.org/html/massacre-innocents-15647.html?wallit_nosession=1.

23. Debra J. Rog, C. Scott Holupka, and Lisa C. Patton, "Characteristics and Dynamics of Homeless Families With Children," US Department of Health and Human Services, Office of the Assistant Secretary for Planning and Evaluation, 2007, 2, 3.

24. Rhonda D. Evans and Craig J. Forsyth, "Risk factors, endurance of victimization, and survival strategies: The impact of the structural location of men and women on their experiences within homeless milieus," *Sociological Spectrum* 24, no. 4 (2004): 483–85; Christopher Jencks, *The Homeless* (Cambridge: Harvard University Press, 1994), 78.

25. Source HUD, "2020 AHAR: Part 1."

26. Kirsten Moore Sheeley at al., "The Making of a Crisis: A History of Homelessness in Los Angeles," UCLA Luskin Center for History and Policy, January 2021, 33, https://luskin center.history.ucla.edu/wp-content/uploads/sites/66/2021/01/LCHP-The-Making-of-A-Cri sis-Report.pdf; New York City Coalition for the Homeless, "View from the Street: Unsheltered New Yorkers and the Need for Safety, Dignity, and Agency," April 2021, 28; New York City Commission on the Homeless, "The Way Home: A New Direction in Social Policy," February 1992, 25–27, and B-19–B-21; Rael Jean Isaac and Virginia C. Armat, *Madness in the Streets: How Psychiatry and the Law Abandoned the Mentally Ill* (New York: Free Press, 1990), 5; Martha R. Burt and Barbara E. Cohen, "Differences among Homeless Single Women, Women with Children, and Single Men," *Social Problems* 36, no. 5 (December 1989), table 4.

27. US Department of Housing and Urban Development, "HUD 2020 Continuum of Care Homeless Assistance Programs Homeless Populations and Subpopulations."

28. Rog, Holupka, and Patton, "Characteristics and Dynamics of Homeless Families With Children," 2-2, https://aspe.hhs.gov/sites/default/files/private/pdf/75331/report.pdf; US Interagency Council on Homelessness, "Homelessness: Programs and the People They Serve: Findings of the National Survey of Homeless Assistance Providers and Clients," September 1999, chapter 12 and table 12.2, https://www.huduser.gov/portal/publications/homeless /homeless_tech.html; Eric N. Lindblom, "Towards A Comprehensive Homelessness Prevention Strategy," *Housing Policy Debate* 2 no. 3 (1991), 961; "US Department of Housing and Urban Development (HUD), US Interagency Council on Homelessness, "Priority: Home! The Federal Plan to Break the Cycle of Homelessness," 1994, 33.

29. US Department of Housing and Urban Development, "The 2018 Annual Homeless Assessment Report (AHAR) to Congress; Part 2: Estimates of Homelessness in the

United States," September 2020, A-9, https://www.huduser.gov/portal/sites/default/files /pdf/2018-AHAR-Part-2.pdf.

30. Ellen L. Bassuk and Ellen M. Gallagher. "The Impact of Homelessness on Children." *Child & Youth Services* 14, no. 1 (1990): 20; New York City Independent Budget Office. "The Rising Number of Homeless Families in NYC, 2002–2012." November 2014, 6, https://ibo .nyc.ny.us/iboreports/2014dhs.pdf; Stephen Metraux, Jamison Fargo, Nick Eng and Dennis P. Culhane, "Employment and Earnings Trajectories During Two Decades Among Adults in New York City Homeless Shelters," *Cityscape: A Journal of Policy Development and Research* 20 no. 2 (2018): 192–93, https://www.huduser.gov/portal/periodicals/cityscpe/vol20num2 /ch11.pdf; US Interagency Council on Homelessness, "Priority: Home! The Federal Plan to Break the Cycle of Homelessness," 23.

31. Weinreb and Rossi, "The American Homeless Family Shelter 'System,'" 96–97; Rog, Ho-lupka and Patton, "Characteristics and Dynamics of Homeless Families With Children," 2–2.

32. Charles Hoch and Robert A. Slayton, *New Homeless and Old: Community and the Skid Row Hotel* (Philadelphia: Temple University Press, 1989), 75.

33. Jessica Semega, Melissa Kollar, Emily A. Shrider, and John F. Creamer, "Income and Poverty in the United States: 2019," United States Census Bureau, September 2020, Table B–7, https://www.census.gov/content/dam/Census/library/publications/2020/demo/p60-270.pdf.

34. US Department of Health and Human Services, "Births: Final Data for 2019," National Vital Statistics Reports 70, no. 2, March 23, 2021, table 11, https://www.cdc.gov /nchs/data/nvsr/nvsr70/nvsr70-02-508.pdf; Social Capital Project, US Senate Joint Economic Committee, "Love, Marriage, and the Baby Carriage: The Rise in Unwed Childbearing," December 2017, figure 1.

35. Rachel M. Shattuck and Rose M. Kreider, "Social and Economic Characteristics of Cur-rently Unmarried Women With a Recent Birth: 2011," US Census Bureau, May 2013, table 2, https://www2.census.gov/library/publications/2013/acs/acs-21.pdf; Carmen Solomon-Fears, "Nonmarital Births: An Overview," Congressional Research Service, July 30, 2014, 13, https:// sgp.fas.org/crs/misc/R43667.pdf; US Department of Health and Human Services, "Births: Final Data for 2019," 15.

36. KIDS COUNT, "KIDS COUNT Data Book, Annie E. Casey Foundation, https:// datacenter.kidscount.org/.

37. "HUD 2020 Continuum of Care Homeless Assistance Programs Homeless Popula-tions and Subpopulations, MI-501 Detroit CoC" US Department of Housing and Ur-ban Development, December 15, 2020, https://files.hudexchange.info/reports/published /CoC_PopSub_CoC_MI-501-2020_MI_2020.pdf; US Department of Housing and Urban Development, "HUD 2020 Continuum of Care Homeless Assistance Programs Homeless Populations and Subpopulations, NY-600 New York City CoC," December 15, 2020, https:// files.hudexchange.info/reports/published/CoC_PopSub_CoC_NY-600-2020_NY_2020.pdf.

38. Carol B. Stack, *All Our Kin: Strategies for Survival in a Black Community* (New York: Harper & Row, 1974); William Ryan, *Blaming the Victim* (New York, Pantheon Books 1971), chapter 3; Kay S. Hymowitz "The Black Family: 40 Years of Lies," *City Journal*, Summer 2005; David Brooks, "The Nuclear Family Was a Mistake," *The Atlantic*, March 2020, https:// www.theatlantic.com/magazine/archive/2020/03/the-nuclear-family-was-a-mistake/605536/.

39. Joanne Pavao, Jennifer Alvarez, Nikki Baumrind, Marta Induni, and Rachel Kimerling. "Intimate Partner Violence and Housing Instability," *American Journal of Preventive Medicine* 32 no. 2 (February 2007): 143–46.

40. US Department of Housing and Urban Development, "The 2018 Annual Homeless Assessment Report (AHAR) to Congress; Part 2: Estimates of Homelessness in the United States," September 2020, B-12–B-13, https://www.huduser.gov/portal/sites/default/files/pdf/2018-AHAR-Part-2.pdf.

41. Hilary Botein and Andrea Hetling, *Home Safe Home: Housing Solutions for Survivors of Intimate Partner Violence* (New Brunswick: Rutgers University Press, 2016), chapter 3.

42. Leigh Goodmark, *A Troubled Marriage: Domestic Violence and the Legal System* (New York: New York University Press, 2011), chapter 1.

43. Office of New York City Mayor Bill de Blasio. "Turning the Tide on Homelessness in New York City," February 2017, 8, https://www1.nyc.gov/assets/dhs/downloads/pdf/turning-the-tide-on-homelessness.pdf; HUD's figures for the nation as a whole are roughly similar: US Department of Housing and Urban Development, "The 2018 Annual Homeless Assessment Report (AHAR) to Congress; Part 2," 3–7.

44. Jaclyn D. Cravens, Jason B. Whiting, and Rola O. Aamar, "Why I Stayed/Left: An Analysis of Voices of Intimate Partner Violence on Social Media," *Contemporary Family Therapy* 37 (2015): 378–79; Deborah K. Anderson and Daniel G. Saunders, "Leaving an Abusive Partner: An Empirical Review of Predictors, the Process of Leaving, and Psychological Well-Being," *Trauma, Violence, and Abuse* 4, no. 2 (April 2003): 163–91.

45. Sascha Griffing, Deborah Fish Ragin, Robert E. Sage, Lorraine Madry, Lewis E. Bingham, and Beny J. Primm, "Domestic Violence Survivors' Self-Identified Reasons for Returning to Abusive Relationships," *Journal of Interpersonal Violence* 17, no. 3 (2002): table 3.

46. Michael L. Benson and Greer Litton Fox, "When Violence Hits Home: How Economics and Neighborhood Play a Role, Research in Brief," National Institute for Justice, September 2004, https://www.ojp.gov/pdffiles1/nij/205004.pdf.

47. Nicole E. Allen, "US Commentary: Insights from the Family Options Study Regarding Housing and Intimate Partner Violence," *Cityscape: A Journal of Policy Development and Research* 19 no. 3 (2017): 245–53, https://www.huduser.gov/portal/periodicals/cityscpe/vol19num3/ch13.pdf; and Dessie Lee Clark, Leila Wood, and Cris M. Sullivan, "Examining the Needs and Experiences of Domestic Violence Survivors in Transitional Housing," *Journal of Family Violence* 34, no. 4 (May 2019), 275–86.

48. National Center for Homeless Education, January 2020, "Federal Data Summary, School Years 2015–2016 Through 2017–2018, Education for Homeless Children and Youth," 2, https://nche.ed.gov/wp-content/uploads/2020/01/Federal-Data-Summary-SY-15.16-to-17.18-Published-1.30.2020.pdf; US Department of Housing and Urban Development, "The 2018 Annual Homeless Assessment Report (AHAR) to Congress; Part 2, B-3.

49. Edin and Kefalas, *Promises I Can Keep*, appendix A, table 4; Josh Leopold, "Housing Needs of Rental Assistance Applicants," *Cityscape: A Journal of Policy Development and Research* 14, no. 2 (2012), exhibits 4 and 6, https://www.huduser.gov/portal/periodicals/cityscpe/vol14num2/Cityscape_July2012_housing_needs.pdf.

50. Natasha V. Pilkauskas and Christina Cross, "Beyond the Nuclear Family: Trends in Children Living in Shared Households," *Demography* 55, no. 6 (2018), 2283–97; Hope Harvey, Rachel Dunifon, and Natasha Pilkauskas, "Under Whose Roof? Understanding the Living Arrangements of Children in Doubled-Up Households," *Demography* 58, no. 3 (June 2021): 821–46.

51. Edin and Kefalas, *Promises I Can Keep*, appendix A, table 4.

52. New York City Independent Budget Office. "Not Reaching the Door: Homeless Students Face Many Hurdles on the Way to School." October 2016, 3, https://ibo.nyc

.ny.us/iboreports/not-reaching-the-door-homeless-students-face-many-hurdles-on-the-way
-to-school.pdf.

53. Stephen Eide, "Is Homelessness Only a Housing Problem?" Institute for Family Studies, June 13, 2016, https://ifstudies.org/blog/is-homelessness-only-a-housing-problem.

54. Natasha V. Pilkauskas, Mariana Amorim, and Rachel E. Dunifon, "Historical Trends
in Children Living in Multigenerational Households in the United States: 1870–2018," *Demography* 57 (2020): 2269–96.

55. Hope Harvey, Rachel Dunifon, and Natasha Pilkauskas, "Under Whose Roof? Understanding the Living Arrangements of Children in Doubled-Up Households," *Demography* 58,
no. 3 (June 2021): 821–46.

56. Anthony Jackson, *A Place Called Home: A History of Low-cost Housing in Manhattan*
(Cambridge: The MIT Press, 1976), 18 and 84; David T. Beito and Linda Royster Beito,
"'The Lodger Evil' and the Transformation of Progressive Housing Reform, 1890–1930." *The
Independent Review* 20, no. 4 (Spring 2016): 485–508.

57. Hope Harvey, "When Mothers Can't "Pay the Cost to Be the Boss": Roles and Identity within Doubled-Up Households," *Social Problems*, June 2020, https://doi.org/10.1093
/socpro/spaa022, 1–21.

58. National Center for Homeless Education, "Federal Data Summary, School Years
2015–2016 Through 2017–2018, Education for Homeless Children and Youth," table 6.

59. National Academies of Sciences, Engineering, and Medicine, "Permanent Supportive
Housing: Evaluating the Evidence for Improving Health Outcomes Among People Experiencing Chronic Homelessness," 2018, 187.

60. Yinghua He, Brendan O'Flaherty, and Robert A. Rosenheck, "Is Shared Housing
a Way to Reduce Homelessness? The Effect of Household Arrangements on Formerly
Homeless People," *Journal of Housing Economics* 19, no. 1 (March 2010): 1–12; Natasha V.
Pilkauskas, Irwin Garfinkel, and Sara S. McLanahan, "The Prevalence and Economic Value
of Doubling Up," *Demography* 51 (2014): 1667–76; Jack Tsai, T. Scott Stroup, and Robert
A. Rosenheck, "Housing Arrangements Among a National Sample of Adults with Chronic
Schizophrenia Living in the United States: A Descriptive Study," *Journal of Community Psy-
chology* 39, no. 1 (2011): 76–88; Sherry Ahrentzen, "Double Indemnity or Double Delight?
The Health Consequences of Shared Housing and 'Doubling Up,'" *Journal of Social Issues*
59, no. 3 (July 2003): 547–68.

61. National Center for Homeless Education, "Federal Data Summary, School Years
2015–2016 Through 2017–2018, Education for Homeless Children and Youth," table 11;
For a survey of the literature, see Peter M. Miller, "A Critical Analysis of the Research on
Student Homelessness," *Review of Educational Research* 81, no. 3 (September 2011): 308–37.

62. New York City Independent Budget Office, "Not Reaching the Door: Homeless Students Face Many Hurdles on the Way to School," October 2016, 4 and 11.

63. John C. Buckner, "The Impact of Homelessness on Children: An Analytic Review
of the Literature," in Debra J. Rog, C. Scott Holupka, and Lisa C. Patton, "Characteristics
and Dynamics of Homeless Families with Children," US Department of Health and Human
Services, Office of the Assistant Secretary for Planning and Evaluation, 2007, A-24–A-26,
emphasis in original, https://aspe.hhs.gov/sites/default/files/private/pdf/75331/report.pdf.

64. Julie A. Lam and Robert Rosenheck, "The effects of victimization on clinical outcomes of homeless persons with serious mental illness," *Psychiatric Services* 49, no. 5 (May
1998), 678–79.

65. United States Census Bureau, "Historical Household Tables," November 2021, https://www.census.gov/data/tables/time-series/demo/families/households.html.

66. Alex F. Schwartz, *Housing Policy in the United States*, 4th Edition (New York: Routledge, 2021), Kindle Edition, figure 2.6.

67. Kevin Corinth, "How Safety Net Programs Tax the Sharing of Housing," *Tax Notes*, December 14, 2015, 1413–20; Ingrid Gould Ellen and Brendan O'Flaherty, "Social Programs and Household Size: Evidence from New York City," *Population Research and Policy Review* 26, no. 4 (August 2007): 387–409.

68. "SHARE! Collaborative Housing," webpage from programs list on SHARE!'s website, https://leaseuplosangeles.org/ https://shareselfhelp.org/programs-share-the-self-help-and-re covery-exchange/share-collaborative-housing/.

69. Matthew Desmond, *Evicted: Poverty and Profit in the American City* (New York: Crown Publishers, 2016), 394–95.

70. Thomas J. Main, *Homelessness in New York City: Policymaking from Koch to de Blasio* (New York: New York University Press, 2017), 154

71. DeParle, *American Dream*, 95; billmoyers.com, "The Vanishing Family: Crisis in Black America." video clip from documentary, July 30, 1989.

Chapter 9. You Can't Catch Schizophrenia from the Streets

1. Gary Blasi, "UD Day: Impending Evictions and Homelessness in Los Angeles," UCLA Luskin Institute on Inequality and Democracy, May 28, 2020, 19, https://escholarship.org/uc/item/2gz6c8cv#main.

2. Peter H. Rossi, James D. Wright, Gene A. Fisher, and Georgianna Willis, "The Urban Homeless: Estimating Composition and Size," *Science* 235 (March 13, 1987): 1336–41; Paul A. Toro, et al., "Obtaining representative samples of homeless persons: A two-city study," *Journal of Community Psychology* 27, no. 2 (1999): 157–77; Paul Koegel, Greer Sullivan, Audrey Burnam, Sally C. Morton, and Suzanne Wenzel, "Utilization of Mental Health and Substance Abuse Services Among Homeless Adults in Los Angeles," *Medical Care* 37, no. 3 (March 1999): 306–17; US Interagency Council on Homelessness, "Homelessness: Programs and the People They Serve: Findings of the National Survey of Homeless Assistance Providers and Clients," chapter 8, https://www.huduser.gov/portal/publications/homeless/homeless_tech.html; New York City Commission on the Homeless, "The Way Home: A New Direction in Social Policy," February 1992, B-20; Doug Smith and Benjamin Oreskes, "Are Many Homeless People in LA Mentally Ill? New Findings Back the Public's Perception," *Los Angeles Times*, October 7, 2019, https://www.latimes.com/california/story/2019-10-07/homeless-population-mental-illness-disability; Ellen L. Bassuk, Lenore Rubin, and Alison Lauriat. "Is Homelessness a Mental Health Problem?" *The American Journal of Psychiatry* 141, no. 12 (December 1984): 1546–50.

3. Charles Hoch and Robert A. Slayton, *New Homeless and Old: Community and the Skid Row Hotel* (Philadelphia: Temple University Press, 1989); US Department of Health and Human Services, Substance Abuse and Mental Health Services Administration, "A Treatment Improvement Protocol: Behavioral Health Services for People Who Are Homeless (TIP 55)," 2013, 1–4 and 1–6, https://store.samhsa.gov/sites/default/files/d7/priv/sma13-4734.pdf.

4. Michael B. Katz, *In the Shadow of the Poorhouse: A Social History of Welfare in America* (New York: Basic Books, 1986), chapter 6.

5. National Association of State Mental Health Program Directors, "Trend in Psychiatric Inpatient Capacity, United States and Each State, 1970 to 2014," assessment #10, August

2017, table 9, https://www.nasmhpd.org/sites/default/files/TAC.Paper_.10.Psychiatric%20 Inpatient%20Capacity_Final.pdf.

6. E. Fuller Torrey, *Nowhere to Go: The Tragic Odyssey of the Homeless Mentally Ill* (New York: Harper & Row, 1988), 141.

7. Jack T. Tsai, Scott Stroup, and Robert A. Rosenheck, "Housing Arrangements Among a National Sample of Adults with Chronic Schizophrenia Living in the United States: A Descriptive Study," *Journal of Community Psychology* 39, no. 1 (2011): 76–88; Robert Reich and Lloyd Siegel, "The Emergence of the Bowery as a Psychiatric Dumping Ground," *Psychiatric Quarterly* 50 (1978): 191–201; Julian Wolpert and Eileen R. Wolpert, "The Relocation of Released Mental Hospital Patients into Residential Communities," *Policy Sciences* 7 (1976): 31–51; Ella Howard, *Homeless: Poverty and Place in Urban America* (Philadelphia: University of Pennsylvania Press, 2013) chapter 6; Torrey, *Nowhere to Go*, 141; Rael Jean Isaac and Virginia C. Armat, *Madness in the Streets: How Psychiatry and the Law Abandoned the Mentally Ill* (New York: Free Press, 1990), 288.

8. Marian Moser Jones, "Creating a Science of Homelessness During the Reagan Era," *The Milbank Quarterly* 93, no. 1 (2015): 148–49.

9. DJ Jaffe, *Insane Consequences: How the Mental Health Industry Fails the Mentally Ill* (Amherst, NY: Prometheus Books, 2017), appendix A.

10. Source: National Institute of Mental Health, "Mental Illness," web page, https://www .nimh.nih.gov/health/statistics/mental-illness.

11. US Department of Health and Human Services, Substance Abuse and Mental Health Services Administration, "Key Substance Use and Mental Health Indicators in the United States: Results from the 2019 National Survey on Drug Use and Health," September 2020, 60, https://www.samhsa.gov/data/sites/default/files/reports/rpt29393/2019NSDUHFFRPD FWHTML/2019NSDUHFFR1PDFW090120.pdf.

12. Stephen B. Seager, *Street Crazy: The Tragedy of the Homeless Mentally Ill* (Redondo Beach, CA: Westcom Press, 1998), 2; Christopher Legras, "We Need to Stop Using the Term 'Homeless Crisis.' It's Wrong, It's Not Backed up by The Data, and It Leads to Bad Policy," *The All Aspect Report*, July 22, 2021, https://allaspectreport.com/2021/07/22/we -need-to-stop-using-the-term-homeless-crisis-its-wrong-its-not-backed-up-by-the-data -and-it-leads-to-bad-policy/.

13. Andrew Doran, "A Modern Mendicant," *First Things*, April 2020, https://www.first things.com/article/2020/04/a-modern-mendicant.

14. Jaffe, *Insane Consequences*, 34.

15. Tsai, Stroup, and Rosenheck "Housing Arrangements Among a National Sample of Adults with Chronic Schizophrenia Living in the United States."

16. Gerald N. Grob, *The Mad Among Us: A History of the Care of America's Mentally Ill* (New York: The Free Press, 1994), 80. For a poignant depiction of family-initiated commitment process in the old days, one involving the developmentally disabled, see Saul Bellow, *The Adventures of Augie March* (New York: Viking Press, 1953), chapter 4. For an account played for laughs, see the 1944 film *Arsenic and Old Lace*.

17. Howard Husock, "Dreams of My Uncle," *City Journal*, Spring 2017, https://www.city -journal.org/html/dreams-my-uncle-15124.html.

18. Joseph P. Shapiro, *No Pity: People with Disabilities Forging a New Civil Rights Movement* (New York: Times Books 1993), chapter 5.

19. Pete Earley, *Crazy: A Father's Search Through America's Mental Health Madness* (New York: Berkley Books, 2007), 15, 23–25, and 28; Jeneen Interlandi, "When My Crazy Father Actually Lost His Mind," *New York Times Magazine*, June 22, 2012.

20. Amanda Peters, "Lawyers Who Break the Law: What Congress Can Do to Prevent Mental Health Patient Advocates from Violating Federal Legislation," *Oregon Law Review* 89, no. 1 (2010): 167.

21. New York City Commission on the Homeless, "The Way Home: A New Direction in Social Policy," appendices B and C.

22. US Department of Housing and Urban Development, "HUD 2020 Continuum of Care Homeless Assistance Programs Homeless Populations and Subpopulations," December 15, 2020, https://files.hudexchange.info/reports/published/CoC_PopSub_Natl TerrDC_2020.pdf; "TIP 55: Behavioral Health Services for People Who are Homeless: A Review of the Literature," 1–6 and 1–8, https://store.samhsa.gov/sites/default/files/d7/priv /sma13-4734_literature.pdf.

23. US Department of Health and Human Services, "Key Substance Use and Mental Health Indicators in the United States," 35–36.

24. US Department of Health and Human Services, "National Survey on Drug Use and Health: Comparison of 2017–2018 and 2018–2019 Population Percentages (50 States and the District of Columbia)," December 15, 2020, tables 20 and 22, https://www.samhsa .gov/data/sites/default/files/reports/rpt32806/2019NSDUHsaeShortTermCHG/2019NSDU HsaeShortTermCHG/2019NSDUHsaeShortTermCHG.pdf.

25. Doug Smith and Benjamin Oreskes, "Are Many Homeless People in L.A. Mentally Ill? New Findings Back the Public's Perception," *Los Angeles Times*, October 7, 2019, https:// www.latimes.com/california/story/2019-10-07/homeless-population-mental-illness-disability.

26. Nikolas Lanum, "Seattle Residents at Breaking Point with Homeless Crisis: 'Makes Me Depressed,'" *New York Post*, March 29, 2021, https://nypost.com/2021/03/29/seattle -residents-at-breaking-point-with-homeless-crisis-makes-me-depressed/.

27. Jacqueline P. Wiseman, *Stations of the Lost: The Treatment of Skid Row Alcoholics* (Englewood Cliffs, NJ, Prentice-Hall, 1970): 4.

28. Anne Case and Angus Deaton *Deaths of Despair and the Future of Capitalism* (Princeton: Princeton University Press, 2020).

29. Chris Arnade, *Dignity: Seeking Respect in Back Row America* (New York: Sentinel, 2019).

30. Sam Quinones, *Dreamland: The True Tale of America's Opiate Epidemic* (New York: Bloomsbury Press, 2015), 239 and 290.

31. Elizabeth Sinclair-Hancq, Kelli South, and Molly Vencel, "Dual Diagnosis: Serious Mental Illness and Co-Occurring Substance Use Disorders," Treatment Advocacy Center, March 2021, https://www.treatmentadvocacycenter.org/storage/documents/TAC_Co-occur ing_Evidence_Brief_March_2021_Final.pdf.

32. James P. Spradley, *You Owe Yourself a Drunk: An Ethnography of Urban Nomads* (Prospect Heights, IL: Waveland Press, 2000 [orig. 1970]), 9.

33. Michael D. Zettler, *The Bowery* (New York: Drake Publishers, 1975).

34. Michael Shellenberger, *San Fransicko: Why Progressives Ruin Cities* (New York: Harper, 2021), 48.

35. George L. Kelling and Catherine M. Coles, *Fixing Broken Windows: Restoring Order and Reducing Crime in our Communities* (New York: Martin Kessler Books, 1996), chapter 2.

36. Applied Survey Research, "San Francisco Homeless Count and Survey Comprehensive Report," 2019, 12, https://hsh.sfgov.org/wp-content/uploads/FINAL-PIT-Report-2019-San -Francisco.pdf; San Francisco Budget and Legislative Analyst's Office, "Policing and Crimi-

nal Justice Costs Related to Open Air Drug Dealing in the Tenderloin, South of Market, and Mid-Market neighborhoods," April 25, 2019, 6–7, https://sfbos.org/sites/default/files/BLA_042519_Open_Drug_Dealing_Sup_Haney.pdf.

37. Stephen Metraux, "Waiting for the Wrecking Ball: Skid Row in Postindustrial Philadelphia," *Journal of Urban History* 25 no. 5 (July 1999): 697.

38. Jill Jonnes, *Hep-Cats, Narcs, and Pipe Dreams: A History of America's Romance with Illegal Drugs* (Baltimore: Johns Hopkins University Press, 1999).

39. Russell K. Schutt with Stephen M. Goldfinger, *Homelessness, Housing, and Mental Illness* (Cambridge: Harvard University Press, 2011), 268.

40. Howard M. Bahr, *Skid Row: An Introduction to Disaffiliation* (New York: Oxford University Press, 1973), 228.

41. US Congress. "Homeless in America: Examining the Crisis and Solutions to End Homelessness; Hearing Before the Committee on Financial Services, US House of Representatives, 116th Congress, First Session," US Government Publishing Office, February 13, 2019, 39, https://www.congress.gov/116/meeting/house/108894/documents/HHRG-116-BA00-20190213-SD003.pdf.

42. Ronn Blitzer, "Gillibrand Mocked for Calling Child Care, Paid Leave 'Infrastructure,'" foxnews.com, April 7, 2021.

43. Danya E. Keene, Mariana Henry, Carina Gormley, and Chima Ndumele, "'Then I Found Housing and Everything Changed': Transitions to Rent-Assisted Housing and Diabetes Self-Management," *Cityscape: A Journal of Policy Development and Research* 20, no. 2 (2018), 107–18, https://www.huduser.gov/portal/periodicals/cityscpe/vol20num2/ch7.pdf; Sandra K. Schwarcz, Ling C Hsu, Eric Vittinghoff, Annie Vu, Joshua D Bamberger, and Mitchell H Katz, "Impact of housing on the survival of persons with AIDS," *BMC Public Health* 9, Article number 220 (2009).

44. Shellenberger, *San Fransicko*, 32–34.

45. Richard G. Frank and Sherry A. Glied, *Better but not Well: Mental Health Policy in the United States since 1950* (Baltimore: Johns Hopkins University Press, 2006), chapter 4 and table 4.1.

46. Jaffe, *Insane Consequences*, 21.

47. D. J. Jaffe and E. Fuller Torrey, "Funds for Treating Individuals with Mental Illness: Is Your State Generous or Stingy?" mentalillnesspolicy.org, December 12, 2017, https://mentalillnesspolicy.org/wp-content/uploads/Funds4TreatingMentalIllnessFinal.pdf.

48. Schutt with Goldfinger, *Homelessness, Housing, and Mental Illness*.

49. Abhijit V. Banerjee and Esther Duflo, *Poor Economics: A Radical Rethinking of the Way to Fight Global Poverty* (New York: Public Affairs, 2011), 69.

Chapter 10. Police Work and Social Work

1. Ann Braden Johnson, *Out of Bedlam: The Truth about Deinstitutionalization* (New York: Basic Books, 1990), 57–58.

2. Henry Hope Reed, *The Golden City* (Garden City, NY: Doubleday, 1959), 101–2.

3. Myron Magnet, *The Dream and the Nightmare: The Sixties' Legacy to the Underclass* (New York: William Morrow and Company, 1993), 106.

4. Erich Goode, *The Taming of New York's Washington Square: A Wild Civility* (New York: New York University Press, 2018).

5. Michael Lewis, "The Death of Public Beauty," *National Review*, September 3, 2020, https://www.nationalreview.com/magazine/2020/09/21/the-death-of-public-beauty/.

6. Jose Martinez, "Homeless Feel Unwelcome at Gleaming New Moynihan Train Hall as They Stick to Penn Station," *The City*, January 10, 2021, https://www.thecity.nyc/2021/1/10/22223920/homeless-feel-unwelcome-at-gleaming-new-moynihan-train-hall.

7. Derek Thompson, "What in the World Is Causing the Retail Meltdown of 2017?," *Atlantic*, April 10, 2017, https://www.theatlantic.com/business/archive/2017/04/retail-meltdown-of-2017/522384/.

8. Scott Greenstone, "Feeling Abandoned By City Hall, Seattle Businesses Try to Respond to Homelessness," *Seattle Times*, October 16, 2018, https://www.seattletimes.com/seattle-news/homeless/feeling-abandoned-by-city-hall-seattle-businesses-try-to-respond-to-homelessness/; Chris Daniels, "Seattle Business Owners Urge New Approach to Crime and Homelessness," K5 News, May 22, 2019, https://www.king5.com/article/news/local/seattle/seattle-business-owners-urge-new-approach-to-crime-and-homelessness/281-06dbc129-3021-43a5-bb96-4a6c072ff33b; Tim Steele, "Small Business Owners Say Portland Is 'Lawless,'" Koin 6, November 28, 2017, https://www.koin.com/news/small-business-owners-say-portland-is-lawless/.

9. Emily Alpert Reyes and Benjamin Oreskes, "LA Expands Cleanup Teams for Homeless Encampments, Vowing to Be 'Less Reactive,'" *Los Angeles Times*, June 28, 2019, https://www.latimes.com/local/lanow/la-me-ln-homeless-encampment-cleanups-plan-20190628-story.html.

10. E. Ann Carson, "Prisoners in 2019," US Department of Justice, Office of Justice Programs, Bureau of Justice Statistics, October 2020, tables 13 and 14, https://bjs.ojp.gov/content/pub/pdf/p19.pdf; Danielle Kaeble, "Time Served in State Prison, 2018," Department of Justice, Office of Justice Programs, Bureau of Justice Statistics, March 2021, https://bjs.ojp.gov/content/pub/pdf/tssp18.pdf.

11. Forrest Stuart, *Down, Out, and Under Arrest: Policing and Everyday Life in Skid Row* (Chicago: The University of Chicago Press, 2016); Issa Kohler-Hausmann, *Misdemeanorland: Criminal Courts and Social Control in an Age of Broken Windows Policing* (Princeton: Princeton University Press, 2018); Chris Herring, Dilara Yarbrough, and Lisa Marie Alatorre, "Pervasive Penalty: How the Criminalization of Poverty Perpetuates Homelessness." *Social Problems* 67, no. 1 (2020): 131–49.

12. Source: "Low-Level Enforcement in New York City" (data story), New York City Mayor's Office of Criminal Justice, https://criminaljustice.cityofnewyork.us/data_stories/low-level-enforcement-in-new-york-city/.

13. National Law Center on Homelessness and Poverty, "Housing Not Handcuffs 2019: Ending the Criminalization of Homelessness in US Cities," December 2019, https://homelesslaw.org/wp-content/uploads/2019/12/HOUSING-NOT-HANDCUFFS-2019-FINAL.pdf.

14. Ted Andersen, Demian Bulwa, and Megan Cassidy, "The Scanner: SF Police Have Backed Off Controversial 'Sit/Lie' Citations," *San Francisco Chronicle*, October 22, 2018, https://www.sfchronicle.com/crime/article/The-Scanner-SF-police-have-backed-off-13322561.php.

15. Gale Holland and Christine Zhang, "Huge Increase in Arrests of Homeless in LA—But Mostly for Minor Offenses," *Los Angeles Times*, February 4, 2018, https://www.latimes.com/local/politics/la-me-homeless-arrests-20180204-story.html.

16. Brendan O'Flaherty and Ting Wu, "Homeless Shelters for Single Adults: Why Does Their Population Change?" *Social Service Review* 82, no. 3 (September 2008): 511–50.

17. Amanda Geller and Marah A. Curtis, "A Sort of Homecoming: Incarceration and the Housing Security of Urban Men," *Social Science Research* 40, no. 4 (2011): 1196–213.

18. New York City Coalition for the Homeless, "State of the Homeless 2021 Housing is Health Care, A Lesson for the Ages," April 2021, 28–29, https://www.coalitionforthehomeless.org/wp-content/uploads/2021/04/StateOfTheHomeless2021.pdf.

19. Stephen Metraux, Caterina G. Roman, and Richard S. Cho, "Incarceration and Homelessness," National Symposium on Homelessness Research, 2007, 9–7, https://www.huduser.gov/portal/publications/pdf/p9.pdf; see also Richard C. Tessler and Deborah L. Dennis, "A Synthesis of NIMH-Funded Research Concerning Persons who are Homeless and Mentally Ill," National Institute of Mental Health, February 9, 1989, 26; Stephen Metraux and Dennis P. Culhane, "Homeless Shelter Use and Reincarceration Following Prison Release," *Criminology and Public Policy* 3, no. 2 (March 2004): 139–60; Brianna Remster, "A Life Course Analysis of Homeless Shelter Use among the Formerly Incarcerated," *Justice Quarterly* 36, no. 3 (2019): 437–65; New York City Commission on the Homeless, "The Way Home: A New Direction in Social Policy," table 1; US Interagency Council on Homelessness, "Homelessness: Programs and the People They Serve: Findings of the National Survey of Homeless Assistance Providers and Clients," September 1999, chapter 8, https://www.huduser.gov/portal/publications/homeless/homeless_tech.html.

20. US Interagency Council on Homelessness, "Homelessness: Programs and the People They Serve," chapter 8; Richard C. Tessler and Deborah L. Dennis, "A Synthesis of NIMH-Funded Research Concerning Persons who are Homeless and Mentally Ill," National Institute of Mental Health, February 9, 1989, 26.

21. Joshua T. Ellsworth, "Street Crime Victimization Among Homeless Adults: A Review of the Literature," *Victims & Offenders* 14, no. 1 (2019): 112.

22. Tammy S. Garland, Tara Richards, and Mikaela Cooney, "Victims Hidden in Plain Sight: The Reality of Victimization Among the Homeless," *Criminal Justice Studies: A Critical Journal of Crime, Law and Society* 23, no. 4 (2010): 295–96; Molly Meinbresse, et al., "Exploring the Experiences of Violence Among Individuals Who Are Homeless Using a Consumer-Led Approach," *Violence and Victims* 29, no. 1 (2014): table 3, https://nhchc.org/wp-content/uploads/2019/08/vv-29-1_ptr_a8_122-136.pdf.

23. Barrett A. Lee and Christopher J. Schreck, "Danger on the Streets: Marginality and Victimization Among Homeless People," *American Behavioral Scientist* 48, no. 8 (April 2005): 1061; Ellsworth, "Street Crime Victimization Among Homeless Adults: A Review of the Literature," 97.

24. Ellsworth, "Street Crime Victimization Among Homeless Adults," 109–10.

25. See, for example, Donald Bogue, *Skid Row in American Cities*, Community and Family Study Center, University of Chicago, 1963, 65ff.

26. Molly Meinbresse, et al., "Exploring the Experiences of Violence Among Individuals Who Are Homeless Using a Consumer-Led Approach," 128–29.

27. David A. Snow, Susan G. Baker and Leon Anderson, "Criminality and Homeless Men: An Empirical Assessment," *Social Problems* 36, no. 5 (1989): 539.

28. Garland, Richards, and Cooney, "Victims Hidden in Plain Sight," 296–97.

29. Lee and Schreck, "Danger on the Streets: Marginality and Victimization Among Homeless People," 1058 and 1076.

30. Lee and Schreck, "Danger on the Streets: Marginality and Victimization Among Homeless People," 1058.

31. Robert C. Ellickson, "Controlling Chronic Misconduct in City Spaces: Of Panhandlers, Skid Rows, and Public-Space Zoning," *The Yale Law Journal* 105 (1996): 1194.

32. "'Since November, I've been sleeping beneath the canopy in front of a building on 45th and Lex. A big nice building. After three days, the security guard told me to move. But he talked to me and when he saw I was clean, he told me I could sleep there, but had to leave at 5 a.m. every day. He looked after me and even gave me his number.'" Claudia Irizarry Aponte and Ben Fractenberg, "Some NYC Homeless Practice Social Distancing in Hotels, With Help from Donors," *The City*, April 20, 2020, https://www.thecity.nyc /services-safety-net/2020/4/20/21247110/some-nyc-homeless-practice-social-distancing-in -hotels-with-help-from-donors.

33. James Q. Wilson, "Foreword" to George L. Kelling, and Catherine M. Coles, *Fixing Broken Windows: Restoring Order and Reducing Crime in our Communities* (New York: Martin Kessler Books, 1996), xiv; emphases in original.

34. Doris A. Fuller, H. Richard Lamb, Michael Biasotti, and John Snook, "Overlooked in the Undercounted: The Role of Mental Illness in Fatal Law Enforcement Encounters," Treatment Advocacy Center, December 2015, 5, https://www.treatmentadvocacycenter.org /storage/documents/overlooked-in-the-undercounted.pdf.

35. Reihan Salam, *Melting Pot or Civil War?: A Son of Immigrants makes the Case against Open Borders* (New York: Sentinel, 2018), 76–77.

36. Elizabeth Findell, "Homeless Become More Visible in Austin, Sparking Political Clash," *Wall Street Journal*, October 24, 2019, https://www.wsj.com/articles/homeless -becomes-more-visible-in-austin-sparking-political-clash-11571914802.

37. Rael Jean Isaac and Virginia C. Armat, *Madness in the Streets: How Psychiatry and the Law Abandoned the Mentally Ill* (New York: Free Press, 1990), 57.

38. Hilary Malson and Gary Blasi, "For the Crisis Yet to Come: Temporary Settlements in the Era of Evictions," UCLA Luskin Institute on Inequality and Democracy, July 21, 2020, 21–22, https://escholarship.org/uc/item/3tk6p1rk.

39. "City of Los Angeles Comprehensive Homelessness Strategy," Council File #15-1138-S1, Los Angeles City Council, February 9, 2016, 43, http://clkrep.lacity.org/online docs/2015/15-1138-s1_misc_03-21-2016.pdf.

40. Bogue, *Skid Row*, 62 and 64.

41. Ellickson, "Controlling Chronic Misconduct in City Spaces."

42. Erica Sandberg, "Fight for What You Love," *City Journal*, August 3, 2020, https:// www.city-journal.org/residents-fighting-for-san-francisco; "Hastings College of the Law, et al., v. City and County of San Francisco," United States District Court for the Northern District of California, Case 3:20-cv-03033, document 1, May 4, 2020, 1 and 12, https://www.city -journal.org/residents-fighting-for-san-francisco; Edward G. Goetz, "Land Use and Homeless Policy in Los Angeles," *International Journal Urban Regional Research* 16, no. 4 (December 1992): 540–54; Stuart, *Down, Out, and Under Arrest*, chapter 1.

43. Teresa Gowan, *Hobos, Hustlers, and Backsliders: Homeless in San Francisco* (Minneapolis: University of Minnesota Press, 2010), xxiii.

44. Stephan Thernstrom and Abigail Thernstrom, *America in Black and White: One Nation, Indivisible* (New York: Simon & Schuster, 1997), 46–50.

45. Data sheets "2020 Greater Los Angeles Homeless Count—Skid Row" and "2020 Greater Los Angeles Homeless Count—Los Angeles County," July 15, 2020, last updated November 20, 2020, accessed at https://www.lahsa.org/news?article=737-2020-greater-los -angeles-homeless-count-data-sheets&ref=hc.

46. Tessler and Dennis, "A Synthesis of NIMH-Funded Research Concerning Persons who are Homeless and Mentally Ill," 9.

47. Rachel M. Cohen, "How the Largest Known Homeless Encampment in Minneapolis History Came to Be," *The Appeal*, July 15, 2020, https://theappeal.org/minneapolis-homeless ness-crisis-powderhorn-park-encampment/.

48. Will Sarvis, "The Homelessness Muddle Revisited," *The Urban Lawyer* 49, no. 2 (Spring 2017): 328.

49. Josiah Flynt, "How Men Become Tramps," *Century Magazine* 50 (October 1895): 941.

Chapter 11. Housing, Housing, Housing

1. Brendan O'Flaherty, "Homelessness Research: A Guide for Economists (and Friends)," *Journal of Housing Economics* 44 (2019): 16–20.

2. Richard Plunz, *A History of Housing in New York City*, revised edition (New York: Columbia University Press, 2016), 126.

3. Thomas J. Main, "The Homeless Families of New York," *The Public Interest*, Fall 1986, 6.

4. See earlier discussion of rapid rehousing versus transitional housing and Schwartz, *Housing Policy in the United States*, figure 2.8; Joint Center for Housing Studies of Harvard University, "America's Rental Housing 2020," 2020, figure 2, table AR-1, https://www .jchs.harvard.edu/sites/default/files/reports/files/Harvard_JCHS_Americas_Rental_Hous ing_2020.pdf.

5. Chris Glynn and Emily B. Fox, "Dynamics of Homelessness in Urban America," *Annals of Applied Statistics* 13, no. 1 (2019): 573–605; Barrett A. Lee, Townsand Price-Spratlen and James W. Kanan "Determinants of Homelessness in Metropolitan Areas," *Journal of Urban Affairs* 25, no. 3 (2003): 335–56; Maria Hanratty, "Do local Economic Conditions Affect Homelessness? Impact of Area Housing Market Factors, Unemployment, and Poverty on Community Homeless Rates," *Housing Policy Debate* 27 no. 4: (2017): 640–55.

6. Source: Calculation based on 2015–2019 American Community Survey data downloaded from https://data.census.gov/cedsci/; The tourist communities of Edwards, Heber, Key West, and Vineyard Haven are technically "micro" areas.

7. Robert M. Hayes, "Hope for New York City's Homeless?; The Issue Is Housing," *New York Times*, November 27, 1986.

8. John M. Quigley and Steven Raphael, "Is Housing Unaffordable? Why Isn't It More Affordable?" *Journal of Economic Perspectives* 18, no. 1 (Winter 2004): 191–214; Schwartz, *Housing Policy in the United States*, chapter 2.

9. Schwartz, *Housing Policy in the United States*, chapter 2.

10. US Department of Housing and Urban Development, "Worst Case Housing Needs 2019 Report to Congress," June 2020, exhibit 1–2, https://www.huduser.gov/portal/sites /default/files/pdf/worst-case-housing-needs-2020.pdf.

11. Brendan O'Flaherty, *City Economics* (Cambridge: Harvard University Press, 2005), 362

12. Gilda Haas and Allan David Heskin, "Community Struggles in Los Angeles," *International Journal of Urban and Regional Research* 5 no. 4 (December 1981): 555.

13. Brendan O'Flaherty, *Making Room: The Economics of Homelessness* (Cambridge: Harvard University Press, 1996), 174–75.

14. Cushing N. Dolbeare and Sheila Crowley, "Changing Priorities: The Federal Budget and Housing Assistance, 1976–2002," National Low-Income Housing Coalition, August 2002, https://nlihc.org/sites/default/files/Changing-Priorities-Report_August-2002.pdf; Conor Dougherty, *Golden Gates: The Fight for Housing—and Democracy—in America's Most Prosperous City* (New York: Penguin Press, 2020), 154.

15. Prisoner Reentry Institute John Jay College of Criminal Justice, "Three Quarter Houses: The View from the Inside," October 2013; Kim Barker, "A Choice for Recovering Addicts: Relapse or Homelessness," *New York Times*, May 30, 2015, https://www.nytimes.com/2015/05/31/nyregion/three-quarter-housing-a-choice-for-recovering-addicts-or-homelessness.html.

16. Prisoner Reentry Institute John Jay College of Criminal Justice, "Three Quarter Houses: The View from the Inside," ix.

17. Los Angeles County Mental Health Commission Ad-hoc Committee on LA County's Board and Care System, "A Call to Action: The Precarious State of the Board and Care System Serving Residents Living with Mental Illness in Los Angeles County," January 22, 2018, http://file.lacounty.gov/SDSInter/dmh/1036005_BoardandCareFacilitiesreport.pdf; Doug Smith, "These Homes Keep LA's Most Vulnerable from Becoming Homeless. Now They're Closing," *Los Angeles Times*, November 6, 2019, https://www.latimes.com/california/story/2019-11-06/homeless-housing-board-care-homes-mental-illness.

18. Los Angeles City Controller. "High Cost of Homeless Housing: Review of Proposition HHH," October 8, 2019, https://lacontroller.org/wp-content/uploads/2019/10/The-High-Cost-of-Homeless-Housing_Review-of-Prop-HHH_10.8.19.pdf.

19. "HUD 2020 Continuum of Care Homeless Assistance Programs Housing Inventory Count Report," US Department of Housing and Urban Development, January 13, 2021, https://files.hudexchange.info/reports/published/CoC_HIC_NatlTerrDC_2020.pdf.

20. For a strong argument that shelters aren't superior to SROs, from a personal autonomy perspective, see Charles Hoch and Robert A. Slayton, *New Homeless and Old: Community and the Skid Row Hotel* (Philadelphia: Temple University Press, 1989), and chapter 11 in particular.

21. Doug Smith, "It Took Three Years of Blown Deadlines, But LA Opens Its First Homeless Housing Project," *Los Angeles Times*, January 7, 2019, https://www.latimes.com/california/story/2020-01-07/homeless-housing-project-proposition-hhh-bond-measure.

22. Benjamin Oreskes, Emily Apert Reyes, Doug Smith, "Judge orders LA City and County to Offer Shelter to Everyone on Skid Row by Fall," *Los Angeles Times*, April 20, 2021, https://www.latimes.com/homeless-housing/story/2021-04-20/judge-carter-la-city-county-shelter-skid-row-homeless-fall.

23. US Department of Housing and Urban Development, "The 2017 Annual Homeless Assessment Report (AHAR) to Congress, Part 2: Estimates of Homelessness in the United States," October 2018, 2–15 and 3–17, https://www.hudexchange.info/resource/5769/2017-ahar-part-2-estimates-of-homelessness-in-the-us/.

24. Kirk McClure, "Length of Stay in Assisted Housing," US Department of Housing and Urban Development, Office of Policy Development and Research, October 2017, https://www.huduser.gov/portal/sites/default/files/pdf/lengthofstay.pdf; US Department of Housing and Urban Development, "The 2018 Annual Homeless Assessment Report (AHAR) to Congress; Part 2: Estimates of Homelessness in the United States," September 2020, 7–6, https://www.huduser.gov/portal/sites/default/files/pdf/2018-AHAR-Part-2.pdf.

25. Barbara Sard, Douglas Rice, Alison Bell and Alicia Mazzara, "Federal Policy Changes Can Help More Families with Housing Vouchers Live in Higher-Opportunity Areas," Center for Budget and Policy Priorities, September 4, 2018, https://www.cbpp.org/research/housing/federal-policy-changes-can-help-more-families-with-housing-vouchers-live-in-higher.

26. Dougherty, *Golden Gates*, 157.

27. Will Fischer, Sonya Acosta and Erik Gartland, "More Housing Vouchers: Most Important Step to Help More People Afford Stable Homes," Center for Budget and Policy

Priorities, April 14, 2021, https://www.cbpp.org/research/housing/more-housing-vouchers
-most-important-step-to-help-more-people-afford-stable-homes.

28. US Department of Housing and Urban Development, "Worst Case Housing Needs 2019 Report to Congress," June 2020, 9, https://www.huduser.gov/portal/sites/default /files/pdf/worst-case-housing-needs-2020.pdf; Mary K. Cunningham, "It's Time to Reinforce the Housing Safety Net by Adopting Universal Vouchers for Low-Income Renters," Urban Institute, April 7, 2020, https://www.urban.org/urban-wire/its-time-reinforce-housing-safety -net-adopting-universal-vouchers-low-income-renters.

29. Eva Rosen, *The Voucher Promise: "Section 8" and the fate of an American neighborhood* (Princeton: Princeton University Press, 2020), 20; Schwartz, *Housing Policy in the United States*, 204.

30. Rosen, *The Voucher Promise*, 128; Schwartz, *Housing Policy in the United States*, 204.

31. Daniel Gubits, et al., "Family Options Study 3-Year Impacts of Housing and Services Interventions for Homeless Families," US Department of Housing and Urban Development, Office of Policy Development and Research, October 2016, exhibit 3–12, pp. 41–44, https:// www.huduser.gov/portal/sites/default/files/pdf/Family-Options-Study-Full-Report.pdf; Anne Fletcher and Michelle Wood, "Guest Editors' Introduction: Next Steps for the Family Options Study," *Cityscape: A Journal of Policy Development and Research* 19 no. 3 (2017): 192, https:// www.huduser.gov/portal/periodicals/cityscpe/vol19num3/guest2.pdf; "Federal Housing Assistance for Low-Income Households," Congressional Budget Office, September 2015, 3 and 15–16, https://www.cbo.gov/sites/default/files/114th-congress-2015-2016/reports/50782 -lowincomehousing-onecolumn.pdf; Robert Collinson, Ingrid Gould Ellen, and Jens Ludwig, "Low-Income Housing Policy," National Bureau of Economic Research, August 27, 2015, 38–39; Edgar O. Olsen, and Jeffrey E. Zabel, "Chapter 14: US Housing Policy" In *Handbook of Regional and Urban Economics, 5A* edited by Gilles Duranton, J. Vernon Henderson, and William C. Strange (New York: North-Holland, 2015), 917–23.

32. Michael Lens, Kirk McClure and Brent Mast, "Does Jobs Proximity Matter in the Housing Choice Voucher Program?" *Cityscape: A Journal of Policy Development and Research* 21, no. 1 (2019): 146.

33. "Federal Housing Assistance for Low-Income Households," Congressional Budget Office, 15–16; Rosen, *The Voucher Promise*, 111–12.

34. Mary Cunningham, et al., "A Pilot Study of Landlord Acceptance of Housing Choice Vouchers," US Department of Housing and Urban Development, August 2018, 6, https:// www.huduser.gov/portal/portal/sites/default/files/pdf/Landlord-Acceptance-of-Housing -Choice-Vouchers.pdf; Brent Mast, "School Performance of Schools Assigned to HUD-Assisted Households," *Cityscape: A Journal of Policy Development and Research* 20, no. 3 (2018): 189–221, https://www.huduser.gov/portal/periodicals/cityscpe/vol20num3/ch10.pdf; Schwartz, *Housing Policy in the United States*, 211–14.

35. Raj Chetty, Nathaniel Hendren, and Lawrence F. Katz, "The Effects of Exposure to Better Neighborhoods on Children: New Evidence from the Moving to Opportunity Experiment," *The American Economic Review* 106, no. 4 (April 2016): 855–902, https://scholar .harvard.edu/files/lkatz/files/chk_aer_mto_0416.pdf.

36. Rosen, *The Voucher Promise*, 210 and 239.

37. Jens Ludwig, et al., "Long-Term Neighborhood Effects on Low-Income Families: Evidence from Moving to Opportunity," *American Economic Review* 103, no. 3 (2013), 226–31.

38. Amity Shlaes, *Great Society: A New History* (New York: Harper, 2019), Kindle edition, 157.

39. Matthew Desmond, *Evicted: Poverty and Profit in the American City* (New York: Crown Publishers, 2016), chapter 11; See also Matthew Desmond and Nathan Wilmers, "Do the Poor Pay More for Housing? Exploitation, Profit, and Risk in Rental Markets," *American Journal of Sociology* 124 no. 4 (January 2019): 1090–124.

40. Kathryn J. Edin and H. Luke Shaefer, *$2.00 a Day: Living on Almost Nothing in America* (Boston: Houghton Mifflin Harcourt, 2015), 183–84; Philip M. E. Garboden, Eva Rosen, Meredith Greif, Stefanie DeLuca, and Kathryn Edin, "Urban Landlords and the Housing Choice Voucher Program: A Research Report," Washington, DC: US Department of Housing and Urban Development, May 2018, 9–10, https://www.huduser.gov/portal/sites /default/files/pdf/Urban-Landlords-HCV-Program.pdf.

41. Alan Mallach, "Rents Will Only Go So Low, No Matter How Much We Build," shelterforce.org, December 13, 2019, https://shelterforce.org/2019/12/13/rents-will-only-go-so -low-no-matter-how-much-we-build/.

42. "Federal Housing Assistance for Low-Income Households," Congressional Budget Office, September 2015, 19.

43. Kirk McClure, "Housing Choice Voucher Marketing Opportunity Index: Analysis of Data at the Tract and Block Group Level," US Department of Housing and Urban Development, Office of Policy Development and Research, 2011, 13; Mary Cunningham, et al., "A Pilot Study of Landlord Acceptance of Housing Choice Vouchers," 7–8.

44. Eva Rosen and Philip Garboden, "Landlord Paternalism: Housing the Poor with a Velvet Glove," *Social Problems* spaa037 (2020): 8–9.

45. Garboden, Rosen, Greif, DeLuca, and Edin, "Urban Landlords and the Housing Choice Voucher Program: A Research Report," 37–38.

46. Brian Goldstone, "The New American Homeless," *New Republic*, August 21, 2019.

47. US Interagency Council on Homelessness, "Homelessness: Programs and the People They Serve: Findings of the National Survey of Homeless Assistance Providers and Clients," September 1999, chapter 4, https://www.huduser.gov/portal/publications/homeless /homeless_tech.html; Institute for Children Poverty and Homelessness, "The Dynamics of Family Homelessness in New York City," June 2019, https://www.icphusa.org/dynamics/.

48. Source: Eviction Lab, "Top Evicting Large Cities in the United States," Eviction Lab website, Princeton University, https://evictionlab.org/rankings/#/evictions?r=United%20States &a=0&d=evictionRate&lang=en.

49. Steven Banks, "Testimony of Steven Banks, Commissioner Department of Social Services," New York City Council, Committee on General Welfare, Fiscal Year 2021 Executive Budget Hearing, May 18, 2020, https://www1.nyc.gov/assets/hra/downloads/pdf/news/tes timonies/2020/Testimony_FY21%20Exec%20Budget_051820_FINAL.pdf; New York City Coalition for the Homeless, "State of the Homeless 2020: Governor and Mayor to Blame as New York Enters Fifth Decade of Homelessness Crisis," March 2020, 35, https://www.coali tionforthehomeless.org/wp-content/uploads/2020/03/StateofTheHomeless2020.pdf.

50. Roger Starr, *America's Housing Challenge: What it is and How to Meet it* (New York: Hill & Wang, 1977): 102–3.

51. Garboden, Rosen, Greif, DeLuca, and Edin, "Urban Landlords and the Housing Choice Voucher Program: A Research Report," 14.

52. Anthony Jackson, *A Place Called Home: A History of Low-cost Housing in Manhattan* (Cambridge: The MIT Press, 1976), 136.

53. Schwartz, *Housing Policy in the United States*, 41; Charles J. Orlebeke, "The Evolution of Low-Income Housing Policy, 1949 to 1999," *Housing Policy Debate* 11, no. 2 (2000): 511.

54. Quigley and Raphael, "Is Housing Unaffordable? Why Isn't It More Affordable?" 204–5.

55. Quigley and Raphael, "Is Housing Unaffordable? Why Isn't It More Affordable?," 205–6; James Ohls, "Public Policy towards Low Income Housing and Filtering in Housing Markets," *Journal of Urban Economics* 2, no. 2 (April 1975): 144–71; Jackson, *A Place Called Home*, chapter 11; William C. Baer and Christopher B. Williamson, "The Filtering of Households and Housing Units," *Journal of Planning Literature* 3, no. 2 (1988): 127–152; Thomas Bier, "Moving Up, Filtering Down: Metropolitan Housing Dynamics and Public Policy," The Brookings Institution Center on Urban and Metropolitan Policy, September 2001, https://www.brookings.edu/wp-content/uploads/2016/06/bier.pdf.

56. Joe Cortright, "How Luxury Housing Becomes Affordable," Cityobservatory.org, July 31, 2017, https://cityobservatory.org/how-luxury-housing-becomes-affordable/; Dougherty, *Golden Gates*, 9–10; M. Nolan Gray, "America Needs More Luxury Housing, Not Less New," *Atlantic*, April 12, 2021, https://www.theatlantic.com/ideas/archive/2021/04/theres-no-such-thing-luxury-housing/618548/.

57. Nolan Gray, "How Luxury Units Turn into Affordable Housing."

58. Vicki Been, Ingrid Gould Ellen, and Katherine O'Regan, "Supply Skepticism: Housing Supply and Affordability," *Housing Policy Debate* 29, no. 1 (2019): 34; Marybeth Shinn and Jill Khadduri, *In the Midst of Plenty: Homelessness and What to do about it* (Hoboken: John Wiley & Sons, 2020), 46.

59. Kenneth T. Jackson, *Crabgrass Frontier: The Suburbanization of the United States* (New York: Oxford University Press, 1985), 285; Jill Jonnes, *South Bronx Rising: The Rise, Fall, and Resurrection of an American City* (New York: Fordham University Press, 2002).

60. Dougherty, *Golden Gates*, 32–33; Peter Cohen, "The 'Filtering' Fallacy," shelterforce.org, October 12, 2016, https://shelterforce.org/2016/10/12/the-filtering-fallacy/; Mallach, "Rents Will Only Go So Low, No Matter How Much We Build."

61. Been, Ellen, and O'Regan, "Supply Skepticism: Housing Supply and Affordability," 28.

62. Quoctrung Bui, "A Secret of Many Urban 20-Somethings: Their Parents Help with the Rent," *New York Times*, February 9, 2017, https://www.nytimes.com/2017/02/09/upshot/a-secret-of-many-urban-20-somethings-their-parents-help-with-the-rent.html?_r=0.

63. Ingrid Gould Ellen and Lei Ding, "Guest Editors' Introduction: Advancing Our Understanding of Gentrification," *Cityscape: A Journal of Policy Development and Research* 18, no. 3 (2016): 3–8, https://www.huduser.gov/portal/periodicals/cityscpe/vol18num3/guest.pdf; John Buntin, "The Myth of Gentrification," Slate.com, January 14, 2015, https://slate.com/news-and-politics/2015/01/the-gentrification-myth-its-rare-and-not-as-bad-for-the-poor-as-people-think.html.

64. Joe Cortright and Dillon Mahmoudi, "Lost in Place: Why the Persistence and Spread of Concentrated Poverty—Not Gentrification—Is Our Biggest Urban Challenge," City Observatory, December 2014.

65. Institute for Children Poverty and Homelessness, "A Theory of Poverty Destabilization: Why Low-income Families Become Homeless in New York City," June 2013, https://www.icphusa.org/wp-content/uploads/2017/03/ICPH_PolicyBrief_ATheoryofPovertyDestabilization_June2013.pdf; Institute for Children Poverty & Homelessness, "A Neighborhood Divided: Gentrification, Poverty, and Homelessness in Elmhurst/Corona," February 2016, https://www.icphusa.org/wp-content/uploads/2016/09/ICPH-Elmurst-Corona_WEB.pdf; Institute for Children Poverty and Homelessness, "The Process of Poverty Destabilization: How

Gentrification is Reshaping Upper Manhattan and the Bronx and Increasing Homelessness in New York City," February 2014, https://www.icphusa.org/wp-content/uploads/2016/09 /ICPH_policybrief_TheProcessofPovertyDestabilization_Revised-022614.pdf.

66. Stephen Eide, "Private Colleges in Peril," *Education Next*, Fall 2018, https://www .educationnext.org/private-colleges-peril-financial-pressures-declining-enrollment-closures/.

67. Dougherty, *Golden Gates*, xi; Nicole Friedman, "Millennials Help Power This Year's Housing-Market Rebound," *Wall Street Journal*, August 27, 2020, https://www.wsj.com /articles/millennials-help-power-this-years-housing-market-rebound-11598520601.

68. Hoch and Slayton, *New Homeless and Old*, 36–37; Kusmer, *Down and Out*, 114–16; Bogue, *Skid Row*, chapter 3; Howard M. Bahr, *Skid Row: An Introduction to Disaffiliation* (New York: Oxford University Press, 1973), 105; Homelessness caused by international immigration is a bigger concern in Europe than in the US: Johan Wennström, "Europe's New Beggars," *Quilette*, April 10, 2019, https://quillette.com/2019/04/10/europes-new-beggars/; "Roma Experiences of Homelessness in Europe," FEANTSA, Winter 2020, https://www .feantsa.org/public/user/Resources/magazine/2020/Winter%20Roma/FEA_008-20_maga zine_winter_v3.pdf.

69. National Academies of Sciences, Engineering, and Medicine, "The Economic and Fiscal Consequences of Immigration," 2016, chapter 3 (especially tables 3–14), https://d279m 997dpfwgl.cloudfront.net/wp/2016/09/0922_immigrant-economics-full-report.pdf.

70. Wendy Wang, "Immigrant Families Are More Stable," Institute for Family Studies, March 3, 2021, https://ifstudies.org/blog/immigrant-families-are-more-stable.

71. The National Academies of Sciences, Engineering, and Medicine, "The Economic and Fiscal Consequences of Immigration," 215, https://d279m997dpfwgl.cloudfront.net /wp/2016/09/0922_immigrant-economics-full-report.pdf.

72. The National Academies of Sciences, Engineering, and Medicine, "The Economic and Fiscal Consequences of Immigration," 226–29, https://d279m997dpfwgl.cloudfront .net/wp/2016/09/0922_immigrant-economics-full-report.pdf; Cynthia Bansak, Nicole Simpson and Madeline Zavodny, *The Economics of Immigration*, second edition (New York: Routledge, 2020), 249–53.

73. Quigley and Raphael, "Is Housing Unaffordable? Why Isn't It More Affordable?," 208; Albert Saiz, "Immigration and Housing Rents in American Cities," *Journal of Urban Economics* 61, no. 2 (March 2007): 345–71; Kirsten Moore Sheeley, et al., "The Making of a Crisis: A History of Homelessness in Los Angeles," UCLA Luskin Center for History and Policy, January 2021, 45, https://luskincenter.history.ucla.edu/wp-content/uploads/sites/66/2021/01 /LCHP-The-Making-of-A-Crisis-Report.pdf.

74. The National Academies of Sciences, Engineering, and Medicine, "The Economic and Fiscal Consequences of Immigration," 54 and 57.

75. The National Academies of Sciences, Engineering, and Medicine, "The Economic and Fiscal Consequences of Immigration," chapter 5.

76. Center for Immigration Studies, "Panel Transcript: Projecting the Impact of Immigration on the US Population," February 18, 2019, https://cis.org/Transcript/Panel-Projecting -Impact-Immigration-US-Population; Reihan Salam remarks in "Panel Transcript: Welfare Use by Legal and Illegal Immigrants," Center for Immigration Studies, September 13, 2015, https://cis.org/Transcript/Panel-Transcript-Welfare-Use-Legal-and-Illegal-Immigrants; Bogue, *Skid Row*, 256–57.

77. Source: "About the Tables on New York City Residents' Income and Tax Liability," New York City Independent Budget Office (IBO), October 2018, https://ibo.nyc.ny.us /RevenueSpending/2018-pit-tables-overview.pdf.

Chapter 12. Conclusion

1. Steve Lopez, "Column: So Trump Wants to Solve Homelessness in California? Here Are Five Things He Can Do," *Los Angeles Times*, February 19, 2020, https://www.latimes.com /california/story/2020-02-19/column-5-things-trump-can-do-if-he-really-wants-to-help -solve-californias-homeless-crisis.

2. Julie A. Lam and Robert Rosenheck, "The Effects of Victimization on Clinical Outcomes of Homeless Persons with Serious Mental Illness," *Psychiatric Services* 49, no. 5 (May 1998): 682; Barrett A. Lee and Christopher J. Schreck, "Danger on the Streets: Marginality and Victimization Among Homeless People," *American Behavioral Scientist* 48, no. 8 (April 2005): 1069.

Bibliography

A-No.1. *The Curse of Tramp Life*. Cambridge Springs, PA: The A-No.1 Publishing Co., 1912.

Abbott, Grace. *From Relief to Social Security: The Development of the New Public Welfare Services and Their Administration*. Chicago: The University of Chicago Press, 1941.

Ahrentzen, Sherry. "Double Indemnity or Double Delight? The Health Consequences of Shared Housing and 'Doubling Up.'" *Journal of Social Issues* 59, no. 3 (July 2003): 547–68. https://doi.org/10.1111/1540-4560.00077.

Alexiou, Alice Sparberg. *Devil's Mile: The Rich, Gritty History of the Bowery*. New York: St. Martin's Press, 2018.

Allard, Scott W. *Out of Reach: Place, Poverty, and the New American Welfare State*. New Haven: Yale University Press, 2009.

Allen, Nicole E. "US Commentary: Insights from the Family Options Study Regarding Housing and Intimate Partner Violence." *Cityscape: A Journal of Policy Development and Research* 19, no. 3 (2017): 245–53. https://www.huduser.gov/portal/periodicals/cityscpe/vol19num3/ch13.pdf.

Andersen, Ted, Demian Bulwa, and Megan Cassidy. "The Scanner: SF Police Have Backed Off Controversial 'Sit/Lie' Citations." *San Francisco Chronicle*, October 22, 2018. https://www.sfchronicle.com/crime/article/The-Scanner-SF-police-have-backed-off-13322561.php.

Anderson, Brian C. "How Catholic Charities Lost Its Soul." *City Journal*, Winter 2000. https://www.city-journal.org/html/how-catholic-charities-lost-its-soul-12150.html.

Anderson, Deborah K., and Daniel G. Saunders, "Leaving an Abusive Partner: An Empirical Review of Predictors, the Process of Leaving, and Psychological Well-Being." *Trauma, Violence, and Abuse* 4, no. 2 (April 2003): 163–91. https://doi.org/10.1177/1524838002250769.

Anderson, Jason Curtis. "A Lucerne for Every Neighborhood." janesdefenders.nyc, May 2021. https://www.janesdefenders.nyc/essays/a-lucerne-for-every-neighborhood.

Anderson, Nels. *The Hobo: The Sociology of the Homeless Man*. Chicago: The University of Chicago Press, 1923.

———. "Book Review: The Demolition of Skid Row by Ronald J. Miller." *Social Forces* 62, no. 4 (June 1984): 1119–21. https://doi.org/10.1093/sf/62.4.1119.

Anuta, Joe, and David Giambusso. "Newark Mayor Sues Progressive ally de Blasio for Exporting Homeless." *Politico*, December 2, 2019. https://www.politico.com/states/new-york /albany/story/2019/12/02/newark-mayor-sues-progressive-ally-de-blasio-for-exporting -homeless-1230258.

Aponte, Claudia Irizarry, and Ben Fractenberg. "Some NYC Homeless Practice Social Distancing in Hotels, With Help from Donors." *The City*, April 20, 2020. https://www.thecity .nyc/services-safety-net/2020/4/20/21247110/some-nyc-homeless-practice-social-distanc ing-in-hotels-with-help-from-donors.

Applied Survey Research. "San Francisco Homeless Count and Survey Comprehensive Report." 2019. https://hsh.sfgov.org/wp-content/uploads/FINAL-PIT-Report-2019-San -Francisco.pdf.

Arnade, Chris. *Dignity: Seeking Respect in Back Row America*. New York: Sentinel, 2019.

Aviv, Rachel. "Netherland." *New Yorker*, December 3, 2012. https://www.newyorker.com /magazine/2012/12/10/netherland.

Baer, William C., and Christopher B. Williamson. "The Filtering of Households and Housing Units." *Journal of Planning Literature* 3, no. 2 (1988): 127–52. https://doi.org /10.1177/088541228800300201.

Baggett, Travis P., et al. "Mortality Among Homeless Adults in Boston: Shifts in Causes of Death over a 15-Year Period." *JAMA Internal Medicine* 173, no. 3 (February 2013): 189–95. https://www.ncbi.nlm.nih.gov/pmc/articles/PMC3713619/.

Bahr, Howard M. *Skid Row: An Introduction to Disaffiliation*. New York: Oxford University Press, 1973.

Baker, Tom, and Joshua Evans. "'Housing First' and the Changing Terrains of Homeless Governance." *Geography Compass* 10, no. 1 (2016): 25–41. https://doi.org/10.1111/gec3.12257.

Bamberger, Joshua. "Reducing Homelessness by Embracing Housing as a Medicaid Benefit," *JAMA Internal Medicine* 176, no. 8 (August 2016): 1051–52. https://doi:10.1001/jama internmed.2016.2615.

Banerjee Abhijit V., and Esther Duflo. *Poor Economics: A Radical Rethinking of the Way to Fight Global Poverty*. New York: Public Affairs, 2011.

Banks, Steven. "Testimony of Steven Banks, Commissioner Department of Social Services." New York City Council, Committee on General Welfare, Fiscal Year 2021 Executive Budget Hearing, May 18, 2020. https://www1.nyc.gov/assets/hra/downloads/pdf/news /testimonies/2020/Testimony_FY21%20Exec%20Budget_051820_FINAL.pdf.

Bansak, Cynthia, Nicole Simpson, and Madeline Zavodny. *The Economics of Immigration*, second edition. New York: Routledge, 2020.

Barbara Poppe and Associates for The Coalition on Homelessness and Housing in Ohio. "Double Jeopardy: The Coronavirus and Homelessness in Ohio." March 24, 2020. https:// cohhio.org/wp-content/uploads/2020/03/DoubleJeopardy-web.pdf.

Barker, Kim. "A Choice for Recovering Addicts: Relapse or Homelessness." *New York Times*, May 30, 2015. https://www.nytimes.com/2015/05/31/nyregion/three-quarter-housing-a -choice-for-recovering-addicts-or-homelessness.html.

Barron, Seth. *The Last Days of New York: A Reporter's True Tale*. New York: Humanix, 2021.

Bassuk Ellen L., Lenore Rubin, and Alison Lauriat. "Is Homelessness a Mental Health Problem?" *The American Journal of Psychiatry* 141, no. 12 (December 1984): 1546–50. https:// doi.org/10.1176/ajp.141.12.1546.

Bassuk, Ellen L., and Ellen M. Gallagher. "The Impact of Homelessness on Children." *Child and Youth Services* 14, no. 1 (1990): 19–33. https://doi.org/10.1300/J024v14n01_03.

Batko Samantha, et al. "Open Letter to Secretary Ben Carson, Joe Grogan, and Robert Marbut." March 18, 2020. https://endhomelessness.org/wp-content/uploads/2020/03/Homelessness-Researcher-Letter.pdf.

Baum, Alice S., and Donald W. Burnes. *A Nation in Denial: The Truth about Homelessness.* Boulder, CO: Westview Press, 1993.

Beck, Angela J., Cory Page, Jessica Buche, Danielle Rittman, and Maria Gaiser. "Estimating the Distribution of the US Psychiatric Subspecialist Workforce." University of Michigan School of Public Health Workforce Research Center, December 2018. https://behavioralhealthworkforce.org/wp-content/uploads/2019/02/Y3-FA2-P2-Psych-Sub_Full-Report-FINAL2.19.2019.pdf.

Been, Vicki, Ingrid Gould Ellen, and Katherine O'Regan. "Supply Skepticism: Housing Supply and Affordability." *Housing Policy Debate* 29, no. 1 (2019): 25–40. https://doi.org/10.1080/10511482.2018.1476899.

Been, Vicki, Ingrid Gould Ellen, Michael Gedal, and Ioan Voicu. "The Impact of Supportive Housing on Surrounding Neighborhoods." Furman Center for Real Estate and Urban Policy, Working Paper 2008–06, October 2008. https://furmancenter.org/files/publications/A3ImpactofSHonNeighborhoods_000.pdf.

Beers, Clifford W. *A Mind that Found Itself: An Autobiography.* New York: Longmans, Green, & Co., 1908.

Beito, David T. *From Mutual Aid to the Welfare State: Fraternal Societies and Social Services, 1890–1967.* Chapel Hill: University of North Carolina Press, 2000.

Beito, David T., and Linda Royster Beito. "'The Lodger Evil' and the Transformation of Progressive Housing Reform, 1890–1930." *The Independent Review* 20, no. 4 (Spring 2016): 485–508.

Bellow, Saul. *The Adventures of Augie March.* New York: Viking Press, 1953.

Benson, Michael L., and Greer Litton Fox. "When Violence Hits Home: How Economics and Neighborhood Play a Role, Research in Brief." National Institute for Justice, September 2004. https://www.ojp.gov/pdffiles1/nij/205004.pdf.

Bercovici, Konrad. *Crimes of Charity.* New York: A. A. Knopf, 1917.

Berkowitz, Edward D., and Larry DeWitt. *The Other Welfare: Supplemental Security Income and US Social Policy.* New York: Cornell University Press, 2013.

Berman, Greg, and Aubrey Fox, "Lessons from the Battle over D.A.R.E.: The Complicated Relationship between Research and Practice," Bureau of Justice Assistance, 2009, https://www.courtinnovation.org/sites/default/files/DARE.pdf.

Berman, Greg, and John Feinblatt. *Good Courts: The Case for Problem-Solving Justice.* New York: New Press, 2005.

Bier, Thomas. "Moving Up, Filtering Down: Metropolitan Housing Dynamics and Public Policy," The Brookings Institution Center on Urban and Metropolitan Policy, September 2001. https://www.brookings.edu/wp-content/uploads/2016/06/bier.pdf.

billmoyers.com. "The Vanishing Family: Crisis in Black America." July 30, 1989. https://billmoyers.com/content/the-vanishing-family-crisis-in-black-america/.

Bittner, Egon. "The Police on Skid-Row: A Study of Peace Keeping." *American Sociological Review* 32, no. 5 (October 1967): 699–715. https://doi.org/10.2307/2092019.

Blair, Gwenda. "Saint Mitch." *Esquire*, December 1, 1986. https://classic.esquire.com/article/1986/12/1/saint-mitch.

Blanco, Lluís Alexandre Casanovas. "A Cut Above the Streets: Robert M. Hayes, Co-Founder of Coalition for the Homeless, in Conversation with Lluis Alexandre Casanovas Blanco,"

Archinect.com, May 1, 2019. https://archinect.com/features/article/150133042/a-cut-above-the-streets-robert-m-hayes-co-founder-of-coalition-for-the-homeless-in-conversation-with-llu-s-alexandre-casanovas-blanco.

Blasi, Gary. "UD Day: Impending Evictions and Homelessness in Los Angeles," UCLA Luskin Institute on Inequality and Democracy, May 28, 2020. https://escholarship.org/uc/item/2gz6c8cv#main.

Blitzer, Ronn. "Gillibrand Mocked for Calling Child Care, Paid Leave 'Infrastructure.'" Foxnews.com, April 7, 2021.

Bloom, Nicholas Dagen. *Public Housing that Worked: New York in the Twentieth Century.* Philadelphia: University of Pennsylvania Press, 2008.

Bly, Nellie. *Ten Days in a Madhouse.* New York: Ian L. Munro, 1887.

Bogard, Cynthia J. *Seasons Such as These: How Homelessness Took Shape in America.* New York: Aldine de Gruyter, 2003.

Bogue, Donald. *Skid Row in American Cities.* Community and Family Study Center, University of Chicago, 1963.

Boone, Steven. "Designer Shades, Quiet Hustle: The Entrepreneurs of the New York City Homeless Shelter." *Politico,* May 12, 2011. https://www.politico.com/states/new-york/city-hall/story/2011/05/designer-shades-quiet-hustle-the-entrepreneurs-of-the-new-york-city-homeless-shelter-067223.

Botein, Hilary, and Andrea Hetling. *Home Safe Home: Housing Solutions for Survivors of Intimate Partner Violence.* New Brunswick: Rutgers University Press, 2016.

Bredderman, Will. "Council's Land Use Committee Approves 'Astoria Cove' Mega-Project." *Observer,* November 12, 2014, https://observer.com/2014/11/councils-land-use-committee-approves-astoria-cove-mega-project/#ixzz3gdjiNmt5.

Bretherton, Joanne, and Nicholas Pleace. "Is Work an Answer to Homelessness? Evaluating an Employment Programme for Homeless Adults." *European Journal of Homelessness* 13, no. 1 (2019): 57–81. https://www.feantsaresearch.org/public/user/Observatory/2019/EJH/EJH_13_1/Feantsa-2019_13-1_Article-3.pdf.

Briggs, Xavier de Souza, Susan J. Popkin, and John Goering. *Moving to Opportunity: The Story of an American Experiment to Fight Ghetto Poverty.* New York: Oxford University Press, 2010. Kindle edition.

Bring LA Home Blue Ribbon Panel. "Bring Los Angeles Home: The Campaign to End Homelessness." 2006. http://planforhope.org/Plan_For_Hope/Resources_files/BRING%20LA%20HOME%20book_final%20%282%29%20%281%29.pdf.

Brooks, David. "The Nuclear Family Was a Mistake." *The Atlantic,* March 2020, https://www.theatlantic.com/magazine/archive/2020/03/the-nuclear-family-was-a-mistake/605536/.

Bruns, Roger. *Knights of the Road: A Hobo History.* New York: Methuen, 1980.

Buckner, John C. "The Impact of Homelessness on Children: An Analytic Review of the Literature." In Debra J. Rog, C. Scott Holupka, and Lisa C. Patton, "Characteristics and Dynamics of Homeless Families with Children." Washington, DC: US Department of Health and Human Services, Office of the Assistant Secretary for Planning and Evaluation, 2007. https://aspe.hhs.gov/sites/default/files/private/pdf/75331/report.pdf.

Bui, Quoctrung. "A Secret of Many Urban 20-Somethings: Their Parents Help with the Rent." *New York Times,* February 9, 2017. https://www.nytimes.com/2017/02/09/upshot/a-secret-of-many-urban-20-somethings-their-parents-help-with-the-rent.html?_r=0.

Buntin, John. "The Myth of Gentrification." Slate.com, January 14, 2015. https://slate.com/news-and-politics/2015/01/the-gentrification-myth-its-rare-and-not-as-bad-for-the-poor-as-people-think.html.

Burnham, James. *Suicide of the West: An Essay on the Meaning and Destiny of Liberalism*. New York: Encounter Books, 2014 (orig. 1964).

Burt, Martha R., and Barbara E. Cohen. "Differences among Homeless Single Women, Women with Children, and Single Men." *Social Problems*, 36, no. 5 (December 1989): 508–24. https://doi.org/10.2307/3096815.

Burt, Martha, et al. "Homelessness: Programs and the People They Serve: Findings of the National Survey of Homeless Assistance Providers and Clients, Summary Report." Urban Institute, December 1999. https://www.urban.org/sites/default/files/publication/66286/310291-Homelessness-Programs-and-the-People-They-Serve-Findings-of-the-National-Survey-of-Homeless-Assistance-Providers-and-Clients.PDF.

Byrne, Thomas, Jamison D. Fargo, Ann Elizabeth Montgomery, Ellen Munley, and Dennis P. Culhane. "The Relationship Between Community Investment in Permanent Supportive Housing and Chronic Homelessness." *Social Service Review* 88, no. 2 (June 2014): 234–63. https://doi.org/10.1086/676142.

California Senate Bill no. 1380, Chapter 847. September 29, 2016. https://leginfo.legislature.ca.gov/faces/billNavClient.xhtml?bill_id=201520160SB1380.

Campbell, Barry. "Testimony of the Fortune Society, Presented by Barry Campbell," New York City Council Committee on General Welfare, March 15, 2016. https://legistar.council.nyc.gov/MeetingDetail.aspx?ID=458065&GUID=C857AABB-1AAC-4462-866D-AA36D439552F&Options=&Search=.

Caplow, Theodore. "Transiency as a Cultural Pattern." *American Sociological Review* 5, no. 5 (October 1940): 731–39. https://doi.org/10.2307/2083695.

Capps, Kriston. "Trump's Plan to Criminalize Homelessness Is Taking Shape." *CityLab*, December 17, 2019. https://www.bloomberg.com/news/articles/2019-12-17/how-trump-is-criminalizing-homelessness.

Carson, E. Ann. "Prisoners in 2019." US Department of Justice, Office of Justice Programs, Bureau of Justice Statistics, October 2020. https://bjs.ojp.gov/content/pub/pdf/p19.pdf.

Case, Anne, and Angus Deaton. *Deaths of Despair and the Future of Capitalism*. Princeton: Princeton University Press, 2020.

Caton, Carol L. M. *The Open Door: Homelessness and Severe Mental Illness in the Era of Community Treatment*. New York: Oxford University Press, 2017.

cbsnews.com, "Dumped on Skid Row," May 17, 2007. https://www.cbsnews.com/news/dumped-on-skid-row/.

Center for Immigration Studies. "Panel Transcript: Welfare Use by Legal and Illegal Immigrants." September 13, 2015. https://cis.org/Transcript/Panel-Transcript-Welfare-Use-Legal-and-Illegal-Immigrants.

———. "Panel Transcript: Projecting the Impact of Immigration on the US Population." February 18, 2019. https://cis.org/Transcript/Panel-Projecting-Impact-Immigration-US-Population.

Chesterton, G. K. *St. Francis of Assisi*. New York: Doubleday, Doran & Company, 1924. Accessed via archive.org.

———. *The Thing*. London: Sheed & Ward, 1946. Accessed via archive.org.

Chetty, Raj, Nathaniel Hendren, and Lawrence F. Katz. "The Effects of Exposure to Better Neighborhoods on Children: New Evidence from the Moving to Opportunity Experiment." *The American Economic Review* 106, no. 4 (April 2016): 855–902. https://scholar .harvard.edu/files/lkatz/files/chk_aer_mto_0416.pdf.

Chiland, Elijah. "Councilmembers Say Other Cities Sending Homeless Residents to LA." *Curbed*, June 5, 2019. https://la.curbed.com/2019/6/5/18654438/homelessness-los-ange les-other-cities-enforcement.

Cho, Richard. "Four Clarifications About Housing First." usich.gov, June 18, 2014. https:// www.usich.gov/news/four-clarifications-about-housing-first.

Clark, Dessie Lee, Leila Wood, and Cris M. Sullivan. "Examining the Needs and Experiences of Domestic Violence Survivors in Transitional Housing." *Journal of Family Violence* 34, no. 4 (May 2019): 275–86.

Cohen, Peter. "The 'Filtering' Fallacy." shelterforce.org, October 12, 2016. https://shelter force.org/2016/10/12/the-filtering-fallacy/.

Cohen, Rachel M. "How the Largest Known Homeless Encampment in Minneapolis History Came to be." *The Appeal*, July 15, 2020. https://theappeal.org/minneapolis-homelessness -crisis-powderhorn-park-encampment/.

Collinson, Robert, Ingrid Gould Ellen, and Jens Ludwig. "Low-Income Housing Policy." National Bureau of Economic Research, August 27, 2015.

Community Housing Innovations, Executive Director's Message, 2017–2018 Annual Report. http://www.communityhousing.org/wp-content/uploads/2018/08/CHI-2017-18-Annual -Report-FINAL-1.pdf.

Comptroller General of the United States. "Returning the Mentally Disabled to the Community: Government Needs to Do More." January 7, 1977. https://www.gao.gov/assets /hrd-76-152.pdf.

Congressional Budget Office. "Federal Housing Assistance for Low-Income Households." September 9, 2015. https://www.cbo.gov/publication/50782.

Corinth, Kevin. "How Safety Net Programs Tax the Sharing of Housing." *Tax Notes* 149 (December 14, 2015): 1413–20.

———. "The Impact of Permanent Supportive Housing on Homeless Populations." *Journal of Housing Economics* 35 (March 2017): 69–84. https://doi.org/10.1016/j.jhe.2017.01.006.

Corinth, Kevin, and David S. Lucas. "When Warm and Cold Don't Mix: The Implications of Climate for the Determinants of Homelessness." *Journal of Housing Economics* 41 (2018): 45–56. https://doi.org/10.1016/j.jhe.2018.01.001.

Corinth, Kevin C. "On Utah's 91% Decrease in Chronic Homelessness." American Enterprise Institute, March 2016.

Correal, Annie. "In Deepest Cold, a Subway Car Becomes the Shelter of Last Resort." *New York Times*, January 8, 2018.

Cortright, Joe. "How Luxury Housing Becomes Affordable." Cityobservatory.org, July 31, 2017. https://cityobservatory.org/how-luxury-housing-becomes-affordable/.

Cortright, Joe, and Dillon Mahmoudi. "Lost in Place: Why the Persistence and Spread of Concentrated Poverty—Not Gentrification—Is Our Biggest Urban Challenge." *City Observatory*, December 2014.

Council of Economic Advisers. "Expanding Work Requirements in Non-Cash Welfare Programs." July 2018. https://trumpwhitehouse.archives.gov/wp-content/uploads/2018/07 /Expanding-Work-Requirements-in-Non-Cash-Welfare-Programs.pdf.

———. "The State of Homelessness in America." September 2019.

Council of State Governments. "The Mental Health Programs of the Forty–Eight States: A Report to the Governors' Conference." 1950.

Couzens, Shannon E. "Priority: Home! A True Priority? An Analysis of the Federal Plan to Break the Cycle of Homelessness." *Journal of Social Distress and the Homeless* 6, no. 4 (1997): 275–82. https://doi.org/10.1007/BF02938596.

Cove, Peter. *Poor No More: Rethinking Dependency and the War on Poverty.* New York: Routledge, 2017.

Cravens, Jaclyn D., Jason B. Whiting, and Rola O. Aamar. "Why I Stayed/Left: An Analysis of Voices of Intimate Partner Violence on Social Media." *Contemporary Family Therapy* 37 (2015): 372–85. https://doi.org/10.1007/s10591-015-9360-8.

Crouse, Joan M. *The Homeless Transient in the Great Depression: New York State, 1929–1941.* Albany: State University of New York Press, 1986.

———. "The Remembered Men: Transient Camps in New York State, 1933–1935." *New York History* 71, no. 1 (January 1990): 68–94.

Culhane, Dennis, Dan Treglia, Ken Steif, Randall Kuhn, and Thomas Byrne. "Estimated Emergency and Observational/Quarantine Capacity Need for the US Homeless Population Related to COVID-19 Exposure by County; Projected Hospitalizations, Intensive Care Units and Mortality." March 27, 2020. https://endhomelessness.org/wp-content/uploads/2020/03/COVID-paper_clean-636pm.pdf.

Culhane, Dennis P. "The Costs of Homelessness: A Perspective from the United States." *European Journal of Homelessness* 2 (December 2008): 97–114. https://www.feantsaresearch.org/download/article-45447406638645867364.pdf.

Culhane, Dennis P., Stephen Metraux, Thomas Byrne, Magdi Stino, and Jay Bainbridge. "The Age Structure of Contemporary Homelessness: Evidence and Implications for Public Policy." *Analyses of Social Issues and Public Policy* 13, no. 1 (December 2013): 228–44. https://doi.org/10.1111/asap.12004.

Cunningham, Mary K. "It's Time to Reinforce the Housing Safety Net by Adopting Universal Vouchers for Low-Income Renters." Urban Institute, April 7, 2020. https://www.urban.org/urban-wire/its-time-reinforce-housing-safety-net-adopting-universal-vouchers-low-income-renters.

Cunningham, Mary, et al. "A Pilot Study of Landlord Acceptance of Housing Choice Vouchers." US Department of Housing and Urban Development, August 2018. https://www.huduser.gov/portal/portal/sites/default/files/pdf/Landlord-Acceptance-of-Housing-Choice-Vouchers.pdf.

Cuomo, Mario M. "1984 Democratic National Convention Keynote Address." July 16, 1984. https://www.americanrhetoric.com/speeches/mariocuomo1984dnc.htm.

Daniels, Chris. "Seattle business owners urge new approach to crime and homelessness." K5 News, May 22, 2019. https://www.king5.com/article/news/local/seattle/seattle-business-owners-urge-new-approach-to-crime-and-homelessness/281-06dbc129-3021-43a5-bb96-4a6c072ff33b.

Denkmann, Libby. "Can A Republican Be Governor Again in California? Kevin Faulconer Will Try to Carve Arnold-esque Path." Laist.com, February 2, 2021. https://laist.com/news/former-san-diego-mayor-kevin-faulconer-will-try-to-carve-arnold-esque-path-to-governorship.

DeParle, Jason. *American Dream: Three Women, Ten Kids, and a Nation's Drive to End Welfare.* New York: Viking, 2004.

Desmond, Matthew. *Evicted: Poverty and Profit in the American City*. New York: Crown Publishers, 2016.

Desmond, Matthew, and Nathan Wilmers. "Do the Poor Pay More for Housing? Exploitation, Profit, and Risk in Rental Markets." *American Journal of Sociology* 124, no. 4 (January 2019): 1090–24. https://doi.org/10.1086/701697.

Deutsch, Albert. *The Shame of the States*. New York: Harcourt Brace, 1948.

Dickens, Charles. *Dombey and Son*. New York: Oxford University Press, 2008 (orig. 1848).

Doherty, Matthew. "What I Learned About Housing First from Lloyd Pendleton." endhomelessness.org, May 6, 2019. https://endhomelessness.org/what-i-learned-about-housing-first-from-lloyd-pendleton/.

Dolan, Maura. "Homeless People from Other Cities Moving to San Francisco for Hotel Rooms, Mayor Says." *San Francisco Chronicle*, April 29, 2020. https://www.latimes.com/homeless-housing/story/2020-04-29/san-francisco-coronavirus-hotel-rooms-homeless-people-from-other-cities.

Dolbeare Cushing N., and Sheila Crowley. "Changing Priorities: The Federal Budget and Housing Assistance, 1976–2002." National Low-Income Housing Coalition, August 2002. https://nlihc.org/sites/default/files/Changing-Priorities-Report_August-2002.pdf.

Doran, Andrew. "A Modern Mendicant." *First Things*, April 2020. https://www.firstthings.com/article/2020/04/a-modern-mendicant.

Doran, Kelly M., Elizabeth J. Misa, and Nirav R. Shah. "Housing as Health Care—New York's Boundary-Crossing Experiment." *New England Journal of Medicine* 369, no. 25 (2013): 2374–77.

Dorn, Sara. "JetBlue Worker Slammed for 'Racist' Homeless Person Halloween Costume." *New York Post*, November 2, 2019. https://nypost.com/2019/11/02/jet-blue-worker-slammed-for-racist-homeless-person-halloween-costume/.

Dougherty, Conor. *Golden Gates: The Fight for Housing—and Democracy—in America's Most Prosperous City*. New York: Penguin Press, 2020.

Douglas, William O. *Go East Young Man: The Early Years; The Autobiography of William O. Douglas*. New York: Random House, 1974.

Duffield, Barbara. "Are We Creating Chronic Homelessness? The Past, Present, and Future of Federal Homelessness Policy." Institute for Children, Poverty and Homelessness, October 2016. https://www.icphusa.org/reports/are-we-creating-chronic-homelessness-the-past-present-and-future-of-federal-homelessness-policy/.

Dugger, Celia. "Conversations/Nancy Wackstein; Memo to Democrats: Housing Won't Solve Homelessness." *New York Times*, July 12, 1992. Accessed via Lexis.

Earley, Pete. *Crazy: A Father's Search Through America's Mental Health Madness*. New York: Berkley Books, 2007.

Eberstadt, Nicholas. *Men Without Work: America's Invisible Crisis*. West Conshohocken, PA: Templeton Press, 2016.

Eckholm, Erik. "New Campaign Shows Progress for Homeless." *New York Times*, June 7, 2006. https://www.nytimes.com/2006/06/07/us/07homeless.html.

Edin, Kathryn, and Maria Kefalas. *Promises I Can Keep: Why Poor Women put Motherhood before Marriage*. Berkeley: University of California Press, 2005.

Edin, Kathryn J., and H. Luke Shaefer. *$2.00 a Day: Living on Almost Nothing in America*. Boston: Houghton Mifflin Harcourt, 2015.

Eide, Stephen. "Is Homelessness Only a Housing Problem?" Institute for Family Studies blog, June 13, 2016. https://ifstudies.org/blog/is-homelessness-only-a-housing-problem.

———. "Housing First and Homelessness: The Rhetoric and the Reality." Manhattan Institute for Policy Research, April 2020. https://media4.manhattan-institute.org/sites/default/files/housing-first-and-homelessness-SE.pdf.

———. "Private Colleges in Peril." *Education Next*, Fall 2018. https://www.educationnext.org/private-colleges-peril-financial-pressures-declining-enrollment-closures/.

———. "Disorder in the Stacks." *City Journal*, Spring 2019.

Eide, Stephen, and Carolyn D. Gorman. "Medicaid's IMD Exclusion: The Case for Repeal." Manhattan Institute for Policy Research. February 2021. https://media4.manhattan-institute.org/sites/default/files/medicaids-imd-exclusion-case-repeal-SE.pdf.

Ellen, Ingrid Gould, and Brendan O'Flaherty. "Social Programs and Household Size: Evidence from New York City." *Population Research and Policy Review* 26, no. 4 (August 2007): 387–409.

Ellen, Ingrid Gould, and Lei Ding. "Guest Editors' Introduction: Advancing Our Understanding of Gentrification." *Cityscape: A Journal of Policy Development and Research* 18, no. 3 (2016): 3–8. https://www.huduser.gov/portal/periodicals/cityscpe/vol18num3/guest.pdf.

Ellickson, Robert C. "Controlling Chronic Misconduct in City Spaces: Of Panhandlers, Skid Rows, and Public-Space Zoning." *The Yale Law Journal* 105 (1996): 1165–248.

Ellsworth, Joshua T. "Street Crime Victimization Among Homeless Adults: A Review of the Literature." *Victims & Offenders* 14, no. 1 (2019): 96–118. https://doi.org/10.1080/1556 4886.2018.1547997.

Ellwood, David T. *Poor Support: Poverty in the American Family*. New York: Basic Books, 1988.

Etulian, Richard W., ed. "Introduction" to *Jack London on the Road: The Tramp Diary, and other Hobo Writing*s. Edited by Richard W. Etulain. Logan: Utah State University Press, 1979.

Evans, Rhonda D., and Forsyth, Craig J. "Risk Factors, Endurance of Victimization, and Survival Strategies: The Impact of The Structural Location of Men and Women on Their Experiences Within Homeless Milieus." *Sociological Spectrum* 24, no. 4 (2004): 479–505. https://doi.org/10.1080/02732170390260413.

Fagan, Kevin. "Bay Area Homelessness: 89 Answers to Your Questions." *San Francisco Chronicle*, July 28, 2019. https://projects.sfchronicle.com/sf-homeless/homeless-questions/.

———. "Newsom Talks Homeless Policy at Encampment Sweep in Mission." *San Francisco Chronicle*, August 21, 2021. https://www.sfchronicle.com/politics/article/Newsom-grabs-a-broom-and-talks-homeless-policy-at-16417072.php.

———. "Ronald Reagan / 1911–2004 / Amid Tributes, Activists Lament Reagan's Failure on Homelessness." *San Francisco Chronicle*, June 10, 2004. https://www.sfchronicle.com/politics/article/RONALD-REAGAN-1911-2004-Amid-tributes-2750499.php#photo-2188953.

Feeney, Francis E., Dorothee F. Mindlin, Verna H. Minear, and Eleanor E. Short. "The Challenge of the Skid Row Alcoholic." *Quarterly Journal of Studies on Alcohol* 16, no. 4 (1955): 645–67. https://doi.org/10.15288/qjsa.1955.16.645.

Findell, Elizabeth. "Homeless Become More Visible in Austin, Sparking Political Clash." *Wall Street Journal*, October 24, 2019. https://www.wsj.com/articles/homeless-becomes-more-visible-in-austin-sparking-political-clash-11571914802.

Fischer, Will, Sonya Acosta, and Erik Gartland. "More Housing Vouchers: Most Important Step to Help More People Afford Stable Homes." Center for Budget and Policy Priorities, April 14, 2021. https://www.cbpp.org/research/housing/more-housing-vouchers-most-important-step-to-help-more-people-afford-stable-homes.

Flannery, Mary, and Mark Glickman. *Fountain House: Portraits of Lives Reclaimed from Mental Illness*. Center City, MN: Hazelden, 1996.

Fletcher, Anne, and Michelle Wood. "Guest Editors' Introduction: Next Steps for the Family Options Study." *Cityscape: A Journal of Policy Development and Research* 19, no. 3 (2017): 191–202. https://www.huduser.gov/portal/periodicals/cityscpe/vol19num3/guest2.pdf.

Flynt, Josiah. "How Men Become Tramps." *Century Magazine* 50 (October 1895): 941–45.

———. *Tramping with Tramps*. New York: The Century Co., 1901.

Foner, Eric. *Free Soil, Free Labor, Free Men: The Ideology of the Republican Party before the Civil War*. New York: Oxford University Press, 1970.

Foote, Caleb. "Vagrancy-Type Law and Its Administration." *University of Pennsylvania Law Review* 104, no. 5 (March 1956): 603–50. https://doi.org/10.2307/3309853.

Forbush, Bliss. *The Sheppard & Enoch Pratt Hospital 1853–1970, A History*. Philadelphia: J. B. Lippincott Company, 1971.

Foscarinis, Maria. "Beyond Homelessness." *Saint Louis University Public Law Review* 12, no. 1 (1993): 37–67.

Frank, Richard G., and Sherry A. Glied. *Better but not Well: Mental Health Policy in the United States Since 1950*. Baltimore: Johns Hopkins University Press, 2006.

Friedman, Nicole. "Millennials Help Power This Year's Housing-Market Rebound." *Wall Street Journal*, August 27, 2020. https://www.wsj.com/articles/millennials-help-power-this-years-housing-market-rebound-11598520601.

Fuchs, Ester, and William McAllister. "The Continuum of Care: A Report on the New Federal Policy to Address Homelessness." US Department of Housing and Urban Development, December 1996.

Fuller, Doris A., H. Richard Lamb, Michael Biasotti, and John Snook. "Overlooked in the Undercounted: The Role of Mental Illness in Fatal Law Enforcement Encounters." Treatment Advocacy Center, December 2015. https://www.treatmentadvocacycenter.org/storage/documents/overlooked-in-the-undercounted.pdf.

Gabe, Thomas. "Welfare, Work, and Poverty Status of Female-Headed Families With Children: 1987–2013." Congressional Research Service, November 21, 2014. https://crsreports.congress.gov/product/pdf/R/R41917/18.

Garboden, Philip M. E., Eva Rosen, Meredith Greif, Stefanie DeLuca, and Kathryn Edin. "Urban Landlords and the Housing Choice Voucher Program: A Research Report." Washington, DC: US Department of Housing and Urban Development, May 2018. https://www.huduser.gov/portal/sites/default/files/pdf/Urban-Landlords-HCV-Program.pdf.

Garland, Hamlin. *A Son of the Middle Border*. New York: The Macmillan Company, 1928. Accessed via achive.org.

Garland, Tammy S., Tara Richards, and Mikaela Cooney. "Victims Hidden in Plain Sight: The Reality of Victimization Among the Homeless." *Criminal Justice Studies: A Critical Journal of Crime, Law and Society* 23, no. 4 (2010): 285–301. https://doi.org/10.1080/1478601X.2010.516525.

Garnett, Nicole Stelle. "Relocating Disorder." *Virginia Law Review* 91, no. 5 (September 2005): 1075–134.

Gazzolo, Dorothy, ed. "Skid Row Gives Renewalists Rough, Tough Relocation Problems." *Journal of Housing* 18, no. 8 (August–September 1961): 327–39.

Geller, Amanda, and Marah A. Curtis. "A Sort of Homecoming: Incarceration and the Housing Security of Urban Men." *Social Science Research* 40, no. 4 (2011): 1196–213. https://doi:10.1016/j.ssresearch.2011.03.008.

Geller, Jeffrey L. "American 'Community' Psychiatry." *The Lancet Supplement* 356 (December 2000): 40. https://doi.org/10.1016/S0140-6736(00)92026-9.

———. "Defining the Meaning of 'In the Community.'" *Hospital and Community Psychiatry* 42, no. 12 (1991): 1197. https://doi.org/10.1176/ps.42.12.1197.

Gelles, Richard J. "Creating an Effective Child Welfare System," in *Urban Policy Frontiers*. New York: Manhattan Institute for Policy Research, 2017. https://media4.manhattan -institute.org/sites/default/files/MI_Urban_Policy_Frontiers_2017.pdf.

Gerson, Michael J. *Heroic Conservatism: Why Republicans Need to Embrace America's Ideals (And Why They Deserve to Fail If They Don't)*. New York: HarperOne, 2007.

Gladwell, Malcolm. "Million-Dollar Murray." *New Yorker*, February 5, 2006. https://www. newyorker.com/magazine/2006/02/13/million-dollar-murray.

Glynn, Chris, and Emily B. Fox. "Dynamics of Homelessness in Urban America." *Annals of Applied Statistics* 13, no. 1 (2019): 573–605. doi:10.1214/18-AOAS1200.

Goetz, Edward G. "Land Use and Homeless Policy in Los Angeles." *International Journal Urban Regional Research* 16, no. 4 (December 1992): 540–54. https://doi .org/10.1111/j.1468-2427.1992.tb00195.x.

Goffman, Erving. *Asylums: Essays on the Social Situation of Mental Patients and Other Inmates*. Garden City: Anchor Books, 1961.

Goldstone, Brian. "The New American Homeless." *New Republic*, August 21, 2019. https:// newrepublic.com/article/154618/new-american-homeless-housing-insecurity-richest-cities.

Goluboff, Risa. *Vagrant Nation: Police Power, Constitutional Change, and the Making of the 1960s*. New York: Oxford University Press, 2016.

Goode, Erich. *The Taming of New York's Washington Square: A Wild Civility*. New York: New York University Press, 2018.

Goodman, Ellen. "Compassion Fatigue." *Washington Post*, February 3, 1990.

Goodmark, Leigh. *Decriminalizing Domestic Violence: A Balanced Policy Approach to Intimate Partner Violence*. Berkeley: University of California Press, 2018.

———. *A Troubled Marriage: Domestic Violence and the Legal System*. New York: New York University Press, 2011.

Gordon, Robert J. *The Rise and Fall of American Growth: The US Standard of Living since the Civil War*. Princeton: Princeton University Press, 2017.

Gothamist. "Is East New York The Next Bushwick?." July 23, 2014. https://gothamist.com /news/is-east-new-york-the-next-bushwick.

Gowan, Teresa. *Hobos, Hustlers, and Backsliders: Homeless in San Francisco*. Minneapolis: University of Minnesota Press, 2010.

Gray, M. Nolan. "America Needs More Luxury Housing, Not Less." *The Atlantic*, April 12, 2021. https://www.theatlantic.com/ideas/archive/2021/04/theres-no-such-thing-luxury -housing/618548/.

Gray, Nolan. "How Luxury Units Turn into Affordable Housing." *CityLab*, June 5, 2019. https://www.bloomberg.com/news/articles/2019-06-05/what-adding-luxury-housing -does-to-rents-elsewhere.

Greenstone, Scott. "Feeling Abandoned by City Hall, Seattle Businesses Try to Respond to Homelessness." *Seattle Times*, October 16, 2018. https://www.seattletimes.com/seattle-news /homeless/feeling-abandoned-by-city-hall-seattle-businesses-try-to-respond-to-homelessness/.

Griffing, Sascha, Deborah Fish Ragin, Robert E. Sage, Lorraine Madry, and Lewis E. Bingham, Beny J. Primm. "Domestic Violence Survivors' Self-Identified Reasons for Returning to

Abusive Relationships." *Journal of Interpersonal Violence* 17, no. 3 (2002): 306–19 https://doi.org/10.1177/0886260502017003005.

Grob, Gerald N. *From Asylum to Community: Mental Health Policy in Modern America.* Princeton: Princeton University Press, 1991.

———. *The Mad Among Us: A History of the Care of America's Mentally Ill.* New York: The Free Press, 1994.

Groth, Paul Erling. *Living Downtown: The History of Residential Hotels in the United States.* Berkeley: University of California Press, 1994.

Gubits, Daniel, et al. "Family Options Study: Short-Term Impacts of Housing and Services Interventions for Homeless Families." US Department of Housing and Urban Development, Office of Policy Development and Research, July 2015. https://www.huduser.gov/portal/sites/default/files/pdf/FamilyOptionsStudy_final.pdf.

———. "Family Options Study: 3-Year Impacts of Housing and Services Interventions for Homeless Families." US Department of Housing and Urban Development, Office of Policy Development and Research, October 2016. https://www.huduser.gov/portal/sites/default/files/pdf/Family-Options-Study-Full-Report.pdf.

Gulcur, Leyla, Sam Tsemberis, Ana Stefancic, and Ronni M. Greenwood. "Community Integration of Adults with Psychiatric Disabilities and Histories of Homelessness." *Community Mental Health Journal* 43, no. 3 (June 2007): 211–28.

Haas, Gilda, and Allan David Heskin. "Community Struggles in Los Angeles." *International Journal of Urban and Regional Research* 5 no. 4 (December 1981): 546–64. https://doi.org/10.1111/j.1468-2427.1981.tb00567.x.

Halpern-Meekin, Sarah. *Social Poverty: Low-income Parents and the Struggle for Family and Community Ties.* New York: New York University Press, 2019.

Hanratty, Maria. "Do Local Economic Conditions Affect Homelessness? Impact of Area Housing Market Factors, Unemployment, and Poverty on Community Homeless Rates." *Housing Policy Debate* 27, no. 4: (2017): 640–55 https://doi.org/10.1080/10511482.2017.1282885.

Harper, Douglas A. *Good Company.* Chicago: University of Chicago Press, 1982.

Harvey, Hope, Rachel Dunifon, and Natasha Pilkauskas. "Under Whose Roof? Understanding the Living Arrangements of Children in Doubled-Up Households." *Demography* 58, no. 3 (June 2021): 821–46 doi:10.1215/00703370-9101102.

Haskins, Ron. *Work over Welfare: The Inside Story of the 1996 Welfare Reform Law.* Washington, DC: Brookings Institution Press, 2006.

"Hastings College of the Law, et al. v. City and County of San Francisco," United States District Court for the Northern District of California, Case 3:20-cv-03033, Document 1, May 4, 2020, https://www.uchastings.edu/wp-content/uploads/2020/05/UC-Hastings-et-al.-v.-CCSF-Complaint-FINAL-FILED-05.04.21.pdf.

Hayes, Robert M. "Hope for New York City's Homeless?; The Issue Is Housing." *New York Times*, November 27, 1986. Accessed via Lexis.

Hayes, Robert. "Litigating on Behalf of Shelter for the Poor." *Harvard Civil Rights-Civil Liberties Law Review* 22 (1987): 79–93.

He, Yinghua, Brendan O'Flaherty, and Robert A. Rosenheck. "Is Shared Housing a Way to Reduce Homelessness? The Effect of Household Arrangements on Formerly Homeless People." *Journal of Housing Economics* 19, no. 1 (March 2010): 1–12.

Heller, Nathan. "A Window onto an American Nightmare." *New Yorker*, June 1, 2020. https://www.newyorker.com/magazine/2020/06/01/a-window-onto-an-american-nightmare.

Henry, O. *Roads of Destiny.* Doubleday, Page & Company, 1918. Accessed via archive.org.

Herring, Chris, Dilara Yarbrough, and Lisa Marie Alatorre. "Pervasive Penalty: How the Criminalization of Poverty Perpetuates Homelessness." *Social Problems* 67, no. 1 (2020): 131–49. https://doi.org/10.1093/socpro/spz004.

Hobbes, Michael. "Why America Can't Solve Homelessness." Huffpost.com, May 15, 2019.

Hobsbawm, Eric. *The Age of Extremes: A History of the World, 1914–1991.* New York: Pantheon Books, 1994.

Hoch, Charles, and Robert A. Slayton. *New Homeless and Old: Community and the Skid Row Hotel.* Philadelphia: Temple University Press, 1989.

Hoffman, Lisa, and Brian Coffey. "Dignity and indignation: How People Experiencing Homelessness View Services and Providers." *The Social Science Journal* 45, no. 2 (2008): 207–22. https://doi.org/10.1016/j.soscij.2008.03.001.

Holland, Gale, and Christine Zhang. "Huge Increase in Arrests of Homeless in LA—But Mostly for Minor Offenses." *Los Angeles Times,* February 4, 2018. https://www.latimes.com/local/politics/la-me-homeless-arrests-20180204-story.html.

Hopper, Kim. "The Counter-Reformation That Failed? A Commentary on the Mixed Legacy of Supported Housing." *Psychiatric Services* 63, no. 5 (2012): 461–63.

———. "The Public Response to Homelessness in New York City: The Last Hundred Years." In *On Being Homeless: Historical Perspectives,* edited by Rick Beard, 88–102. New York: Museum of the City of New York, 1987.

———. *Reckoning with Homelessness.* Ithaca: Cornell University Press, 2003.

Houghton, Ted. "A Description and History of the New York/New York Agreement to House Homeless Mentally Ill Individuals." Corporation for Supportive Housing, May 2001.

Howard, Ella. *Homeless: Poverty and Place in Urban America.* Philadelphia: University of Pennsylvania Press, 2013.

Hunt, Morton M. *Mental Hospital.* New York: Pyramid Books, 1962.

Hunter, Robert. *Poverty.* New York: The MacMillan Company, 1905.

Husock, Howard. "How the Agency Saved My Father." *City Journal,* Spring 1999. https://www.city-journal.org/html/how-agency-saved-my-father-12151.html.

———. "Dreams of My Uncle." *City Journal,* Spring 2017. https://www.city-journal.org/html/dreams-my-uncle-15124.html.

———. *Who Killed Civil Society?: The Rise of Big Government and Decline of Bourgeois Norms.* New York: Encounter Books, 2019.

Hymowitz, Kay S. "The Black Family: 40 Years of Lies." *City Journal,* Summer 2005.

Institute for Children Poverty & Homelessness. "The Dynamics of Family Homelessness in New York City." June 2019. https://www.icphusa.org/dynamics/.

———. "A Neighborhood Divided: Gentrification, Poverty, and Homelessness in Elmhurst/Corona." February 2016. https://www.icphusa.org/wp-content/uploads/2016/09/ICPH-Elmurst-Corona_WEB.pdf.

———. "The Process of Poverty Destabilization: How Gentrification is Reshaping Upper Manhattan and the Bronx and Increasing Homelessness in New York City." February 2014. https://www.icphusa.org/wp-content/uploads/2016/09/ICPH_policybrief_TheProcessofPovertyDestabilization_Revised-022614.pdf.

———. "A Theory of Poverty Destabilization: Why Low-income Families Become Homeless in New York City." June 2013. https://www.icphusa.org/wp-content/uploads/2017/03/ICPH_PolicyBrief_ATheoryofPovertyDestabilization_June2013.pdf.

Interlandi, Jeneen. "When My Crazy Father Actually Lost His Mind." *New York Times Magazine*, June 22, 2012.

Isaac, Rael Jean, and Virginia C. Armat. *Madness in the Streets: How Psychiatry and the Law Abandoned the Mentally Ill*. New York: Free Press, 1990.

Isay, David, Stacy Abramson, and Harvey Wang. *Flophouse: Life on the Bowery*. New York: Random House, 2000.

Jackson, Anthony. *A Place Called Home: A History of Low-Cost Housing in Manhattan*. Cambridge: The MIT Press, 1976.

Jackson, Kenneth T. *Crabgrass Frontier: The Suburbanization of the United States*. New York: Oxford University Press, 1985.

Jacobs, Jane. *The Death and Life of Great American Cities*. New York: Vintage Books, 1992 (orig. 1961).

Jaffe, DJ. *Insane Consequences: How the Mental Health Industry Fails the Mentally Ill*. Amherst, NY: Prometheus Books, 2017.

Jaffe, DJ, and E. Fuller Torrey. "Funds for Treating Individuals with Mental Illness: Is Your State Generous or Stingy?" mentalillnesspolicy.org, December 12, 2017. https://mentalill nesspolicy.org/wp-content/uploads/Funds4TreatingMentalIllnessFinal.pdf.

Jamison, Peter. "DC Housed the Homeless in Upscale Apartments. It Hasn't Gone as Planned." *Washington Post*, April 16, 2019. https://www.washingtonpost.com/local/dc -politics/dc-housed-the-homeless-in-upscale-apartments-it-hasnt-gone-as-planned/2019 /04/16/60c8ab9c-5648-11e9-8ef3-fbd41a2ce4d5_story.html?hpid=hp_hp-top-table-main _dcscdgwick-nhp-1130pm%3Ahomepage%2Fstory-ans.

Jencks, Christopher. *The Homeless*. Cambridge: Harvard University Press, 1994.

Jindra, Michael. "Inside the Safety Net." *Hedgehog Review*, Fall 2014.

Johnson, Ann Braden. *Out of Bedlam: The Truth about Deinstitutionalization*. New York: Basic Books, 1990.

Johnson, Byron, William H. Wubbenhorst, and Alfreda Alvarez. "Assessing the Faith-Based Response to Homelessness in America: Findings from Eleven Cities." Program on Prosocial Behavior, Baylor Institute for Studies of Religion, February 1, 2017.

Johnson, Sydney. "SF Could Expand Program That Pays Drug Users to Stay Clean." *San Francisco Examiner*, September 7, 2021. https://www.sfexaminer.com/news/sf-could-expand -program-that-pays-drug-users-to-stay-clean/.

Joint Center for Housing Studies of Harvard University. "America's Rental Housing 2020." 2020. https://www.jchs.harvard.edu/sites/default/files/reports/files/Harvard_JCHS_Amer icas_Rental_Housing_2020.pdf.

Joint Committee on Taxation. "Estimates Of Federal Tax Expenditures for Fiscal Years 2020– 2024." November 5, 2020. https://www.jct.gov/publications/2020/jcx-23-20/.

Jones, Marian Moser. "Creating a Science of Homelessness During the Reagan Era." *The Milbank Quarterly* 93, no. 1 (2015): 139–78.

Jonnes, Jill. *Hep-Cats, Narcs, and Pipe Dreams: A History of America's Romance with Illegal Drugs*. Baltimore: Johns Hopkins University Press, 1999.

———. *South Bronx Rising: The Rise, Fall, and Resurrection of an American City*. New York: Fordham University Press, 2002.

Kaeble, Danielle. "Time Served in State Prison, 2018." Department of Justice Office of Justice Programs Bureau of Justice Statistics, March 2021. https://bjs.ojp.gov/content/pub/pdf /tssp18.pdf.

Kamiya, Gary. "Don't Call Them Bums: Hobos Once Filled the South of Market." *San Francisco Chronicle*, July 26, 2019. https://www.sfchronicle.com/chronicle_vault/article/Don-t-call-them-bums-Hobos-once-filled-the-14185808.php?psid=9hkpU.

Katz, Michael B. "Poorhouses and the Origins of the Public Old Age Home." *The Milbank Memorial Fund Quarterly* 62, no. 1 (Winter 1984): 110–40.

———. *In the Shadow of the Poorhouse: A Social History of Welfare in America*. New York: Basic Books, 1986.

———. *The Undeserving Poor: America's Enduring Confrontation with Poverty*. New York: Oxford University Press, 2013.

Kaufman, Nancy K. "State Government's Response to Homelessness: The Massachusetts Experience, 1983–1990." *New England Journal of Public Policy* 8, no. 1 (1992): 471–82.

Keene, Danya E., Mariana Henry, Carina Gormley, and Chima Ndumele. "'Then I Found Housing and Everything Changed': Transitions to Rent-Assisted Housing and Diabetes Self-Management." *Cityscape: A Journal of Policy Development and Research* 20, no. 2 (2018): 107–18. https://www.huduser.gov/portal/periodicals/cityscpe/vol20num2/ch7.pdf.

Kelling, George L., and Catherine M. Coles. *Fixing Broken Windows: Restoring Order and Reducing Crime in our Communities*. New York: Martin Kessler Books, 1996.

Kellor, Frances A. *Out of Work: A Study of Unemployment*. New York: G. P. Putnam's Sons, 1915.

Kelly, Edmond. *The Elimination of the Tramp*. New York: G. P. Putnam's Sons, 1908.

Kemp, Harry. "The Lure of the Tramp." *Independent*, June 8, 1911: 1270–71.

Kennedy, William. *Ironweed*. New York: Penguin, 1983.

Kenworthy, Lane. *Social Democratic Capitalism*. New York: Oxford University Press, 2019.

Kertesz, Stefan G., et al. "Housing First for Homeless Persons with Active Addiction: Are We Overreaching?" *The Milbank Quarterly* 87, no. 2 (June 2009): 495–534. doi:10.1111/j.1468-0009.2009.00565.x.

———. "Permanent Supportive Housing for Homeless People—Reframing the Debate." *New England Journal of Medicine* 375 (December 1, 2016): 2115–17. doi:10.1056/NEJMp1608326.

Kertesz, Stefan G. and Guy Johnson. "Housing First: Lessons from the United States and Challenges for Australia." *Australian Economic Review* 50, no. 2 (May 2017): 220–28. https://doi.org/10.1111/1467-8462.12217.

Kirchheimer, Donna Wilson. "Sheltering the Homeless in New York City: Expansion in an Era of Government Contraction." *Political Science Quarterly* 104, no. 4 (Winter 1989–1990): 607–23. https://doi.org/10.2307/2151101.

Knight, Heather. "Poop. Needles. Rats. Homeless Camp Pushes SF Neighborhood to the Edge." *San Francisco Chronicle*, June 24, 2018. https://www.sfchronicle.com/news/article/Neighbors-disgusted-over-despair-on-block-hit-13015964.php.

Knight, Heather. "A View of Progress." *San Francisco Chronicle*, June 28, 2018, https://www.sfchronicle.com/news/article/SF-homelessness-chief-Thrilled-with-13031080.php.

Koegel, Paul, Greer Sullivan, Audrey Burnam, Sally C. Morton, and Suzanne Wenzel. "Utilization of Mental Health and Substance Abuse Services Among Homeless Adults in Los Angeles." *Medical Care* 37, no. 3 (March 1999): 306–17.

Kohler-Hausmann, Issa. *Misdemeanorland: Criminal Courts and Social Control in an Age of Broken Windows Policing*. Princeton: Princeton University Press, 2018.

Kozol, Jonathan. *Rachel and her Children: Homeless Families in America*. New York: Crown, 1988.

Kusmer, Kenneth L., *Down and Out, on the Road: The Homeless in American History*. New York: Oxford University Press, 2002.

———. "The Underclass in Historical Perspective: Tramps and Vagrants in Urban America, 1870–1930." In *On Being Homeless: Historical Perspectives*, edited by Rick Beard, 20–31. New York: Museum of the City of New York, 1987.

"LA Alliance for Human Rights, et al. v. City of Los Angeles, et al.," United States District Court, Central District of California, Case 2:20-cv-02291-DOC-KES, Document 277, April 20, 2021.

Lacey, Forrest W. "Vagrancy and Other Crimes of Personal Condition." *Harvard Law Review* 66, no. 7 (May 1953): 1203–26.

Lam, Julie A., and Robert Rosenheck. "The Effects of Victimization on Clinical Outcomes of Homeless Persons with Serious Mental Illness." *Psychiatric Services* 49, no. 5 (May 1998): 678–83. https://doi.org/10.1176/ps.49.5.678.

Lanum, Nikolas. "Seattle Residents at Breaking Point with Homeless Crisis: 'Makes Me Depressed.'" *New York Post*, March 29, 2021. https://nypost.com/2021/03/29/seattle -residents-at-breaking-point-with-homeless-crisis-makes-me-depressed/.

Laubach, Frank Charles. *Why There Are Vagrants: A Study*. New York: Columbia University, 1916.

Lee, Barrett A. "The Disappearance of Skid Row: Some Ecological Evidence." *Urban Affairs Quarterly* 16, no. 1 (September 1980): 81–107. https://doi.org/10.1177/10780874800 1600105.

Lee, Barrett A., and Christopher J. Schreck. "Danger on the Streets: Marginality and Victimization Among Homeless People." *American Behavioral Scientist* 48, no. 8 (April 2005): 1055–81. https://doi.org/10.1177/0002764204274200.

Lee, Barrett A., Townsand Price-Spratlen, and James W. Kanan. "Determinants of Homelessness in Metropolitan Areas." *Journal of Urban Affairs* 25, no. 3 (2003): 335–56.

Lee, Ellen E., et al. "Comparison of Schizophrenia Outpatients in Residential Care Facilities with Those Living with Someone: Study of Mental and Physical Health, Cognitive Functioning, And Biomarkers of Aging." *Psychiatry Research* 275 (May 2019): 162–68. https:// doi.org/10.1016/j.psychres.2019.02.067.

Legras, Christopher. "California's Homeless are Fodder for an Insatiable Bureaucracy." allaspectreport.com. December 14, 2020. https://allaspectreport.com/2020/12/14/califor nias-homeless-are-fodder-for-an-insatiable-bureaucracy/.

———. "We Need to Stop Using the Term 'Homeless Crisis.' It's Wrong, It's Not Backed Up by the Data, and It Leads to Bad Policy." allaspectreport.com. July 22, 2021. https://all aspectreport.com/2021/07/22/we-need-to-stop-using-the-term-homeless-crisis-its-wrong -its-not-backed-up-by-the-data-and-it-leads-to-bad-policy/.

Leibowitz, Ed. "Reinventing Skid Row." *Politico*, March 5, 2014. https://www.politico.com /magazine/story/2014/03/los-angeles-skid-row-reinvention-104266/.

Lelyveld, Nita. "How to Unharden Our Hearts Toward Homeless People." *Los Angeles Times*, January 25, 2020. https://www.latimes.com/california/story/2020-01-25/homless-solu tions-los-angeles-providing-aid.

Lens, Michael, Kirk McClure, and Brent Mast. "Does Jobs Proximity Matter in the Housing Choice Voucher Program?" *Cityscape: A Journal of Policy Development and Research* 21, no. 1 (2019): 145–62.

Leopold, Josh. "Housing Needs of Rental Assistance Applicants." *Cityscape: A Journal of Policy Development and Research* 14, no. 2 (2012): 275–98. https://www.huduser.gov/portal/peri odicals/cityscpe/vol14num2/Cityscape_July2012_housing_needs.pdf.

Lescohier, Don D. *The Labor Market*. New York: The Macmillan Company, 1919.

Lewis, Michael. "The Death of Public Beauty." *National Review*, September 3, 2020. https:// www.nationalreview.com/magazine/2020/09/21/the-death-of-public-beauty/.

Levinson, David. "The Etiology of Skid Rows in the United States." *International Journal of Social Psychiatry* 20, nos. 1–2 (April 1974): 25–33. https://doi.org/10.1177/00207640 7402000104.

Lindblom, Eric N. "Towards A Comprehensive Homelessness Prevention Strategy." *Housing Policy Debate* 2, no. 3 (1991): 957–1025. https://doi.org/10.1080/10511482.1991 .9521079.

London, Jack. *London On the Road: The Tramp Diary and Other Hobo Writings*. Edited by Richard Etulian. Logan: Utah State University Press, 1979.

Lopez, Steve. "Column: So Trump Wants to Solve Homelessness in California? Here Are Five Things He Can Do." *Los Angeles Times*, February 19, 2020.

———. "They Come from Around US to Live Homeless on Hollywood's Streets. How Much More Can We Take?" *Los Angeles Times*, November 17, 2019. https://www.latimes.com /california/story/2020-02-19/column-5-things-trump-can-do-if-he-really-wants-to-help -solve-californias-homeless-crisis.

Los Angeles City Controller. "High Cost of Homeless Housing: Review of Proposition HHH." October 8, 2019. https://lacontroller.org/wp-content/uploads/2019/10/The -High-Cost-of-Homeless-Housing_Review-of-Prop-HHH_10.8.19.pdf.

Los Angeles City Council. "City of Los Angeles Comprehensive Homelessness Strategy." Council File #15-1138-S1, February 9, 2016. http://clkrep.lacity.org/onlinedocs/2015/15 -1138-s1_misc_03-21-2016.pdf.

Los Angeles City Councilmember Mike Bonin. "Mike Proposes New Commission Composed of People Who Are or Have Been Homeless." Press Release. September 4, 2019. https://11thdistrict.com/news/mike-proposes-new-commission-composed-of-people-who -are-or-have-been-homeless/.

Los Angeles County Chief Executive Office. "Approved Strategies to Combat Homelessness." February 2016. https://homeless.lacounty.gov/wp-content/uploads/2017/01/HI-Report -Approved2.pdf.

Los Angeles County Mental Health Commission Ad-hoc Committee on LA County's Board and Care System. "A Call to Action: The Precarious State of the Board and Care System Serving Residents Living with Mental Illness in Los Angeles County." January 22, 2018. http://file.lacounty.gov/SDSInter/dmh/1036005_BoardandCareFacilitiesreport.pdf.

Lowell, Josephine Shaw. *Public Relief and Private Charity*. New York: G. P. Putnam's Sons, 1884.

Lubove, Roy. *The Professional Altruist: The Emergence of Social Work as a Career, 1880–1930*. Cambridge: Harvard University Press, 1965.

Lucas, David S. "The Impact of Federal Homelessness Funding on Homelessness." *Southern Economic Journal* 84, no. 2 (October 2017): 548–76. https://doi.org/10.1002/soej.12231.

Ludwig, Jens, et al. "Long-Term Neighborhood Effects on Low-Income Families: Evidence from Moving to Opportunity." *American Economic Review* 103, no. 3 (2013): 226–31. doi:10.1257/aer.103.3.226.

Ly, Angela, and Eric Latimer. "Housing First Impact on Costs and Associated Costs Offsets: A Review of the Literature." *Canadian Journal of Psychiatry* 60, no. 11 (November 2015): 475–87. doi:10.1177/070674371506001103.

Magnet, Myron. *The Dream and the Nightmare: The Sixties' Legacy to the Underclass.* New York: William Morrow and Company, 1993.

Main, Thomas J. "The Homeless Families of New York." *The Public Interest*, Fall 1986.

———. *Homelessness in New York City: Policymaking from Koch to de Blasio.* New York: New York University Press, 2017.

Maisel, Albert Q. "Bedlam: Most US Mental Hospitals Are a Shame and a Disgrace." *Life*, May 6, 1946.

Mallach, Alan. *The Divided City: Poverty and Prosperity in Urban America.* Washington, DC: Island Press, 2018.

———. "Rents Will Only Go So Low, No Matter How Much We Build." shelterforce.org, December 13, 2019. https://shelterforce.org/2019/12/13/rents-will-only-go-so-low-no -matter-how-much-we-build/.

Malson, Hilary, and Gary Blasi. "For the Crisis Yet to Come: Temporary Settlements in the Era of Evictions." UCLA Luskin Institute on Inequality and Democracy. July 21, 2020. https:// shelterforce.org/2019/12/13/rents-will-only-go-so-low-no-matter-how-much-we-build/.

Marris, Peter, and Martin Rein. *Dilemmas of Social Reform: Poverty and Community Action in The United States,* second edition. London: Routledge and Kegan Paul, 1972.

Martinez, Jose. "Homeless Feel Unwelcome at Gleaming New Moynihan Train Hall as They Stick to Penn Station." *The City,* January 10, 2021. https://www.thecity.nyc/2021/1/10/22223920 /homeless-feel-unwelcome-at-gleaming-new-moynihan-train-hall.

Martinez, Mel. "Taking on the Problem That 'Cannot Be Solved,'" US Department of Housing and Urban Development, Secretary [Mel] Martinez's Speeches and Testimony, July 20, 2001.

Mast, Brent. "School Performance of Schools Assigned to HUD-Assisted Households." *Cityscape: A Journal of Policy Development and Research* 20, no. 3 (2018): 189–221. https:// www.huduser.gov/portal/periodicals/cityscpe/vol20num3/ch10.pdf.

Mast, Brent D. "Measuring Homelessness and Resources to Combat Homelessness with PIT and HIC Data." *Cityscape: A Journal of Policy Development and Research* 22, no. 1 (2020): 215–26. https://www.huduser.gov/portal/periodicals/cityscpe/vol22num1/ch7.pdf.

McCarty, Maggie, Katie Jones, and Libby Perl. "Overview of Federal Housing Assistance Programs and Policy." Congressional Research Service, March 27, 2019. https://crsreports .congress.gov/product/pdf/RL/RL34591.

McClure, Kirk. "Housing Choice Voucher Marketing Opportunity Index: Analysis of Data at the Tract and Block Group Level." US Department of Housing and Urban Development, Office of Policy Development and Research, 2011.

———. "Length of Stay in Assisted Housing." US Department of Housing and Urban Development, Office of Policy Development and Research, October 2017. https://www.huduser .gov/portal/sites/default/files/pdf/lengthofstay.pdf.

McDougal, Dennis. "Comic Relief Will Give Aid to the Homeless in US." *Los Angeles Times,* January 15, 1986.

McGray, Douglas. "The Abolitionist." *The Atlantic,* June 2004.

Meinbresse Molly, et al. "Exploring the Experiences of Violence Among Individuals Who Are Homeless Using a Consumer-Led Approach." *Violence and Victims* 29, no. 1 (2014): 122–36. https://nhchc.org/wp-content/uploads/2019/08/vv-29-1_ptr_a8_122-136.pdf.

Metraux, Stephen. "Waiting for the Wrecking Ball: Skid Row in Postindustrial Philadelphia." *Journal of Urban History* 25 no. 5 (July 1999): 690–715.

Metraux, Stephen, and Dennis P. Culhane. "Homeless Shelter Use and Reincarceration Following Prison Release." *Criminology and Public Policy* 3, no. 2 (March 2004): 139–60.

Metraux, Stephen, Caterina G. Roman, and Richard S. Cho. "Incarceration and Homelessness." National Symposium on Homelessness Research, 2007. https://www.huduser.gov/portal/publications/pdf/p9.pdf.

Metraux, Stephen, Jamison Fargo, Nick Eng, and Dennis P. Culhane. "Employment and Earnings Trajectories During Two Decades Among Adults in New York City Homeless Shelters." *Cityscape: A Journal of Policy Development and Research* 20, no. 2 (2018): 173–202. https://www.huduser.gov/portal/periodicals/cityscpe/vol20num2/ch11.pdf.

Metraux, Steve. "Digging Up Vine Street in Search of Old Skid Row." hiddencityphila.org, April 26, 2017. https://hiddencityphila.org/2017/04/digging-up-vine-street-in-search-of-old-skid-row/.

Metropolitan Transportation Authority. "Safety Committee Meeting Materials." July 2019. http://web.mta.info/mta/news/books/pdf/190724_0800_Safety.pdf.

Miller, Myles. "A Christmas Day Vigil in Grand Central Remembers the Plights of the Homeless." ny1.com, December 25, 2018. https://www.ny1.com/nyc/all-boroughs/news/2018/12/25/the-doe-fund-honors-mamma-doe-homeless-people-struggling-in-nyc-grand-central-vigil.

Miller, Peter M. "A Critical Analysis of the Research on Student Homelessness." *Review of Educational Research*. 81, no. 3 (September 2011): 308–37. https://doi.org/10.3102/0034654311415120.

Millich, Nancy A. "Compassion Fatigue and the First Amendment: Are the Homeless Constitutional Castaways?" *UC Davis Law Review* 27, no. 2 (1994): 275–81.

Minkler, Meredith, and Beverly Ovrebo. "SRO's: The Vanishing Hotels for Low-Income Elders," *Generations: Journal of the American Society on Aging* 9, no. 3 (Spring 1985): 40–42.

Monkkonen, Eric H. "Introduction." In *Walking to Work: Tramps in America, 1790–1935*. Edited by Eric H. Monkonnen, 1–20. Lincoln: University of Nebraska Press, 1984.

———. "Regional Dimensions of Tramping, North and South, 1880–1910." In *Walking to Work: Tramps in America, 1790–1935*, edited by Eric H. Monkonnen, 189–211. Lincoln: University of Nebraska Press, 1984.

Mosley Jennifer E. "From Skid Row to the Statehouse." In *Nonprofits and Advocacy: Engaging Community and Government in an Era of Retrenchment*. Edited by Robert J. Pekkanen, Steven Rathgeb Smith, and Yutaka Tsujinaka, 107–34. Baltimore: Johns Hopkins University Press, 2014.

Moynihan, Daniel P. *Maximum Feasible Misunderstanding: Community Action in the War on Poverty*. New York: The Free Press, 1969.

Murphy, Jarrett. "Data Drop: Which NYC Neighborhoods Host the Most Homeless-Shelter Beds?" *City Limits*, September 10, 2019. https://citylimits.org/2019/09/10/data-drop-which-nyc-neighborhoods-host-the-most-homeless-shelter-beds/.

Nahmias, Laura. "Christine Quinn to Head Nonprofit for Homeless Women." *Politico*, September 17, 2015. https://www.politico.com/states/new-york/city-hall/story/2015/09/christine-quinn-to-head-nonprofit-for-homeless-women-000000.

———. "HUD Slashes Funding for Some New York City Homeless Shelters." *Politico*, May 9, 2016. https://www.politico.com/states/new-york/city-hall/story/2016/05/hud-slashes-funding-for-some-new-york-city-homeless-shelters-101531.

National Academies of Sciences, Engineering, and Medicine. "The Economic and Fiscal Consequences of Immigration." 2016. https://d279m997dpfwgl.cloudfront.net /wp/2016/09/0922_immigrant-economics-full-report.pdf.

———. "Permanent Supportive Housing: Evaluating the Evidence for Improving Health Outcomes Among People Experiencing Chronic Homelessness." 2018. https://d155kunx f1aozz.cloudfront.net/wp-content/uploads/2018/07/25133.pdf.

National Alliance to End Homelessness. *Fact Sheet.* April 2016. http://endhomelessness.org /wp-content/uploads/2016/04/housing-first-fact-sheet.pdf.

———. "A Plan, Not a Dream: How to End Homelessness in Ten Years." 2000. https:// b.3cdn.net/naeh/b970364c18809d1e0c_aum6bnzb4.pdf.

National Alliance to End Homelessness, et al. "Letter to Reps. Collins, Price, Reed, and Diaz-Balart." December 3, 2019. https://cdn.theatlantic.com/assets/media/files/los_for_2018 _coc_nofa_in_thud_appropriations.pdf.

National Association of State Mental Health Program Directors. "Trend in Psychiatric Inpatient Capacity, United States and Each State, 1970 to 2014." Assessment #10, August 2017. https://www.nasmhpd.org/sites/default/files/TAC.Paper_.10.Psychiatric%20Inpatient%20 Capacity_Final.pdf.

National Center for Homeless Education. "Federal Data Summary, School Years 2015–2016 Through 2017–2018, Education for Homeless Children and Youth." January 2020. https://nche.ed.gov/wp-content/uploads/2020/01/Federal-Data-Summary-SY-15.16 -to-17.18-Published-1.30.2020.pdf.

National Law Center on Homelessness and Poverty. "Housing Not Handcuffs: A Litigation Manual." 2018. https://homelesslaw.org/wp-content/uploads/2018/10/Housing-Not -Handcuffs-Litigation-Manual.pdf.

———. "Housing Not Handcuffs 2019: Ending the Criminalization of Homelessness in US Cities." December 2019. https://homelesslaw.org/wp-content/uploads/2019/12/HOUS ING-NOT-HANDCUFFS-2019-FINAL.pdf.

National Low-Income Housing Coalition. "Congressional Leaders Agree to Coronavirus Response Package with Funding for Homelessness and Housing." March 25, 2020. https:// nlihc.org/resource/congressional-leaders-agree-coronavirus-response-package-funding -homelessness-and-housing.

———. "President Biden Signs American Rescue Plan Act with Nearly $50 Billion in Housing and Homelessness Assistance." March 15, 2021. https://nlihc.org/resource/president -biden-signs-american-rescue-plan-act-nearly-50-billion-housing-and-homelessness.

Nelson, Geoffrey, and Timothy MacLeod. "The Evolution of Housing for People with Serious Mental Illness." In *Housing, Citizenship, and Communities for People with Serious Mental Illness: Theory, Research, Practice, and Policy Perspectives.* Edited by John Sylvestre, Geoffrey Nelson, and Tim Aubry, 3–22. New York: Oxford University Press, 2017, 3-22.

New York City Coalition for the Homeless. "State of the Homeless 2020: Governor and Mayor to Blame as New York Enters Fifth Decade of Homelessness Crisis." March 2020. https://www.coalitionforthehomeless.org/wp-content/uploads/2020/03/StateofTheHome less2020.pdf.

———. "State of the Homeless 2021: Housing is Health Care, A Lesson for the Ages." April 2021. https://www.coalitionforthehomeless.org/wp-content/uploads/2021/04 /StateOfTheHomeless2021.pdf.

———. "View from the Street: Unsheltered New Yorkers and the Need for Safety, Dignity, and Agency." April 2021. https://www.coalitionforthehomeless.org/wp-content /uploads/2021/04/View-from-the-Street-April-21.pdf.

New York City Commission on the Homeless. "The Way Home: A New Direction in Social Policy." February 1992.

New York City Comptroller, "FY 2022 Agency Watch List: Homeless Services Provider Agencies," March 2021. https://comptroller.nyc.gov/wp-content/uploads/documents/Watch _List_Homeless_Services.pdf.

———. "NYC Department of Correction FYs 2009–2019 Operating Expenditures, Jail Population, Cost Per Incarcerated Person, Staffing Ratios, Performance Measure Outcomes, and Overtime." December 6, 2019. https://comptroller.nyc.gov/reports/nyc-department -of-correction/.

New York City Continuum of Care. "Governance Charter of the New York City Continuum of Care." May 22, 2020. https://www1.nyc.gov/assets/nycccoc/downloads/pdf/Gover nance%20Charter_Final_Adopted%205.22.20.pdf.

New York City Department of Homeless Services. "NYC HOPE 2019 Results," 2019. https:// www1.nyc.gov/assets/dhs/downloads/pdf/hope-2019-results.pdf.

New York City Housing Authority. "NYCHA 2020 Fact Sheet." March 2020. https://www1 .nyc.gov/assets/nycha/downloads/pdf/NYCHA-Fact-Sheet_2020_Final.pdf.

New York City Independent Budget Office. "The Rising Number of Homeless Families in NYC, 2002–2012." November 2014. https://ibo.nyc.ny.us/iboreports/2014dhs.pdf.

———. "Not Reaching the Door: Homeless Students Face Many Hurdles on the Way to School." October 2016. https://ibo.nyc.ny.us/iboreports/not-reaching-the-door-homeless -students-face-many-hurdles-on-the-way-to-school.pdf.

———. "Close to Home: Does Proximity to a Homeless Shelter Affect Residential Property Values in Manhattan?" September 2019. https://ibo.nyc.ny.us/iboreports /close-to-home-does-proximity-to-a-homeless-shelter-affect-residential-property-values -in-manhattan-2019.pdf.

New York Housing Conference. "United for Housing: from the Ground Up 2021." December 14, 2020. https://thenyhc.org/2020/12/14/united-for-housing-releases-report/.

New York Times, "New Priority Means Fewer Beds in City Shelters." Editorial. May 17, 2016.

O'Flaherty, Brendan. *City Economics*. Cambridge: Harvard University Press, 2005.

———. "Homelessness Research: A Guide for Economists (and Friends)." *Journal of Housing Economics* 44 (2019): 1–25. https://doi.org/10.1016/j.jhe.2019.01.003.

———. *Making Room: The Economics of Homelessness*. Cambridge: Harvard University Press, 1996.

O'Flaherty, Brendan, and Ting Wu. "Homeless Shelters for Single Adults: Why Does Their Population Change?" *Social Service Review* 82, no. 3 (September 2008): 511–50.

Office of New York City Mayor Bill de Blasio. "Mayor's Management Report." September 2019. https://www1.nyc.gov/assets/operations/downloads/pdf/mmr2019/2019_mmr.pdf.

———. "Turning the Tide on Homelessness in New York City," February 2017. https:// www1.nyc.gov/assets/dhs/downloads/pdf/turning-the-tide-on-homelessness.pdf.

Office of New York State Senator Liz Krueger. "Home Stability Support Bill Moves Out of Senate Social Services Committee." Press Release. March 5, 2019. https://www.nysenate .gov/newsroom/press-releases/liz-krueger/home-stability-support-bill-moves-out-senate -social-services.

Ohls, James. "Public Policy towards Low Income Housing and Filtering in Housing Markets." *Journal of Urban Economics* 2, no. 2 (April 1975): 144–71. https://doi.org/10.1016/0094 -1190(75)90044-3.

Olasky, Marvin. *The Tragedy of American Compassion.* Wheaton, IL: Crossway Books, 2008 (orig. 1992).

Olsen, Edgar O., and Jeffrey E. Zabel. "Chapter 14: US Housing Policy." In *Handbook of Regional and Urban Economics 5A.* Edited by Gilles Duranton, J. Vernon Henderson, and William C. Strange, 887–986. New York: North-Holland, 2015.

Olsen, Henry. "A New Homestead Act—To Jump Start the US Economy." *National Interest,* December 15, 2015. https://nationalinterest.org/feature/new-homestead-act%E2%80%94 -jumpstart-the-us-economy-14618.

Oreskes, Benjamin, Doug Smith, and David Lauter. "95% of Voters Say Homelessness Is LA's Biggest Problem, Times Poll Finds. 'You Can't Escape It.'" *Los Angeles Times,* November 14, 2019. https://www.latimes.com/california/story/2019-11-14/homeless-housing-poll-opinion.

Oreskes, Benjamin, Emily Apert Reyes, and Doug Smith. "Judge Orders LA City and County to Offer Shelter to Everyone on Skid Row by Fall." *Los Angeles Times,* April 20, 2021. https://www.latimes.com/homeless-housing/story/2021-04-20/judge-carter-la-city-county -shelter-skid-row-homeless-fall.

Orlebeke, Charles J. "The Evolution of Low-Income Housing Policy, 1949 to 1999," *Housing Policy Debate* 11, no. 2 (2000): 489–520. doi:10.1080/10511482.2000.9521375.

Orwell, George. *Down and Out in Paris and London.* New York: Penguin, 2001 (orig. 1933).

Padgett, Deborah, Benjamin Henwood, and Sam Tsemberis. *Housing First: Ending Homelessness, Transforming Systems, and Changing Lives.* New York: Oxford University Press, 2015.

Patel, Jugal K., Tim Arango, Anjali Singhvi, and Jon Huang. "Black, Homeless, and Burdened by LA's Legacy of Racism." *New York Times,* December 22, 2019.

Patterson, James T. *America's Struggle Against Poverty, 1900–1980.* Cambridge: Harvard University Press, 1981.

Pavao, Joanne, Jennifer Alvarez, Nikki Baumrind, Marta Induni, and Rachel Kimerling. "Intimate Partner Violence and Housing Instability." *American Journal of Preventive Medicine* 32, no. 2 (February 2007): 143–46.

Perl, Libby, et al. "Homelessness: Targeted Federal Programs." Congressional Research Service. October 18, 2018. https://sgp.fas.org/crs/misc/RL30442.pdf.

Perlman, Merrill. "2020 AP Stylebook Changes: Person-First Language, and the Great 'Pled' Debate." *Columbia Journalism Review,* May 6, 2020. https://www.cjr.org/language _corner/2020-ap-stylebook-changes.php.

Perry, Mitch. "Ted Yoho Urges Ben Carson to Reverse Obama-Era 'Housing First,' Reinstate Homeless Shelter Funds." floridapolitics.com, June 19, 2017. https://floridapoli tics.com/archives/240348-ted-yoho-calls-ben-carson-revise-hud-housing-first-approach -homelessness/.

Peters, Amanda. "Lawyers Who Break the Law: What Congress Can Do to Prevent Mental Health Patient Advocates from Violating Federal Legislation." *Oregon Law Review* 89, no. 1 (2010): 133–74.

Picture the Homeless Research Committee. "The Business of Homelessness: Financial & Human Costs of the Shelter-Industrial Complex." 2018.

Pilkauskas, Natasha V., and Christina Cross. "Beyond the Nuclear Family: Trends in Children Living in Shared Households." *Demography* 55, no. 6 (2018): 2283–97. https://doi .org/10.1007/s13524-018-0719-y.

Pilkauskas, Natasha V., Irwin Garfinkel, and Sara S. McLanahan. "The Prevalence and Economic Value of Doubling Up." *Demography* 51 (2014): 1667–76.

Pilkauskas, Natasha V., Mariana Amorim, and Rachel E. Dunifon. "Historical Trends in Children Living in Multigenerational Households in the United States: 1870–2018." *Demography* 57 (2020): 2269–96.

Plunz, Richard. *A History of Housing in New York City*. Revised edition. New York: Columbia University, Press, 2016.

"Presidential Debate in Winston-Salem, North Carolina." September 25, 1988, Transcript: https://www.presidency.ucsb.edu/documents/presidential-debate-winston-salem-north-carolina.

President John F. Kennedy. "Special Message to the Congress on Mental Illness and Mental Retardation." February 5, 1963. https://www.presidency.ucsb.edu/documents/special-message-the-congress-mental-illness-and-mental-retardation.

Prisoner Reentry Institute, John Jay College of Criminal Justice. "Three Quarter Houses: The View from the Inside." October 2013.

ProPublica, "Right to Fail. "New Documentary Chronicles the Challenges of New York's Supported Housing Program for People with Mental Illness." February 20, 2019.

Public Policy Institute of California. "Californians and Their Government: PPIC Statewide Survey." October 2020. https://www.ppic.org/wp-content/uploads/ppic-statewide-survey-californians-and-their-government-october-2020.pdf.

Quigley, John M., and Steven Raphael. "Is Housing Unaffordable? Why Isn't It More Affordable?" *Journal of Economic Perspectives* 18, no. 1 (Winter 2004): 191–214.

Quilgars, Deborah and Nicholas Pleace. "Housing First and Social Integration: A Realistic Aim?" *Social Inclusion* 4, no. 4 (2016): 5–15. https://pdfs.semanticscholar.org/d094/4c1a0ad1f79ce9a3001b7203255ba4e2f409.pdf.

Quinnipiac University. "New York City Mayor Gets Worst Grades on Corruption, Quinnipiac University Poll Finds; 96% Say Homelessness Is Serious Problem." March 1, 2017. https://poll.qu.edu/poll-results/.

Quinones, Sam. *Dreamland: The True Tale of America's Opiate Epidemic*. New York: Bloomsbury Press, 2015.

Rader, Victoria. *Signal Through the Flames: Mitch Snyder and America's Homeless*. Kansas City, MO: Sheed & Ward, 1986.

Rankin, Sara K. "Punishing Homelessness." *New Criminal Law Review: An International and Interdisciplinary Journal* 22, no. 1 (Winter 2019): 99–135.

Rarick, Ethan. *California Rising: The Life and Times of Pat Brown*. Berkeley: University of California Press, 2005.

Ravani, Sarah. "Theo Homeless at Age 7." *San Francisco Chronicle*, July 29, 2020. https://www.sfchronicle.com/projects/2020/theo/.

Raven, Maria C., Matthew J. Niedzwiecki, and Margot Kushel. "A Randomized Trial of Permanent Supportive Housing for Chronically Homeless Persons with High Use of Publicly Funded Services." *Health Services Research* 55, no. S2 (October 2020): 797–806. https://doi.org/10.1111/1475-6773.13553.

Rector, Robert, and Vijay Menon. "Understanding the Hidden $1.1 Trillion Welfare System and How to Reform It." Heritage Foundation, April 5, 2018. https://www.heritage.org/sites/default/files/2018-04/BG3294.pdf.

Reed, Henry Hope. *The Golden City*. Garden City, NY: Doubleday, 1959.

Reich, Robert, and Lloyd Siegel. "The Emergence of the Bowery as a Psychiatric Dumping Ground." *Psychiatric Quarterly* 50 (1978): 191–201.

Remster, Brianna. "A Life Course Analysis of Homeless Shelter Use among the Formerly Incarcerated." *Justice Quarterly* 36, no. 3 (2019): 437–65. https://doi.org/10.1080/07418 825.2017.1401653.

Reyes, Emily Alpert, and Benjamin Oreskes. "LA Expands Cleanup Teams for Homeless Encampments, Vowing to Be 'Less Reactive.'" *Los Angeles Times*, June 28, 2019. https://www.la times.com/local/lanow/la-me-ln-homeless-encampment-cleanups-plan-20190628-story.html.

Richter, Dirk, and Holger Hoffmann. "Preference for Independent Housing of Persons with Mental Disorders: Systematic Review and Meta-Analysis." *Administration and Policy in Mental Health and Mental Health Services Research* 44, no. 6 (2017): 817–23. doi:10.1007 /s10488-017-0791-4.

Ridgway, Priscilla, and Anthony M. Zipple. "The Paradigm Shift in Residential Services: From the Linear Continuum to Supported Housing Approaches." *Psychosocial Rehabilitation Journal* 13, no. 4 (April 1990): 11–31. https://doi.org/10.1037/h0099479.

Rog, Debra J., C. Scott Holupka, and Lisa C. Patton. "Characteristics and Dynamics of Homeless Families with Children." US Department of Health and Human Services, Office of the Assistant Secretary for Planning and Evaluation, 2007. https://aspe.hhs.gov/sites /default/files/private/pdf/75331/report.pdf.

Roncarati, Jill S., et al. "Housing Boston's Chronically Homeless Unsheltered Population 14 Years Later." *Medical Care* 59 (April 2021): S170–74. doi:10.1097/MLR.000000 0000001409.

Rooney, James F. "Group Processes among Skid Row Winos: A Re-Evaluation of the Undersocialization Hypothesis." *Quarterly Journal of Studies on Alcohol* 22, no. 3 (1961): 444–60. https://doi.org/10.15288/qjsa.1961.22.444.

Rosen, Eva. *The Voucher Promise: "Section 8" and the Fate of an American Neighborhood.* Princeton: Princeton University Press, 2020.

Rosen, Eva, and Philip Garboden. "Landlord Paternalism: Housing the Poor with a Velvet Glove." *Social Problems* spaa037 (2020): 1–22. https://doi.org/10.1093/socpro/spaa037.

Rosenheck, Robert, et al. "Cost-Effectiveness of Supported Housing for Homeless Persons with Mental Illness." *Archives of General Psychiatry* 60, no. 9 (September 2003): 940–51. doi:10.1001/archpsyc.60.9.940.

Rossi, Peter. *Without Shelter: Homelessness in the 1980s.* New York: Priority Press Publications, 1989.

Rossi, Peter H. "Troubling Families: Family Homelessness in America." *American Behavioral Scientist* 37, no. 3 (January 1994): 342–95. https://doi.org/10.1177/0002764294037003003.

Rossi, Peter H., James D. Wright, Gene A. Fisher, and Georgianna Willis. "The Urban Homeless: Estimating Composition and Size." *Science* 235 (March 13, 1987): 1336–41. doi:10 .1126/science.2950592.

Rothman, David. "The First Shelters: The Contemporary Relevance of the Almshouse." In *On Being Homeless: Historical Perspectives*, edited by Rick Beard, 10–19. New York: Museum of the City of New York, 1987.

Ryan, William. *Blaming the Victim.* New York, Pantheon Books: 1971.

Saffran, Dennis. "Massacre of the Innocents." *City Journal*, Winter 2018. https://www.city -journal.org/html/massacre-innocents-15647.html?wallit_nosession=1.

Saiz, Albert. "Immigration and Housing Rents in American Cities." *Journal of Urban Economics* 61, no. 2 (March 2007): 345–71. https://doi.org/10.1016/j.jue.2006.07.004.

Saleh, Amam Z. Paul S. Appelbaum, Xiaoyu Liu, T.Scott Stroup, and Melanie Wall. "Deaths of People with Mental Illness During Interactions with Law Enforcement." *International Journal of Law and Psychiatry* 58 (May–June 2018): 110–16. https://doi.org/10.1016/j.ijlp.2018.03.003.

Salam, Reihan. *Melting Pot or Civil War?: A Son of Immigrants Makes the Case against Open Borders.* New York: Sentinel, 2018.

Sandberg, Erica. "Fight for What You Love." *City Journal,* August 3, 2020. https://www.city-journal.org/residents-fighting-for-san-francisco.

Sandler, Lauren. *This is All I Got: A New Mother's Search for Home.* New York: Random House, 2020.

San Francisco Budget and Legislative Analyst's Office. "Policing and Criminal Justice Costs Related to Open Air Drug Dealing in the Tenderloin, South of Market, and Mid-Market neighborhoods." April 25, 2019. https://sfbos.org/sites/default/files/BLA_042519_Open_Drug_Dealing_Sup_Haney.pdf.

San Francisco Chamber of Commerce. "Public Safety, Homelessness and Affordability Are Biggest Issues in 2018 SF Chamber Poll." Press Release, February 2, 2018.

Santos, Melissa. "Across the Entire State, WA Voters Rank Homelessness as the No. 1 Issue Lawmakers Must Address." crosscut.com, January 9, 2020. https://crosscut.com/2020/01/across-entire-state-wa-voters-rank-homelessness-no-1-issue-lawmakers-must-address.

Sard, Barbara, Douglas Rice, Alison Bell, and Alicia Mazzara. "Federal Policy Changes Can Help More Families with Housing Vouchers Live in Higher-Opportunity Areas." Center for Budget and Policy Priorities. September 4, 2018. https://www.cbpp.org/research/housing/federal-policy-changes-can-help-more-families-with-housing-vouchers-live-in-higher.

Sarvis, Will. "The Homelessness Muddle Revisited." *The Urban Lawyer* 49, no. 2 (Spring 2017): 317–54.

Satel, Sally. "Happy Birthday, Methadone!" *Washington Monthly,* November/December 2014.

Schlesinger, Arthur. *The Crisis of the Old Order, 1919–1933.* New York: Houghton Mifflin, 1957.

Schneider, John C. "Tramping Workers, 1890–1920." In *Walking to Work: Tramps in America, 1790–1935,* edited by Eric H. Monkonnen, 212–34. Lincoln: University of Nebraska Press, 1984.

Schutt, Russell K., with Stephen M. Goldfinger. *Homelessness, Housing, and Mental Illness.* Cambridge: Harvard University Press, 2011.

Schwarcz, Sandra K., Ling C. Hsu, Eric Vittinghoff, Annie Vu, Joshua D. Bamberger, and Mitchell H. Katz "Impact of Housing on the Survival of Persons with AIDS," *BMC Public Health* 9, Article number 220 (2009). doi:10.1186/1471-2458-9-220.

Schwartz, Alex F. *Housing Policy in the United States.* Fourth edition. New York: Routledge, 2021. Kindle edition.

Seager, Stephen B. *Street Crazy: The Tragedy of the Homeless Mentally Ill.* Redondo Beach, CA: Westcom Press, 1998.

Secret, Mosi. "Clock Ticks for a Key Homeless Program." *New York Times,* May 31, 2011. https://www.nytimes.com/2011/06/01/nyregion/new-york-city-close-to-ending-key-housing-program.html.

Segal, Steven P., Jim Baumohl, and Elsie Johnson. "Falling through the Cracks: Mental Disorder and Social Margin in a Young Vagrant Population." *Social Problems* 24, no. 3 (February 1977): 387–400. https://doi.org/10.2307/800091.

Semega, Jessica Melissa Kollar, Emily A. Shrider, and John F. Creamer. "Income and Poverty in the United States: 2019." United States Census Bureau, September 2020. https://www .census.gov/content/dam/Census/library/publications/2020/demo/p60-270.pdf.

Shapiro, Joan Hatch. *Communities of the Alone*. New York: Association Press, 1971.

Shapiro, Joseph P. *No Pity: People with Disabilities Forging a New Civil Rights Movement*. New York: Times Books, 1993.

Shattuck, Rachel M., and Rose M. Kreider. "Social and Economic Characteristics of Currently Unmarried Women with a Recent Birth: 2011." US Census Bureau, May 2013. https:// www2.census.gov/library/publications/2013/acs/acs-21.pdf.

Sheehan, Susan. *Is There No Place on Earth for Me?* New York: Houghton Mifflin Harcourt, 1982.

Sheeley, Kirsten Moore, et al. "The Making of a Crisis: A History of Homelessness in Los Angeles." UCLA Luskin Center for History and Policy, January 2021. https://luskincenter .history.ucla.edu/wp-content/uploads/sites/66/2021/01/LCHP-The-Making-of-A-Crisis -Report.pdf.

Shellenberger, Michael. *San Fransicko: Why Progressives Ruin Cities*. New York: Harper, 2021.

Shiffer, James Eli. *The King of Skid Row: John Bacich and the Twilight Years of Old Minneapolis*. Minneapolis: University of Minnesota Press, 2016.

Shinn, Marybeth and Jill Khadduri. *In the Midst of Plenty: Homelessness and What to do about It*. Hoboken: John Wiley & Sons, 2020.

Shklar, Judith N. *American Citizenship*. Cambridge: Harvard University Press, 1991.

Shlaes, Amity. *Great Society: A New History*. New York: Harper, 2019. Kindle edition.

Shorter, Edward. *A History of Psychiatry: From the Era of the Asylum to the Age of Prozac*. New York: John Wiley & Sons, 1997.

Siegal, Harvey, and James Inciardi. "The Demise of Skid Row." *Society* 19, no. 1 (1982): 39–45.

Sinclair-Hancq, Elizabeth, Kelli South, and Molly Vencel. "Dual Diagnosis: Serious Mental Illness and Co-Occurring Substance Use Disorders." Treatment Advocacy Center, March 2021. https://www.treatmentadvocacycenter.org/storage/documents/TAC_Co-occuring _Evidence_Brief_March_2021_Final.pdf.

Slattery, Denis. "Queens Assemblyman Calls Out Cuomo over Donations from Homeless Shelter Providers amid Homeless Crisis." *New York Daily News*, July 28, 2019. https:// www.nydailynews.com/news/politics/ny-hevesi-homeless-shelters-cuomo-campaign-dona tions-20190728-nbr47cqytzdpfdfjtqvdpjiy2q-story.html.

Smith, Doug. "These Homes Keep LA's Most Vulnerable from Becoming Homeless. Now They're Closing." *Los Angeles Times*, November 6, 2019. https://www.latimes.com/califor nia/story/2019-11-06/homeless-housing-board-care-homes-mental-illness.

———. "It Took Three Years of Blown Deadlines, but LA Opens Its First Homeless Housing Project." *Los Angeles Times*, January 7, 2019. https://www.latimes.com/california /story/2020-01-07/homeless-housing-project-proposition-hhh-bond-measure.

Smith, Doug, and Benjamin Oreskes. "Are Many Homeless People in LA Mentally Ill? New Findings Back the Public's Perception." *Los Angeles Times*, October 7, 2019. https://www .latimes.com/california/story/2019-10-07/homeless-population-mental-illness-disability.

Smith, Greg B. "Woes at Wards Island Homeless Shelters Overseen by Gov. Cuomo's Sister," *The City*, May 31, 2019. https://www.thecity.nyc/special-report/2019/5/31/21211051 /woes-at-wards-island-homeless-shelters-overseen-by-gov-cuomo-s-sister.

Smith, Richard M. "Skid Row: An Overview for Geographers." *Journal of Geography* 78, no. 1 (January 1979): 7–12.

Smith, Sharon G., et al. "The National Intimate Partner and Sexual Violence Survey (NISVS): 2010–2012 State Report." National Center for Injury Prevention and Control, Centers for Disease Control and Prevention, April 2017. https://www.cdc.gov/violenceprevention/pdf /NISVS-StateReportBook.pdf.

Smith, Steven Rathgeb. "Social Services." In *The State of Nonprofit America*, edited by Lester M. Salamon, 192–228. Washington, DC: Brookings Institution Press, 2012.

Smith, Steven Rathgeb, and Michael Lipsky. *Nonprofits for Hire: The Welfare State in the Age of Contracting*. Cambridge: Harvard University Press, 1995.

Snow, David A., Susan G. Baker, and Leon Anderson. "Criminality and homeless men: An empirical assessment." *Social Problems* 36, no. 5 (1989): 532–49. https://doi.org/10 .2307/3096817.

Social Capital Project, US Senate Joint Economic Committee. "Love, Marriage, and the Baby Carriage: The Rise in Unwed Childbearing." December 2017. https://www.jec.senate.gov /public/_cache/files/bc6c3b18-b268-4178-b65f-56fec2b26002/4-17-love-marriage-and -the-baby-carriage.pdf.

Solenberger, Alice. *One Thousand Homeless Men: A Study of Original Records*. New York: Charities Publication Committee, 1911.

Solomon-Fears, Carmen. "Nonmarital Births: An Overview." Congressional Research Service, July 30, 2014. https://sgp.fas.org/crs/misc/R43667.pdf.

Soskis, Benjamin. "Both More and No More: The Historical Split between Charity and Philanthropy." Hudson Institute, October 2014. https://www.hudson.org/research/10723 -both-more-and-no-more-the-historical-split-between-charity-and-philanthropy.

Speek, Peter. "The Psychology of Floating Workers." *Annals of the American Academy of Political and Social Science* 69 (January 1917): 50–57.

Spence, Clark C. "Knights of the Tie and Rail: Tramps and Hoboes in the West." *Western Historical Quarterly* 2, no. 1 (January 1971): 4–19.

Spitzer, Robert L., George Cohen, J. David Miller, and Jean Endicott. "The Psychiatric Status of 100 Men on Skid Row." *The International Journal of Social Psychiatry* 15, no. 3 (Summer 1969): 230–34. https://doi.org/10.1177/002076406901500309.

Spradley, James P. *You Owe Yourself a Drunk: An Ethnography of Urban Nomads*. Prospect Heights, Il: Waveland Press, 2000 (orig. 1970).

Stack, Carol. *All Our Kin: Strategies for Survival in a Black Community*. New York: Harper & Row, 1974.

Standing, Guy. *Basic Income: A Guide for the Open-Minded*. New Haven: Yale University Press, 2017. Kindle edition.

Stanhope, Victoria, and Kerry Dunn. "The Curious Case of Housing First: The Limits of Evidence Based Policy." *International Journal of Law and Psychiatry* 34, no. 4 (July–August 2011): 275–82. https://doi.org/10.1016/j.ijlp.2011.07.006.

Starr, Roger. *America's Housing Challenge: What It Is and How to Meet It*. New York: Hill & Wang, 1977.

Steele, Tim. "Small Business Owners Say Portland Is 'Lawless'." Koin 6, November 28, 2017. https://www.koin.com/news/small-business-owners-say-portland-is-lawless/.

Steinbeck, John. *Cannery Row*. New York: Penguin, 2002 (orig. 1945).

Stessin, Lawrence. "That Vanishing American: The Hobo." *New York Times Magazine*, August 18, 1940.

Stevens, Carol. "Families: New Breed of Street People." *USA Today*, December 15, 1982.

Stewart, Nikita. *Troop 6000: The Girl Scout Troop that began in a Shelter and Inspired the World.* New York: Ballantine Books, 2020.

Stid, Daniel. "Dismantling the Social Services Industrial Complex." *Washington Post,* April 25, 2012. https://www.washingtonpost.com/national/on-innovations/dismantling -the-social-services-industrial-complex/2012/04/25/gIQAuTcMhT_story.html?utm _term=.1d75d46c087f.

Stopera, Matt. "61 Things I Learned at The National Hobo Convention." *Buzz Feed News,* August 21, 2012. https://www.buzzfeed.com/mjs538/things-i-learned-at-the-national -hobo-convention.

Storbakken, Jason. *Bowery Mission: Grit and Grace on Manhattan's Oldest Street.* Walden: Plough Publishing House, 2019.

———. "The Pain of Homelessness: A Plea For New York City to Deal Compassionately with People in Deep Need." *New York Daily News,* November 7, 2019. https://www.nydailynews .com/opinion/ny-oped-on-the-bowery-14-decades-of-lives-transformed-20191107-vzjt 3na7wzgpzg6yetdxm5dery-story.html.

Stuart, Forrest. *Down and Out and Under Arrest: Policing and Everyday Life in Skid Row.* Chicago: University of Chicago, 2016.

Sullivan, Brian J., and Jonathan Burke. "Single-Room Occupancy Housing in New York City: The Origins and Dimensions of a Crisis." *CUNY Law Review* 17, no. 1 (Winter 2013): 113–43.

Sun, Wei, Anthony Webb, and Natalia Zhivan. "Does Staying Healthy Reduce Your Lifetime Health Care Costs?" Center for Retirement Research at Boston College, May 2010. https:// crr.bc.edu/wp-content/uploads/2010/05/IB_10-8.pdf.

Tanner, Michael D. *The Inclusive Economy: How to Bring Wealth to America's Poor.* Washington, DC: Cato Institute, 2018.

Teles, Steven M. "The Eternal Return of Compassionate Conservatism." *National Affairs,* Fall 2009. https://www.nationalaffairs.com/publications/detail/the-eternal-return-of-compas sionate-conservatism.

Tempest, Rone. "Millions Hit Bottom in the Streets." *Los Angeles Times,* December 26, 1982.

Terkel, Studs. *Hard Times: An Oral History of the Great Depression.* New York: The New Press, 2000 (orig. 1970).

Tessler, Richard C., and Deborah L. Dennis. "A Synthesis of NIMH-Funded Research Concerning Persons Who Are Homeless and Mentally Ill." National Institute of Mental Health, February 9, 1989.

Thernstrom, Stephan, and Abigail Thernstrom. *America in Black and White: One Nation, Indivisible.* New York: Simon & Schuster, 1997.

Thompson, C. Bradley. "The Decline and Fall of American Conservatism." *The Objective Standard,* August 20, 2006. https://theobjectivestandard.com/2006/08/decline-fall-amer ican-conservatism/.

Thompson, Derek. "What in the World Is Causing the Retail Meltdown of 2017?" *The Atlantic,* April 10, 2017. https://www.theatlantic.com/business/archive/2017/04/retail -meltdown-of-2017/522384/.

Tierney, John. "Save the Flophouses." *New York Times,* January 14, 1996.

Toibin, Colm. *Brooklyn: A Novel.* New York: Scribner, 2009.

Toro, Paul A., et al. "Obtaining Representative Samples of Homeless Persons: A Two-City Study." *Journal of Community Psychology* 27, no. 2 (1999): 157–77.

Torrey, E. Fuller. *Nowhere to Go: The Tragic Odyssey of the Homeless Mentally Ill.* New York: Harper & Row, 1988.

Treffert, Darold. "Dying with Their Rights On." *American Journal of Psychiatry* 130, no. 9 (September 1973): 1041.

Tsai, Jack, and Robert A. Rosenheck. "Considering Alternatives to the Housing First Model." *European Journal of Homelessness* 6, no. 2 (December 2012): 201–8. https://www.feantsa research.org/download/ejh6_2_resp_housingfirst5541264244834483939392.pdf.

Tsai, Jack, Alvin S. Mares, and Robert A. Rosenheck. "Does Housing Chronically Homeless Adults Lead to Social Integration?" *Psychiatric Services* 63, no. 5 (May 2012): 427–34. https://doi:10.1176/appi.ps.201100047.

———. "A Multi-Site Comparison of Supported Housing for Chronically Homeless Adults: 'Housing First' Versus 'Residential Treatment First.'" *Psychological Services* 7, no. 4 (November 2010): 219–32. https://doi:10.1037/a0020460.

Tsai, Jack, T. Scott Stroup, and Robert A. Rosenheck. "Housing Arrangements Among a National Sample of Adults with Chronic Schizophrenia Living in the United States: A Descriptive Study." *Journal of Community Psychology* 39, no. 1 (2011): 76–88. https://doi .org/10.1002/jcop.20418.

Tsemberis, Sam. "From Streets to Homes: An Innovative Approach to Supported Housing for Homeless Adults with Psychiatric Disabilities." *Journal of Community Psychology* 27, no. 2 (March 1999): 225–41. https://doi.org/10.1002/(SICI)1520-6629(199903)27 :2%3C225::AID-JCOP9%3E3.0.CO;2-Y.

Tsemberis, Sam, and Sara Asmussen. "From Streets to Homes: The Pathways to Housing Consumer Preference Supported Housing Model." *Alcoholism Treatment Quarterly* 17, nos. 1–2 (1999): 113–31. https://doi.org/10.1300/J020v17n01_07.

Tsemberis, Sam, Douglas Kent, and Christy Respress. "Housing Stability and Recovery Among Chronically Homeless Persons with Co-Occurring Disorders in Washington, DC" *American Journal of Public Health* 102, no. 1 (January 2012): 13–16.

Tsemberis Sam, Leyla Gulcur, and Maria Nakae. "Housing First, Consumer Choice, and Harm Reduction for Homeless Individuals with a Dual Diagnosis." *American Journal of Public Health* 94, no. 4 (May 2004). https://doi:10.2105/ajph.94.4.651.

Tucker, William. *The Excluded Americans: Homelessness and Housing Policies.* Washington DC: Regnery Gateway, 1990.

Tully, Jim. *Beggars of Life.* New York: A. & C. Boni, 1924.

US Congress, 116th Congress of the United States. "Further Consolidated Appropriations Act, 2020." (HR 1865). https://www.congress.gov/116/bills/hr1865/BILLS -116hr1865enr.pdf.

———. "Congressional Record: Proceedings and Debates of the 104th Congress, First Session." 141, no. 137, September 6, 1995. https://www.govinfo.gov/content/pkg/CREC -1995-09-06/pdf/CREC-1995-09-06-senate.pdf.

———. "Homeless in America: Examining the Crisis and Solutions to End Homelessness; Hearing Before the Committee on Financial Services, US House of Representatives, 116th Congress, First Session." US Government Publishing Office, February 13, 2019. https://www.congress.gov/116/meeting/house/108894/documents/HHRG-116-BA00 -20190213-SD003.pdf.

———. "Homelessness in America: Hearing Before the Subcommittee on Housing and Community Development of the Committee on Banking, Finance, and Urban Affairs, House of Representatives, Ninety-seventh Congress, Second Session, December 15, 1982."

———. "Joint Hearing Before the Subcommittee on Housing and Community Development of the Committee on Banking, Finance and Urban Affairs and the Subcommittee on Manpower and Housing of the Committee on Government Operations, House of Representatives, Ninety-Eight Congress, Second Session, May 24, 1984."

———. "Problems in Urban Centers: Oversight Hearings Before Committee on the District of Columbia, House of Representatives, Ninety-Sixth Congress, Second Session on Problems in Urban Centers, Washington, DC, and the Federal Government Role, June 25, 26, 27, July 23, 24, 30, and September 30, 1980."

US Department of Health and Human Services. "National Survey on Drug Use and Health: Comparison of 2017–2018 and 2018–2019 Population Percentages (50 States and the District of Columbia)." December 15, 2020. https://www.samhsa.gov/data/sites /default/files/reports/rpt32806/2019NSDUHsaeShortTermCHG/2019NSDUHsaeShort TermCHG/2019NSDUHsaeShortTermCHG.pdf.

———. "Welfare Indicators and Risk Factors Nineteenth Report to Congress 2020." February 8, 2021. https://aspe.hhs.gov/sites/default/files/private/pdf/265031/welfare-indicators -and-risk-factors-19th-report.pdf.

———. "Births: Final Data for 2019." National Vital Statistics Reports 70, no. 2, March 23, 2021. https://www.cdc.gov/nchs/data/nvsr/nvsr70/nvsr70-02-508.pdf.

US Department of Health and Human Services, Administration for Children and Families. "Child Maltreatment 2019." 2021. https://www.acf.hhs.gov/sites/default/files /documents/cb/cm2019.pdf.

US Department of Health and Human Services, Substance Abuse and Mental Health Services Administration. "Key Substance Use and Mental Health Indicators in the United States: Results from the 2019 National Survey on Drug Use and Health." September 2020. https:// www.samhsa.gov/data/sites/default/files/reports/rpt29393/2019NSDUHFFRPDFWHT ML/2019NSDUHFFR1PDFW090120.pdf.

———. "A Treatment Improvement Protocol: Behavioral Health Services for People Who Are Homeless (TIP 55)." 2013. https://store.samhsa.gov/sites/default/files/d7/priv/sma13 -4734.pdf.

US Department of Housing and Urban Development. "The 1988 National Survey of Shelters for the Homeless." March 1989. https://www.huduser.gov/portal/Publications /pdf/HUD%20-%205356.pdf.

———. "The 2017 Annual Homeless Assessment Report (AHAR) to Congress, Part 2: Estimates of Homelessness in the United States." October 2018.

———. "The 2018 Annual Homeless Assessment Report (AHAR) to Congress; Part 2: Estimates of Homelessness in the United States." September 2020. https://www.huduser.gov /portal/sites/default/files/pdf/2018-AHAR-Part-2.pdf.

———. "Fiscal Year 2020 Annual Performance Report." January 15, 2021. https://www.hud .gov/sites/dfiles/CFO/documents/HUD_FY20_Annual_Performance_Report_1-15-21.pdf.

———. "Letter to The Honorable Darrell Issa." August 9, 2017.

———. "Housing and Employment." Evidence Matters. Summer/Fall 2018. https://www .huduser.gov/portal/sites/default/files/pdf/EM-Newsletter-summer-fall-2018.pdf.

———. "HUD 2020 Continuum of Care Homeless Assistance Programs Homeless Populations and Subpopulations." December 15, 2020. https://files.hudexchange.info/reports /published/CoC_PopSub_NatlTerrDC_2020.pdf.

———. "HUD 2020 Continuum of Care Homeless Assistance Programs Homeless Populations and Subpopulations, NY-600 New York City CoC," December 15, 2020. https://files .hudexchange.info/reports/published/CoC_PopSub_CoC_NY-600-2020_NY_2020.pdf.

———. "Notice of Funding Availability for Continuum of Care Homeless Assistance; Funding Availability." Federal Register 61, no. 52 (March 15, 1996): 10866–77. https://www .govinfo.gov/content/pkg/FR-1996-03-15/pdf/96-6396.pdf.

———. "A Report to the Secretary on the Homeless and Emergency Shelters." April 23, 1984.

———. "Worst Case Housing Needs 2019 Report to Congress," June 2020. https://www .huduser.gov/portal/sites/default/files/pdf/worst-case-housing-needs-2020.pdf.

US Interagency Council on Homelessness. "Deploy Housing First Systemwide." August 15, 2018. https://www.usich.gov/solutions/housing/housing-first/.

———. "The Evidence Behind Approaches that Drive an End to Homelessness." September 2019. https://www.usich.gov/resources/uploads/asset_library/Evidence-Behind-Approaches-That-End-Homelessness-Brief-2019.pdf.

———. "Homelessness: Programs and the People They Serve: Findings of the National Survey of Homeless Assistance Providers and Clients." September 1999. https://www.huduser.gov /portal/publications/homeless/homeless_tech.html.

———. "Home, Together: The Federal Strategic Plan to Prevent and End Homelessness." July 2018. https://www.usich.gov/resources/uploads/asset_library/Home-Together-Federal -Strategic-Plan-to-Prevent-and-End-Homelessness.pdf.

———. "Priority: Home! The Federal Plan to Break the Cycle of Homelessness." 1994. https://books.google.com/books?id=esfC-UbC-yoC&printsec=frontcover&source=gbs_ge _summary_r&cad=0#v=onepage&q&f=false.

———. "Successfully Connecting People Affected by Opioid Use to Housing: Central City Concern in Portland, Oregon." March 2017. https://www.usich.gov/resources/uploads/as set_library/case-study-central-city-concern-march-2017.pdf.

———. "US Interagency Council on Homelessness Historical Overview." December 2016. https://www.usich.gov/resources/uploads/asset_library/USICH_History_2016.pdf.

US Senate, Special Committee on Aging. "Single Room Occupancy: A Need for National Concern." 1978.

Urban Institute. "The Nonprofit Sector in Brief 2019." June 4, 2020. https://nccs.urban.org /publication/nonprofit-sector-brief-2019#the-nonprofit-sector-in-brief-2019.

Vander Kooi, Ronald. "The Main Stem: Skid Row Revisited." *Society* 10 (September–October 1973): 64–71.

Venice Neighborhood Council, Public Health and Safety Committee. "Special Report: LAPD Calls for Service by Venice Homeless Service Providers." February 9, 2021. https://www .venicenc.org/ncfiles/viewCommitteeFile/12775.

Venkatesh, Sudhir Alladi. *Off the Books: The Underground Economy of the Urban Poor*. Cambridge: Harvard University Press, 2006.

Voegeli, William J. *The Pity Party: A Mean-spirited Diatribe against Liberal Compassion*. New York: Broadside Books, 2014.

von Wachter, Till, Geoffrey Schnorr, and Nefara Riesch "Employment and Earnings Among LA County Residents Experiencing Homelessness." California Policy Lab, February 2020. https://www.capolicylab.org/wp-content/uploads/2020/02/Employment-Among -the-Homeless-in-Los-Angeles.pdf.

Walker, Alissa, and Emma Alpern. "The Language Around Homelessness Is Finally Changing." curbed.com, June 11, 2020. https://archive.curbed.com/2020/6/11/21273455 /homeless-people-definition-copy-editing.

Wang, Wendy. "Immigrant Families Are More Stable." Institute for Family Studies, March 3, 2021. https://ifstudies.org/blog/immigrant-families-are-more-stable.

Warner, Amos. *American Charities: A Study in Philanthropy and Economics*. New York: Thomas Y. Crowell & Company, 1894.

Watkins, T. H. *The Great Depression: America in the 1930s*. Boston: Little, Brown and Company, 1993.

Waugh, Evelyn. *Brideshead Revisited*. New York: Little, Brown and Company, 2012 (orig. 1945).

Weaver, R. Kent. *Ending Welfare as We Know It*. Washington, DC: Brookings Institution Press, 2000.

Weinreb, Linda, and Peter H. Rossi. "The American Homeless Family Shelter 'System.'" *Social Service Review* 69, no. 1 (March 1995): 86–107.

Wennström, Johan. "Europe's New Beggars." *Quilette*, April 10, 2019. https://quillette.com /2019/04/10/europes-new-beggars/.

Wetzler, Scott. "Defeating Dependency: Work First." American Enterprise Institute, September 2018. https://www.aei.org/wp-content/uploads/2018/09/Defeating-Dependency.pdf.

White, Richard W. Jr. *Rude Awakenings: What the Homeless Crisis Tells Us*. San Francisco: ICS Press, 1992.

Wickenden, Elizabeth. "Reminiscences of the Program for Transients and Homeless in the Thirties." In *On Being Homeless: Historical Perspectives*, edited by Rick Beard, 81–87. New York: Museum of the City of New York, 1987.

Willse, Craig. *The Value of Homelessness: Managing Surplus Life in the United States*. Minneapolis: University of Minnesota Press, 2015.

Willis, Jay. "Who Will Run the Soup Kitchens?" *The Atlantic*, March 20, 2020. https:// www.thcatlantic.com/family/archive/2020/03/the-coronaviruss-impact-on-homeless-ser vices/608467/.

Wilson, James Q. "Foreword" to George L. Kelling and Catherine M. Coles. *Fixing Broken Windows: Restoring Order and Reducing Crime in our Communities*. New York: Martin Kessler Books, 1996.

Winship, Scott. "Poverty After Welfare Reform." Manhattan Institute for Policy Research, August 2016. https://media4.manhattan-institute.org/sites/default/files/R-SW-0816.pdf.

Wiseman, Jacqueline P. *Stations of the Lost: The Treatment of Skid Row Alcoholics*. Englewood Cliffs, NJ: Prentice-Hall, 1970.

Wolpert, Julian, and Eileen R. Wolpert. "The Relocation of Released Mental Hospital Patients into Residential Communities." *Policy Sciences* 7 (1976): 31–51.

Wooster, Martin. "The Homeless Issue: An Adman's Dream." *Reason*, July 1987. https:// reason.com/1987/07/01/the-homeless-issue-an-admans-d/?print=.

Wright, Christopher C. "Down but Not Out: The Unemployed in Chicago during the Great Depression." The Graduate College of the University of Illinois at Chicago, 2017. https://91c74b8b-cd08-4a7c-b14c-3efaa5fb1ee2.filesusr.com/ugd/9b146c_dc5363dddd1f 4d9699ee341f0e7dd64f.pdf.

Wright, James. *Address Unknown: The Homeless in America*. New York: Aldine de Gruyter, 1989.

Wyman, Mark. *Hoboes: Bindlestiffs, Fruit Tramps, and the Harvesting of the West*. New York: Hill & Wang, 2010.

Zettler, Michael D. *The Bowery*. New York: Drake Publishers, 1975.

Zhong, Fan. "Richard Gere and Alec Baldwin Care About the Homeless." *W Magazine*, November 18, 2015. https://www.wmagazine.com/story/richard-gere-alec-baldwin-artwalk-ny.m

Zunz, Olivier. *Philanthropy in America: A History*. Princeton: Princeton University Press, 2012.

Index

About the Author

Stephen Eide is a senior fellow at the Manhattan Institute and a contributing editor of *City Journal*. He has written widely on homelessness and related issues such as mental illness, including articles in *National Affairs*, the *New York Daily News*, *The Hill*, and the *Los Angeles Times*.

www.ingramcontent.com/pod-product-compliance
Lightning Source LLC
Chambersburg PA
CBHW031546260326
41914CB00002B/290